Carnival in Romans

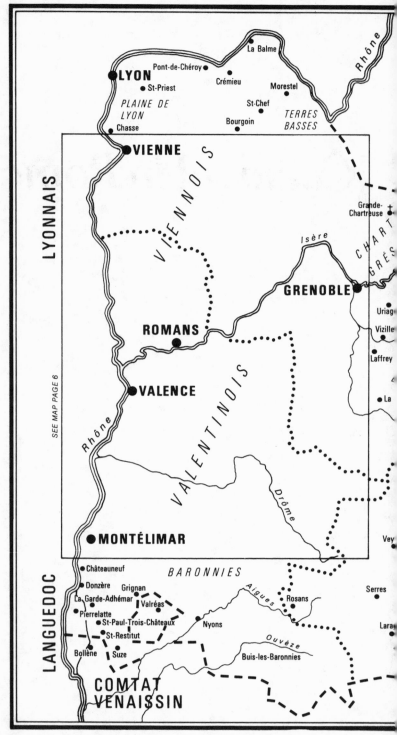

The province of Dauphiné, based on Dreyfus, *Histoire du Dauphiné*, Hachette.

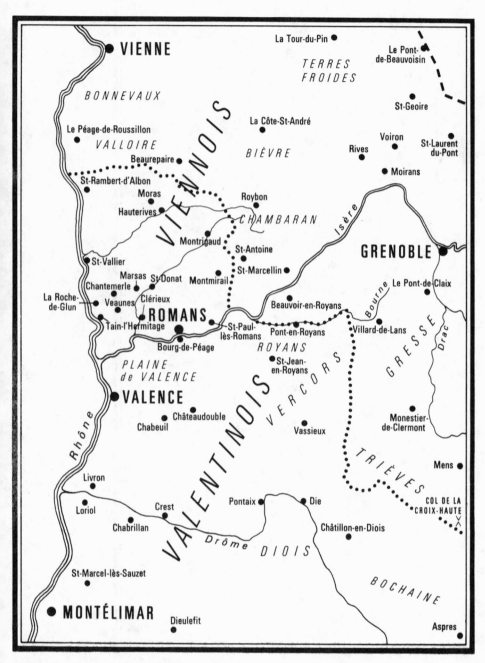

Sites of League Action (1579–1580)
Based on «Le Peuple Française», June 1977.

Carnival
in
Romans

Emmanuel Le Roy Ladurie

Translated from the French by Mary Feeney

George Braziller, Inc.

New York

Paperback reprint 1980 by George Braziller, Inc.
Originally published in the United States in 1979 by George Braziller, Inc.

English translation by Mary Feeney Copyright © 1979 by George Braziller, Inc.

Originally published in France under the title
   Le Carnaval de Romans.
   © Editions Gallimard, 1979.

George Braziller, Inc.
One Park Avenue, New York 10016

Library of Congress Cataloging in Publication Data
Le Roy Ladurie Emmanuel.
   Carnival in Romans.
   Translation of Le Carnaval de Romans. De la Chandeleur au
   mercredi des Cendres 1579–1580.
   1. Romans, France (Drôme)—History. 2. France—
History—Wars of the Huguenots, 1562–1598. I. Title.
DC801.R75L4713   944′.98   79–52163
ISBN 0–8076–0991–9

Printed in the United States of America

Designed by Nancy Kirsh

Acknowledgments

I would especially like to thank L. Scott Van Doren and Daniel Hickey for their help and their kindness; Vital Chomel, the archivist of the Archives Départementales de l'Isère, for giving me free access to his own vast stores of knowledge; the archivist of the Archives Départementales de la Drôme; my friend Bernard Bonnin; the head librarian of Romans's Bibliothèque Municipale; and the former and present mayors of Romans.

Contents

Foreword   *xiii*

I   The Urban and Rural Setting   *1*
II   Taxes: Commoner versus Noble   *35*
III   Jean de Bourg's Petition of Grievance   *61*
IV   1578: Jacques Colas and the Moderate Revolt   *79*
V   1579: The Shadow Carnival   *93*
VI   Strikes and Debts   *153*
VII   Antoine Guérin, Master of Ceremonies   *175*
VIII   Mardi Gras 1580 or, God on Our Side   *229*
IX   A Slaughter of Peasants   *249*
X   "Magpies and crows have pecked out our eyes . . ."   *265*
XI   Paradigms, Confraternities, Kingdoms   *289*
XII   The Winter Festival   *305*
XIII   A Word on the Peasants   *325*
XIV   Forerunners of Equality   *339*

       Appendix   *371*

       Chapter Notes   *375*

       Manuscript Sources   *409*

       Abbreviations   *411*

       Bibliography   *413*

Foreword

Romans is a former textile center located to the southeast of Lyons in what was once the province of Dauphiné; during the sixteenth century it had a population of nearly 8,000. Each February, it was the scene of a colorful and animated Mardi Gras Carnival. In 1580 the winter festivities were even livelier than usual; they degenerated into a bloody ambush where the notables killed or imprisoned the leaders of the craftsman party. This blend of public celebration and violence burst like a skyrocket over France, which was in the throes of a prolonged religious conflict. Contemporary accounts of the Romans episode make it seem a combination of Shakespearean tragedy and street theater, with men in the leading roles. The incident was and is highly charged in terms of social and cultural history. But what interest does it hold for the reader who lives far from southeastern France, for example in Lancashire, New York, or Minnesota?

Gauging the full importance of the Carnival in Romans means, first of all, keeping in mind that it happened at the juncture of two essential phases of the Wars of Religion, a bitter struggle between Protestants and Catholics involving France and much of the Western world during the second half of the sixteenth century.

The Huguenots had the upper hand in France from 1560 until

1572, when the infamous St. Bartholomew's Day massacre decimated their ranks. Maimed and intimidated, the Protestant party went into an irreversible decline. Then from 1580 on, a great Catholic party, the *League*, gathered strength. It resurrected the "popish" fundamentalism—erroneously thought to have been dealt a fatal blow by the Lutherans and Calvinists— still lurking in the popular sensibility. Instead, fundamentalism surfaced intact, triumphant, in its most archaic and fanatic forms. The formidable Catholic League which it spawned was only nominally directed by the great noble house of Guise; zealous monks and preachers formed the base of the organization. It was a true apparatus in the modern sense of the term, not a liberal one, of course, but democratic, prerevolutionary, manipulative, even totalitarian. We have just witnessed events of the same type in Iran in 1979, where a vast popular movement is directed by the *mullahs,* homologues of the leaguer-monks, under the supreme command of the eminently medieval Ayatollah Ruhollah Khomeini. Perhaps in the light of these very recent events we can better understand how four centuries ago, in the France of 1580, reactionary Catholicism and the revolutionary spirit formed their odd couple.

The Carnival in Romans immediately preceded these developments; as I have stated, it came at the juncture of the Huguenot phase (1560–1572) and the Catholic phase (1580 on) in the bitter chronology of the Wars of Religion. Fifteen-eighty was the eye of the hurricane, a period of relative calm between two equally devastating phases, the first infused with Calvin's spirit, the second inspired by Loyola. As for the Dauphiné revolt's popular leagues, which flourished just before and after the Carnival in Romans, with a few specific exceptions they were led neither by devout Catholics nor by monks. They simply regrouped craftsmen, peasants, and bourgeois, each of whom defended its own professional or social interests, and was willing to fight for them if need be.

On the most basic level, the Carnival was in fact the climax of a vast regional revolt. It was a rebellion against government and against taxes. The Western world experienced dozens more such "tax revolts" in the sixteenth and seventeenth centuries, mainly in France, but also in Spain, even England. Elitist thinking at the time characterized such insurrections as the base expression of a primitive peasant class's more savage impulses. Today the term used might be *poujadisme*, referring to Pierre Poujade's postwar union of small businessmen and skilled workers, and connoting a short-sighted political attitude. But an antitax movement recently developed in California, one of the world's most advanced societies. The Proposition 13 vote showed that tax revolts are often highly sophisticated, and that statement applies to sixteenth-century France as well. As Parkinson's law demonstrates, bureaucracies proliferate if left unchecked; in the case at hand the result was more and higher taxes. Dauphiné in 1580 was the scene of a dual struggle against taxes and against the nobility. The aristocrats were exempt from taxes by privilege of birth. This incurred the egalitarian wrath of the commoners, peasants, bourgeois, etc., all of whom detested taxes, but hated fiscal injustice even more. Resentment of the nobles welled up on account of taxes; the same resentment reappeared just before the French Revolution, framed in Jean-Jacques Rousseau's egalitarian thought.

The Dauphiné revolt of 1580, however, was also rooted in the distant past, in the antiseignorial struggles of the Middle Ages, which likewise took on new and perfectly contemporary meanings during the last decade of the eighteenth century. In 1579, rebellious Dauphiné peasants attacked and destroyed country manors; the same thing happened during the *Jacqueries* of 1358 and again during the terrifying spring of 1789.

Romans was the focal point of the conflict. On the local level the craftsmen used their trade confraternities to organize their challenge to the town notables, who were led by Judge Antoine Guérin, the powerful boss of the local political machine. February 1580 saw Carnival arrive on schedule . . . and transfigure everything. The winter festivities were a reminder of the days when prospective Christians buried their pagan ways in a Saturnalian outburst. In this way they prepared for Lent, which was in turn a cleansing process culminating in baptism at Easter, the time of spiritual birth or rebirth. Pagan excesses were brought to a halt by the trial and execution of a Mardi

Gras effigy. But Carnival also dealt with social sins or ills, on which the community unfortunately could reach no consensus. In other words, the elimination of social ills implied class struggle, with greedy notables on one side and rebellious peasants on the other. Each group entered violently into Carnival, confronting the other with theatrical and ritual gestures leading up to the final massacre.

Although it was a strictly localized incident, the Carnival in Romans represents a deep probe into the geological stratifications of a dated culture. It informs us about a specific city and a particular province. More generally speaking, it elucidates the urban dramas of the Renaissance, at the time of the Reformation, the beginning of the Baroque age, and the rise of the Catholic Counter-Reformation.

I

❧❧❧❧❧❧❧❧❧❧❧

The Urban and Rural Setting

Writing the history of a small city has long been a dream of mine. Romans, near Grenoble, in what was once the province of Dauphiné, is just such a place and a particularly appealing one. There are plentiful archives documenting seven or eight centuries of local life—social, economic, cultural, municipal. All things considered, there is an over-abundance of material for the monographer I strive to be, so I eventually chose to describe only two weeks of Romans's history. Two short weeks, but what weeks they were!

In February 1580, Carnival in Romans was a time of masks and massacres for the divided citizenry. These two colorful, eventful, bloody weeks inspire a discussion of the antecedents and consequences of the drama; its intricacies, context, and significance; the neighboring towns and villages concerned; and its place in comparative history. The Carnival and all the elements involved are the point, the plot of my book. I will begin by briefly depicting Romans and rural Dauphiné in 1579–1580, as well as the social and political forces converging to set the scene for the tragedy of 1580. I beg indulgence for the flood of statistics in this first chapter. They are not characteristic of the book as a whole but are a necessary part of it, for any history is in part quantitative.

Romans, on the Isère River, lies a few leagues from the Rhône, and has through the centuries followed a classic pattern of urban demography. After the Black Death of 1348, there were 1,163 heads of household paying taxes in Romans in 1357.[1] Multiplying by 4.5 persons per household, and allowing for those who were not taxable and therefore not included in the count (nobles, the poor, etc.), produces a population of approximately 6,013.[2] In 1366, following the disastrous plague of 1361, only some 430 heads of household attended the town's electoral assembly. This gives a figure of 2,223 inhabitants calculated at the same rate as above,[3] and is certainly too low to be realistic. A fair number must have absented themselves from the electoral assembly. In 1450, 529 hearths (real ones, not just in the fiscal sense) were taxed in Romans, making a population of 2,735—less than half of that recorded a century earlier.[4] The thriving city had become a mere village. This reflects the demographic nose dive of the late Middle Ages, at the end of a period of plagues, wars, famine, and financial crises.

By 1498 the Renaissance was under way in Romans as elsewhere. The *taille* rolls (records of the direct royal tax, called the *taille*) show 814 heads of household, for a population of 4,208. Eleven years later, virtually the same figure: 815 taxable, population 4,214.[5] After this brief halt, renascent growth was again in evidence by 1557. At the close of four decades of expansion, the town had 1,612 taxpayers, or twice as many as at the turn of the century. A population of something like 8,334 nearing the 10,000 mark: a town of considerable size for the times.[6] Continuing into the 1550s, demographic growth had some surprising consequences, including the enlargement of the local brothel. "A larger house is needed for whores and bawds to be kept in, given the scandals and bad examples occurring in town," read a municipal decision of April 1554.[7] Nine years later, the Wars of Religion were under way. In 1556, the growth trend of the Renaissance was reversed: the effects of the plague in 1564 stunned Romans,[8] leaving it with no more than 1,519 taxpayers, or 7,853 inhabitants.[9] In 1570, the downward trend continued and there were now only 1,454 taxpayers, or 7,517 inhabitants: war, like the plague it is, had skimmed the population.[10] In 1578, Romans had about 6,742 inhabitants, judging from the 1,304 taxpayers. Still falling! In 1582, following the Carnival, 1,335 taxpayers were counted, for a population of 6,902.[11] For the second—though not the last—time since 1557, Romans's population had fallen beneath the vital 7,000 mark. But perhaps the reckonings for these years slightly underestimate the population. The *taille* roll for 1583, however, was meticulous. It gave 1,547 taxpayers, or 7,998, say 8,000, inhabitants, or 212 per hectare.[12] The figure for 1588, after the devastating plague of 1586, was much lower: 1,183 taxpayers, or a population of less than 6,000.[13] In short, the Carnival in Romans took place during the Wars of Religion, during the downward or static phase of a demographic cycle. The upward swing preceding it represents the Renaissance in France between 1450 and 1560. The Carnival affected a town with a maximum population of 8,000 people, probably more like 7,500.

Romans was in the fifth category of cities as they were ranked in sixteenth-century France. The first category was Paris, with its population of 200,000 to 300,000. Lyons was second with 60,000. Rouen, Nantes, and Bordeaux, each with about 20,000, were the third. The fourth category, 15,000 to 20,000, included Toulouse, Montpelier, Marseille, and Orleans. Romans and other towns with populations from 6,000 to 12,000, came next.[14]

There are no parish registers to give us a complete picture of family structures in Romans. Instead, we learn about them from another first-class source: the list, by household, of names of those who died in the 1586 plague.[15] The count was ordered by Judge Guérin, Romans's real political boss and a major character in this book.

The 1586 plague, an overwhelming tragedy which recalled the Black Death of 1348, claimed 4,096 victims, a good half (51 percent) of the population at the time. This outbreak of the plague killed many of the protesters who had survived the 1580

Carnival, bringing down a final curtain on the rebellion six years after the event. Romans quickly recovered from this plague, due to the prompt remarriage of widows, the high local birth rate, and much immigration from the countryside.

The pandemic of 1586 killed half of Romans, affecting rich and poor alike. It therefore represents a thorough and valid poll (with 51 percent responding!) of certain family structures. Seven hundred and three *nuclear families* (a couple and children with no other relations living in the household) were struck by the plague, as were the households of 84 *widows* and at least 161 *extended families*. This last group had an ascendant (such as a grandparent) or a collateral relative (unmarried brother of one of the partners) sharing the household. Without counting the widows, there were 864 households (161 + 703), with at least 18.6 percent extended families (161 to 864) as opposed to 81.4 percent nuclear families (703 to 864). Let me stress the *at least*. A certain number of nuclear families must have included ascendant or collateral relatives. But they survived the plague and are the missing pieces in our puzzle. Because they did not die in 1586, we have no way of knowing if they ever existed. Furthermore, many of the nuclear families no doubt had been or were to be extended families at some point in their life cycle. If the grandmother in a household died, an extended family became a nuclear one. The process was reversed if the couple's grown son then married and continued to live under the parental roof with his wife. The figure of two extended families per ten households thus seems reasonable for Romans around 1580—a far cry from the individualism of modern England, for example, with its overwhelming majority of nuclear families.[16] Romans inclined toward the Latin structuring which favors the extended family.

The extended families in Romans had a proportionately higher number of wealthy households in their ranks. They were prosperous enough to take an elderly or single relative under their wing. Out of the 161 extended families, 52, or 32.3 percent of the households included one or more domestic servants, mostly female. The overall percentage of families with servants was much lower, 13.6 percent (174 to 1,282), with every type of household, including widows and unmarried persons living alone, figured into the total. It was lower still for widows. Generally poorer as a group, 9.5 percent (8 to 84) of them had servants. Thus, one extended family in three, but only one average family in seven, and one widow in ten, had live-in help. The difference is striking.

Let us take a closer look at these live-in employees. Most of them were really domestic servants, not journeymen in the carding and weaving trades who might have been temporarily sharing the home. Out of 212 domestic servants who died in the plague of 1586, only 61 were male, and the remaining 151 (71.2 percent) were *chambrières*, maids-of-all-work.

We can estimate, then, that one Romans family in seven or eight belonged or aspired to the moneyed elite of the town. The Carnival protest took aim at this very elite. Another important minority, the protest leaders, came almost entirely from the 86 percent of remaining families, those without servants.

Whether rich or poor, nuclear or extended, all families had a large number of children. The 1586 plague struck a total of 49 widows with children and killed an average of 2.0 children in each household. In nuclear households, an average of 2.2 children fell victim. From this minimum of two children dead in each type of household, we can estimate that there were at least three children per household at the onset of the plague. Considering the toll taken by infant and child mortality, the actual birth rate must have been higher, perhaps six or seven births per family, assuming that both parents had lived long enough to produce a family of that size.

Now let us turn to sociology. The urban community nestled within the ramparts of Romans can be dissected in several ways. There are the following possibilities:

—the sixteenth century's own criteria: division of local society into several categories, called *estats* or ranks;

—an index of *strata* (an upper socioeconomic stratum, for instance, consisting of the wealthiest 10 percent, is determined by contrast with the remaining 90 percent of townspeople);

—the criteria of social *classes,* combining indications of hier-archic position (*estat* or rank) and financial position (socioeconomic level).

First, the categories or *estats.* The 1578 tax roll divided the population of Romans (as represented by its 1,304 taxpayers) into four ranks.[17] The first rank included well-to-do landowners: members of the patrician bourgeoisie who lived as nobles, with income from rents and money-lending activities. Also included were those of the town's few nobles who for some reason were not tax exempt; royal officeholders and doctors of law; and the occasional physician—in short, what passed for the town's upper crust. Among the first-rank families were the Guérins (not yet very rich), the Velheus, Loyrons, de Manissieus, Garagnols . . . 52 heads of household in all, or 4 percent of the population. Yet according to the amount of tax they paid as a group (the per capita average was 6 *écus*), they held four times that percentage of the city's land.[18]

The second rank was essentially mercantile. There were successful tradesmen, thriving shopkeepers of various sorts, and the merchants themselves. Small though they seemed in comparison to their Lyons counterparts, they dominated the local cloth industry, selling unprocessed wool to carders and drapers, then buying the finished cloth and reselling it. They were like the merchants of the nearby Comtat Venaissin (part of modern Vaucluse) as described by Marc Venard: "They siphon off rural production (wheat, wool) and market locally manufactured products (cloth). They are also directly involved as landlords or owners of textile mills. One-man businesses, they advance expenses, lend money, grain, livestock, cloth, to be repaid with interest by any other name. They manage land belonging to the nobility, farming it out."[19] The merchants of Romans did not restrict their interests to the local areas. They sailed the Isère with their wares; an old tradition linking them with the merchants of Grenoble and Valence. They controlled the flow of salt northward up the Rhône and the Isère, and also dealt in wheat, wine, and wool. They regulated the log trade coming down from the Alps as well as the iron, steel, cheese, cloth and notions from Germany and the north of France.[20]

This second rank was not exclusively mercantile, however. It extended to the intellectual and related professions, with four or five notaries of modest means and a headmaster among its number.[21] Some of Romans's proudest names belonged to merchant families: the Guigous, Odoards, Jomarons, Monluels, and the local tycoon Antoine Coste, a favorite target of the 1580 protest. He paid the highest taxes in town.

A total of 137 taxpayers, or 10.5 percent of the town's heads of household, belonged to the second rank—easily twice as many as the first rank. In real property (the merchants' often very valuable moveable property counted very little for land roll purposes) the merchants and notaries owned 18.5 percent of the town's buildings and land.[22] Not even twice their percentage of the population.

As a whole, the merchants and others of this group were somewhat better off than the members of the first rank with their private incomes. The second rank's share was 18.5 percent as opposed to 16.2 percent for the first. But their particular share of taxes, divided among more individuals, was markedly smaller. Thus they paid an average 2.6 écus per household, as compared to the first rank's 6 écus. The average merchant pulled 43 percent the weight a member of the first group did.

The third rank included every branch of the crafts, from textile producers (drapers, carders) to food suppliers (butchers, bakers). They represented a high percentage of the population. Before the French Revolution, Romans was one of the most "industrial" cities in Dauphiné. Yet industry, particularly the textile industry, was simply a craft. The line between the merchant and craftsman ranks was clearly drawn. Crossing it required solid evidence of substance, without which would-be climbers were put in place by the town council, controlled as it was by watchful members of the first and second groups.[23] Rank or *estat* was a matter of the utmost seriousness. Furthermore, too many moves might have upset the town's four-part fiscal balance.

Craftsmen were economically dependent on the merchants, who sold them unprocessed wool, bought their cloth, rented them their mills. However, this did not lead *ipso facto* to political dependence. The craftsmen were either the owners of minuscule businesses or else employees, journeymen, or partners in such businesses. They were thus their own proletariat. They made a good living as skilled workers: for forty days' work they "earn in money the grain they eat in a year." They owned the odd plot of land, sometimes had elaborate or costly funerals, and were in good standing with the confraternity for their trade. The carders and drapers of Romans had their own such organization, the St. Blaise confraternity. What distinguished them from the merchants and other bourgeois patricians was their peasant, or at least rural, background. They attained a degree of literacy. A certain number of butchers and wool workers who were key figures in the protest could read and write, although this was hardly the case for masons, blacksmiths, and carpenters.[24]

The third category furnished nearly all the leaders of the 1579–1580 rebellion. In all, this rank included 637 persons, or 48.8 percent of the total of heads of household in all four ranks. A virtual majority, they were the real backbone of the town. Their share in houses, shops, fields, vineyards, and so on amounted to 39.5 percent of the total (they paid 764 of the 1932.4 *écus* tax). Thus, in relation to their proportion of the population (48.8 percent), they had less than their fair share of the total wealth in Romans. Nevertheless, considering they were one of the two so-called lower ranks and thoroughly looked down upon by the others, their financial position was fairly comfortable. Two-fifths of the town belonged to them. Solid enough grounds for opposition, even attack! Their individual share of taxes was lower though: 1.2 *écus* compared to the second rank's 2.6 and the 6 *écus* paid by the average first-rank member. It took more than two craftsmen to make a merchant, we might say, and six to equal someone whose sole income was annuities from land or usury!

Lastly, the citizens of Romans who did agricultural work—called *plowmen* at the time—made up the fourth rank. There were 478 of them, or 36.7 percent of the population. This is a huge proportion, illustrating the fact that Romans was still essentially agrarian, despite the ramparts demarcating town and country. It could be called rural-urban. Every summer morning many citizens left town to work in the fields just beyond the stout walls. The land they worked often was not their own. At harvest time, Romans seemed to empty (as it did in 1577 even though possibly loot-hungry soldiers were in the area). Thirty years before that, in 1547, the clergy of Romans's main church, at the request of the town council, excommunicated all caterpillars for eating up the crops! The insects were first given a legal counsel, and were then instructed to gather in one small field and remain there. Otherwise, they were warned, the wrath of the Holy Father (and the holy fathers) would fall on them.[25] What better proof of the agrarian or sacro-agrarian nature of life in Romans?

The 478 plowmen in the 1578 tax roll can be divided into two groups. A minority of prosperous ones—nineteen in all—paid 2.6 *écus* tax or more. They kept one-fourth to one-half of the crops they raised on land belonging to Romans's bourgeois patricians. These self-styled "farmers, grain merchants, lenders" were quite as well off as the more comfortable craftsmen; they owned pewter dishware and linens. Below this well-to-do group were 459 of what were simply called *travailleurs* (workers) in the local language of southern France. They formed the core of the proletariat and were a cheap and plentiful source of labor for the owners and lords of the land. The late sixteenth century was a period of drastic declines in wages.

These underdogs, Marc Venard wrote, "spend the whole summer harvesting grain, then grapes. The sun tans them like leather." In the wintertime, "they do terracing, prune or dig in the vineyards, run out of work," and sometimes they had to beg. In the spring "they borrow wheat from the usurers to keep going."[26] They resisted, at least by grumbling, their employers' arbitrary cutting of their wages. They protested against seizure of their grain from within the town or without.[27] They were nearly penniless, barely scraping by, and were usually illiterate. Their daughters had insignificant dowries and were forced to go to work as servants or *chambrières* (there were 300 of these in 1585, half of whom died in the plague of 1586).

The picture was not entirely bleak, however. The 459 less

prosperous members of the fourth rank contributed participants, if not leaders, to the revolt of 1579–1580. They were often homeowners, with a bit of land or a small vineyard as well, depending on their profession. All in all, the 478 plowmen owned 25.7 percent of the property in Romans. This was less than their theoretical due, given the 36.2 percent of the population they represented but was still not an unreasonable share: a quarter of all real estate for slightly more than a third of the recorded population. On an individual basis, their per capita tax was negligible as was their share of the total wealth: 1 *écu* in taxes, a little less than the average craftsman paid, two or three times less than the merchant, and six times less than the landlord of the first rank.

The protest during the Carnival of 1580 reflected the fundamental differences separating these four categories. The two upper ranks, 14.5 percent of the population controlling 34.7 percent of real property, were almost entirely on the side of law and order. The lower two furnished members and support to the league of rebels. Together they were 85.5 percent of the population, holding 65.2 percent of the property. Up to this point, the division of wealth does not appear too undemocratic. Controlling 65.2 percent of real property, the craftsman and plowman ranks had a good chance of making themselves heard. Perhaps even a better one than the people in many French villages of the same period, where a few noblemen and bourgeois patricians owned 80 percent of the land. And certainly a better chance than the poor have in some wealthy Third World countries of our own day.

Analyzing the *estats* or ranks as they appear in the *taille* rolls affords us a glimpse of how the society of the time saw itself. Details, however, are missing. For example, the first rank included taxpayers so poor they paid less than .5 *écu* tax per capita, as well as the wealthy landowners of Romans's upper crust. The second rank also had its poor members, for not all the town's merchants were wealthy ones. Likewise, some craftsmen and plowmen were prosperous, although they were categorized as lower-class. Thus, an analysis of *strata* is called for, at least as far as the upper strata are concerned.

Among the 1,304 heads of household in Romans, there were 125 "top" individuals paying 13 or more florins in tax in 1578, or 2.6 *écus* or more.[28] These 125 citizens represented 9.6 percent of all taxpayers, or 10 percent for simplicity's sake—what statisticians call the upper *decile;* the remaining 90 percent paid less than 2.6 *écus*. The top 10 percent constituted a certain elite. Each household had a servant, and we have seen that the 1586 plague revealed that only 13.6 percent of all Romans households had them. The top 125 paid, in all, 768 out of the 1932.4 *écus* in tax collected in Romans in 1578, or 39.7 percent. In other words, they controlled 39.7 percent of all real property— or two-fifths (40 percent) if we round it off. The top 10 percent thus swung *four times* its proportional weight. The rest of the population controlled 60.3 percent of all property and were the overwhelming majority, demographically speaking. Thus, three-fifths of the land was owned by nine-tenths of the population, making the community of Romans in 1578 far more egalitarian than underdeveloped societies of its day or even of today.[29]

After looking at ranks and strata separately, let us now combine them in the hope of isolating social groups, or even classes. Among the 125 heads of household in the top 10 percent stratum, 31 were members of the first rank. As we have seen, there were 52 heads of household in this upper rank of wealthy landowners. The majority of them (31) were thus in the top tenth. Of the 137 members of the second rank, 39 belonged to the golden decile, a much lower proportion than for the first group. We must therefore make a distinction between the forty or so well-to-do merchants and the remaining hundred, who were less than outstanding wholesalers, small retailers, and picayune shopkeepers. There were also a few prosperous members of the craftsman rank in the top tenth. They were 36 out of 637, or one prosperous craftsman for 17 who were not. A handful of plowmen were comfortable as well; 19 out of 478 paid 2.6 *écus* or more tax and thus placed in the top tenth. The best the other 459 could hope for was a tiny plot of land or a small house.

To sum up, of the 125 members of the well-to-do top decile,

24.8 percent (thirty-one) belonged to the first rank, 31.2 percent
(thirty-nine) to the second, and 28.8 percent (thirty-six) were
elite, conservative members of the generally protest-minded
craftsman rank. Finally, 15.2 percent (nineteen) were members
of the plowman rank, living proof that a small minority of this
group (19 to 478 or 4.0 percent) had feathered their nests. These
nineteen prosperous farmers, unlike the greater part of their
group, had nothing to do with the fomentors of the revolt. The
majority of agitators came from the 601 craftsmen and 459
plowmen who were part of the lower 90 percent—1060 heads
of household in all, providing leaders and popular support for
the protests. Counting women, children, and elders, the thousand households actually represented 4,800 to 5,000 people.

Now back to the faction who were on the side of law and
order. The fat cats of Romans, if you will, belonged to this
one. It had a base of support in various sectors of society, but
primarily depended on the 125 heads of household in the top
decile, and more particularly on the 70 of those 125 belonging
to the two upper ranks of landowners and merchants. These
were the citizens who, with their wives, sat down to the Carnival
banquet for 140 guests on February 15, 1580, a counterrevolutionary celebration on the day before Mardi Gras. The "gentlefolk" of Romans gathered in protest against the unrest: "the
most notable merchants and citizens of the town," in the words
of Judge Antoine Guérin and Eustache Piémond, a Dauphiné
notary. The "gentlefolk," women and children included, numbered 300 to 350, or 4.5 percent of the population of 7,000 to
7,500.

The lines dividing the classes were at once clearly drawn and
intersecting as Romans and its region experienced the upheavals
of 1579–1580. In the country, peasants attacked noble landlords, whether of old stock or recently ennobled. In the town,
the craftsmen and plowmen clashed with the bourgeois patricians. The offices of the first and second consul were held by
notables such as Jean Thomé, Umbert Dubois, Gaspard Jomaron, and Antoine Coste of the second, merchant rank; and
Jerome Velheu, Bernardin Guigou, "Monsieur Bruère, Doctor
of Law," and Ennemond Pellissier, all of the first rank of

landowners, and so on. The first rank contained no more than a sprinkling of nobles, descended from merchant families; Antoine de Manissieu, noble Jean de Solignac, Jean de Villiers. . . . On a regional plane, interest groups formed. Urban merchants and country noblemen rallied around Judge Antoine Guérin, while craftsmen and peasants joined under the direction of Jean Serve, called Paumier.

Who were these craftsmen? What did they do? The 1582 or 1583 tax rolls do not list the professions of all taxpayers, although they give a substantial number of clues. In 1582, Romans had 664 members of the craftsmen rank, 28 more than in 1578. We have information on the occupations of 275 of these craftsmen in 1582, and of 241 in 1583. This sweeping poll concerns about 40 percent of the craftsman rank and is very revealing as to the principal branches of the trades. The remaining 60 percent, that is, the 400 or so craftsmen of indeterminate profession, were quite often *journeymen,* salaried workers employed one or two per shop by master craftsmen.

The principal craft or trade in Romans was clothmaking. One hundred and sixty-two heads of household, or 59 percent of all craftsmen whose occupations were reported in 1582, were involved in it. This included sixty-six carders, who were often tenants, and thus most probably impoverished nonhomeowners. They carded the wool produced in Dauphiné that was then bought up by Lyons merchants[30] or by local drapers. There were thirty-nine drapers (recorded as such) in 1582. Their very small output was sold for a very small profit to the wealthy dealers of Romans and Lyons who sold unprocessed wool and bought up cloth. Jean Serve, called Paumier, leader of the 1580 protest of his fellow drapers, was doubtless far more humble than Étienne Marcel, the wealthy merchant-draper who led the Parisian revolution of the fourteenth century. The rebel drapers of Romans bring to mind, rather, the silkworkers who revolted in Lyons in 1832. They were small manufacturers fighting the wealthy dealers' monopoly. The carders and drapers of Romans had good reason to be discontent. The economic crisis provoked by civil war was disastrous for them. Their buying power, in terms of value of the cloth they sold in relation to the wheat they bought, had considerably weakened during the sixteenth century.[31]

Compared to the textile sector, the other important trades in Romans—metalworking, leather, food—employed many fewer craftsmen. There were 20 to 30 heads of household in each, or fewer than 100 in all, in contrast to the 162 clothworkers. Butchers and bakers, few in number but influential, played a crucial role in Romans's tax revolt of 1579–1580.

Romans, Januslike, has two faces, the craftsman community being one, the other agricultural. Farming was the link between the bourgeois landowner of means and the many small farmers who lived in town and worked the vast holdings of the rich, or their own small plots, beyond the walls. The pertinent land roll for Romans[32] is unfortunately late (1596) and less than exhaustive. Still, it can give us an approximate idea of the division of real estate within the walls, and the distribution of the largely agricultural adjacent territory beyond them.

As might be expected, the largest fortunes in land belonged to the bourgeois patrician families, mainly of the merchant and notary rank—rarely noble, occasionally old—whose holdings were usually sizeable. They owned good chunks of Romans and of a dozen surrounding villages as well.[33] Limiting ourselves to their possessions within the town of Romans, we can see they were assessed as high as 100, 200, 300 or even 350 *écus* for land roll purposes, provided the owners were not tax exempt (sometimes the case, as for nobles). Jérôme Velheu's widow owned three huge properties (grain-growing) assessed at 357 *écus*. A Canon Loyron had an estimated 327 *écus* in eighteen pieces of land, a house, two barns, three vineyards. Maître Bertomieu Loyron had twelve fields, a house, and a vineyard, assessed at 276 *écus*. An "honorable" merchant was rated at 294 *écus* in twenty-nine fields, eight vineyards; Sire Charles Jomaron at 280 *écus* in two houses, twenty-two fields, a vineyard, a stable; and so it went for the Milhards, Bonnivauds, and other families of former town consuls. Below 100 *écus*, and especially under 50, came the small merchants. Their possessions were mainly in town (houses, shops), but also included land. The vast majority of craftsmen and peasants, the peasants living within Romans's walls but working the surrounding land owned by prosperous citizens of the first and second ranks, were worth 20 or 10 *écus* or even less. Their holdings at most were a small house, a vineyard, a field. Some widows were assessed lower yet, at 1, 2, and 5 *écus*.

The fact that 478 heads of household lived within the walls but worked in the adjacent fields is partially explained by the large number of vineyards surrounding Romans. Some were owned by the upper classes, but even more were owned by the lower. Growing densely just outside the ultraplebian Le Chapelier quarter and producing good wine, the vineyards hugged the trench round the town's ramparts. Digging, pruning, and harvesting grapes required many a hand. As early as 1449, the citizens of Romans claimed that their town, situated as it was in a poor and unyielding part of the country, would not survive "but for all its culture or the greater part being in vines."[34] Not so far from the truth. The 1516 *compoix*,[35] an important survey of several hundred pieces of land, shows 40.3 percent in fields, 48.6 percent in vineyards, 7 percent in woodland, and 4.1 percent in meadows. Often belonging to the "little people," these vineyards were very small plots of ground, smaller than the grain-producing fields owned by many of the wealthy. Yet the vineyards covered an appreciable portion of the land.

This brief sociological survey of Romans has given us a clearer picture of its craftsmen. We have looked at the two wealthiest groups and have also seen the farmworkers living in town and working in the country on their own or others' land. But what about the *poor*, strictly speaking, or as strictly as this loose term allows? Among those who died during the plague of 1586 (4,096 or a good half of the 8,000 citizens of Romans at the time), only thirty persons were in the town's two almshouses, St. Nicholas and St. Foy, and yet the death rate, which rose under crowded conditions, was certainly as high here as elsewhere. The thirty victims included a few female servants as well as paupers. With a death rate from the plague of 50 percent or more, we can thus estimate that between 1580 and 1585 there were no more than fifty to sixty persons in the almshouses, or less than 1 percent of the population. This is quite a contrast to major cities of the eighteenth century; Madrid, for example, had at least a tenth of its population in almshouses.[36] Romans in 1580 predated the heyday of almshouses. The town had many poor, but they had not yet been herded in off the streets.

The urban poor had its professionals: the beggars who worked the streets, churches, feasts, and funerals.[37] The town fathers were in favor of giving them alms; others wanted to give them the boot. Next came a certain number of heads of household called the "circumstantial poor." They rented, even owned, houses in Romans, and were members of the two lower ranks. They paid less than 4 florins tax in 1578, or less than 0.8 of an *écu* per capita. *Above* this 0.8 *écu* level was the social milieu which bred the leaders of the 1580 protest, those later condemned by the Parlement of Grenoble. The cadre of the rebellion thus came from the lower and middle sections of the craftsman and plowman groups, but not from the rich or poor extremes of either.

This eight-tenths of an *écu* is a true cutoff point. Below it I find 143 plowman and 106 craftsman heads of household. In other words, one craftsman in six (16.6 percent) and almost one plowman in three (29.9 percent) had less than the standard of even minimal prosperity and success. In the first rank, only eight heads of household out of fifty-two (15.4 percent) fall below the cutoff, and in the second, merchant rank, which was the most consistent financially, the percentage was lower, at 12.4 percent.[38]

Let us now focus on those doubly underprivileged citizens who belonged to one of the two so-called lower ranks and who paid less than 0.8 *écu* tax. My count shows 143 plowmen plus 106 craftsmen, for a total of 249 poor heads of household. The majority, then, belonged to the fourth rank. Statistically, this rank was the poorest. In all, these 249 less-privileged taxpayers corresponded to 19.5 percent of Romans's 1,304 heads of household in 1578. One out of five inhabitants was poor. Counting their families—wives, children, ascendants, and so on—we have at least a thousand poor people. There were also the fifty or so unfortunates shut up in the two almshouses, plus an indeterminate, if not very high, number of people too poor even to be included in the tax roll, and finally, the dozens of beggars working the streets and churches, eating the broad-bean soup that the town government doled out. Altogether, the poor numbered perhaps 1,300 to 1,500 out of the town's 7,000 to 7,500 inhabitants. Many of these 1,300 took part, sporadically, in street demonstrations during the protests and during Carnival. But the indigent played no role in the leadership of the revolt, which was almost entirely organized (as we shall see in Chapter VII) by the middle and lower sections of the craftsman and plowman ranks.

We have examined the differences between ranks or *estats*, strata, and poverty or nonpoverty in Romans. One more distinction will aid us in our analysis: landlord versus tenant. A fine document, register CC 5 of 1583, provides the necessary elements. Romans had 1,547 heads of household paying tax in 1583.[39] The list of taxpayers naturally indicates which ones were landowners. The majority of landowners, as we have seen, were modest craftsmen or plowmen who owned a single house, perhaps a small garden. The list also includes, as a check of the two pertinent registers reveals, a large number of tenants.[40] The tax they paid was based on their moveable personal property, since they owned no house or land. The 1583 register CC 5 lists 595 such tenants. We can immediately subtract the sixty or so craftsmen who rented shops or workshops in order to practice their trades. Most of these shops were along a strip slanting through the center of Romans, from the Jacquemard quarter in the north to the St. Barnard quarter in the south. This bourgeois, commercial heart of town was the stronghold of the law and order party. Certain buildings near the Town Hall and the large church of St. Barnard housed as many as seven or eight shops behind their Low Gothic or Renaissance arcades, each shop let to a different retailer. Excepting these 60 or so tradesmen, who probably owned homes elsewhere in town, there were 535 heads of household, or 34.6 percent of all taxpayers, who were real *tenants* in the full (or, rather, wanting) sense of the term.

This means that, by contrast, a good half, if not two-thirds, of all heads of household were the *owners* of their homes—undeniable evidence of a middle-class society. In the working-class quarter of St. Nicholas on the east side of town, the average rent in 1583 was 2.3 *écus* per capita per year, or slightly more than the per capita tax that the quarter paid in the same year (2 *écus*). Landlords seemed to see this rent as a repayment, on the order of 6 percent, of their capital investment in real estate.[41] A tenant may have had anything from a whole house to a single room, including an "upper" or a "lower" (a whole ground floor or second floor, with or without a shop). At the end of the sixteenth century Romans had no buildings higher than two stories. Let us note in passing that Romans did have a few "tenement houses," most of them in the St. Nicholas quarter along the Isère. Four or five tenants would each rent a room in these latter-day apartment buildings. Generally, there were no more than two tenants to a house. The most prosperous of the bourgeois patricians had five or six houses rented out to one or two tenants apiece. Antoine Coste, captain, merchant, and town tycoon, was a typical multidwelling landlord. Coste became a popular scapegoat during the Carnival of 1580.

The total of 535 tenants in 1583 included a few who were in fairly good financial shape. Nonetheless, it was an essentially proletarian group. The town's real poor were tenants, but so were a great number of nonpoor, plowmen, journeymen, crafts-men. They were too impoverished to be considered part of the middle class, however, much less the upper crust. Nor were they part of the lower middle class of homeowning craftsmen which produced the leaders of the revolt. One hundred eighteen of the 535 tenants were craftsmen, journeymen, and plowmen, such as we have already met. An impressive number of them (fifty) were carders; only five carders who owned homes were counted. Then there were the plowmen who were really simple agricultural workers, not farmers (thirteen); "unattached women" (servants whose room was paid, a few paupers); drapers (ten) who were craftsmen and journeymen, not merchant-drapers; street-porters (six); rope-makers (five); and a sprinkling of other crafts and trades.

The remarkable thing is that the leaders of the revolt of 1579–1580, as their subsequent trials presented them, were *not* tenants, even though the tenant group as a whole, and the carders in particular, provided troops and popular support for the protest, the public demonstrations, and the final battles. Only one of the 1580 defendants appeared as a tenant in the 1583 tax roll: Louis Fayol, farmworker. All the other known defendants owned property: the butcher François Drevet, in the St. Foy quarter; Jean Troyassier, farmer; the widow of Antoine Nicodel,[42] blacksmith and protester, executed in 1580; the anti-notary butcher Jean Terrot; Sire Jean Robert-Brunat, related to one of the executed protesters; and Sire Jean Guigou, prosperous upper-class Protestant or Huguenot sympathizer, who sided with the rebels in 1579, only to turn on them the following year.

With the exception of Jean Guigou, a notable of some means, the protesters (or widows of same) we meet in 1583 appeared as *small* property owners.[43] In spite of this smallness, or perhaps because of it, they considered themselves superior to the next group down on the totem pole, the poor or semipoor mass of tenants. The two groups may have banded together during street demonstrations, but the homeowner-craftsman group ran the show. The Carnival in Romans seems to me, then, as I will elaborate, a conflict between the upper crust of the merchant-landowner society and the bourgeois patricians, on the one hand, and on the other, the small property owner sector in the middle ranges of common craftsmen. This group may on occasion have encouraged the next group down to take part in the fighting, but never in the decision making. The opposition leaders prided themselves on the fact they all belonged to the middle level of craftsmen prosperous enough to own homes. But this was also their weakness, perhaps a fatal one. At the strategic moment, the rich were able to turn the resentment of the tenant group against the craftsmen.

There is an overall concept that should be kept in mind. It takes in all the urban craftsmen and peasants who were at once the masses and the leaders of the popular movements sweeping Dauphiné cities. This concept is that of the *menu populat* or common folk. The term was found in records of the 1579 protests in Vienne. Jean de Bourg and his friends write: "We deemed it dangerous, with the populace aroused, to divest the city of men [armed men, the local militia]. Indeed, this done, the common folk (*menu populat*) might become inflamed and rise up."[44] A *common folk*, in sixteenth-century Dauphiné as in four-teenth-century Tuscany, implied an uncommon folk, an elite minority above it. Merchants, lawyers, and bourgeois patricians sometimes pretending to the nobility, formed an elite which was a plausible adversary when opinion ran high and the streets of a walled town welled with people.

And now for the question of *power* in Romans around 1579–1580. Theoretically, a royal *governor* oversaw the town. He had no discernible influence on the events under study.[45] Practically speaking, power was shared on the one hand by the four consuls (collective equivalent of today's mayor) and two town councils, one restricted, the other large. On the other hand was a royal judge, in this case Antoine Guérin—whose reign seemed to be an eternal one.[46]

Guérin's father was a country peddler who became a jeweler in Romans. His descendants were dedicated social climbers. Antoine Guérin, doctor of law, was appointed to the town's highest judicial post in the mid-1560s. He had already succeeded in marrying well, and in fact it was his father-in-law, Antoine Garagnol, who preceded him as judge.[47] Garagnol's son in turn became vice-bailiff of the bailiwick of St. Marcellin in 1580, and was hand in glove with his brother-in-law Guérin. Antoine Guérin probably paid out a considerable sum for the official purchase of his post. He later arranged to have one of his descendants succeed him after his death. By 1579–1580,

Guérin was solidly entrenched. He was the master of judiciary *constraints*, which allowed him to have the orders of the consuls carried out through the good graces of the sergeants-at-arms and other noncommissioned officers. In this sense, Guérin's power was executive as well as judicial.

A concrete text, dated March 5, 1577, sheds light on the separation of power in Romans.[48] It reads: *A royal sergeant of Romans, by virtue of constraints obtained from the Common Court of Romans* (that is, Guérin's local and royal court), *and at the request of Maître Jérôme Velheu, doctor of law and former consul of Romans, orders Jean Mailhot called Sassenage to pay the aforesaid Velheu the sum of 40 florins 10 sous for payment of 30 taxes of 1571.* In other words, Jérôme Velheu, jurist and bourgeois patrician, was consul in 1571. As such, like his fellow consuls he was responsible for levying taxes (the royal taxes were dubbed "30 taxes" or "20 taxes" according to the proportion collected in each quarter). Velheu's mandate as consul lasted only one year, but *six years* after his term he was still responsible for collecting back taxes. To make sure they were paid, he obtained a judicial constraint from judge Guérin. A sergeant who was the judge's direct subordinate executed the order. Terms as consul (municipal power) lasted one year, retroactive in the case of back taxes. The offices of judge (judicial power) and sergeant (police) were for life and few men ever gave them up.

Antoine Guérin, as we shall see again and again, was the real town boss. He ran Romans's political machine and his appointment was permanent.

Revolving around him were the four consuls. They managed Romans's political life. Their functions were partly judicial (drawing up communal rules and regulations), and partly military (upkeep of the ramparts, appointing the captains and corporals of the town militia). They collected direct and indirect taxes and managed and farmed out the indirect municipal taxes (town dues, meat tax, flour tax). They supervised rationing and epidemics, and kept the peace. They oversaw cultural and religious life (management of the secondary school, town feasts). Their makeup reflects the four-part social balance in Romans: the first consul was "a noble living as such or noble of the robe, lawyer, doctor, or bourgeois living off income from land, rent, or debts, not engaging in trade of any kind." The second consul was a merchant or a practician (term for law clerk). The third was a craftsman, the fourth a plowman.[49] Elected for one year, the consuls were assisted by a lesser council of twenty-four members and a great council of forty. Both councils took a quarter of their members (6+6+6+6=24, or 10+10+10+10=40) from each of the four social categories. The two councils in turn elected the four consuls.

Like other Dauphiné towns, Romans had a revolving system of cooptation within the branches of government. They elected a "sovereign people," as Brecht would have it, which in turn elected the government! In 1580, uneasy over the protesters, the town council "dissolved" the people's participation in government, again in Brechtian terms. The craftsmen and farmers who constituted half of each council were, of course, chosen from among the common people of Romans, the cream of the crop, if possible. But they were not *elected* by the people.[50] This undemocratic situation gradually took shape in Dauphiné during the first half of the sixteenth century, as the reawakening of urban centers and increasingly centralized power of the monarchy encouraged the predominance of local oligarchies. Thus, the rapidly growing lower-class population was becoming a threat, and as such needed to be repressed. As late as 1536, the election of Romans's four consuls and forty members of the great council was still theoretically democratic. All heads of household were to gather at the Town Hall and proceed with the business of elections. These elections, however, were somewhat less than valid given the high absentee rate. Only seventy-one people, or less than 7 percent of all eligible voters, attended the assembly of 1536.[51] A few years later absenteeism helped overthrow democratic institutions in Romans or, to be more exact, dealt a final blow to them.

A visit, symbolic of the move toward oligarchy and centralization, was made to Romans in 1542.[52] The Parlement of Grenoble (the sovereign judicial court) sent one of its members, Raymond Mulet, to complain about seditious goings-on. Romans at this time was the most industrial, most restive town in Dauphiné. The cure Mulet had in mind was the enactment of several rulings proposed by the consuls on the advice of the king's men. This was how the local elite and the state bureaucracy joined forces to crush popular sovereignty, or what passed for it. Raymond Mulet, with all the legal weight of the Parlement, thus declared that all general assemblies (which elected the town government) were forbidden. A general council of forty members would henceforth name the consuls and members of the governing bodies, who would be replaced every three years *by mutual cooptation,* an ingenious innovation of the act of 1542. The 1542 assembly, it goes without saying, was the last of its kind. It had just wrung its own neck. But of course, it had been skillfully manipulated by Raymond Mulet and the consuls.

The forty-member council of the assembly, with its ten members from each socio-professional group, included twenty craftsmen and plowmen. But more important it had twenty representatives of the bourgeois patricians and merchants. These twenty nabobs included members of the Velheu family and the de Manissieus, the Bourgeois (Bourgeois-Mornets), Guigous, Romanet-Boffins, Jomarons, Millards. Together with a few other families they dominated the town oligarchy for the next forty years. There you have it. The Parlement of Grenoble, with a hand from the local "dons," had just pulled off a small-scale coup d'état in Romans in 1542. The coup could not have eliminated existing conflicts, but it at least masked the strains caused by the rise and growth of the craftsman class within an outdated but undeniably democratic system of government.

The tensions which subsequently arose within the upper-class group of twenty should not be underestimated. The merchant rank officiously considered the members of the first rank to be parasites.[53] The facts remain: in 1542 a coterie of merchants and noble landlords united and, with the help of twenty master craftsmen and farmers, they seized the power they had only partially controlled up to that point. Cooptation was their method of reproduction. The whole philosophy of the revolution of 1579–1580 was basically an attempt to undo the con-

sequence of the 1542 takeover. In the early spring of 1579, the
craftsman rebel chief Jean Serve-Paumier scored a brief victory
when a number of "extraordinary-supernumerary" members,
deemed "agreeable to the people," were appointed to join the
forty indirect descendants of the coup of 1542. The appointment
of the new council members was the direct result of the unin-
vited and rather brusque appearance of a group of craftsmen
at a regular meeting of the council.[54] Among the new extraordinary-supernumerary council members were several key figures in the protest, all craftsmen: Guillaume Robert-Brunat,
Jean Serve-Paumier, Geoffroy Fleur, Jacques Jacques, François
Robin, Jean Jacques. There were also a few upper-class Hu-
genots like Jean Guigou. The Huguenots had briefly rallied to
the cause of the people, who, they hoped, would support them
in their religious struggles. But the next year, lured by the post
of second consul, Guigou went over to judge Guérin and the
party of law and order. He was named consul in the spring of
1580, after the craftsmen's revolt was put down.

The final repression of the popular movement in February-
March 1580 cut short the terms of the "extraordinary-supernumerary" council members. It also eliminated the captains in
each quarter who were briefly appointed in 1579, when popular
sentiment forced the reluctant consuls to oust Antoine Coste as
captain of the militia.[55] Once Romans was over the "scare" of
1580, the town was again run by the inbred, self-serving system
set up in 1542. The extraordinary-supernumerary council members of 1579 were only an incomplete, if energetic, resurrection
of the popular supremacy abolished in 1542. During Lent of
1580, the one-time council members, stripped of office, were
sent to prison or to the gallows. Quelling the revolt did away
with a momentary situation of "double power," the class struggle taking place within the legal institutions.[56] The miraculous
thing about the Carnival was that it worked within the system.

I now have a little room left for a sketch of Romans's religious
and cultural life. The Carnival of 1580 is also a kind of object
lesson in the town's culture. By the early 1600s Romans was

highly accomplished in the religious and cultural spheres. A large-scale mystery play, *Les Trois Doms* (the three martyr-saints Séverin, Exupère, and Félicien), centered on the spring celebrations of Pentecost and the month of May 1509, and on prayers against droughts and the plague (which had occurred in 1504, 1505, and 1507). For the entire first decade of the century, Romans poured all its resources—financial, municipal, religious, elitist, even demographic—into the production of the mystery play.[57]

In 1516, the construction of a *Calvary*, a great outdoor Way of the Cross, created a holy place near Romans. It was to become famous for its miracles, especially bringing infants back to life.[58] The religious fervor of the Renaissance foreshadowed the furor or counterfuror of the Reformation, well under way in the town even before the start of the Wars of Religion (1560).[59] During the 1560s, notably in 1562–1563 and 1567–1568, Huguenot influence seemed dominant, even in the town council, after a momentary waning due to military raids. Jean Guigou transmitted the Huguenots' wishes to the council, where his word was law. Corrupt priests had earned lasting resentment in Romans; as late as 1550 "They sold masses and souls the way a butcher sells meat."[60]

But the Huguenots were in the minority in Romans. They amounted to 12.4 percent of the population, or 181 out of 1,454 heads of household in 1569.[61] They were members of the upper and especially the craftsman class: drapers, carders, tailors, knife-grinders. Only one of them was a leader in the revolt of 1579–1580: Jean Jacques, the draper. Then there was Sire Jean Guigou, the upper-class turncoat. From 1569 onward, Protestant influence declined sharply. The captains of the town's various quarters, such as Sire Beauregard, were under the thumb of Guérin and the papist consuls. They held the small flock of local Protestants in check. In 1573 they numbered only 128 heads of household, or less than 10 percent of all Romans households.[62] The first exodus to Geneva, the tragic St. Bartholomew massacre, and forced denials of faith all had their effect. Huguenots were turned out of local offices during the 1570s. They had one more go at it, forming a discreet alliance with the Catholic protesters in 1579–1580, which they then reneged on. That was their swan song—in Romans, at any rate.

As for Catholicism and the church, a few distinctions should be made. Romans was obviously full of fervent Catholics or Catholico-pagans. Carnival, leading to Lent, which climaxed at Easter, was a marvelous representation of the town's complex religious sensibilities. During Carnival the sacred blended with the grotesque. In the church of the first millennium, Lent's original purpose was to prepare catechumens for Easter, at which time they were baptized.[63] Practicing members also participated in the cleansing rites—doing penance for the forty days of Lent. The Mardi Gras Carnival was quite simply the time when prospective Christians *buried their pagan ways*, with the help of members of the church, on the eve of Lent. It is no surprise, then, that Carnival celebrations recalled the gastronomic masquerades of the Saturnalia, Lupercalia, and other winter feasts of pagan Rome, now remade to order for Catholicism. Any contradiction between the pagan and Christian elements was mere dialectics.

The pagan nature of Carnival in Romans and the rest of Europe is easy enough to discern. We must look further at the precise state of Catholicism in Romans in 1570 to 1580. In Dauphiné at that time, the church was suffering from the traumas afflicting it since 1560: the Reformation and the Wars of Religion. The mighty church had taken a mighty fall. It had lost property, monks, priests, vocations. At the same time, it had not yet found the second wind that would power its eventual comeback. Only after 1580 was it really back on its feet, when a concerted effort was made to put the directives of the Council of Trent into motion.[64] For the time being, in 1579–1580, the Holy Church in Romans was in rather poor shape, even though its teachings were still faithfully and enthusiastically followed. In addition, the mass sensibility behind Carnival had not yet been subdued by the rigid, repressive precepts the Council of Trent had been trying to impose for the last few decades.

The clergy, then, was in a state of social eclipse in Romans during the difficult times of 1579–1580, even with its members still present in town. No branch of the clergy played an important role in the incidents occurring between February 1579 and February 1580. The Chapter of St. Barnard, the pastors of Romans's three parishes—St. Barnard, St. Nicholas, and St. Roman—and even the Cordeliers (the presence of this truly urban Franciscan order identifies Romans as a city) played no active part in the incidents, for or against. The influence of the church, however, was evident in both the protester and the law and order camps. The socially active guilds claimed church allegiance; religious feasts were at once sacred and profane; and finally, the Catholic hierarchy was identified with the law and order faction.

Although learning was predominantly religious, partly traditional, possibly astrological at this time, let us note the recent appearance in Romans of the new scholarly thought. It was taught at the secondary school.[65] Since its institution in the late Middle Ages, both the town and the Chapter of St. Barnard had taken an equal share in running the school. The young of the upper two ranks were virtually the sole beneficiaries of what was taught there. What the outcome of such an education might have been is very difficult to say. More generally speaking, it is difficult to study the problem of literacy in Romans at the time in question. The most we can state is that, as might be expected, the leading bourgeois put magnificent signatures on consular documents.[66] Some of the rebel craftsmen also had handsome signatures. The richer participants in the Carnival in Romans were literate, even in French. But the masses, we can surmise, spoke only a Franco-Provençal patois, and the vast majority of the two lower groups could not read or write. This literate/illiterate dichotomy was significant in the choice of symbolic themes of the 1580 protest. Sixty years later, in 1641–1644, when the existence of parish registers permits us to gather statistics, 71 percent of the population of Romans was illiterate, with a slightly higher proportion of women.[67] The overall percentage must have been close to 80 percent in 1580, when education was even less developed than in 1643. Yet no matter how low, the urban literacy rate was much higher than that of the surrounding country districts, where probably nine out of ten adults were illiterate.

Let us now have a look at these country districts. The ribbons of plains and hills east of the Rhône framed the protest belt which included the cities of Romans, Valence, Montélimar, even Grenoble, in the Dauphiné piedmont. The country districts are of prime importance in our study, for the 1580 Carnival in Romans was simply the urban showcase of a vast peasant war. In the towns, revolts pitted upper class against craftsman class; the standard rural struggle was peasant against noble. Urban unrest was a logical consequence of the rise of towns during the Renaissance. As such, they were premonitory, suggesting the self-styled antibourgeois class struggles in modern cities. Rural conflict, however, was rooted in a much more distant past, even when, tinged with antigovernment protest, it seemed contemporary. In this context, I can almost hear Fustel de Coulanges neatly summing up the Middle Ages, especially the first millennium when towns had almost entirely disappeared. He writes: "The rural estate was the most powerful if not the only organ of social life. It is the place where almost all the society's work is done, where riches and the hunger for riches grow. A stronghold. Inside this rural estate the classes mingled. Land and the desire for land are what created inequality."[68]

Noble estates did take up a generous portion of the land around Romans and also in the nearby Vienne region, where rural protest was particularly vigorous. In these two geographic sectors (a total of 271 villages), the nobility of the robe or of the sword, along with the clergy, owned 38.45 percent of all land at the end of the sixteenth century, almost two-fifths. Peasants and lowborn burghers who lived in the towns and had holdings in the country shared the remaining 61.55 percent. For Romans alone the proportion of noble and other tax-exempt landowners was slightly lower (34.12 percent). Rural unrest in the Vienne region was the expression of the village and citydwellers' strong opposition to such tax exemptions. In effect, 40.85 percent of Vienne land belonged to exempt owners. The unrest there turned explosive between 1576 and 1580.

Generally speaking, the percentage of land owned by nobles and the clergy, while not exorbitant, was relatively high. A point of comparison: on the brink of the French Revolution, tax-exempt land in the whole of the realm amounted to only 30 to 35 percent of the total. The bourgeoisie owned 30 percent, and peasants 40 to 45 percent. In England at the same period, a full 80 percent of land belonged to the aristocracy and gentry![69]

Even so, the 38.45 percent of tax-exempt landowners in the Romans and Vienne regions were in for their share of hatred and rancor during the heated protests of 1579–1580, particularly because these landowners represented less than 2 percent of the overall population and owned 40 percent of the land or close to it. This well-heeled minority had been rounding out its estates, in the best capitalist tradition, throughout the sixteenth century. Challenges put to the landlords in times of social unrest became understandable.[70]

We should further note that exempt holdings were far more extensive (38.45 percent) in the Vienne and Romans regions, hotbeds of peasant rebellions, than in the rest of Dauphiné (27.35 percent). The excessive protest in these two districts reflected the unreasonable amount of tax-exempt land.[71]

Let us now examine the *droits seigneuriaux,* or rents, shares, and services due noble landlords, in the hundred or so villages of the Romans region. These rents and services also sparked protest against the nobles; it should be kept in mind that 93 percent of all landlords were tax-exempt members of the nobility and clergy.[72] In Romans itself, where the Chapter of St. Barnard was lord of the town, a minimum was due. The chapter received the tongue of slaughtered cattle, a few quit-rents, and a *lods et ventes,* or inheritance tax amounting to 10 percent of the capital value of inheritance claimed or sold. Social protest in

Romans, then, was directed more against the aristocracy than against the clergy, which at any rate had taken a beating in the Protestant Reformation. Elsewhere, in open country, the landlord's share was much greater. A few documents from the Wars of Religion and testimony recorded in a later "review of hearths" around 1700 give us an idea of what the share must have been.[73]

In 1700, things had changed little since the end of the sixteenth century in the 106 villages north of Romans which were officially attached to the town. In at least fifty-seven villages, and probably a good many more, the landlord was due *cens et rentes*. *Cens* were quit-rents, the customary share of money or produce paid by farmers. They amounted to little. *Rentes* or annuities, however, could become perpetual interest on accumulation of debts owed to the landlord, and came due even after the debtor's death. Furthermore, there were at least twenty-seven banal (that is, belonging to the landlord) flour mills in use in the district; the landlord received 5 percent of the output. There were also fourteen banal ovens, with varying amounts going to the landlord: one-sixteenth of the bread, one-twenty-fifth of the flour. A share called *vingtain* is mentioned in seventeen localities. As its name indicates, it involved one-twentieth of all produce; it fell on especially rich or recently cleared land. The above-mentioned *lods et ventes* inheritance tax appeared thirty-six times, at the rate of 16.7 percent. In nineteen wine-producing villages the landlord also had a privilege called *banvin*, which allowed him a monopoly on wine sales in August or during Lent, according to local custom.

In at least forty-seven villages, the landlord was also due a certain share of the rye, oats, poultry, and other foods produced there. In addition, he had the right to use peasants for two or three days per year of forced labor on his estate. In these forty-seven villages, payment of shares was graduated depending on the size of the peasant's operation. There were plowmen of some substance with three pairs of oxen and sheepfolds; others of middling means with one or two pair of oxen (meaning one or two plows); dirt farmers with donkeys, mules, or even horses to pull their plows; and finally, there were simple day-laborers with no team at all, who paid the smallest share to the land-lord.

This evidence points toward a village society divided into two standard groups (with some overlapping) of *plowmen* who owned oxen and sheep, and might have been tenant farmers on lordly estates or else cultivated very small farms, and *day-laborers* who owned no oxen or cattle. The ownership of livestock and sheep was the essential criterion of social differentiation in the villages. Yet the graduated pressure from the landlord affected every member of the peasant community, distinctions between them notwithstanding. As a result, peasants were likely to form a cohesive group in time of crisis. They banded together against the landlord. His men were often the direct targets: the judge, registrar, and steward, in charge respectively of the judicial, clerical, and administrative affairs of a noble estate.

All in all, the noble landlords laid a heavy yoke on the Dauphiné peasant.[74] The quit-rents themselves were nothing much, but unpaid rents accumulated, and the 16.7 percent *lods et ventes* was often onerous. Moreover, the Dauphiné real estate market was an active one. In each generation, about a third of all farmland changed hands. Nobles took advantage of this situation to get hold of a major part of the plain or semiplain-land of the lower Dauphiné area around Romans and Valence, and in the Grésivaudan River valley. Here the future homes of Judge Guérin's descendants, with their new noble name of de Tencin, were to be built. The landlords effectively molded an archipelago of fields yielding low quit-rents into a veritable continent for their neocapitalistic use.

Among the nobles buying up land, those newly ennobled and therefore freshly exempted from taxes were a particularly dynamic lot. The share of taxes they had formerly paid was now shouldered by the peasants who were therefore not overly fond of them.[75] It is difficult to say how many of these new noble families there were. A study of the Valence and Die regions in 1594 shows a 50.6 percent increase in nobles over 1523.[76] It is true that only 4.4 percent of them can be said with certainty to have been new titles. But the 50.6 percent increase in sixty years cannot be accounted for simply by a sudden migration of bluebloods to the area. There must have been a number of newly titled families not officially counted as such. Having risen from the common dregs, the *nouveau* nobles did not get good press.[77] They were reputed to sow their wild oats with abandon, piss in cemeteries, never pay their debts, and beat the commonfolk. In Pisançon, near Romans, there were quite a few of these brand new squireens at the beginning of the seventeenth century: the Guérins (son of the judge), Jomarons, Velheus, Costes, and Loyrons. They were sometimes very low types indeed, with the blood of the 1580 protesters still on their hands. This clique along with some other Pisançon notables held 3,438 *séterées* of land (tax exempt) out of a total of 7,353, or 46.8 percent of arable land: enough to cause a bit of resentment . . . it had already manifested itself in 1579–1580.[78]

The new nobles, old nobles, and landlords of all sorts were much like another group that made huge profits from exploiting the countryside between 1560 and 1600. Moneylenders, using the sort of loans approved by the church and the law, cleaned out many an honest man, many a poor debtor, during the Wars of Religion.[79]

Compared to the landlords' due, church tithes were low. As a rule, a tithe was a 10 percent share of the harvest given to churchmen: bishops, canons, abbots, monasteries, and parish priests themselves. It was based on the principal crops and adjusted according to harvests. The 1700 "review of hearths" in Dauphiné, which we have already made use of, is a broad survey allowing us to specify the rate of the tithe in 335 separate tithe-zones. A scattering of late sixteenth-century sources validate the 1700 sources for the period we are studying. In the 335 tithe-zones in question, the rate for cereal crops was not the tenth that the etymology of the word *tithe* would warrant, but rather a perfect twentieth, more precisely 1 to 20.1 or 4.98 percent. The rate was lower in Romans's 106 villages or 209 tithe-zones. The figures are 1 to 22 or 4.55 percent and 1 to 18.2 or 5.49 percent, respectively. These were moderate levels.[80] For the peasants in Languedoc and the Comminges region of the

Pyrenees, the tithe was far higher, reaching 8, 9, and 10 percent, or very close to the double of the Dauphiné rate. This explains why the peasants living in Romans's countryside bore relatively little hostility toward the clergy in 1579–1580. Demonstrations against church oppression were few and far between.[81] In any case, the clergy was still reeling from the Huguenot and anti-Catholic violence prevalent since 1560. It deserved to be left in peace. There were few Huguenot peasants. The essentially Catholic rural masses turned their wrath against the nobility and the landlords in general, rather than against the clergy.

Even so, the case against the nobles should not be overstated. Heavy as the landlords' rents and dues may have seemed in comparison to tithes, they were far from being the real target of peasant protests.[82] The thorn in the peasants' side was the tax-exempt status of the landlords. In the first wave of demonstrations against such exemptions, the peasants burned one or two castles and a few *terriers,* registers of the rents and shares due.[83]

The Carnival in Romans was at the crux of a situation in the Dauphiné of 1579–1580 that I shall progressively describe. But after this brief introduction we are already justified in calling it a revolutionary situation. Large groups of the peasantry had taken up arms. They combated the outlaw soldiers of noble birth who had been terrorizing the countryside. They fought against certain aspects of domination by the landlords, and most of all against the tax-exempt status of the nobles. The urban bourgeoisie was to varying degrees in conflict with the two privileged ranks. The craftsmen and the common folk were locked in a struggle with the bourgeois patricians. Finally, the nobility itself was no longer unified. The rift between Protestant nobles and their Catholic brothers was destructive. These are the same elements Lawrence Stone identifies in the "revolutionary situation" when it arose in the *ancien régime.*[84] In our case, upper class battled with lower; the elite was divided. On top of all this there were conflicts between the central government (the royalty holding court in Paris or Blois) and the outlying provinces (Dauphiné, jealously guarding its fiscal privileges). The royal army crushed the peasant adversaries of the established order. Without its intervention and its weight, more important social change might have come about in 1580, to the detriment of the nobility's tax-exempt status. As it turned out, the changes came later, but peacefully, during the 1630s. Dauphiné, after all, was a next-door neighbor to Switzerland, and antinoble and antilandlord revolutions had been taken for granted for centuries in the Swiss sphere.

II

❦❧❦❧❦❧❦❧❦❧❦❧

Taxes:
Commoner versus Noble

Could there have been a Huguenot plot at the bottom of the 1579–1580 revolt in Dauphiné? Judge Guérin seemed to think so, or at least he wanted to make us think so. For Guérin is all too clearly the author of the anonymous report which provides one of the main accounts we have of the protest in Romans. He saw the meddling hand of the Protestants behind the troubles in the lower Dauphiné and Vienne regions. The report grandiloquently states: *If the source and foundation of the following discourse of the rising of the people[1] that has come about in Dauphiné is to be well and truly understood, in the first place it must be presumed that those of the supposedly reformed religion* (Huguenots), *unable to gain a foothold in Vienne during all the troubles occurring in the said region, and seeking by all means to do so, found no better solution than to encourage some division between those of the said region of Vienne and who were in league with those of the said region of Vienne and who were in league with those of the "village party," meaning villages near Romans.*

In truth, the Huguenots did not come close to having their way with the people of the Rhône valley and the Alps, of whom a good number were still Catholic, especially in the valleys. Moreover, the Huguenots themselves were divided on the question of popular unrest and the Catholic leagues which gave it a voice. The term, *league*, if not a new word at the time, was in vogue and decidedly controversial. Some of the most influential Huguenot leaders thought the unrest dangerous and portentous

35

of what some today would call the peril of anarchy. In this conservative camp was the chief of Geneva's local partisans, François de Lesdiguières, then in the prime of youth. Lesdiguières was blunt: *We have good news, the leagues make much noise, but no move* (A 29, note), he wrote to Gouvernet on June 13, 1579.[2] It should be pointed out that the leagues in question were in the Montélimar region, under the direction of the ultrapapist Jacques Colas, a natural enemy of the Huguenots.

Thus, the Huguenots were of two minds on the question, and in any case, their scheming would not have sufficed to sow discord in the Vienne and Romans regions had there not already been a great deal of popular discontent predisposing the area to riot. The prime cause of discontent was the soldiery that had been sapping the countryside's resources for twenty years, since the start of religious strife in 1560. The soldiers' material demands, backed up by threats, had brought Dauphiné to its knees. Guérin, the "Anonymous Author," stated it quite plainly for once. Huguenot plotting, he wrote, encouraged the country rebels to "act up" simply because they claimed *they had been trodden on and oppressed, suffering greatly, by the fighting men, foot guards as well as horse guards, who, crossing the said country again and again during the preceding years, had committed extortion of goods and excesses without number* (A 29). Using one of the less serious incidents as an example, in 1577 soldiers of the Grillon, Larche, and Martinière regiments did not think twice about stealing, then selling, a good many cattle.[3] The situation was such that when these regiments were to pass through Romans, on their way down to Languedoc, the town fathers decreed that not more than one company at a time might march through their walled city, and when they did *the inhabitants by order of the consuls kept their shops closed, stood armed at their posts and at the gates to the city.* This would not, the consuls euphemistically put it, keep the townspeople from *showing these regiments every courtesy and honor on the part of the said town* (of Romans).

Thievery and threats were not the only ways the plowmen and townsfolk (themselves semirural) lost cattle and victuals to the soldiery. The population was also required to deliver food to the soldiers, who consumed, and wasted, a great deal of meat. They ate 80 kilograms each per year, even more than the well-fed Parisian of today. On July 22, 1577, "under orders from Monsieur de Moideux, commissioner general of rations, the town of Romans was required to send cattle, sheep, bread, and wine to Monsieur de Gordes's troops camped at Pont-en-Royans. The siege there was suddenly lifted, and 4,500 loaves of bread supplied by Romans were left to go stale and be sold for next to nothing."[4] Waste and more waste . . . of money as well: in July 1577 Romans had to pay 600 *écus* for the ransom of two of its consuls who had been captured by soldiers. Or in 1575, for instance, Baron de Gordes, then the royal lieutenant governor of the province, came to Romans. He requested that the town underwrite his men's living expenses with a subscription amounting to 20 *livres* of tax per fiscal hearth.[5]

The levying of these crushing taxes (called *foules*, literally "pressings" in the language of the time) had a severe effect indeed on taxpayers. In August 1578 a collection of 4 *écus* per fiscal hearth was ordered throughout Dauphiné, for the payment of taxes and debts due or contracted by the two warring factions, Catholic and Huguenot. Let everyone pay, and God will take care of His own! Needless to say the Huguenots complained, and the Catholics just as loudly, when they realized each would be paying a share of the expenses incurred by the other side. Yet the 4 *écus* were paid up without too much gnashing of teeth, if we are to believe Eustache Piémond, Dauphiné's own "good soldier Schweik." But then, on top of this, another tax was projected for October 1578, at the rate of 2 *écus*, 4 *sols* per hearth (P 63), " for the affairs of the region," meaning the repayment of regional and provincial debts and expenditures. This was very nearly the last straw. *The thing is too sudden and unbearable for the people, given the great levies the war has already caused* (P 63). When a conflict is financially ruinous, why give a cent to support it? Why add fuel to the flame you want to douse? Peace seemed more and more remote from Dauphiné, even though the kingdom of France had been on the whole peaceful since the royal edict of pacification in 1577. Certain Dauphiné towns and villages therefore had recourse to the third estate *Cahiers*; this provincial document was presented nationally at Blois on March 16, 1577. ("The *cahier* was a petition of grievances coupled with recommendations on how

the listed wrongs could be righted.")† This *Cahier* was Dauphiné's great hope. It requested that all those who had levied
taxes for one or the other of the warring factions give an account
and give financial satisfaction. The accounts would be checked
by auditors brought in from outside the province and who would
thus be above suspicion of complicity with those they would be
investigating.

That was not all the commoners demanded. With an eye to
the provincial Estates (the representative assembly of Dauphiné's three orders, commoner, clergy, and noble) which were
soon to be held in Grenoble, the communities protested against
the enormity of royal taxes and other *tailles* and special levies
relating to the war. They complained that as a result, nothing
was left the taxpayers but *the clay and rocky soil*, and they requested that the nobility and the clergy pay a share of taxes—
their just share—so that the third estate would no longer bear
the brunt of the taxes.

Of course, demanding that the three estates share equally
was out of the question; this was 1579, for heaven's sake, not
1789. A fervent wish was that the new nobles (who were all or
nearly all former bourgeois patricians with fortunes in land
and houses) should not be automatically exempted from taxes
when they acceded to the nobility, as the fiscal relief thus
afforded them quite literally put what they had formerly paid
in taxes onto the commoners. The *Cahiers* requested that the
third estate, whether in the town or the country, should not be
so burdened and that the nobility and the Church pay taxes on
any land they owned which was lately "rural," meaning non-
noble. When such land was bought by nobles it automatically
became tax-exempt. Consequently, since the total amount of
tax to be collected in a given locality was constant, this increased the already heavy tax on the remainder of land owned
by those not fortunate enough to belong to the nobility or the
clergy.

---

†Translator's note. J. Russell Major, *Representative Institutions in Renaissance France* (Madison, University of Wisconsin: 1960), p. 76.

It follows that noblemen and even clerics did not always see things the way the commoners did and this was especially true of the new nobles, who had scarcely shaken the dirt off their boots and were thus very proud of their noble status. They disdained being taxed like vulgar commoners.

Even before the convocation of the Estates, held in the spring of 1579, the commoners' request gave rise to the compilation of the *Cahiers* between August 1578 and the following February. The authors hoped to present their grievances and recommendations at the provincial assembly. They attacked exemptions and accused the nobility and clergy of tax evasion, as we have just seen. This evasion was considered all the more scandalous because in time of war each citizen, in theory, was duty bound to contribute to the defense of the province (P 64). Those leaders of the 1579 revolt who were literate produced texts which invoked Dauphiné's former privileges: theoretically, nobles and clergy as well as plebeians were to contribute to the public defense. They called on regional privilege to combat social privilege. A fitting argument indeed! The leaders referred to themselves as members of the plebeian third estate, that is, the commoners of town and country alike. Yet it would be stretching the term "commoners" to include the upper crust of the third estate: the bourgeois patricians living idly off their rents, the solid dignitaries of the robe, the rich merchants, the parasitic financiers. All of them were on the side of nobility, which was the state of grace they hoped to attain or have their children attain.

The spokesmen for the "third estate of commoners," which *wept it could take no more,* indulged in agitation and propaganda, openly or clandestinely, depending on circumstances. They seemed to promote the idea of a tax strike or even of abolishing taxes, that is, the *taille. They wooed the people by pursuing their just remonstrances, and by insinuating no more tailles would be paid* (P 64). Political propagandists and militants went from town to town, village to village. They publicized the contents of the *Cahiers,* gathering the communities' formal approval of the contents. They announced the tax strike Jean de Bourg outlined for the Estates in Grenoble in April 1579. These beginnings of

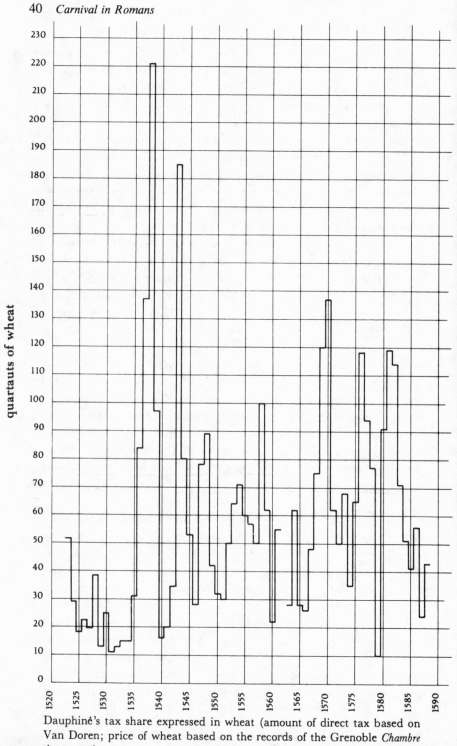

Dauphiné's tax share expressed in wheat (amount of direct tax based on Van Doren; price of wheat based on the records of the Grenoble *Chambre des comptes*).

"objective" rebellion were awash with devout submission to the reigning king, Henri III. Secretly, from community to community, the oath was taken to live and die in pursuit of the aims outlined in the *Cahiers,* by means of humble remonstrances to His Majesty.

At this point a pause in our narrative is in order. It is apparent that the initial causes of the 1579–1580 revolt were numerous, but fiscal problems soon became a focal point, as did the presentation of the *Cahiers* listing the third estate's grievances. As a digression from the events culminating in the Carnival of 1580, I would first like to ask two questions, both of them interlocutory. First: was the tax squeeze really that hard on the commoners during the 1580s, and especially just before the uprising? Second: third estate protest centered around the nobility and clergy's tax-exempt status; can the history of this exemption be briefly stated, if only to give us a fuller understanding of the common people's resentment and the causes of the revolt?

First, the peasant war in Dauphiné and its urban offshoot, the Carnival in Romans, were directly tied to tax increases immediately preceding them and to the taxpayers' negative reaction to these increases. The graph of the *taille* or direct tax in Dauphiné from 1523 to 1580 is very convincing in this respect. The *taille* has of course been recalculated in terms of *real* value (here, in wheat). In *nominal* value, the fiscal curve would be distorted by the inflation affecting prices as well as taxes at the time. Graph I illustrates these points.

In real value, there can be no doubt that between 1566 and 1584 one of the heaviest waves of taxes since the first quarter of the sixteenth century hit Dauphiné (see Graph I). It is true that taxes were even heavier around 1536 and again in 1543, when France was deep in François I's costly wars. The Alpine province had to come up with, or put up with, its share of taxes for the royal coffers, but in those days such levels of taxation were still tolerable. The Renaissance, at its height prior to the Wars of Religion, found Dauphiné in a phase of growth and relative prosperity, both economic and demographic. The province was able to pay, and pay it did—somewhat less than cheerfully, but what did that matter to the authorities? Rebellion was out of the question. However, things changed in the period between 1566 and 1584. The Dauphinois developed a taste for arms, or at least got into the habit of using them after more than ten years of civil war. The people were no longer so easy to fleece. Furthermore, the province had plenty to complain about as it had been bled dry by war, plague, and famine. Before 1560, the number of taxpayers increased along with the general growth in population; after that date it leveled off (in Romans, for instance, there was a marked decline). Taxable wealth was also shrinking. This happened on every level, whether we consider overall revenue or revenue calculated per capita for each taxpayer. The authorities' behavior at this point went against economic theory: they imposed taxes in 1566–1572 and again in 1575–1578 which were far heavier than those of the preceding, flourishing period before 1560 (with the exception of the two spurts of high taxation mentioned above).

The 1579 revolt was a timely, if short-lived, remedy against high taxation, and ended the deplorable tax squeeze of 1574–1578. The tax for 1579 was the lightest, in real value, during the entire period from 1523 to 1589, a full three-quarters of a century. In contrast, once the revolt was put down in the spring of 1580, the infernal tax machine proceeded full steam ahead. A new and intense tax squeeze was in store between 1580 and 1584.

The second problem concerns the tax-exempt status of the clergy and aristocrats as the matrix of plebeian frustration, and the privileged or nonprivileged status of the various strata of society as regards taxation. What was the background of the third estate's outlook on this problem? To portray it I will indulge in something akin to a flashback.

Although their belief lacked a basis in fact, the people of Dauphiné believed they were totally tax-exempt, and that they had been since 1341 when the *dauphin* (as the counts who ruled the province before it was ceded to France were called), Humbert II, fell ill. Hounded by his confessors, he extended a general exemption from taxes to all his subjects. The majority of the towns already enjoyed such tax privileges, by virtue of their *chartes de liberté*, the charters underlying their very existence. As successors to Humbert II, all the kings of France up until the seventeenth century theoretically maintained this blanket exemption. In practice, however, they showed no compunction in levying taxes (modestly disguised as "free gifts" to the crown). Despite this royal hypocrisy, the act of 1341, freeing Dauphiné of taxes, was very much alive in the minds of commoners in 1550 and even in 1630.[6]

During the sixteenth century there was speculation about a tax exemption which would extend to all three estates, not just the nobility and clergy. In this sense—but in this sense only— our revolt had a utopian aim, that of reviving a conservative past.[7] This ran counter to the realism displayed by the statesmen and bureaucrats of the period—whose brand of realism was the harbinger of centralized government. Yet, as we shall soon see, the rebels' supposed conservatism was confined to this question and was idealistic rather than factual. The rebels of 1580 were not really for maintaining the status quo or returning to a utopian past. They were reformers, and at times revolutionaries.

It is true that at the local level certain very real exemptions, applying to the commoners of an entire town, were in effect in the mid-sixteenth century. Montélimar only forfeited its privilege in 1550.[8] No wonder the tax revolt thirty years later was particularly virulent there. The parents and grandparents of the town's taxpayers had kept alive the memory of the golden age a generation back, when no one in Montélimar paid taxes.

This *real* exemption was limited to Montélimar and did not apply to the rest of Dauphiné in any way. In fact, despite the exemption supposedly granted them in 1341, the Dauphinois paid substantial taxes during the late Middle Ages and the Renaissance, though always in the guise of voluntary contributions. One of the first cases of such a so-called contribution to the royal treasury was in 1357, to the crown prince Charles,

for the ransom of John the Good. These "gracious gifts" theoretically manifested the people's good will, their nonservitude,
their status as freemen, and their general consent, as witnessed
by the provincial Estates' vote of tax monies. Marcel Mauss
elaborates on this theme in his *Essai sur le don*.

Now comes the second explosive element, or rather the second
ingredient in the explosive charge. It was felt in all fiscal
protest between the Rhône and the northern Alps in the sixteenth century. I am of course referring to the *particular* tax
exemption enjoyed by the two privileged estates, and the people's resentment of it. There was nothing utopian about this
exemption. It was very real, having come into being, as far as
we can tell, some twenty years after the fatal act of 1341, and
no later than June 1370 (when it became law at the provincial
Estates convened in Romans). Subsequently, and until Richelieu's time, the exemption was considered a fait accompli. A
rule proved by the exceptions to it. For, on occasion, nobles and
priests were forced to pay an exceptional tax, but there was no
question of such levies setting precedents. The act of 1370, so
typical of what was to become the French nobility's general
philosophy, would be held valid for several centuries, despite
the fact that the exemption was originally granted for purely
political, contemporary reasons. In 1370 the king of France
needed to win the support of the clergy and nobility of Dauphiné. Historically, tax exemption was a by-product of the
centralization of the French monarchy, and in 1370 what the
king was trying to do was funnel Dauphiné's voluntary subsidy
into the accounts of the ordinary revenue of the realm.[9] He was
therefore in need of some well-placed accomplices in the province. The nobles and the clergy were declared tax-exempt, and
the squeeze was put all the more tightly on the people.

The scene was set for what was to become the very long-term
social tragedy of fiscal protest in Dauphiné. The sixteenth century, much more intensely than the fifteenth, witnessed conflict
between the third estate, which claimed to be exempt from
taxes like everyone else in the province, and the remaining two
estates. The nobility and clergy benefited from specific, effective exemptions which the third estate was naturally loath to
acknowledge. The obvious conclusion of plebeian reasoning

was that according to the act of 1341, *no one* should pay taxes. A corollary (with a much better chance of becoming fact) was that *everyone*, nobles and clergy included, should contribute his quota of the "gracious gift" to the royal treasury.

The arena for this battle was furnished by the Dauphiné Estates. A word or two should be said on the subject of that august institution, which had met annually and regularly since the end of the fourteenth century. An understanding of it will help us understand the tragic outcome of the Carnival in Romans.

What was the nature of the thriving Dauphiné Estates in the sixteenth century? It goes without saying that its structures were far from rigid. The religious and civil troubles from 1560 to 1580 gave the Estates more than one push in the right or the wrong direction.

The list or *roll* of the convocation of the Estates, says Dussert, contained 36 representatives of the clergy, 270 nobles, who were theoretically seigneurs with great estates which they administered, and 115 personages of the third estate.[10] All of the 115 were town consuls, some in smaller towns or even villages. Many such communities lay within the direct domain of the king, some were on the lands of noblemen. Because of this arbitrary selection, a certain number of rural parishes that joined the revolt of 1579–1580 were not represented at the Estates, since they were the fiefs of private landlords or even of the king. There were examples of this in the Valloire north of Romans. All this made for even more tension. Generally speaking, no matter how the voting was conducted during the different sessions of the Estates, the nobility had a clear numerical and hierarchic superiority.[11] It had prestige on its side, not to mention an absolute majority. The larger or privileged towns sent the most representatives of the third estate. This included Dauphiné's "Ten Towns," Vienne, Valence, and Romans among them. But the *other* towns, and the rural villages, too, were in very good voice when it came to official complaints and demands. These demands helped the commoners maintain their identity as distinct from the two privileged groups, as well as from the bourgeoisie of the "Ten Towns."

The provincial Estates played a political role (grievances and such), but their other and more important role was financial. In theory, they voted on taxes. They had at least partial responsibility for the assignment, collection, and control of all taxation in Dauphiné, whether the revenues were destined for national or local coffers. They also handled military, religious, and economic affairs.[12]

Let us limit ourselves to the Estates' dealings with taxes. During the sixteenth century one part of Dauphiné had a relatively equitable tax system. This was the southern Alps region in the southeast of the province. The regions of Gap, Embrun, Briançon, Oisans, and the Baronnies had a very old tradition of taxation through the drawing up of *cadastres* or land rolls. Each community, town or village had its own roll. They were not always meticulous in their accuracy. Still, they provided for prorating taxes according to the size and fertility of each piece of land and, excluding the small number of fields specifically designated as noble and tax-exempt, *all* property, belonging to commoners, peasants, bourgeois, nobles, and clerics, was included for tax purposes. In these fortunate regions tax disputes were nowhere near as bitter, naturally, as in central and northern Dauphiné. Around Grenoble and Romans, the tax-exempt noble and clerical classes were pitted against the commoners in town and country; the commoners considered their tax burden unfair. In the sunlit Alps, however, each head of household, blueblood or not, in the tax-free service of Christ or not, paid more or less his just due. The reasons for this happy state of affairs are numerous, and it would take too long to describe them. Suffice it to say that these southern Dauphiné regions were Occitanian, meaning they spoke Provençal, in which *oc* was the word for *yes*. This made them quite distinct from the area around Grenoble where Franco-Provençal dialects were spoken (Romans itself was on the border between these two language groups). The southern part of Dauphiné was thus linguistically and culturally related to Provence and Languedoc, the two great Occitan provinces . . . which both had *cadastres*.

In Provence and Languedoc, land rolls, called *compoix*, had long been in existence. They were rooted in Roman law and had been revived at the end of the Middle Ages by provincial jurists. The Occitanian regions of Dauphiné eagerly followed their neighbors' example. Indeed, the kingdom of France could be viewed as divided between the "southerners" who paid *real* taxes and the "northerners" who paid *personal* taxes. Taxes were real when they were applied equitably and were based on *real* property by means of land rolls. This was the case in Oisans, for instance. Taxes can be called personal, and unjust, when they are based on rank in society, with some categories of persons exempt and others paying tax. The borderline between the *personal* taxation of the north and the *real* taxation of the south cut through the whole of southern France, and, as we have just seen, through the heart of Dauphiné. It should also be pointed out that the very powerful regional and community institutions in places like Oisans made them veritable mountain republics on the Swiss model; such institutions reinforced peasant control and fostered payment of taxes by nobles as a result.

Conflict was thus far more pronounced in the north. Romans, Vienne, Grenoble, and the surrounding countryside paid what were in fact personal taxes. And conflict was further aggravated because comparisons were possible: the hard-pressed taxpayers of Vienne and Romans knew that only a few leagues away, the citizens of Oisans or Gap and their regions had a tax system that was far more just. From this point of view, the split personality of Dauphiné distinguished it from its neighbors in the far north, Normandy or Île de France for example. Matters there were equally unpleasant, but much less explosive. The peasants of the north may have been overtaxed, but so were all their neighbors, and nobles were tax-exempt without exception. The grass in the next region seemed no greener. But to the peasants in any discontented village near Romans, the grass over the fence looked very green indeed.

The peasant revolt in Dauphiné in 1579–1580 was of no interest to the southern regions of the province with their land rolls and real taxes. They had little sympathy with the protesters to their north. And as it happened in the late 1570s, they were partially under Huguenot control, which gave them problems of their own quite different from those under discussion. The 1579 uprisings were the main concern of the mid-Rhône and lower Isère regions. The clash over tax exemption had slowly come to a head during an earlier period, while the problem of exemption was destroying the social fabric: one problem was the partial freedom from taxes enjoyed by the towns and especially the urban bourgeoisie as compared to the overtaxed country dweller. A further problem was the tax-exempt status of nobles, members of the clergy, and the upper bureaucracy, giving us two opposing fronts. The split between city and country had been widening since 1530, as the one between privileged and commoner groups had been since 1550.

The town versus country situation was the first to worsen in the sixteenth century for two reasons: the transfer of rural property and the tax squeeze. As for the first, the population growth of the Renaissance resulted in the active clearing of even marginally productive soil. Land became rarer, more precious and coveted. The leading citizens of the towns, nobles and especially bureaucrats and bourgeois patricians, did not give a thought to snatching as much land as they could from the peasants. Naturally, the peasants would have preferred to keep their land, since their own population was increasing. A thorny situation. Taxes, once more, were at the heart of the matter. The urban notables, in effect, were not taxed on their new country property. Their town address in Valence or Grenoble was their residence for tax purposes. The fact that they had recently bought and thus possessed land in the outlying villages added nothing to the share of taxes they paid in town. The tax relief thus afforded the notables resulted in an extra burden of taxes on the peasants remaining in the village. They still had to pay the tax on the land now owned by the city-dweller who could better afford to pay but did not have to, because he did not reside in the village. Instead, it was divided up and tacked onto the share paid by the peasants.

Each time a *forain* (nonresident landowner) acquired what had once been peasant land in a rural community, it meant heavier taxes for the peasants remaining in the community. The rural unrest resulting from this situation in the sixteenth century was particularly acute. It was a period when the population, the towns, and the economy were expanding, and the urban notables were buying up the countryside at a far faster and more relentless pace than during the less prosperous days of the preceding century. Now that the peasants had a minimum of prosperity, it was threatened. That was what taxation taught them. The lines were most clearly drawn in the large outlying districts of Grenoble by 1540, and around Romans by 1513–1515. In 1579–1580 Romans was one of the places where strife between the countryside and the urban elite was most acute, and it was in the region around Romans that conflict specific to the mid-sixteenth century could still be observed toward the end of the century.

The conflicts of the era can thus be viewed through the problem of taxation. On one hand, there was the world of the peasants, its economy based on the family. The steady growth of the population was rapidly bringing about its ruin, since it caused property to be divided into smaller and smaller plots for an increased number of children, and because an increased work force meant a decline in wages. On the other hand, we find the urban notables turning into something like capitalistic land developers in the countryside. They snatched up, bought, and regrouped as many pieces of land as they could. And in all this, unjust taxation played the role of catalyst.[13]

The second factor in the growing intensity of the conflict was the tax squeeze. In Dauphiné, where there was quite a distinct and orderly sequence of events as compared to Languedoc, the increasing pressure was precisely recorded. Retrospectively, as compared to the relatively mild taxation of the first half of the century, we can see the situation take a turn for the worse in 1536. In that year, François I and Charles V, the Holy Roman Emperor, once again went to war following Charles's invasion of Provence. From 1536 to 1538, the total of *direct* taxes rose prodigiously as calculated in nominal value (*livres tournois*, the currency of the time) and even more in real value (wheat). The overall value in wheat increased by five- or eightfold depending on the year. Afterward there was a slight letup in tax pressure, but the moderate taxes of the years before 1536 were never to return. A step toward high taxation had been taken and could not be revoked.

The tax squeeze of 1535–1538 was so intense that it seemed to release all the repressed resentment in the kingdom. Skeletons came out of the closet. The people were exasperated with handing so much money over to the royal or provincial treasury. They began to rail against certain exemptions and the injustices of the system that were making various officials and notables rich. The Dauphiné Estates repeated the requests they had already made in 1524: that Montélimar and Gap should no longer enjoy freedom from taxes, or at least from all taxes. François I, in letters dated from his camp at Hesdin in April 1537, gave in to this demand. But the fiscal privilege of the two towns was not completely abolished until the 1550s, when its death toll sounded from the belfry of Gap's great church, sorrowfully announcing to the townspeople that from now on they would have to pay taxes, just like everyone else. As late as 1614 the consuls of Gap and Montélimar still wistfully referred to their lost privilege.[14]

During the decade of the 1530s, however, Montélimar and Gap were not the only towns under fire. The country districts in general were hostile toward the towns, especially the larger ones, because of the purchase of so much rural land by the urban elite (land then *ipso facto* tax-exempt, as we have seen), and because the towns so nonchalantly took advantage of their dominant position in the province's various representative institutions. They used their influence to foist certain responsibilities onto the villages. For instance, the towns avoided lodging the royal army. Troops were billeted in the open country instead, a situation hardly likely to leave the peasants' pocketbooks, or the country women's virtue, intact. The repayment of the soldiers' lodging involved endless petty quarrels, with village leaders learning to outwit the accounting ploys of the town notables. Likewise, *emprunts royaux*, so-called loans to the crown, were in theory imposed only on "enclosed towns," but somehow they were spread out over entire districts—which meant the rural areas. These illegal transfers of taxes were the unsavory though not necessarily inevitable by-product of the financing of royal wars. They were common practice throughout the 1540s, and the natural reaction to them was peasant protest aimed at the towns; these practices bred protest "as surely as clouds bring rain."[15]

The protest at this stage was political and judicial, practically nonviolent, and was all the more effective for it. Violent protest on the part of the peasants did not come for another forty years, within the general context of physical aggression and bloodshed that characterized the Wars of Religion. During the 1540s, however, the villagers of the Romans and Grenoble regions were represented by local consulates, an expression of the rural elite, and they formed short-lived associations or unions (nonviolent predecessors, of the rural leagues). These associations brought the twenty villages together in legal pursuit of a specific goal. They hired courageous counsels, like Louis Faure, to plead their cause at the regular tribunals of the province, such as the Parlement (sovereign judicial court) or the Estates. Here we see how the immense French judicial system of the time served society. It was often able to route village demands and complaints through peaceful channels, avoiding armed conflict. It should be obvious that the peasants of the sixteenth century, like those of other eras, were far from being the inert, loutish "sack of potatoes" Karl Marx once unfortunately labeled them.

Despite the urban counteroffensive to these demands—which was mounted by means of little gifts to grease the palms of susceptible judges, or presents of truffles and melons—the peasants' case for fiscal justice during the 1540s finally won some of the Parlement magistrates in Grenoble over to its side, as well as certain factions in the Estates. It was not all that remarkable since the urban bourgeoisie was not automatically in favor of the nobles and the clergy in their fight against rural demands; in fact, far from it. The bourgeois harbored thoughts of future action against noble and clerical privileges, and that made them less than ready to join in the struggle against the country districts. The peasant demands went so far as to involve the king himself, and his council, when Henri II traveled to the Midi in 1548.

The 1540s were a favorable juncture for the recognition of

rural interests: the new tax squeeze of 1542, intended to finance the war (see Graph I), was almost as intense as that of 1536. The food shortages of 1544–1545 made unjust tax quotas more unpopular than ever. Urban growth, the increased activity of towndwellers buying up rural land, made the "country bump-kins" highly aware of the tax burden they eventually inherited. The towns' tax privileges, combined with the employment opportunities the growing towns offered, drew many peasants to move to the urban centers. This underlined the paradoxical nature of the exploitation of rural areas by means of the *taille*.[16] In 1548, Henri II struck a well-advised blow for fiscal justice. The Edict of Lyons of September 30, 1548, decreed that all rural properties bought by citydwellers after 1518 would be taxed in the villages, in the name of their urban proprietors. The sigh of financial relief could almost be heard in the countryside. Measures for the application of the edict followed and were most welcome.

By 1552, the third estate, in town and country, was becoming unified; the better to fight against the tax-free status of the privileged classes, especially the clergy. Anticlericalism was beginning to rear its head, encouraged by the Huguenot cause which was stirring up the countryside. In 1552, advocates and consuls, some representing the towns, some the country, agreed to accept the terms of Henri II's edict. This taxation affected urban landowners alone, not the rural farmer. The urbanites' ready consent to the edict proved, incidentally, that the conflict was in no way unresolvable through legal means. Far harsher was the struggle over the end of tax exemptions. It pitted commoners, whether they lived in towns or open country, against bluebloods and men of the cloth.[17] This struggle was under way in Dauphiné in the mid-sixteenth century and ended with the strife of 1579–1580, but rose again and came to a more satisfactory, if temporary, conclusion between 1595 and 1639.

Thus the anti-urban struggle of the 1540s became an antinoble offensive during the 1550s and in 1570 to 1580. This was as much a turning point, or at least as typical a one, as that which saw French public opinion turn, in 1788–1789, from anti-absolutist to antiprivileged class.

In the sixteenth century, however, the first, anti-urban stage of conflict in Dauphiné displayed several characteristics which remained quite stable. First, the friction was initially most concentrated in the most urbanized, most open, and most commercial zones of Dauphiné, in both town and country. Along the great water routes, the Isère and the Rhône, it affected the quadrangle formed by Vienne-Valence-Romans-Grenoble. In contrast, and for various reasons, the mountain regions of Allevard to the north and Die to the south (which were slightly less developed and whose taxes were based on land rolls) remained relatively passive throughout the struggles. In the second place, a seminal peasant consciousness began to take form even at this early date. It involved organization of the peasants, which emerged by 1550 through the creation, however ephemeral, of *commis de village* or village delegates to the Estates, whose function was to represent the interests of communities other than the "Ten Towns." In 1578, an important year for our study, these delegates appeared again, in a somewhat more substantial reincarnation.

A final constant was the decisive role of what we might second the American historian Scott Van Doren in calling "Renaissance centralization of the State." The royal interventions of 1537 and 1548 were bold and far-reaching. But the greater part of the drama was set, if not resolved, in the province, and particularly in the Dauphiné Estates. Whether willingly or not, the Estates levied and spent huge sums, in their own name, for the royal wars. Yet these sums did not even appear in the crown accounts, since the money was spent on the spot, in Dauphiné. Thus in 1537–1538, the sum of 662,000 *livres* was collected in the province for the *parcelles extraordinaires* or exceptional levies for the wars, without one *sou* ever reaching the central government at Blois or Paris. In fact, from Paris or Blois in 1537–1538, Dauphiné must have looked like some tax-free paradise. But from Grenoble or Romans, Dauphiné taxes looked very heavy indeed. Simply studying the central government budgets or crown accounts therefore does not suffice for an understanding of the dimensions of the sixteenth-century struggles. Deep in the provinces, peasants seethed with resentment against the towns, and commoners worked against the privileged orders of society.

The initial phase or first heat of the battle between noble and commoner took place between 1550 and 1556. The stakes were high. Of course, no member of the lower class voiced aloud the opinion that a tax or *taille* should be imposed on the holdings of the "old" nobility (even if such thoughts did exist in the back of some minds). To say a thing like that would have been regarded as a sacrilege. Imagine: the tax-hungry king taking a pound of flesh from his faithful servants the nobles. The mind boggles! Everyone knew, of course, that many a noble of so-called old stock was really the descendant of a butcher or innkeeper ennobled a century earlier . . . but it takes time to break taboos. For the moment, peasants were still heady with the gains they had made in 1548, when they forced taxation upon rural property bought by nonresident bourgeois. In the same vein, they hoped to see commoners' lands, *recently* bought by members of the nobility or clergy, eligible for taxes (and on this issue they met no opposition from urban commoners, even the very rich).

They also hoped to see the *taille* imposed on land purchased by the recently ennobled. This group, or those who were most eager to join it (like Antoine Guérin) were later among those who most strongly opposed the rebel peasants of 1579. Birds of a feather . . . In 1553, however, the very principle of nobility was not challenged as it was in 1789. But with ennoblement and new holdings under attack, the nobility's exposed (or least attractive) side was crumbling. The century's main trend, which came to a halt in 1560, was the long-term economic growth of the Renaissance. It encouraged the nobility to buy up peasant land, and particularly land-hungry were the new, energetic nobles who lived in town and had only recently become part of the urban bourgeoisie. This corresponded to the growth of the towns that hoped to find sources of property income in the

open country, as well as a food supply. It also derived from
the depreciation of the old perpetual quit-rents. The other side
of the coin was the ever-growing profitability of the larger
properties some buyers put together and either farmed themselves or rented to farmers. Let us add that, in this offensive
against the tax exemptions enjoyed by the pseudonobles, each
urban commoner class—meaning each town (not to mention
the surrounding countryside)—had its own demands, and these
demands sometimes contradicted each other. A cacophony
could result, and this was one of the causes of the temporary
defeat of the commoners' cause in the 1550s.

The people of Grenoble, for instance, wanted to have taxes
paid by the *avocats consistoriaux* in their town. These were the
highest-ranking barristers in Grenoble, king's counsel and attached to the Parlement. The obvious pride they took in their
tax exemption made the common people of Grenoble see red.
In Valence, the people's argument was with the professors at
the local university, who were laboring under the strange de-
lusion that sitting in a university Chair automatically conferred
nobility, and that they should pay no taxes.[18]

Let us add that the towns, unfortunately, kept fighting fruit-
lessly on two fronts, against taxes and seignorial injustice. They
did not despair of seeing taxation on the rural landholdings of
nonresident bourgeois abolished or at least reduced (this was
the taxation stemming from peasant demands which were instituted in 1548, and which the bourgeois found unjust). Further, the commoners' struggle against nobles started badly in
the towns, as they were a heterogeneous group and were
wracked with internal dissension. They were not one, but many:
town against country; honorable notables against craftsmen;
smaller towns against the "Ten Towns" of Dauphiné. Valence
stood against Grenoble, and so on. There was no end to the
contradictions, which makes one wonder if it is at all possible
to use such broad, unifying terms as *bourgeoisie* and *nobility*: "The
ancien régime is called diversity."

Various acts, called accords or compromises, punctuated the
tension between commoner and privileged classes during the
1550s. First, there was the 1553 transaction, then the accord of

1554: the delegates of the two dominant estates forced this on the terrorized or corrupt representatives of the third estate, using extortion or intimidation. Finally, the royal decree of 1556, which undid the third estate in the first heat of the struggle. The decree was categorical. Noble property of every type remained exempt from the *taille*, even if it had been recently acquired or if it belonged to new nobles. This upholding of the exemptions represented a major defeat for the third estate, even though the question had politicized the commoners to some degree in both town and country. However, a few concessions were obtained. A limit was set on the number of consistorial advocates in Grenoble, and the number of professors at the University of Valence, although both groups remained tax-exempt. The main concession was the limitation of the clergy's fiscal privileges. Huguenot influence was at its height. Slyly, Henri II sensed he would have the support of both nobles and third estate if he taxed the clergy.

The extent of the third estate's defeat is more easily understood if it is realized that the aim of the peasants and even the bourgeoisie was a general provincial land roll. That would have made it easy to tax noble holdings. As it turned out, the demand was unceremoniously tabled. At this juncture the commoners were not as motivated as they had been in the past, or as they would be. Fiscal pressure during the 1550s was still moderate (see Graph I) and was far from reaching the heights it had in 1530, or would in 1576–1580, or 1630, when peasant protest was more vigorous. The third estate of the 1550s, not unduly oppressed by the *tailles* could therefore tolerate tax exemptions (for everyone but themselves!). Even so, the commoners had made a fine showing of local activism. A pro-Huguenot zone in 1550 comes to mind: the "union" of the town of Die and eighteen surrounding villages against the tax privileges of certain priests. It gave rise to the eventual taxation of real estate acquired by clerics, and of any property they inherited from their common-born families. The clergy of Die were less than amused.

But these are specific cases. In general, the villages too readily believed they could go straight on from their first victory—

the taxation of nonresident bourgeois property in the villages—
to the taxation of noble gentlemen. The nobility were not taxed
until 1639, and would still be partially exempt until 1789. The
villagers and their new friends in the towns, Romans among
others, still forged ahead in the 1550s. But getting the bull by
the horns—that is, the nobility by its tax exemptions—was no
easy task. After their defeat, the commoner alliances kept a
very low profile for a quarter century or so. Yet there were
certain signs of events to come. During the 1550s one of the
principal envoys to court, defending the commoners' interests
against those of the nobles, was Gabriel Loyron, consul of
Romans. The Loyron family belonged to the solid bourgeoisie,
but Jean Serve-Paumier, the leader of the revolt of 1579–1580
in Romans, married a Loyron daughter in the early 1560s—a
rather unusual alliance for a craftsman, yet perfectly in keeping with both Loyron and Paumier's social and political activism.[19]

Under François I, and then Henri II, the Italian campaigns,
followed by the war with Charles V, produced a boomerang
effect in Dauphiné. The wars acted as a catalyst. They were
paid for by specially levied taxes, and the tax system widened
the gaps in Dauphiné's social foundation, both between and
within the various classes. It was almost like a classical drama.
One after the other, country, towns, third estate, nobility, clergy
squared off during the annual ritual of the assembly of Estates.

By 1560, the Wars of Religion touched off a second cycle of
regional protest. Heresy was the first rallying point, but after
1575, social divisions were again at the forefront. This was a
general pattern: the League, in Paris, though in a different
context, followed a similar winding course.

What and who was responsible for Dauphiné's course of revolt
in 1579–1580? Let us first mention the two further tax squeezes
occurring in 1567–1570 and 1576–1578 (there was another just
after the Carnival, in 1580–1582). During the two periods in

question, regional *tailles* almost reverted to their true level, or "buying power," of 1537–1543, with allowance made for inflation. And this level was reached in a province no longer in the flourishing state of health that characterized it during the late Renaissance in the second third of the sixteenth century. Dauphiné was economically and demographically devastated between 1567 and 1578. It had been bled dry since 1560 by civil strife and its attendant miseries. The new worsening of the tax load was almost more than the province could bear.

The two new and intensive tax squeezes encouraged some bad habits in the crown and in the regional officials administering taxes. From 1567 to 1576, as the pressure mounted, the king's commissioners and the lieutenant governor of Dauphiné devised some remarkable measures against the representative and legal processes. They imposed *tailles* without the formal consent of the Estates, with the sole support of either Parlement officials or the lieutenant governor himself, and the "country representatives." The country representatives supposedly represented the people between sessions of the Estates; in reality they often acted as the crown's men of straw. The officials' ultimate innovation came in October 1578, when a mock "king's council," a caricature of the provincial Estates, authorized the levying of taxes in the region. This council, far from being royal, was the purely local concoction of a few representatives of the Grenoble Parlement and the odd notable citizen, of whatever rank, willing to play yes-man.[20] These ploys seemed like so many injustices to the commoners. Their reactions to them were multiple, and they were strong.

Conflict over the *tailles*, between 1576 and 1590, can be said to follow the standard in many ways. For instance, the third estate and the nobility were adversaries, as were the lower and upper ranks of the third estate. The lower classes, in town and country alike, were opposed to the urban bourgeoisie and the bureaucrats who aspired to the nobility. In 1579–1580, pure and simple negotiation between the three estates, as it had existed in mid-century, was fruitless, but it was still pursued.

Negotiation was fruitless because by 1578 the conflict involved bloodshed. The tax question was the burning issue as the elite's energy was no longer concentrated on religious problems. The upper ranks were slowly beginning to abandon the Huguenot cause they had embraced during the 1560s. Moreover, since the beginning of the civil war, every craftsman had gone about armed with a dagger by day and a sword by night, and these weapons were liable to be drawn now that tax and money matters were assuming an ominous significance.[21]

Negotiation was nonetheless pursued with gusto. Here we must introduce that great commoner Jean de Bourg, who loomed large on the scene between 1576 (when the Estates General were held in Blois) and 1579 (when Catherine de'Medici toured Dauphiné): Jean de Bourg, archepiscopal judge of the town of Vienne and delegate to the national assembly in Blois in 1576.

III

Jean de Bourg's
Petition of Grievance

Very little is known about Jean de Bourg's background or his career before the mid-1570s. It is not unreasonable to surmise that the de Bourg family belonged to the patrician bourgeoisie, whose members filled so many offices in so many towns. At any rate, by the time he appears in the records, Jean de Bourg was a barrister, Doctor of Law, and the Archepiscopal judge of Vienne. The ruling lord of Vienne was the Archbishop and de Bourg's authority was second only to his. De Bourg was elected Vienne's third estate representative to the provincial Estates in Grenoble, then to the Estates General at Blois. Another de Bourg, Laurent, was the town's first consul.[1] The family seems to have had "clout" in Vienne.

Jean de Bourg personally drew up the *Cahier de doléance* he was to present at Blois on behalf of Dauphiné's third estate. Once again, a *cahier* was a petition of grievances combined with suggestions for rectifying injustices. The text Jean de Bourg delivered is a fascinating document.[2] From our modern standpoint we might call it the product of a politically liberal intellectual tradition. It first defined the third estate's complaints and demands regarding the other two categories of society which included complaints concerning the tax exemption of the nobility, the ever-growing number of new nobles, and the clergy, including monastic orders which theoretically were bounded by the strictest vows of poverty. Nobles and clerics, de Bourg claimed, had *les plus beaux biens*, the best land in the province. They should therefore pay their quota of taxes, as well as their share of expenses for the stores of wheat, wine, meat, oats, hay, straw, and candles laid in for the troops passing through the province, and which were entirely paid for by the third estate. Nor should the grievance of travel expenses go unmentioned. Grenoble was a good distance from Paris or Blois, which were the seats of the central government. Whose taxes paid for the various delegations Dauphiné had to send there? The privilege was all the third estate's. And who actually went? Nobles and priests. The third estate got to foot the bills for their jaunts to France's capitals. It was more than just a tax scandal: as de Bourg explained, under this system the third estate was kept from appearing in person on the king's doorstep and acquainting the monarch with its particular complaints and demands.

According to de Bourg's petition, there was no end to the taxes the nobility and clergy did not pay. One reason behind these injustices was the way regional power was divided. The Dauphiné Estates maintained a permanent delegation of eight at court, consisting of six nobles and two priests—not a single commoner. Along with an ad hoc *procureur* or solicitor, they represented Dauphiné's interests between sessions of the national Estates, and it is easy to guess whose interests they represented. The bourgeois consuls of Dauphiné's ten largest towns could do nothing about this situation, even though they were delegates to the provincial Estates. The third estate was discriminated against, fiscally and politically. In addition, the permanent delegates seized every tax privilege for themselves, and found a wealth of opportunities for spending the third estate's money.

De Bourg's remedy was that the third estate should convene separately from the other two and they might then be able to elect their own legal representative, even though such an office did not at that time exist under the law. Their own *procureur général* would have local counterparts in each Dauphiné bailiwick or seneschalsy, and these new delegates would attend and have a say at meetings of the Estates' permanent delegation to court. The third estate would thus be better able to check on the way taxes were apportioned and to limit the tax exemptions enjoyed by the privileged classes.

But Jean de Bourg and his constituents in Vienne had more than one grievance in 1576. De Bourg, a municipal judge, also disapproved of certain of his colleagues who formed the very top rank of Dauphiné's judicial bureaucracy. Articles 28 and 31 of the *Cahier* charged the Parlement of Grenoble with awarding itself high salaries out of the third estate's taxes. De Bourg also attacked officeholders whose posts were superfluous or recently created on the grounds that they were expensive and wasteful since offices serving the same purpose already existed.

The judge's next target was the financiers who had plunged Dauphiné towns into considerable debt (3,550,000 *livres* in ten years, if de Bourg's figure is to be believed). He thought they should be made to hand over every bit of money they came by dishonestly; it would be enough for the cities to buy their way out of debt. De Bourg also attacked "foreign merchants," probably from Switzerland or Savoy. In the seventeenth century, these merchants were called *gabeleurs*, a name deriving from the *gabelle* or salt tax; in de Bourg's time they had just gained control of the trade between the salt flats of Languedoc and the countries to the north and east of the French Alps, with the consent of the king's agents. Dauphiné merchants and shippers were thus deprived of one of their customary sources of income.

The judge tartly criticized Grenoble tax collectors, who were expert at granting themselves healthy commissions, skimming the top of tax receipts. A practical man, Jean de Bourg requested the appointment of separate collectors, one in each bailiwick, where taxpayers could better regulate their activities. Finally, de Bourg took on one last category of crooked financiers: the Lyons moneylenders who had the towns in their debt. He did not argue with the 8 percent annual interest they charged, but requested they be required by law to wait ten years before demanding repayment of principal on a loan (Article 74).

The entire power complex—nobility, clergy, finance, justice—came under fire from de Bourg, a champion as intrepid as Don Quixote and sure to find a host of followers like Sancho Panza in Dauphiné towns. But what about peasant support for his program?

This was a question that certainly occurred to de Bourg. Articles 64 to 71 of his *Cahier* protested against the new *seigneurs'* land-buying operations. Often they were given some portion of crown lands, as an outright gift or for a pittance.[3] The new landlords then allowed stewards to administer the domains as they wished. The stewards often trod on the communal rights usually enjoyed by villages, such as grazing rights, the cutting of firewood, and the right to build communal mills, dovecotes, ovens, and wine presses. Displaying the classic belief that monarchy rests on popular support, de Bourg hoped that the king would reclaim his former domains, arguing that His Majesty was far better than the noble landlords at administering justice to his subjects. De Bourg also demanded, in Article 77, that the landlords and their figureheads cease to interfere with village meetings and assemblies. He strongly disapproved of the landlords' abuse of police and judicial power in peasant matters.

However, de Bourg had little or nothing to say about other peasant complaints and demands, although they were legion (regarding the system of justice, the rents and services due landlords, and so on). He belonged to the urban bourgeoisie, and the interests of his class differed from those of the country-dwellers. In Article 73, the judge denounced the tax surcharges village consuls meted out to city commoners who had bought land in the country. In Article 89, he demanded that the taxpayer's *residence* be the sole basis of taxation. This was a test.[4] It meant that the urban bourgeoisie would pay tax only on property in town, and not on holdings, however extensive, owned in the country; the tax burden would once again fall on the peasants and villagers. The conflict between town and country weakened the third estate when the revolt came to a head in 1580.

Jean de Bourg's petition thus contained contradictions which were an inevitable product of the times but which do not in any way detract from the *Cahier's* very great worth. The *Cahier* is a manifesto of political activism of the third estate. The judge from Vienne was a man of the Renaissance, a provincial Jean Bodin. Bodin (1530–1596) was an economist, political theorist, and author of *De la république*. His treatise argued in favor of a monarchy whose power would be balanced by that of the Estates General. De Bourg was also eager to see regional representative institutions taken seriously. He sought justification for his political philosophy in the works of classical authors. In this de Bourg was outstanding: he was far ahead of his time, considering that the overwhelming majority of popular protest in sixteenth- and seventeenth-century France had no theoretical basis.[5] An educated man, de Bourg carefully reasoned out the revolutionary practices of his constituents. He forcefully upheld the idea of *equality* in a style foreshadowing that of the eighteenth century. The regional Estates, he wrote in the petition, were originally created in order to maintain the third estate in an *official equality* with the other two (Article 3). Farther on (Article 5), de Bourg discussed the equality between cities which should ideally dictate the apportionment of taxes. Above all, sensitive to the unfairness of the tax system, the judge from Vienne formulated the principle that *equality, which is required in any society, will be observed, so that each shall easily pay* (the taxes) *appropriate to his condition* (Article 51).

De Bourg, of course, was not talking about Rousseau's brand of equality among individuals, with liberty and justice for all. He was, rather, sanctioning functional equality among the social categories as they were represented in the Estates. De Bourg expressly attributed this request to Cicero's egalitarian thought; in secondary school, or later, he had read the Latin author's political writings (Article 53). *For as Cicero shows, what supports one part of the people and scorns the other, causes a ruin and loss of the latter. It is well known that the poor Third Estate in the society and union aforementioned resembles nothing more than a dead branch attached to the tree trunk, and receiving no sap* (from the roots) *which should unanimously nourish the whole body. The Third Estate receives but burdens and inconveniences from this society. And consequently it is in obvious peril of drying up and withering. . . .*

An organic metaphor of this kind is typically medieval and not particularly original. Society was a tree. The third estate, it followed, was a large branch, with which the rest of the organism refused to share the life-giving sap. The reference to Cicero, however, is of prime importance. De Bourg was talking about the Cicero who wrote the third part of his *Laws*, master before the fact of egalitarian thought, the theory of social contract. In the name of a fundamental equality and *parity* for all, Cicero evolved the theory of a harmonious balance between the various bodies compromising human societies. It inspired all the Western thinkers of the Middle Ages, in the era of corporate equality preceding Rousseau, from the humanism of fifteenth-century Florence[6] to Hugo Grotius. De Bourg was merely a provincial judge in Vienne, a town steeped in Latin culture, yet he was in the mainstream of this line of thought. In comparison to his illustrious counterparts, like Grotius, he had the singular merit of having first-hand experience, of having put theory and practice together. He wanted to translate his ideal of egalitarianism into reality.

De Bourg's thought was rooted in a regional tradition. For half a century, the third estate, the towns and the villages of Dauphiné had incessantly demanded, individually and collectively, the equalization of hearths, war expenses, and taxes. This equalization would have been proportional to the ability to pay. François I had indicated that he would be favorably inclined to such demands.[7] De Bourg enlarged on his immediate tradition in other ways. Proposing a global concept and elaborating on the classical heritage of equality between the estates, his thought was on a higher level than not only that of his predecessors, but also that of many of his most eminent successors. Twenty-five years later the jurist and great French historian Pasquier became a counsel for Dauphiné's third estate, at which time he pointed to historical facts to justify the need for *real* taxes in the province. The whole of Dauphiné, he said, belonged to the southern regions of the kingdom with their *real* taxes; people there were taxed on their real property instead of their rank in society . . . But Pasquier[8] did not soar, as de Bourg had so effortlessly,[9] into the heady reaches of an egalitarian system, based on the universal Ciceronian principle of a social Nature.

It was a Platonic principle as well. Consider for a moment de Bourg's concepts of time and of inherent justice. On historical time and its destructive or corrupting force, the *Cahier* is clear, and very close to Plato's thought: *It will do them* (the two privileged estates) *no good to say they rule over the Third Estate by long precedent, seeing as how there is no custom, privilege, law or ordinance which is not subject to change and correction when evidence and necessity require, as lawgivers have shown and as Plato says in the fourth book of his laws, a thing should always be taken up and righted by human laws, which he compares to paintings easily erased by the passing of time if they are not touched up.* Elsewhere (Article 2), de Bourg took the same idea further: *It has happened with the passage of time (which spoils and alters all things) that the said attorney and delegates of the Estates did not restrict themselves to the sole office and purpose they had been established to fill.* According to de Bourg, this consisted of "maintaining the third estate in an official equality with the two others." Instead, these men *appointed themselves the judge and opponent of the Third Estate, to which they gave endless troubles and oppression your people suffer on account of these delegates.*

The reference to Plato is typical. De Bourg was steeped in Greek learning; elsewhere, in Article 76 of the petition, he cited the worthy example of Solon of Athens, who ordered that debts oppressing the people be redistributed equally throughout society. The fourth book of Plato's *Laws* which de Bourg mentioned maintains that "human affairs are but temporal vicissitudes, dictated by a god, by fortune, by circumstances and by profession." And that "political régimes have been overthrown one after the other by war, epidemics, the effects of inclement weather on crops." The Middle Ages would have said war, plague, famine.

De Bourg cited the evil practices established little by little through the years by a *tyrannical and leonine* society which forgot that in a community *each and all must share in the conveniences and inconveniences,* must share good and bad alike (Article 54). Would it have been better to return to the practices of olden days, the golden age which Louis XII's practically tax free reign was

supposed to have been? . . . If that were de Bourg's viewpoint
(and there is some evidence that it was, in Article 76 of the
petition, for instance),[10] we could say his thought was as pla-
titudinous as one historian finds that of sixteenth-century
protesters in Germany and Acquitaine. They were reactionaries
(we are told) who cared only about "rejecting the modern State
and returning to a former state of things whose symbols and
values, now supplanted, they mourned."[11] This is too strict a
definition to apply to Jean de Bourg. His ideal was more than
mere nostalgia for the customs of what people remember as the
good old days. De Bourg's real model was first of all Justice
(Article 29) in its universal, abstract, shining glory, and in its
more positive incarnations: *Justice and its officials are as necessary
for the consideration of man as one of the fours elements . . . all must
procure and desire its growth and establishment. But as no one can do or
live without the four elements, so is there no personage who can last long
nor be sure of his life without the administration of justice.*

*For if it is so that justice is established for the good of all the states in
imitation of the sun (which sheds its rays universally on all the bodies of
the earth), that it functions for each and everyone, is it not then reasonable,
(if you deem fit that your justice and treasury officials be supported and
paid for by the province of Dauphiné) that the first two orders, who hold
and possess the finest and largest properties, should have to pay their quota
in the sum of 34,000 livres* (for the wages of Parlement and treasury
officials), *a sum that the said delegates* (to the Estates), *ignoring both
usage and duty, have permitted to be newly cast upon your poor people*
(the third estate). These paragraphs suggest that de Bourg had
read not only Cicero and Plato, but Bodin as well.

De Bourg was close to the great authors of Antiquity, and just
as close to the aspirations of the common people of his own
day, who had never read a word of Plato or Cicero. In his
Histoire des Croquants,[12] Yves Bercé analyzes the vocabulary of
the Acquitaine revolts in 1594, as found in manifestos written
by the lesser bureaucrats of the lesser towns, who were conver-
sant with the popular cause. His analysis identifies key words;
they refer to the moral and religious sentiments of the masses,
who were enamored with what they thought of as real justice,

and irritated with the kind of justice they saw in their own legal system. Among the recurring words are *God* (eighteen times), *just* and *justice* (ten times), *gentlefolk* (eighteen times), and the hostile, ironic use of *thieves* and *thievery* (fourteen times).

Perhaps the best way to sum up is to say that popular revolts in late sixteenth-century France did not merely express a longing for lost traditions; they also drew on an ethical, religious value system implicitly understood by the people and explicitly revealed when it came in contact with the return to classical learning so typical of the period. Jean de Bourg's Greek and Latin authors helped him speak for the people.

After the Estates General at Blois in 1576, the details of the next two years of Jean de Bourg's life are somewhat hazy.[13] But in April 1579, with Dauphiné in turmoil, he traveled to the regional Estates in Grenoble. Dauphiné's third estate was still flushed with the Montélimar league's military victory at Châteaudouble a few weeks previous (see below). De Bourg was emboldened; he presented a new and lengthy list of grievances, with forty-four articles (the one he took to Blois had one hundred), the latest catalogue of third estate requests for the year to come. Moreover, four months later de Bourg made further "brief recommendations" to the Queen Mother, Catherine de'Medici, who was on an official visit to Dauphiné. They complemented the forty-four articles of April,[14] which were not entirely of de Bourg's own devising. They were, however, written in his distinctive style; they followed logically from the hundred articles of his first *Cahier;* but they were also the outgrowth and expression of popular enthusiasm, of the primitive petitions we have already discussed. The *cahiers* directly inspiring de Bourg's petition seem to have been drawn up in Dauphiné towns and country districts between October 1578 and March 1579.

De Bourg's forty-four articles are not as rich philosophically as his first hundred. No more Plato, Cicero, Solon of Athens; the new *Cahier,* instead, was packed with concrete details. The "reviews" of the petition, so to speak, have also come down to us; the regional nobility's comments were recorded a few months afterward, in August 1579. They were often antagonistic and caustic, and Catherine de'Medici, touring the Midi, was the most outspoken of all.

Conceptually, de Bourg's thought in 1579 was terser but bolder than it had been three years earlier. At the beginning of the text, he put emphasis on the good old days, on Dauphiné's healthy tradition of *liberties*. But the future appeared open and freely positive. Timeless values *(justice, equality)* win out over *custom*, which refers to a real past. The lawyer in de Bourg comforts the philosopher on this point: *The state of the present time is greatly altered and dissimilar from the past. When necessity requires, as it does at present, there is no law, statute, custom, or privilege over which it is not seemly to make new ordinances when evidently and manifestly needful, as legal provisions make well-known, as in this matter.*

The *pièce de résistance* of the forty-four articles concerned, as always, tax exemptions enjoyed by *Messieurs of the Church, of the nobility, and the office holders.*[15] (The tax dividing line ran between the upper bureaucrats of the Parlement and the like, who were exempt and automatically sided with the privileged groups, and the lesser bureaucrats who remained faithful to their fellow taxpayers in the third estate.) On this count, de Bourg and his friends improved the 1576 text. "A *cadastre* of rural and commoners' property will be made, as in Languedoc and southern Dauphiné." A land roll would make it possible for farmland bought by the first two estates to be taxed. For the first time, the desirable principle of *real* taxation for the province was proposed in plain terms.[16] Substantial progress had been made since the 1576 petition. The 1579 document further suggested that those subject to the *taille* also include all families ennobled within the past hundred years (and they were increasing rapidly). It also proposed that land belonging to exempted proprietors, but formerly owned by commoners, also be taxed. Such proprietors were in an outrageous position: they paid neither the *taille* affecting the third estate, nor the *arrière-ban* or general levy which the nobles contributed, nor the tithe on ecclesiastical revenues due from the clergy. They simply did not exist for tax purposes. Furthermore, the new *Cahier* demanded that *all* of the privileged elements, including those ennobled for more than one hundred years, should share in war-related expenses. De Bourg would hear no more of the nobles eating the *fish* (that is, benefiting from the army protection provided them by the province) without having to deal with the *bones* (that is, attendant taxes). Yet de Bourg adroitly made a concession to the lesser clergy: parish priests whose income was less than 200 *livres* a year should not be taxed.

It is hardly surprising that the nobles, whether of recent or ancient date, sent up a wail of protest (although the older nobility was willing to make concessions . . . where the new nobles were concerned). Catherine de'Medici, who was stopping in Dauphiné at the time, joined the chorus.[17] To the Queen Mother, the idea of taxing the nobility went against all the traditions of French custom, as she put it. But what custom? And which France? In Languedoc, a part of French territory since the thirteenth century, nobles paid taxes. Although Catherine was gifted with political acumen, she did not apply it in this instance. A half-century later Richelieu, although a noble, did not feel so duty-bound to his class; he was understanding in his dealing with the tax demands of Dauphiné's third estate. However, in exchange for his sympathetic treatment of the *equality* issue, he took advantage of circumstances to eliminate the regional Estates and extinguish what was left of *liberty* in Dauphiné. Give with one hand, take away with the other . . .

The articles dealing with *power*,[18] and the recommendations to the Queen Mother which elaborated on them, were sharply divisive. The third estate was solidly behind de Bourg. Catherine and the nobles could not have been more opposed, especially to measures such as the election of a special representative *procureur* or solicitor for the third estate, and the doubling of the number of third estate delegates to the provincial Estates in order to bring it in line with the number of delegates from the two upper ranks. These two measures would have greatly increased the third estate's power in the provincial assembly, which explains why the Queen Mother and the nobility were not favorably disposed toward them.

They did not, on the other hand, oppose limitations on the

number of royal officeholders and on their salaries. The third estate hoped to see that number as low as it had been during the utopian reign of Louis XII, when France had had a minimum of bureaucrats.[19]

A measure everyone in the province could agree on was that the salt contract be taken away from foreign traders and given back to the provincial Estates, which had administered the salt trade from 1547 to 1574. Doing so would have created 10,000 jobs in Dauphiné, the third estate claimed, however inaccurate their estimate might have been.

We are already familiar with the third estate demands for the landlords' judicial administrative functions to be turned over to crown officials in cases where the landlords' domains had once been crown lands. Generally, the owners of these vast properties were bourgeois patricians, who were still commoners. They were a wealthy, land-hungry minority, unpopular with both the rest of the third estate (which disliked oppression) and the nobles (who disliked competition). Thus there was little opposition to this particular demand. The peasants, furthermore, had staged an uprising against the rural administrators in question in the spring of 1579.

The forty-four articles of 1579 also contained various complaints and demands specifically related to the peasants (Articles 18, 33, and 42). Their urgency had been more in evidence since 1578, when village delegates were appointed, giving the country people more of an opportunity to be heard, even within the third estate. Loud and clear, they demanded that deserted castles be demolished; that the nobles be forbidden to ride the chase through their wheat fields and vineyards; that forests, swamps, and grazing land usurped by the landlords be restored to them as common ground . . . It is remarkable that the nobles showed *no* opposition to these articles; even more remarkably, neither did Catherine. The real sore spot, as the mounting conflict between commoner and noble would amply demonstrate, was in the areas of third estate *power*, which the other two groups considered dangerous; and tax *exemption*, the earthly reward of the privileged ranks. Tax-exempt status and provincial power were the pillars on which the supremacy of the privileged ranks reposed.

The meeting of the Estates at Grenoble in April 1579 was not entirely unproductive. Naturally, the nobles and especially the newer ones (who were quite aware that the gentlemen of longer standing would gladly betray them) frantically and victoriously defended their tax exemption (P 73). But the church was more accommodating . . . and the third estate's determination increased tenfold. By April 12 the third estate was ready for de Bourg to announce a postponement in paying taxes to the Estates. This was in effect a tax strike, which was to remain in effect until such time as His Majesty replied to the forty-four articles of the 1579 petition. And that was not the end of it.[20] There would also be a delay in the repayment of debts to the province's creditors, such as the Henrys, wealthy Lyons financiers. The same applied to the "captains," who were something like *condottieri* commanding the troops hired by the province for its defense. The principle, and the existence, of the tax strike and all its particulars were upheld by Vienne's town council shortly after the recess of the Estates. The council met to hear de Bourg's report on the provincial assembly on Easter Monday, 1579.

The assembly of the bailiwick of Vienne also voted its support. This body was composed of delegates from seventeen of the larger villages. There were about twenty delegates, members of the rural elite, including farmers and châtelains. The latter were not nobles, but often commoners designated by a noble lord to live in and manage his castle and the affairs of the domain. The bailiwick assembly elected the *commis des villages* or village delegates to the Estates. Their choice was one Maître Barrin, who represented the semipeasant and rather restive community of Beaurepaire at the Vienne meetings.

Through their automatic noble majority, the Dauphiné Estates of 1579 had pronounced themselves firm on the principle—to them a sacred one—of tax exemptions (with the tax strike as a result). On the other hand, they had given in a bit on the thorny question of power. They had allowed the third estate's official delegates, which were elected in each bailiwick, to be seated at the Estates, be permitted to mix freely with the

two privileged orders and presumably benefit from their wisdom. At the meeting of April 24, 1579, the seventeen localities
of the bailiwick of Vienne elected eighteen to twenty representatives, whom they instructed to go as a delegation to plead the
cause of the tax strike before the throne. Jean de Bourg was
among them, together with Claude Ravinel, Vienne's consul,
and the village delegate Barrin. These three would also encounter the lieutenant-governor of Dauphiné, Laurent de Maugiron.

At the same time the urban commoner class developed a very
systematic policy of demilitarizing the towns, counter to the
official soldiery. Valence, Romans, and Montélimar had already taken care of this problem during the incidents of February 1579 (as we shall see) by expelling their garrisons. On
April 26, 1579, Vienne followed suit. Pierre de St. Marc, the
local military governor, was stripped of his command by his
charges, and gladly left his post. Simultaneously, Jean de
Bourg and his friends kept a nervous eye on the military preparations being made by Vienne's nobility and the Count of
Tournon. Together they had raised money and 400 men, probably in preparation to answer the third estate . . .

Yet de Bourg's vigilance had nothing to do with revolution:
on May 9 and May 12, 1579, he and the other third estate
delegates denounced the murders of noblemen and burning of
castles by village militias in the Romans area. A gap opened
up between the urban bourgeoisie, who were reformers but only
moderates, and the riotous elements of the peasant communities, ready to take violent action against the landlords.[21] In
addition, on May 19, 1579, Vienne's notables refused the pro-
posals for joint action submitted by Jacques Colas, head of
Montélimar's urban-peasant coalition and its militia, because
they were regarded as seditious and liable to cause civil war.
Did de Bourg consider Colas a daredevil? The judge from
Vienne was in favor of legal process and peaceful rather than
warlike methods, and he was proved right when in 1630 the
case of the *taille* was decided in favor of the third estate and
against tax exemptions for the privileged few—long after the
last protestor of 1579 had died.

At the beginning of August 1579, Catherine de'Medici was in Grenoble after visiting Montélimar and Romans, on the occasion of her historic voyage into the southern provinces of the realm. Her response to the forty-four articles of the 1579 *Cahier*, as we have seen, was negative on the vital subjects of tax exemption and third estate power. As for de Bourg himself, he was moderate, even when firm; his encounter with the Queen Mother, however, was stormy. Catherine de'Medici called de Bourg *factious* and upbraided him (August 4–5, 1579). She could not get him to retract the promises he had made to the Vienne assembly: to go and see the king directly at Blois and not to allow the Queen Mother to settle the problems. He was aware that Catherine's august son had not made her plenipotentiary ambassador to Grenoble. De Bourg was not a man to waste time. He would have rather spoken directly to God than have a saint intercede for him, and speak to the king before the Queen Mother. Catherine was shocked by his failure to be awed by her, which she found rude. Although their meeting ended with an apparent reconciliation, the judge from Vienne and the strong-minded ruler from Florence remained loyal to their own beliefs: he upheld the third estate's complaints and demands; she rejected them, as the staunch supporter of noble privilege that she was.

We have seen that de Bourg was very much the political activist, but nowhere near so radical as the peasant communities when they were roused to action. Catherine was aware of the distinction. A revealing incident, however, illustrates how profoundly Dauphiné towns were affected by the stands de Bourg took. Suppose we are in Grenoble. It is about nine in the evening of April 4, 1579. De Bourg's obstinancy is the talk of the town; he will not budge on the idea of meeting with the king and not being content with the Queen Mother. There is also gossip to the effect that the Grenoble consuls have betrayed their commoner constituents and are now supporting the Queen against de Bourg on this point. "That evening, between eight and nine o'clock, Messieurs de Saint-Jean, d'Octavéon and de Triors (all nobles) were at the Sign of the Stag (a Grenoble inn) along with Messieurs de Deauville and de Caulis (also nobles) when Mr. Bastien, a Grenoble surgeon, came in. They became engaged in conversation. *Monsieur de Saint-Jean told Bastien that the Grenoble men* (the consuls) *had shown themselves to be honest men by opposing those* (de Bourg and his group) *who did not want the Queen Mother acquainted with their dispute* (the third estate's quarrel with the other two). *Whereupon the surgeon Bastien answered that nothing had been decided and that the Nobility ought to contribute to common expenses of the province and other funds, or otherwise there would shortly be strange goings-on which would cost the lives of a hundred thousand men, if the nobility did not contribute. Bastien added these words:*

—Remember the Swiss!

And he repeated them two or three times. Whereupon the said seigneur de Saint-Jean replied, growing very angry:

—What do you want? The massacres of nobles they had in Switzerland?

And the surgeon answered:

—I have said my piece.

Whereupon the said Caulis (another noble) *said to Bastien:*

—Be quiet. You are disturbing their game.

Because the said Messieurs de Deauville and de Triors were playing tarots. A few minutes later the said surgeon told Saint-Jean:

—Do not take what I have told you amiss for I heard of it from Gamot, who was going all about this town proclaiming it, assembling the people with his trumpet and a green bough and crying:

—Remember the Swiss.[22]

And Bastien repeated that two or three times.

This outrage is swiftly brought to the Queen Mother's attention. In a fury, she summons the third estate delegates to Maugiron's residence. She commands them all, from de Bourg on down, to disclaim Bastien and Gamot's bloodthirsty talk; they quite naturally do so. The two incendiaries are thrown in jail, on the combined and emphatic recommendations of Catherine and the Duke of Savoy, who happens to be on an official visit to Grenoble, accompanied by a thousand well-armed horsemen. Gamot is condemned to death by the summary court; but when he appeals his case to the king, he is pardoned, thanks to an energetic campaign by Dauphiné's main towns (probably Vienne, Valence, Romans, Montélimar, Grenoble). They support him *in what he did for the Third Estate and its interests. They know him to be a worthy man and devoted to the people.* Gamot's release coincides with Catherine de'Medici's departure.

Gamot's is an interesting case. Although de Bourg ultimately disowned him, Gamot was identified in de Bourg's mind with the defense of third estate interests and with the campaigns against the nobles as well. A suspicious individual, Gamot was accused of being Switzerland's agent in Dauphiné. He was a protestor and a Carnival character at the same time; he brandished the symbols of the egalitarian, peasant revolution: the green bough, the rake which was supposed to level social distinctions, and the onion; his trademark was a trumpet made of wood, similar to the Swiss model. He had them made by the dozen and handed them out to the towns and villages of Dauphiné. Gamot's profession had been that of attorney with the Parlement of Grenoble, and he was thus typical of the *basoche* or lower level of the legal bureaucracy, which identified with the complaints and demands of the third estate, and the beginnings of the egalitarian movement. Gamot and those like him were the opposite of the high Parlement officials who went over to the privileged camp. Gamot was of the people; he was the leader of the lower ranks of Grenoble's third estate, like Paumier in Romans. The common people loved him, from the urban consuls who energetically fought to save his neck, to the villagers of Valloire where he stirred up antilandlord revolt. During the same period, William Tell's fame was spreading faster than ever in Switzerland; the mythical, democratic and antinoble champion was even becoming known beyond Swiss borders. Gamot was the poor man's Tell, symbolic of the fantasy of exterminating the nobles, something the people did not really want but which was waved like a red cloth by those who spoke in the name of the masses.

Jean de Bourg's personal contribution to the cause ended here. As late as October 1579, Vienne's town assembly held firm on

the demands made in the *Cahiers,* both the one-hundred articles
of 1576 and the forty-four of 1579. Vienne opposed tax exemptions for the privileged, despite the pressure Leyssin, lieutenant-
governor Maugiron's younger brother, had put on Vienne. Leyssin wanted the townsfolk to pledge their support to the fragile
peace between the three estates worked out by the Queen
Mother. A few days later, before November 14, 1579, de Bourg
died. He had led the second phase of antitax, antiprivileged
class agitation in Dauphiné from 1576 to 1579. The first phase
went back to the mid-sixteenth century. But it was the third
phase that was victorious: in 1639, Dauphiné nobles were
obliged to pay taxes, at least on property bought from commoners. The final phase occupied a considerable portion of the
reigns of Henri IV and Louis XIII.

By de Bourg's time a *split* was evident. Contact with Languedoc, Provence, and southeastern Dauphiné, where nobles had
long paid taxes based on the land rolls, had finally roused the
northern and western regions of Dauphiné. They were the first
in France to wake up. This was the Dauphiné which by 1576
was acutely aware of the fiscal and anticommoner injustices
plaguing it. The subsequent revolts had altogether different and
greater expectations—philosophical and political—from those
of the Acquitaine *Croquants* and other "primitive rebellions."
The latter have been described, as they occurred in various
regions, by Hobsbawn, Porchnev, Mousnier, Bercé, Pillorget.

Political action in Dauphiné was on a high level. The town
of Vienne, its Bench, its surrounding countryside were only one
of its modes of expression. Montélimar and, most of all, Romans had a few words to say as well, and highly significant
ones at that.[23]

IV

1578: Jacques Colas and the Moderate Revolt

Before the digression in the previous chapter that concerned
Dauphiné under François I, and Vienne in Jean de Bourg's
ascendancy, we caught a glimpse of the first, halting steps of
a union of communities formed in 1578. This union grew out
of the same feelings about antinoble and anti–tax privilege
enunciated in Jean de Bourg's petitions of grievance. The new
protest grouping could hardly be called an organization; it had
a segmented structure, with decisions made at the local level,
and was run as a flexible confederation. It was more the man-
ifestation of a state of mind than a bureaucratic method of
organization. There was even a name for the movement: *league*,
the same term Parisian protesters of the 1580s and 1590s would
use when they championed the cause of citydwellers from the
capital and the larger provincial towns, in the name of the
Catholic faith. There were later leagues, too; for example in
1594 the *Croquants* and *Tard-Avisés*[1] in Périgord. The former were
"royalist" peasants, that is, supporters of the formerly Huguenot king, Henri IV; they disagreed with the ultrapapist
fanatics who ruled in Paris. And yet these divergent groups all
formed *leagues* to defend their corporate interests as communities.

In Dauphiné (1579–1580), initiative toward forming active
protest leagues came first from Pont-en-Royans, then more

strongly from Montélimar. Starting from this town and its surrounding country districts, the movement quickly spread north and northeast. In Valence, as in Romans, things rapidly deteriorated—from the patricians' pont of view—around February 1579. *This form of Union of the people was called League, which began at Montélimar and then at Valence,* the notary Eustache Piémond wrote (P 64). In Pont-en-Royans the inhabitants stopped the underhanded dealings of an outlaw soldier called Bouvier. In April and May 1578, Captain Bouvier, *a violent man and who loved but war,* stormed the local castle, aided by a dozen or so soldiers of fortune or ruffians of his own breed. He hoped to use this stronghold as his home base for plundering, as his friend and accomplice Laprade had done from Châteaudouble. Their strategy was to set up a protection racket, mafia-style, around Châteaudouble and Pont-en-Royans, despite the fragile truce the Catholic Maugiron and the Huguenot Lesdiguières had managed to put together.

What they had not counted on was the new energy the region's communities had discovered by running their own Huguenot organization. The population of Pont-en-Royans was by and large Huguenot or controlled by local Huguenots. The people learned very quickly that Bouvier's strongarm compatriots had taken the town castle, killing a sentinel in the process. As soon as the alert was given, the inhabitants were joined by the *communes* (as they are called in the records), the volunteers from neighboring villages. The combined forces laid siege to the castle that Bouvier had so very recently taken. The outlaw-captain did not hold out for long. He surrendered, having no provisions, and in exchange for his life left Pont-en-Royans, despite the reinforcements Laprade had sent him from Châteaudouble who arrived late. That is the story of the first armed conflict led by a community or communal militia, in the spring of 1578, which began or at least implied the peasant war which was fully under way in late 1578 and early 1579.[2]

Yet it was not in Pont-en-Royans, but to the south, in Montélimar and its neighborhood, that the movement really developed. And not by fits and starts, either; it grew steadily, sturdily. Pont-en-Royans was only a smallish town and Montélimar a city, and this was logistically important to the early stages of revolt. After the new developments in Montélimar, in August 1578, the word *league* appeared, and not merely *communes,* the only term chroniclers had used up to that point. *League* was already current in the political and religious usage of the day, but in 1576–1577 it only applied to the vast and specifically Catholic League in the northern provinces, meaning papist Paris and the upper reaches of the kingdom. It is quite possible that the words *league* and *union,* so widely used by Dauphiné writers in 1579–1580, were borrowed from the "northerner" vocabulary of Paris, filtering down to Lyons in a written or oral form. But the Dauphiné leagues and unions, even when they had urban confraternities as their foundation (as was also the case in Paris), were of a much less confessional nature than their contemporaries in the Paris region. Some of the Dauphiné leagues were indeed Catholic; they were in Montélimar and the environs. Sometimes, though, they were "pro-Protestant" despite the fact their members were Catholic; this was the case around Romans. But everyone, even revolutionaries, defended corporate interests, whether blatantly urban or rural, much more than they upheld any religious concept—that is, until the immense Catholic League led by the de Guise family came from Paris to cast its shadow over Dauphiné during the 1580s.

What initially motivated the first Dauphiné league movement, which started in 1578, was fear: fear of outlaw soldiers and of equally devastating taxes. By August 1578, popular sentiment became unified in Montélimar, and there were signs of an organization. The summer tax levy provoked, or probably uncovered, the appearance of an antitax league, with a certain Faure (called Barletier) as its leader; he was probably of modest means. The wave of discontent was aggravated by the decision, hastily approved by other Dauphiné towns, to grant 36,000 *livres* to the Grenoble audit office for the wages to be paid its officials.[3]

Against this less than tranquil background came the news

that a levy of 4 (or 6) *écus* per hearth had been decreed by the provincial Estates for July–August 1578. The sum was not exorbitant, but the timing was bad, and even worse for the heavier "collections" to follow. The gross agricultural product, judging from the level of tithes paid in surrounding Dauphiné regions, was at its lowest.[4] The new tax levy met resistance from the league recently formed by Faure-Barletier. The league probably recruited members from among the craftsmen's guilds and the lower class in general, just as other leagues did in Romans or Paris.

Vidal Baume, *exactor* (collector) of the summer 1578 levy, affirmed to Montélimar's town council[5] that *there are several private persons, on account of the league they have made with Jean Barletier, who want to pay nothing at all.* Barletier did not win immediately; he took the matter through the high courts at Grenoble. These were the legal, judicial means characterizing one side of the popular movement; the other, more spectacular side was the resort to illegal violence. Faure-Barletier, before the important personages of Parlement, asked that the consular accounts of his town be subjected to a thorough examination, as their regular auditing had been suspended. The Parlement made a small concession on this point, because it agreed with the principle of special audits; it also accepted that only one-half of the taxes assigned to Montélimar for the summer be collected. It is of note that the lower-class craftsmen of Montélimar made demands similar to those their counterparts in Romans put forward shortly after. Negotiating a "pay raise" or anything like it was impossible in the cultural context of the times, even though some of the craftsmen and day-laborers who were protesting taxes no doubt worked for less than subsistence wages. Instead, the commoners challenged the top of the provincial bureaucratic hierarchy. They refused to pay a part of their taxes, perhaps even envisaged a total refusal. They questioned the way Montélimar's power elite had been handling municipal finances. Rightly or wrongly, the ruling clique was accused of skimming local taxes—wrung out of the poor—to fatten their own pocketbooks. During the following year the common folk of Romans became familiar with these themes; whether they were based on fact or not is another matter.

Protest was already spreading beyond Montélimar. In October 1578, popular sentiment in the Rhône valley villages surrounding Montélimar was strong and well organized enough for it to surface in the records. The rallying point, which quickly turned into open revolt, was the plunder, pillaging, kidnapping, and rape of young women perpetrated by the outlaw soldiers who had been camping in a local village since early August. In October, the consuls of the parishes concerned, duly instructed by their constituents, corresponded with each other; thus they formed a segmented organization whose network was lateral, not hierarchical. The peasants in these communities were already keeping an armed watch over their daughters, their crops, and their goats; they formed themselves into a small army, which eventually brought the wayward soldiers in the neighborhood to their senses.[6] The town council of the village of Donzère joined this union; it voted in October 1578 to pay volunteers who would head the peasant militia. Donzère had not forgotten the terrible threats the Huguenot chief Montbrun once made in a letter to its Catholic consuls: *If you do not pay your taxes to the Huguenots, I shall massacre your people and animals, burn all the houses and barns.* The villagers wanted to protect themselves from future blackmail of this sort, widespread in lower Dauphiné.[7] Reading Montbrun's distasteful letter, it is easy to understand why the Catholic backlash was extreme in the area, and how it explains the change that Jacques Colas, the Montélimar leader, underwent: first an anti-Huguenot in 1578, then an ultra-Catholic League militant in 1590.

It was only natural that the democratic, segmented union of villages in the Montélimar region should have joined the urban league which Faure-Barletier had formed. At the same time, this coalition brought the struggle "to a higher level" (the use of this cliché is pertinent, under the circumstances). The other large towns, as municipal entities (and not without internal conflict), were eventually brought into the fray, beginning with Montélimar, and moving northward to Valence, Grenoble, and most important of all, Romans.[8]

On November 1, 1578, a general council met in Montélimar's town hall. It was really a meeting of the whole town, open to various sectors of the population, with the active minorities of the lower classes swelling its numbers. The official record shows that eighty members of the league run by Faure-Barletier were present. The episode was like a dress rehearsal for what was to take place in Romans three months later, though with a different ending.

The agenda called for a statement by delegates from the peasant union we have just examined. Through their spokesman, a man named Coste, they invoked the royal edict of pacification of 1577, which had yet to take effect in Dauphiné; they denounced the thefts, kidnappings, and other harassment by the soldiers and outlaw soldiers from both warring factions, Catholic and Huguenot, and particularly those committed locally by the latter. Coste also pointed out that his fellow members of the union had already sent a delegation before Lieutenant-General Maugiron. The villagers wished to see all thieves and robbers in the custody of *Messieurs de la Justice;* and "gladly" placed themselves under the authority of *Messieurs du Parlement.* Maugiron (Coste adds) acceded to their request and said that they should "tell it to the other towns." Contact between and among the towns was under way. Romans, Valence, and Crest had already promised to join in the movement. Coste and his friends asked the corporate body of Montélimar to join, and because of support from Faure-Barletier's party and the influential Colas family, the request was granted. Montélimar was now a full member of the union.

The call to action was theoretically prudent. The network of regular provincial and even crown institutions was brought into play or at least cited: edict of pacification; Maugiron; Parlement; organized "Justice"; peasant communities; network of towns. (Dauphiné's ten largest towns had long been recognized as a single legal entity.) In the Vienne region, similarly, the situation was "taken in hand" by the bailiwick assemblies.

The movement then divided into two branches, one working northward, toward Valence and the Valloire area. Despite the best intentions in the world, this branch nonetheless became a subversive, even revolutionary force. It included activities in and around Romans, supported by discontented rural and urban Catholics who saw nothing wrong in seeking out a compromising alliance with the Huguenots against the bourgeois patricians. The other branch of the movement, centered in Montélimar, was by contrast quite clearly anti-Huguenot, reflecting the religious consciousness of the area. The people of Dauphiné's extreme south remained traditional and orthodox. Force of circumstance also played a decisive role; in Romans and Valloire (the northern sector of league activities), Catholic soldiers posed the real threat, while in Montélimar and its district, Lesdiguières and the Huguenot soldiery were the principal causes of distress. Their operations were in the mountains on the eastern edge of the Rhône valley, and in the southern Alps around Die, Gap, and in the Baronnies.

Romans was different because it fought *with* the Huguenots *against* the local Catholic patricians. Montélimar was moderate by contrast: the Catholic patricians in this area did not have to be asked twice to take action *against* the Huguenots, to head the peasant urban leagues, and to act as a stabilizing influence over them. Donzère is a good example of southern Dauphiné's moderate stance: this smaller town had joined the Montélimar league in October 1578, but by February 1579, and more strongly in April 1580, it dissociated itself from Romans and the antinoble, pro-Protestant factions in the Romans region.[9] Donzère had good cause to be anti-Huguenot; it had Lesdiguières on the horizon. It also worried about the troubles between the third estate and the nobility; it was alarmed at the *excesses, pillaging, and massacres committed by the Third Estate united with the Huguenots*. The text demonstrates that the pro-Huguenot north and pro-Catholic south were beginning to move apart by the winter of 1578–1579.

The situation in Montélimar required a daring and well-connected Catholic; Jacques Colas fitted this role admirably. He was a man of about thirty, from a Montélimar family of sixteenth-century tanners who had been shoemakers in the fifteenth century.[10] The family had slowly but surely climbed the social ladder before Jacques Colas was born; they became consuls and men of the robe instead of mere tradesmen. Claude

Colas, Jacques's father, was a lawyer. Jacques himself had been a student at the University of Valence, around 1572, where he was chosen *Prince of Youth* or *Rector*. The Prince always came from the immediate region of Valence. Jacques Colas's election gives credence to the thesis that the mainsprings of the 1579–1580 revolts in Dauphiné were youth organizations, folk gatherings, and their leaders.

Colas was a hothead, a delinquent, and a leader with no fear of the sort of bloodshed that was in all too abundant supply during the troubled times we are studying. He was a wildly enthusiastic Catholic, but hardly an angel. This smooth-talking patrician, whom Catherine de'Medici pronounced *presumptuous and mad* in 1579, had killed a fellow student while at the university. He was acquitted, thanks to his powerful family friends in Valence. In 1575, before he was thirty, he was helped by his father into the post of vice-seneschal of Montélimar, which had been left vacant by the death of the previous holder. In fact, Jacques bought the office. It was the liaison between local and provincial authorities, and as such performed a crucial function. In 1576 Colas was one of the third estate delegates from Dauphiné to the Estates General in Blois, where he regularly met with Jean de Bourg. He was a moderate opposing such extremists as the Parisian Versoris, a fanatic leaguer (as Colas himself would become some fifteen years later) who wanted to give himself *body and soul, guts and bowels* to the king in his war against the Huguenots.[11] Colas personally took on Versoris during one session.

The events of 1578 followed Colas's return to Dauphiné: the formation of the league and the peasant union. At first the Colas family wavered. As pillars of local law and order, Claude Colas and his son were not very favorably disposed toward Faure-Barletier's activities in August 1578. But in October, at the strategic moment, they reversed their position and joined the league, nudging Montélimar into the union camp. *I am their follower, therefore I become their chief*, Colas modestly exclaimed. Given his high position in local affairs, he could legally assume control of the league movement which he had nothing to do with founding. Could religion have been his motivation? The prospect of crossing swords with the gentle-man-gangsters who were Huguenots must have been an attrac-tive one to a zealous Catholic like Colas (although at thirty he had not yet matured into a fanatic).

So Jacques Colas's functions slowly changed or evolved. Until May 1578 he was simply the guardian of the royal edict of pacification, which had been decreed but barely implemented in Dauphiné.[12] His legal functions as vice-seneschal predis-posed him to the role of peacemaker and during that period he appeared in a favorable light, as a reasonable man and not as the impetuous sort he had been as a youth and would be again later in life. Thus in August 1578 Colas was worried about Laroche, an outlaw soldier more or less supported by the Hu-guenots, who had taken up residence in the castle at Roussas, terrorizing the countryside around his stronghold. In February 1579 Colas skillfully managed a communal military reprisal against Laroche. He led a militia of 1200 league members to Roussas. Laroche had about thirty noble gentlemen—a typical situation—in his gang, but he had to surrender and take flight after four days. As a result of this victory, Colas was the official enemy of Protestants, nobles, and gangsters.[13] As we saw in Chapter III, Colas also evicted outlaw soldiers from Château-double that winter; in fact, only two weeks later. These two successful forays confirmed him as a true leader. Politician and chief of the joint village forces, he coordinated the efforts of Montélimar's urban and rural population in its struggle against the warlords. The people were only too happy to fight.

Colas also enlisted the support of a number of small towns in lower Dauphiné; Pierrelatte, on the border of the Comtat Venaissin, was one. It was a favorite target of the outlaws; they found provisions there and promised the villagers immunity in exchange for goods and services. The outlaw Laroche had sev-eral accomplices in Pierrelatte, to the point that Maugiron, in a letter dated August 8, 1578, upbraided the townsfolk for collaborating with the gangsters. Then matters went from bad to worse. Pierrelatte bristled against Laroche's imperious de-mands; the villagers even beat one of the bandit's men. Laroche burned a few houses in revenge; the same day, he sent the town

consuls a letter outlining his latest demands. Colas jumped at
the opportunity, immediately offering his services to Pierrelatte.
In the fight against Laroche, he wrote (February 22, 1579), *I
offer you all that is in me, and my life, which I will gladly put to use for
you.* Colas's victory at Roussas (February 28) was sufficient to
convince the citizens of Pierrelatte; they subsequently sent Colas all the volunteers he wanted for his fight against the outlaws.[14]

From April 1579 until the beginning of 1580, Colas continued
to use his official office of vice-seneschal, and his officious title
of leader of the Montélimar leagues. By virtue of his dual
authority, he sent many circulars to outlying villages, asking
each village to raise troops; to be on the watch for outlaws;
and to hold meetings of community delegates at the neighboring
large village. His activities, although legal, did not please the
nobles or the upper echelons of the provincial and even national
hierarchy. Catherine de'Medici, for example, in a letter dated
July 18, 1679, mentioned Colas, whom she had just met. She
rather disparagingly described him as *one of the principal leaders
of the Leagues: he is a presumptuous and mad soul of whom the gentlemen
of the Nobility are right to dislike.*[15]

Despite the relatively moderate stance taken by Colas, the
acknowledged leader of the third estate, his relations with the
nobility were often strained. His probourgeois positions were
not revolutionary, yet they were nonetheless firm regarding the
two privileged ranks. In a significant "policy paper" of May
1579, which had a certain dignity to it, Colas pointed out that
the third estate paid the greater share of taxes imposed by the
king, or the Catholic or Protestant warring factions which paid
for the upkeep of the army. The third estate had to make many
more sacrifices than the nobles; their grievances were therefore
not unfounded if the third estate bore arms *as all your Majesty's
faithful subjects must* to see that the edict of pacification be obeyed.
Colas's rhetoric veils the seditious side of this call to arms with
the necessities of pacifism and royalism (but did the king of
France approve of the uprisings in his name? I doubt it).

He who can do more, can do less, the proverb says: to Colas,
the right to bear arms automatically implied the right to assem-

ble, where, when, and how the commoners wished. In the same circular of 1579, Colas declared that he had become aware that the nobles, because of the peasant uprisings in Valloire, had come to distrust the third estate (and, by imputation, himself). But according to Colas, the remedy for the nobles' mistrust was certainly not that the third estate quiet down. Instead, Colas invited the other two estates to join the third as proof of its predominance. He desired *that the Third Estate seek out all honest men and convene them in an assembly of the four towns, namely Valence, Romans, Crest, and Montélimar,*[16] *where all town and village consuls will be sent as representatives.* His plan was to have the bourgeois elite of the three major protest centers take the initiative, presiding over an assembly of village leaders and lesser rural notables (the consuls). This would ensure the unity of the third estate in town and country alike. It would then meet with a few representatives of the nobility and clergy, duly screened for the purpose. They would be asked to call a meeting of their friends in the two upper estates, who in turn would be able to discuss a course toward making and keeping the peace with the bourgeoisie. This was a moderate program, but one which recognized the primary importance of the commoners' interests.

Colas's efforts indicate what a skillful and determined soldier-politician can accomplish under certain favorable conditions. Within the framework of his juridical authority as vice-seneschal, Colas had the support of the leading citizens and power figures in his town, and that of the urban and rural masses in his region as well, insofar as a minority of the lower-class population answered his call to arms. If anyone could overcome the two upper estates' unwillingness to negotiate with the commoners, Colas was that man.

Colas and his achievements enable us, by comparison, to understand the specific problems faced by the north (Romans), where mutual and even violent dissent separated bourgeois patrician from urban craftsman, unlike the unified front the third estate presented in Montélimar. Paumier, the plebeian rebel leader in Romans and its vicinity, used a different strategy from Colas. After all, Paumier had no official title or legal authority to protect him. The result, too, was different in the two towns:

after 1580, Paumier caused no more trouble, while Colas, with his *savoir-faire*, saved himself and his friends in the league as well. He made sure that royal and Parlement repression (initiated by the law and order party) was not visited on the protesters in Montélimar and its neighborhood. He even managed to have Montélimar granted the right to hold two additional market fairs. A powerful man with an eye for a good opportunity, he next affiliated himself with the military fortunes of the Dukes of Mayenne and Guise and other great leaders of the nationwide League or ultra-Catholic party. As a self-styled leader of men, Colas was attracted by the democratic ways of the gigantic, superpapist organization. He became something of a fanatic, as we have seen. Colas eventually became a peer of the realm, founding a new noble line. Brilliantly and nobly married for the second time, he died just after being elevated to the nobility. He was killed in combat in 1600: a major figure in the League, ex-governor of La Fère in Picardy, a bitter enemy of Henri IV, and having sworn loyalty to the king of Spain.

Colas's career is worthy of note. He was a third estate leader, but a moderate one, he later became a fanatic, and he finally ended up, after changing his allegiances, in the ranks of the nobility he had once fought. How many other political careers in other centuries have followed the same pattern?

In the context of the Dauphiné revolt of 1579–1580, Colas and his campaigns are a good illustration of the split within the provincial judiciary. There were magistrates like de Bourg and Colas who sided with the popular front. Others, like Romans's judge Antoine Guérin and the jurists of the Parlement of Grenoble, took pleasure in quashing the revolt. Yet it was in the judiciary's very nature to be torn between the third estate (where its roots were) and the nobility (to which many of its members aspired). The specific circumstances in Montélimar, and even more so in Vienne, where there had been no St. Bartholomew's Day massacres and where the craftsman class had no great influence, doubtless explain why the Vienne bourgeoisie, including the judiciary, felt closer to the remainder of the third estate than to the nobility. In Romans, quite to the contrary, the elite had led a St. Bartholomew's Day slaughter of plebeian Protestants. Relations with the local craftsman class were at their worst. The natural inclinations of Romans's elite were therefore toward the extremist factions of the Catholic party and toward what would later be called the aristocracy.

V

❧❧❧❧❧❧❧❧

1579: The Shadow Carnival

Our study of unrest in Dauphiné will focus from now on on Romans itself and its environs. While it was still beset by real misfortunes—including war—some ominous natural phenomena had also given cause for alarm over the past two years.

On November 8, 1577, a comet was sighted, *like a star*, trailing the new moon; *it cast its light against the rising sun, and was two fathoms in length* (P 56). It took a month for this astonishing apparition to fade from view. In relatively distant Lyons, one François Junctin capitalized on the general sense of foreboding by publishing a sixteen-page in-octavo brochure or *Discourse on what harm may come of the comet sighted on the 12th of this present month of November 1577 which can still be seen today in Lyons and other places.* Far more serious were the heavy storms of the winter of 1577–1578, which left snow on the ground until April. Walnut trees and vineyards froze; as a result of the extreme cold, walnut oil was in short supply and doubts (unfounded?) were raised about the next fall's grape harvest. All of this was taken as a sign of further misfortunes to come: *this was an admonition and forewarning to predict to us the troubles which later came about through the people's revolt, through war, plagues, famines, and other scourges with which God visited and punished his people.*

That summer, watchful observers saw more troubling signs: *in the month of August 1578, marks in the shape of snakes were seen on the leaves of cherry, plum, apple and walnut trees.* The confounding news spread; there were other omens as well. *Several reported that in eggs and in herrings little snakes had been found* (P 62), so some frightened consumers boycotted herrings and eggs.

Even so, 1578 was far from a bad year, agriculturally speaking. A cold winter followed by a hot, dry summer was just the right weather for wheat, nor was it bad for the grapes that survived the April frosts either. There was an adequate harvest of both in 1578 despite the pessimistic predictions. Wine was good and cheap. The only real problem was fruit *which was wormy from the drought.*

A good yield was not enough in itself; crops had to be sold, and this posed a problem. The royal edict of Poitiers proclaiming pacification in 1577 had had little or no effect on the outlaw soldiers around Romans. Merchants were assaulted. The cattle trade on both sides of the Isère had come to a halt (P 62). Money circulated with difficulty. The anti-inflationary edict of September 1577 had set the value of the *écu* once and for all (at three *livres tournois* or 60 *sous*); shipments of silver arriving from the Spanish mines in Mexico might well have stimulated the economy had there been real peace. The manifold unrest besetting Romans at the time prevented either measure from having the beneficial effect it would have had under normal conditions.

The league movement was bound to find energetic support in the turbulent Romans area. It got started in the village of Marsas in the barony of Clérieu, whose partial population of Huguenots had suffered from anti-Protestant repression, ordered by the court of justice in Romans. The town dictated to the country as well, all in the name of the king. The Romans tribunal pronounced death sentences on the Marsas dissenters, leaving their surviving relatives in the village desperate for revenge on the city magistrates. It was the kind of rural vendetta that is often found as the source of rebellions: fire fighting fire. Marsas put a challenge to judge Antoine Guérin, who was chiefly responsible for the decision handed down from the Romans court and who remained on the firing line until the Carnival revolt was over. In addition, antiseigneur feeling ran high in Marsas as it did in all the country districts to the north of Romans.

Neighboring rebel parishes wasted no time associating themselves with the revolt under way in Marsas. An initial gathering took place, with men from a locality called Chantemerle joining the Marsas group: *a gathering which convened a great number of low-life types from several surrounding villages* (A 30).

Guérin's allusion to the *low life* suggests the involvement of extremist elements, not representative of the peasantry as a whole, with its plowmen and laborers. The fact that rural Huguenots were implicated in the uprising does not in itself denote a socially marginal element. Quite the contrary. Even in the sixteenth century Protestant farmers generally came from the more prosperous ranks of the peasantry. In fact, such village communities, with their regular institutions (elected consuls, perhaps replaced in this instance by energetic militants who took control under the special circumstances) participated in the rural revolt from the beginning. It was no brutal *jacquerie*, no peasant uprising in the usual and often pejorative sense of the word. Village government participation was probably there at the outset and was definitely important in further developments. Guérin says as much when he tells us that after the first meeting in January 1579, *there gathered together the greater part of villagers for six leagues in every direction* (A 30). The "greater part" implies a democratic majority. If Guérin says so it must be true, for the judge was hardly fond of the rebels; he depicted them as a minority of rabble-rousers. Village democracy did indeed have a hand in things. As for Eustache Piémond, his description of the massacre, which was to end the Carnival in Romans and with it the revolt some thirteen months later, includes the report that *around Romans, a great number of* (rural) *communities gathered to bring armed relief, about 1500 men* (P 89). It was a demonstration of the communities' administrative power as the regular institutions of village society.

From the start, the peasant insurrection had certain characteristics of a folk festival. The first gatherings took place at Carnival or at least pre-Carnival time (January 1579), since in Dauphiné pre-Lenten celebration began as early as the feast of the Epiphany, January 6.[1] The pretext for the gathering of villagers at Marsas, Chantemerle, and other places, was a *reynage*, the Franco-Provençal word for kingdom (comparable to English *reign*). Coynart suggests that the *reynage* was a folk festival consisting of "jousts for the title of *King of Youth;* the champion reigned over his peers until the next festival."[2] Perhaps it was so; one thing we know for certain is that the first seditious gathering at Marsas and Chantemerle coincided with the winter games held by young male athletes. They culminated in the annual high-comic election of an Epiphany or Carnival king. The Catholic Church was a leading participant in the ceremonies.

Once the rebel movement was incorporated into the burlesque, yet serious and sacred, institution of the festival, the next step was logical and simple. Light weapons appeared (during this first phase of the revolt there was no question of artillery). The arms works at St. Etienne-en-Forez, with its iron and coal mines, was not far away. The smiths there worked like devils next to the gaping furnaces, turning out swords, helmets, and arquebuses from their anvils. A St. Etienne arms dealer (referred to as a "hardware seller") was only too happy to cart or ship military wares to Romans, trade center for the farmers. However little money the peasants had, they did have enough to pay for arms. *The villagers began to provide themselves with arms in the said town of Romans through a smith or hardware seller from Forez who brought them to this town in great quantity* (A 30).

A peasant war "for six leagues in every direction" was in the offing. Guérin's figure (A 34), undoubtedly exaggerated, would mean that 1800 square kilometers (or 0.3 percent of modern-day France) were involved; about 100 villages could have easily raised 14,000 armed volunteers. France saw a few more peasant wars like this one, on an equally large scale, during the seemingly endless seventeenth century, not to mention the even more involved and drawn-out conflicts of our own century in Algeria and Indochina.

The arms purchases were a prelude to warlike action. The first battle took place in Marsas, the village at the center of the revolt. Royal troops were attacked; their excesses, whether real or fictional, had earned them the enmity of the people. The revolt was unleashed to the sound of the village tocsin and the wooden horns or trumpets so prized in Alpine and Swiss folklore.[3] The occasion was the visit of the light cavalry commanded by Jean de Bourrelon, seigneur de Mures and governor of Embrun. The company was passing through Marsas on its way to Flanders and was so dauntlessly charged by the peasants that *after having lost certain men and horses it was forced to take flight toward the castle at Jarcieu belonging to Mme. d'Anjou.* A short time later, Bourrelon's men were able to retreat toward Lyons. But the members of the peasant leagues had made off with many of their horses and weapons during the scuffle, to the point where the victors began to squabble over the spoils.

These disagreements were quickly resolved and, their appetite whetted, the rebels renewed their efforts. This time their quarry was nothing less than the troops of the illegitimate son of king Henri II, the Grand Prior of France and governor of Provence.[4] The peasants attacked his soldiers with no respect for the commander's royal blood. The gentlemen of this honorable company, which included many noblemen, made all sorts of vain attempts at soothing their pursuers. They even promised to pay double for whatever they bought for their own needs. This good behavior was too long in coming. *The company was forced to go off by the back streets* (A 31), subjected to jeers and curses from the peasants and to some persuasive action as well.

Up to this point, however, in January 1579, the situation had not gone out of control, at least in the Romans region. The countryside, or parts of it, had seen a moderate number of uprisings. But the town itself, and its surrounding villages, remained *in obedience to His Majesty.* Fear was nonetheless spreading quietly through the aristocracy and the local judiciary in this little corner of Dauphiné. In these powerful, privileged circles it was generally thought that it would be fitting *if exemplary punishment were promptly carried out on such agitators, so the fire would not spread.* But of course it was already too late; it is always too late in such cases. The Huguenot network *began to misbehave on a trumped-up excuse,* despite its underdog position. The Huguenots formed the link, if indeed there was any need of one, between town and country. Furthermore, peasants arrived weekly, even daily, in Romans to sell their livestock or grain. At the marketplace, in the shops, at taverns over flagons of wine, tongues loosened. Rural unrest and the urban example of Montélimar were infectious. The case of Romans is of special interest in that the country was the detonator of urban troubles and not vice versa. So it would remain until the final rout. Then, of course, a good third of Romans's citizens were farmers.

The town's rebel element was composed of drapers, carders, and wool-combers, of whom there were many in this center of the textile industry. The successive economic crises Romans had suffered since 1560 (the beginning of the civil wars) were related to their political environment. Men were open to the possibility of regional if not national protest, but the women had reservations.

The craftsman milieu was a complex one. It was controlled from above, economically speaking, by a few wholesale merchants (sellers of raw materials, buyers of finished goods), whose sympathies lay with the law and order party.[5] The bulk of master craftsmen had a small output, but they were proud of their family-run shops. The proletariat or preproletariat, to be exact, was made up of journeymen.

Contemporary sources are categorical: the master craftsmen (sometimes with journeymen apprentices in tow) were the first to raise the banners of revolt—or at least of street demonstrations—in Romans. Twenty years earlier, they had been the first ones susceptible to Huguenot propaganda. Around 1560 both Romans and Toulouse had carders in the vanguard entoning Marot's psalms as they toasted the revolution. They had disseminated "Calvin's garbage" from the beginning. Besides the carders, Romans had always had other craftsmen likely to join any protest, and then outsiders who had immigrated from the surrounding countryside or even farther away. They were unskilled laborers, filling the least desirable jobs in town. No love was lost between them and the local notables; they were an eager audience for the agitators. Starting in the crucial month of February 1579, the fire of rebellion was set alight, and the flames soon spread back to the countryside where it had all started. *So encouraged were the villagers that,* as a result, *they did things they would not have dared to think of at the outset* (A 32).

In Romans it all began on February 3, 1579. It was the feast of St. Blaise, the patron saint of drapers . . . *The members of this trade, and a few others, thus have a large gathering, numerous as they are in the said town. They staged an armed parade.* A captain and an ensign were elected, as they were each year. Up to this point everything was in order and followed the rules. A large crowd attended the ceremony. That was only normal. Besides the twenty or twenty-five prosperous drapers who were at the top of the profession, there were also many lesser clothmakers, then the apprentices; the carders, too, were closely related to the drapers by profession, since they refined the raw wool. The processional gathering became a military review. Carrying arms was *de rigueur.* Urban *confréries* (trade confraternities), not unlike medieval corporations, had the right to bear arms, or at least claimed the right. In this respect they differed from the peasant organizations which theoretically had no right to possess swords or even the arquebus; as we have seen, they had to acquire weapons from St. Etienne merchants.

The choice of St. Blaise's Day for the demonstration was not without significance in terms of folklore. Gaignebet, in a superb and imaginative book, sees St. Blaise as a kind of bearlike character, keeper of the winds. Like the bear coming out of its winter lair in February (Candlemas, February 2), St. Blaise marks the beginning of the vital rebirth of the year by breaking wind. According to Gaignebet, the bear's resounding *fart of dehibernation* celebrated the primordial rite of spring. Without going quite so far, let us note, as Van Gennep does,[6] that St. Blaise, in the Alpine version of his cult, was a sort of textile, agrarian deity, also representing fertility and music. He was supposed to have been tortured to death by being torn to pieces with iron pincers, combs, and cards; it was natural enough, then, for the carders, and by extension the drapers or clothmakers, to choose him as their patron saint. They chose his feast day for the beginning of their revolt as well.

The textile workers were not the only ones to claim St. Blaise.

Plowmen, too, and agricultural workers, who were to throw in their lot with the craftsmen when trouble started in Romans, were also under the protection of this very popular saint. In Dauphiné, Savoy, and the lower Alps, masses were said on St. Blaise's Day for the success of the harvest to come; the grain to be sown in the spring was blessed (see also the description below of the *flailing* dances in Romans in 1580); table upon table of plowmen ate bread decorated with a cross, then, carrying a pine tree trimmed with flowers, formed a procession to the statue of St. Blaise. The fertility of the fields[7] was tied to human fecundity. St. Blaise was said to smile on maidens who left him an offering. In exchange they were given a draught of wine and promised a swain before the year was out. St. Blaise was also the saint in charge of the windpipes; he cured laryngitis and similar ailments. "He who sows the wind shall reap the whirlwind," and Blaise, a lesser deity of life in Romans, was also the saint of death. He was the patron of the confraternity of the Holy Spirit, responsible for burying the dead.[8] Their headquarters was the church of St. Foy in the lower-class eastern quarter of Romans, which was firmly behind the protesters during the final outburst of 1580. Workers rested on feast days, so the saints were their friends. St. Blaise was a comrade in the revolt.

St. Blaise's Day had become a type of military parade in 1579, but it was also a folk gathering, a *reynage*. It was followed by an unprecedented, audacious move. During the feast or spree, a captain was elected for the draper's militia and their parade, according to custom. They may also have named a comic king for the celebration of their *reynage*. And they enthroned a political leader to boot! *They elected a chief not so much for the occasion, they said, as to embrace a cause which they called the rest and relief of the people* (A 32).

Eustache Piémond, the notary from St. André, reports on the election held on February 9, 1579.[9] Piémond goes straight to the point, stating that this election was not only held by the drapers, but by the common people of Romans in general: in other words, there was in all probability a substantial group of men from the crafts and trades, even the plowman ranks, gathered in through their confraternities but also independent of them.

The lucky winner of this election was Captain Jean Serve, known as Paumier or le Paumier. According to Piémond, he was a native of Montmirail.[10] Thus he had come from a nearby village and a rural, if not agricultural, background. He migrated to the city as a youth. All this set him apart from the more or less refined elite of bourgeois born in Romans proper and proud of its "urban" identity. But Paumier had become a master craftsman among the drapers, and had achieved a certain social status in his chosen place of residence.

Paumier's reputation was not purely professional; he also displayed a certain degree of athletic and military prowess. In September 1575 Jean Serve had fought off a band of marauders who claimed to be Huguenots;[11] he came out of the scuffle with a bullet wound. Early in 1579, even before the festivities described above, his supporters had elected him King of the Arquebus. Can we assume that he was good at handling a gun and had the eye of a true marksman? In Romans, archery contests had been replaced by marksmanship with firearms; the target was a popinjay, either a live bird or a wooden or clay effigy attached to the top of a post. The contest took place either during May or on Saint Sebastian's Day (January 20), since Sebastian was martyred by arrows (he was also the saint who guarded against the plague). The popinjay games were yet another instance of Romans's sociability with military, religious, and folkloric overtones. They were also part of a sporting rivalry between Valence and Romans which aided the two towns in joining armed forces in times of civil war and urban alliance.[12] Paumier thus gained prestige from his prowess with firearms, yet events did not subsequently show him to be much of a warmonger. Still, he was a noted local athlete. His skill at *jeu de paume* (an ancestor of tennis) earned him the nickname *Paumier,* which suited him so perfectly that his patronymic *Serve* was much less frequently used and gradually forgotten.

For a country boy, Jean Serve, Master Draper, had certainly made his way in the world of Romans. Even his first marriage was a master stroke; he and Antoinette Thomé were wed on

February 27, 1560. The Thomés were a judiciary clan, lately
merchants; during the entire sixteenth century they filled important posts in Romans's courts and even in the Parlement of
Grenoble.[13] The Carnival in Romans saw Serve-Paumier clash
(mildly) with one of the most notable Thomés. Antoinette,
however, quickly left him a widower, leaving him a daughter
named Monille. Paumier was remarried on November 20, 1562,
to Marguerite Loyron, who also belonged to one of the vener-
able families of Romans's bourgeoisie.[14]

Judging from the taxes he paid, Paumier was neither rich nor
poor.[15] Romans craftsmen, especially his fellow drapers, promoted him because in addition to his athletic skill at *jeu de
paume* and the arquebus, he was one of the most notable and
influential men in the trades. At forty-five or thereabouts Paumier was a favorite with the people and also had rather good
connections in the upper reaches of society.

Paumier's charisma and his outstanding qualities as a leader
were eventually recognized far beyond the city walls, in the
countryside and neighboring towns. Guérin regretfully acknowledged his influence outside Romans. *Paumier* (he writes),
*having attracted to himself by alliances and secret leagues a part of the
people of the town of Valence where he caused a division between the
citizens, had also attracted the villagers around Romans, and as far as
Valloire,*[16] *which he armed to the number of 14,000 arquebuses, signed on
to his cause.* Catherine de'Medici, in Romans on July 18, 1579,
also correctly gauged Paumier's prestige; in a letter to her son
Henri III dated that day, she writes: *their captain named Paumier,
who is a merchant draper,*[17] *has such great influence and authority over
these leagues that his least word will set those of this town and the
surrounding region on the march.*

Paumier's enemies paint a portrait of *as unpresentable and vulgar
a man as may be imagined* (A 33), so insolent that he did not show
proper respect toward the Queen Mother; in short, an uncouth,
lowborn sort of fellow, an ill-groomed boor, the image of the
Carnival wildman or bear.

We are also told that he was manipulated, that this demiking
was nothing but a court jester *who should wear the cap and bells.*
He was mostly capable, his adversaries added, of *executing what*

the masterminds intended to do, since he would have been able to do nothing on his own initiative: the classic accusation against a leader of the common people.

It would probably be nearer the truth to say Paumier had a great deal of nerve. He would have had to in order to assume leadership as he did. He nevertheless exhibited moderation at critical moments; he could be overly moderate, even indecisive. This does not fit in with the picture of the brutal, violent dolt that Guérin paints. As for the "masterminds" or "manipulators" who are reported to have controlled Paumier like a puppet on a string, there is no proof they ever existed. One thing that is true (even Guérin bears it out) is that Paumier had extensive support in the province, as much in Grenoble as in Valence or Montélimar. To the northwest, the east, and the south, his Huguenot contacts kept him in touch with reformist pockets in the Lyons area (P 65) and above all the Protestant bastions of Champsaur, Trièves, the Barronies, and a part of the Valence region; the country surrounding Die and especially Gap, where Lesdiguières was invincible; in short, with all the little Alpine precincts where the Mass had been partially eliminated, where the Catholic clergy had been relieved of its property and income by the followers of Calvin.[18]

Guérin describes the early days of Paumier's "reign" in horrific terms. *He began to command with so much indiscretion and bestiality that he made the gentlefolk dread him* (A 34). He was accused of perpetrating an "18 Brumaire" incident at the town hall. *He began to go into the consular hall* (town hall) *of Romans, replaced the council, and instead of the gentlefolk who had filled it, he had others of his own following take over,*[19] *who were as unworthy of this responsibility as a shoemaker would be as presiding officer of a High Court* (A 34). The repeated allusion to shoemakers, gentlefolk, and presidents of sovereign courts, is typical. Two social territories are defined, one belonging to the cloth and leather workers and other craftsmen, the other the exclusive preserve of the gentlefolk, snugly clustered around the core group formed by the town's judges, administrators, nobles, rich bourgeois, prosperous landowners, and well-to-do merchants. The small businessmen were on one side, the notables on the other. Of course, a certain number of Romans's craftsmen and peasants did not follow the rebel "ringleaders" who came from their own social group; out of sheer habit, they kept on supporting the local notables in a more or less passive manner, since the latter had kept the town under tight control up to that point.

On the subject of Paumier's revolutionary or at least protest activity, Eustache Piémond is less vociferous, less hostile than Guérin, but just as categorical and even more specific. *In Romans,* the notary writes on the events of February 1579, *the common folk, having elected Paumier as their chief, took the keys* (to the city's gates) *from the captains of the said town, and especially captain Antoine Coste and other notable personages who were the keepers of the town* (P 65).

The fact that several of Romans's important personalities were stripped of their functions by the people, in particular those who controlled the strategic gates to the town—consuls, or those designated by the consuls as chief gatekeepers or *portiers*—is also inferred by another of Piémond's statements. He tells us that in Valence, no matter how many "pieces of impudence" the leaguers committed, they at least left the most honorable representatives of the town's staid bourgeoisie in power (P 65). By contrast, what happened in Romans must have been more extreme.

On February 10, 1579, the first and decisive confrontation between the popular faction and the governing bodies took place in a large room at the town hall. It was supposed to be an audience, in this case a tumultuous example of the kind regularly accorded to malcontents by the town councilors. *There presented themselves before the Judge* (Guérin) *and the Consuls a great many of the people of the said city, as many craftsmen as plowmen numbering at least about one thousand.* [20] A thousand people, a few hundred of them waiting in the street outside for lack of room, was quite a high proportion of the population considering the active male population (young or mature adults) could scarcely have been greater than 2,000. A remarkable turnout had been achieved. It expressed discontent, but also the degree to which the populace was organized (through confraternities, etc.). The

people's complaints and demands, our sources tell us, originated with the craftsmen; but they also came from the "urban
peasants" who accounted for more than a third of the town's
population, as we have seen. The various groups of demonstrators asked that the *taille* of 15 *écus*, plus a 3 *écu* surtax, which
had begun to be collected on January 3, "be suspended until
the next meeting of the provincial Estates" (in April–May
1579).[21] The 15 *écu* tax had unleashed the townsfolk's barely
contained anger and provoked *public outcry.*[22] On this point Romans was in perfect agreement with the rest of Dauphiné's
population who were protesting against their tax situation. As
for the preceding tax (which some sources put at 18 *écus*, others
at 6 or 7), the demonstrators requested a deferrment in rather
strong terms "and that it not become outstanding until next
July 18." Finally, the specific demand of the craftsmen, small
employers, and the workers or apprentices who formed the real
backbone of the popular movement (especially the first two
groups), did not go unmentioned: "That merchandise produced
in Romans no longer be subject to special taxes"[23] (indirect
municipal taxes). In short, things had to change: Romans's
producers of goods had had enough of seeing the fruit of *all
their labor go to the payment of tailles and taxes.* In November 1579
Romans's butchers and bakers went on strike against the increase in indirect or excise taxes on bread, livestock, and meat.
Three months later, one of the leaders of the great Carnival
revolt of February 1580 was a butcher named Geoffrey Fleur.[24]

In a city the size of Romans, all the participants in a revolution knew each other. They hated each other passionately,
cordially, and personally. It was the kind of hatred which only
the small can feel toward the mighty, and was far more concrete than a simple, abstract "class consciousness." Hatred was
aimed at those too-comfortable citizens who had for so long
handled the community finances. The thousand malcontents
thus requested (as the town clerk recorded in a sort of official
gibberish) *that the balance of accounts be gone over pertaining to the
handling of the communal funds between the year 1564 up to the present;
and that the accounts be gone over by those who will be named by the
public so that the oppression caused to the poor people may be stopped.*[25]

The date mentioned, 1564, was just after the beginning of Antoine Guérin's reign as town judge.

Moreover, the complaints registered in Romans were far from being the only ones about falsification of local or regional budgets. The *fat purses* of Grenoble, in other words, the crooked financiers, rich holders of royal offices, all those highly placed in business, administrative, fiscal circles were also deeply resented. They were the scourge of the Dauphiné capital. One of the most notorious was a certain sieur de St. André. Sébastien de Lyonne, Treasurer and Receiver General of the Estates wrote[26] that *the people complain of badly administered finances, and those who have handled them; that all or the greater part of funds are to be found in three or four purses in Grenoble with M. de St. André being the main offender, and the others those of the high clerks and other officers of the region* . . . (It appears that the clerks of Dauphiné's Estates dipped into *local* finances as well, a scandalous departure from their defined functions).

Inflation had increased over the preceding few years or even decades and although this ought to have encouraged thrift, the towns and villages had accumulated enormous debts. They imagined that money reclaimed from Grenoble's "loan sharks" would be recycled, putting an end to the indebtedness (P 65). If necessary, the more intemperate claims ran, "*one need only seize M. de St. André's holdings, sell them, and distribute the money over the province so it could buy its way out of debt.*"[27] It is easy to understand why Dauphiné was obsessed with its indebtedness. At this point the province was "crushed under 50,000 *écus* of debt" (or 150,000 *livres*); it paid an annual interest rate of 14 percent to its creditors, the Henrys, a Lyons banking dynasty.[28] In themselves, the various complaints and demands were not enough to shake the foundations of public order. What more ordinary, more legitimate complaints could the people have than with high royal and local taxes, municipal officials with their hands in the till, and pirating financiers in Grenoble and Lyons?

The demand for equal taxation and the end to tax exemptions enjoyed by the nobility surfaced in Romans, as elsewhere, to the annoyance of the long-time holders of tax privileges and the intense aggravation of the new nobles. On February 4, 1579, Romans's consuls, overwhelmed by popular sentiment, actually protested against a tax exemption their fellow notable Jean Souffrey was liable to be granted. He had just been named to a lesser royal office, and this automatically freed him from taxes.[29] Another local case attracted attention during the entire later part of the sixteenth century: that of Antoine de Manissieu the younger. It seems his noble ancestors had departed from custom and gone into trade, which brought taxes crashing down upon their heads. *My grandsire Guillaume de Manissieu,* Antoine's complaint ran, *had 17 children. His son and heir Antoine* (the elder) *thus had to become a merchant to feed his brothers. Jean de Manissieu, eldest son of this Antoine, then had 25 children of his own! In order to support his brothers he had to continue in trade. But my father Guillaume de Manissieu,* Antoine the younger concluded, quoting appropriate letters of Henri III dated 1576, *served the king, and lived as a nobleman just as I have done.*[30] Therefore "we Manissieus should be tax-exempt." One can imagine what a high opinion the citizens of Romans, who would have paid the populous clan's share of taxes as a result, held of this argument. The spontaneous demonstrations against these two tax exemptions and similar cases took on an insurrectionist tinge, just as the law and order party hoped they would.

The street agitators very often carried arms, and that of course made them look even worse. They had confiscated the keys to the city's gates. Then they required that a close watch be kept over comings and goings through the gates, interfering as little as possible with ordinary traffic. The checkpoints were intended as a means of keeping out the soldiery so feared for its looting and repressive measures against the workingmen activists. The less innocent intention of the gate patrol was to keep the urban insurrectionists in close touch with their league friends from the country villages.

Insurrection was also in the air in nearby towns. Piémond praised the popular faction in Valence for its moderation (P 65). He says they had the good sense to keep the most important patricians of their city in place and in power. Piémond was inclined to side with the leaguers, or at least the moderate element; could he have glossed over the situation in Valence? The fact is that on February 15, 1579, five days after the events in Romans, the situation in Valence started to go sour, if not positively rotten. Paumier's emissaries were already stirring things up (A 34). A leader of the people, the miller Bonniol, had taken firm control of matters at his mill at Albon half a league out of town.

A detachment of horse guards garrisoned in Valence, which ultimately answered to Maugiron, the lieutenant-governor of Dauphiné,[31] was responsible for the beginning of Valence's troubles in 1579. Flanking this cavalry regiment were three or four companies of infantry commanded by Messieurs de Champes, de La Bastide, and de Triors. No matter what reasons, good or bad, there had been for stationing the troops in Valence, the town's inhabitants were at wit's end over the havoc the soldiers had wrought, and in complete despair over the daily cost of their upkeep, which was entirely the town's responsibility. On February 4, 1579, during that phase of Carnival which *warms the blood* (the day after the St. Blaise incidents in Romans), Valence's consuls courteously addressed themselves to *Maugiron to beg him to remove and recall his company from the said town of Valence, and to put this company elsewhere, where it may be better able to do the king's service.*[32] The boldfaced excuse the consuls came up with was that the troops in question were a "horse company" while Valence, with its narrow streets, *could be better guarded by infantry.* These words were rapidly followed by action: on February 15, 1579, the miller Bonniol led part of the town's population in a mutiny (probably the lower segments of the third estate, craftsmen and plowmen). Their goal: to run the royal army out of town. The peasant leagues had been requested to help and they did not default (A 35). *They had all the* (village) *leagues come in to massacre the royal troops,* Guérin writes, not without a certain malicious exaggeration.

But no massacre of any kind took place. With the help of the peasants, Valence's insurgents politely showed the four companies to the door (P 64). Only one of the commanders tried to resist: *Monsieur de La Bastide did not want to leave his bodyguard, although he had been invited to depart.* Stronger measures were then taken, but not too strong. *It was no time to disobey. He was wounded in the arm by a halberd* (P 65). This one small incident resulted in the soldiers' total withdrawal. *Henceforth the town guarded itself without a garrison.*

The soldiers newly expelled from Valence had not seen the end of their troubles. They left the area and *took various routes* (A 35). The horsemen wanted to make their retreat along well-beaten paths: *they could not retreat without passing by Romans, where they supposed they would be given food for themselves and their mounts* (A 35). Unfortunately for them, the keys to Romans had changed hands—those fabled keys, now more symbolic than ever. *The cruelty of Romans's seditionists was such,* Guérin rather comically writes (no doubt hoping to impress Catherine de'Medici with his zeal, since it was for her eyes that he prepared his brief), *that they made the horsemen pass many paces outside their town*—meaning that they forbade the troops to enter; then letting them go by or flee as they jeered at them from atop the ramparts. The soldiers were not even given a sack of oats for their horses or a glass of wine for themselves as alms. Instead, the mutineers *brandished their halberds at the horsemen* while calling out many insults as well. The mockery and reversal of the social order seen in this incident were typical Carnival phenomena. A year later the Carnival in Romans was to reveal to how great an extent these themes had been developed.

The real "cruelty" of Romans's rebels was nonviolent and took place outside the city walls. Thanks to the intelligence network linking the town with the country parishes, they incited the *surrounding villagers to sound the tocsin so that* (Maugiron's horsemen) *would be dispersed* (A 36). From then on, the horse guards, many of them nobles, were harassed by rather lackadaisical rustic guerrilla warfare. The cavalrymen scattered, their ears ringing with the sound of the tocsin. *They were forced to go on in very small troops and march all night on unfamiliar side roads.* These weary men at arms ended up in the backwoods, where they finally found a resting place for themselves and their horses.

It was an inglorious rout, involving no real combat. But it marked a first victory for the leagues. One typical episode: a nobleman attached to Maugiron's company of men-at-arms,

Monsieur de Vallins, owned an agricultural property a half-mile or so from Romans. The urban protestors expressly forbade him to take refuge there. They physically prevented him from *communicating with his farmers and servants* (A 36). Thus, there was already evidence, albeit indirect, of the antinoble slant that would become a characteristic of the Romans uprising, particularly of the peasant leagues in surrounding country districts, where farmers were questioning their long-standing subordination to the privileged ranks.

In Romans, as in Valence, the situation in February 1579 was not one of out-and-out insurrection. Negotiations persisted. Romans's consuls kept the promise they had made to the thousand demonstrating malcontents. They dispatched an envoy to Maugiron to acquaint the lieutenant-governor with the craftsmen's complaints and demands. By February 13, Maugiron had answered, in writing, with a few soothing phrases. The essence of his message was: "Come see me with *someone of the people,*" meaning "one of your plebeians." "The taxes you are paying were decreed by my predecessor, Gordes; they are not my fault; I truly wish *to please all the people of Dauphiné; I so dearly love her people, for I am the son of a father who ruled their affairs for forty years and more, . . .*" The letter did contain one solemn pledge: not to levy one more cent from Romans "for the moment."[33]

Maugiron, the lieutenant-governor, represented only one axis of public power in Dauphiné, and not always the most important one. The crucial decisions handed down from Grenoble also came from the Estates and the Parlement, whose members were feeling highly uneasy. They feared the disaffected factions in Romans might join with Lesdiguières and his Huguenot bands which occupied the mountain regions around Gap, and also with the peasant leagues in the Valloire and lower Vienne regions, which had already shown signs of support for the insurrection. If that were the case, dissidence would reign in all of southern and western Dauphiné, replacing royal authority.

The incidents in Romans had caught the provincial authorities off their guard, the Estates and the governor's lieutenant included. It was no time for high-handed dealings with the

popular movement; ferment was too widespread, and, if provoked, would pose too great a threat to provincial authority.
Basset, a high clerk of the Estates, therefore drafted a very
accommodating letter to the consuls and people of Romans.[34]
We have been advised of some rising in your towns . . . We send you
Maître Michel Thomé (of the Parlement and of the old Romans
family) *on account of the old friendship he bears toward you being your*
fellow townsmen . . . to attend to you by the best and most agreeable
means.

Thomé was an apt choice as plenipotentiary envoy to Romans, sent to keep the local authorities in line. This "ambassador" from the High Court was the descendant of an old
Romans family which had provided the town's courts with
presiding judges and crown solicitors for several generations,
since 1484 to be exact.[35] The family, and Michel Thomé himself, had taken an active part in the extended quibbling between
Romans and the chapter of St. Barnard, with the common
people and the bourgeois on the one side, and the canons on
the other. The chapter of Romans's largest church was the co-
seigneur of the town; the other was the king of France. For
Thomé it was a victorious fight: the chapter had had to capit-
ulate to the local bourgeoisie. Now that the bourgeoisie was
was again confronted, not by the chapter clerics but by the
obstreperous complaints and demands of the lower classes,
dispatching Thomé to Romans seemed an inspired move. As we
have seen, he was related by marriage to Jean Serve-Paumier,
leader of the revolt and at first he seemed to score a clear
political victory in his town.[36] He took part in the regular
session of the greater council held in the town hall on February
16, 1579. At his side was another Parlement judge, Jean de
Lacroix, also from Romans. Seated near Lacroix and Thomé
was Jean Rabot, a representative of the provincial Estates.
Finally there was the man who would ultimately be the evil
genius of Romans's patricians and the angel of death to the
common folk: Antoine Guérin, royal judge in the local court,
a gifted writer and historian, and a cunning operator, whose
hands had already been bloodied by his involvement in the St.
Bartholomew's Day slaughter in Romans in 1572.

Facing the Grenoble visitors was the assembled council, consisting of some forty members plus the four consuls; they too had full rights of attendance at Michel Thomé's address.

Thomé spoke on the usual safe topics: he deplored the calamities of the Wars of Religion; he mentioned the good will of the king, of Maugiron, and the Parlement—all of whom were trying to alleviate the tax squeeze as best they could. He dwelled on the virtues of harmony among all the citizens of Romans. In conclusion, he dragged out that time-honored tearjerker: *My family comes from this town, I was born here, I am your fellow townsman, I am one of you.*

Thomé's rhetoric can still be heard at any state fair in any election year; in 1579, his eloquence seems to have hit the mark. At the end of Thomé's homily the crowd in the council chamber shifted and there was an ovation for the orator.[37] There was also some response from two representatives of the opposition (Paumier's group): André Ferrier, an attorney, and especially the draper Guillaume Robert-Brunat.[38] He was in charge of defending the drapers' corporate interests, and directed the protest movement in tandem with Paumier.

The troubled weeks of February 1579 were a period of power based in the streets as much as in the town hall. Given a solicitous welcome by the local elders, Thomé did not get anything resembling good treatment from the seditionists (as he already considered Paumier and company to be). *He did everything in his power to put the people back on the right track . . . but from the people he received many indignities, from the said mutineers, so much so that he was forced to return to Grenoble* (A 36). Thus Thomé's diplomatic mission did not have a happy ending, nor indeed any success at all save at the very beginning. All this inspired Guérin to a few remarks full of Alpine imagery expressing his disillusionment: *In the same say that it is impossible to prevent a waterfall from felling all the barriers erected in its path . . . thus this insurgent people, paying no heed to the wise remonstrances of Michel Thomé, could not hold back . . .*

Michel Thomé had to return to the provincial capital, and to the Parlement at which Romans's rebels had scoffed, with no concrete results and a heart full of bitterness at the conduct of the agitators. And in his later account Guérin takes no pains to hide his lack of respect for Michel Thomé; he found the Parlement official spineless. Once Thomé was gone, the whole game was played out between the citizens of Romans and the town's relationships with surrounding villages, heady with hope inspired by the newly formed leagues.

One concession had been made during Thomé's visit. Romans had asked the Parlement *to force the treasurers, and those who have handled the municipal funds, to give an account of them.* The request was granted (P 65). As a result there were endless audits in Romans and other communities, *which only did harm* and were used by the agitators as fuel for their antinoble, antigovernment propaganda. In Romans proper, it heightened the tension. The bourgeoisie split into factions, supporting various courses of action.

Some of the gentlefolk, so called, were frankly disheartened, for *they say that this mutinous band* (the rebels)[39] *was growing day by day as their misdeeds went unpunished, and that they could not be corrected by justice which did not have sufficient strength.*

For these defeatist patricians the solution was voluntary exile, at least temporarily. *Some went to Grenoble, others to other places* where the situation was not so "insurgent" as in Romans. They wanted a change of scene. They resigned themselves to waiting for it *to please God to restore order* (A 35). One day, ever so quietly, they planned to return.

Judge Guérin was as hostile toward his fellow bourgeois who chose exile as he was toward Paumier and his supporters. He was also craftier and braver than the fugitive patricians. Later, when he was sure of support, he showed himself to be cruel and intransigent. For the moment, he pursued conciliation, a middle ground. There was no question he would ever consider leaving Romans: he even stayed put in 1586 when plague wiped out half the town's population.

Guérin lamented the *mutinous band's* vulgar ways: like real rabble (A 35), they came and went at all hours in the town hall and the Cordelier's Friary, a convenient and centrally located meeting place with a large main chamber. The judge noted the rebels' obstinate style: they *all wanted to speak at once,* shouting "We want, we want..." But he could do nothing

about it. It was like a Carnival *charivari*; no one could hear or
understand what his neighbor was saying. The very least these
people could have done was to appoint a speaker to represent
them, who would, ideally, be rather less stubborn, rather more
moderate than Paumier. Guérin, with the help of a few members
or notables of the bourgeois faction, took it upon himself to use
every means (including tricks), though these proved fruitless,
to convince the unruly protesters they should name . . . a single
individual to speak for all of them. Guérin had some education
in Latin, and perhaps he had in mind something vaguely resembling Rome's *tribune* channelling plebeian demands . . . This
would do away with the *irreverence and filth* of the disorganized
collective sessions the craftsman group had been holding. The
people's choice, which the notables underhandedly tried to
steer, was once again (like Paumier) a draper, Guillaume Robert-Brunat, a native of Romans (the drapers' association was
decidedly the element deemed most responsible and influential
for better or worse). According to Guérin, *this personage had a
rather good mind, and could have remedied many things, had he wanted
to apply himself to it.* This is tantamount to saying that Guérin
and his colleagues hoped Robert-Brunat would supersede Paumier and serve as liaison between Guérin and the lower classes.
Their hopes were disappointed. The judge would keep trying to
find a workingman leader he could control, eventually satis-
fying himself with Laroche, a ropemaker and former friend of
Paumier's. Brunat, however, was no puppet; he fanned the
flames of the class struggle instead of calming it.

   The "gentlefolk" and the "revolters" had barely concluded
this extremely lame compromise, with Brunat as the shaky link
between the two camps, when new problems arose. Paumier,
who remained the agitators' real chief, was given food for
thought. The Huguenots, under Lesdiguières's command, were
cornered in the southern Alpine highlands. They wanted to use
Paumier to their advantage, and Guérin claims that the draper
was full of *ambition and the desire to make himself great* (A 37). The
Protestants began negotiations with him; they gave him *promises
and assurances of reciprocity....* Paumier and Lesdiguières's men
held several conferences or *pourparlers* in two local villages,

Petit–St. Jean and La Côte–St. Michel. Could it really be true that Romans's popular hero succumbed to vulgar bribes? Or did he need money for his troops? Whatever the reason, to get Paumier *in their tow* (the Huguenots) *paid to Paumier a certain sum which was said to be 1200 écus*—or at least that was the rumor the "gentlefolk" circulated concerning their adversary. They were good Catholics or at any rate determined members of the Catholic faction (one did not necessarily imply the other); the Huguenot wheeling and dealing made them nervous, they considered it *the best way for the town of Romans to be lost*: in other words to let the Huguenots from Geneva take over Romans while they pretended to serve Paumier.

The already complicated situation became even more involved when a third or fourth renegade party came into the picture: none other than the outlaw leader Laprade.[40] Antoine de la Salle, alias Captain Laprade, was born near Romans to a quite well-connected family: he was related to Claudia de la Salle, the wife of the sieur de Triors. Laprade had spent his Protestant youth in Lesdiguières's fighting forces; he maintained contacts with the Huguenot brethren. By 1577 he had struck out on his own. He became a soldier of fortune, fighting and pillaging for his own gain. The forthcoming peace (or the one thought to be forthcoming after the edict of pacification in 1577) threatened to send Laprade into retirement, if not to jail. To avoid this ignominious fate he somehow pulled off the capture of the fortress at Châteaudouble, one of the most formidable in Dauphiné. He barricaded himself inside, sallying forth to strike at towns over a considerable range of territory; he assaulted the neighborhoods of Valence, Romans, even Montélimar. He looted and kidnapped travelers and merchants for ransom; he held them prisoner when they resisted his stringent demands.

Laprade's first brush with the townsfolk of Romans occurred in 1578. On March 12 of that year he kidnapped the merchant Jean Guigou, member of a prominent Romans family, who was on a business trip attending to the Duke of Savoy's affairs (the link between one of Romans's great notables and one of the Alpine region's most powerful potentates is of itself interesting). By late 1578 and early 1579, Laprade had created an unbearable situation in the Valence and lower Vienne regions. Trade had been disrupted; in the immediate vicinity of Châteaudouble it was totally suspended, inciting businessmen to join with the rabble of craftsmen and peasants to combat Laprade's thievery and extortion. In January 1579 the gentleman outlaw grew even bolder. He crossed the Rhône and captured the town of Soyans in Vivarais. He had plans to take control of the château Pipet, which would have made him master of Vienne, no less, but swift action on the part of Vienne's consuls put an end to Laprade's scheme.

Foiled in Vienne, Laprade nonetheless had success elsewhere. In May 1578, he commandeered a group of Swiss envoys making their way back to their cantons after a diplomatic mission in the southwest of France. The king of Navarre—the future Henri IV of France—was incensed. Dauphiné's most powerful figures, Maugiron and Lesdiguières, were natural enemies, but for once they agreed, begging Laprade, "their brother and good friend" to cease and desist. Laprade paid not the least attention to their highly respectful letters. He had good reason to think, furthermore, that Lesdiguières and the Huguenots were only turning against him for show, and that they secretly continued to regard him as an ally. And he was joined in thinking this by a few other outlaws who claimed support for the Huguenots.[41]

Such was the ambiguous yet charged ambience in the midst of which Paumier and his followers had to adopt an attitude toward Laprade. It was a most delicate matter, since Paumier was making a deal with the Huguenots, and Laprade was Protestant or at any rate a lapsed one. It seems likely that the Romans protesters and the Châteaudouble gangsters came close to formulating a pact which would have combined the forces of the peasant leagues, Paumier's Romans plebians, and the Huguenots!

Whether truth or half-fiction, these rumors made the bourgeoisie of Romans quiver in their boots—and quite rightly—to think *that Laprade who commanded Châteaudouble had promised to be chief, and afterwards to take over the said town of Romans* (A 37). Were their fears justified? It appears that a rather large gathering took place at a village called Charpey for the purpose of negotiation. In attendance were craftsmen, *farmworkers and others of the Third Estate of the said League,* that is, Paumier's league of workingmen and peasants, as well as *certain captains and soldiers of the said Laprade* (A 37). The confederation of outlaws and leaguers would bring the town and country *to wrack and ruin. The Good Lord,* Guérin wrote, *could not have willed such a disaster,* and the judge then rushed to the aid of the gentlefolk. Paumier's league had a peasant majority, if only by virtue of the fact that 85 percent of the population was rural. It was reported (perhaps the figure is inflated) that there were 14,000 volunteers ready to take up the arquebus. As their insignia the impromptu soldiers *wore no cord on their hats.* They could be quickly called up thanks to 300 wooden cowherd's trumpets which Gamot, the Grenoble agitator, had encouraged them to keep on hand so they could call or *sound off to each other* from parish to parish. These countrymen, more or less outfitted as soldiers but more often than not ill-equipped, were far from ready, even for the best of strategic reasons, to take orders from a highwayman, renegade warrior, and tragicomic lord of a castle such as Laprade.

Some peasant leaders, who differed strongly with Paumier on this point, therefore refused to make it up with Laprade. The noble outlaw, furious, or suspecting an ambush, or simply giving in to his rapine instincts, promptly assembled all his horsemen, stormed Charpey, and killed 100 to 120 men, women, and children; he pillaged and ravaged their homes, livestock, and foodstuffs (A 38).

That was the end of cordial relations between Paumier and Laprade. (The final break was yet to come: Paumier, something of the diplomat, accepted and encouraged the country militia's subsequent attack on Laprade, but carefully refrained from taking part in it himself.)

The growing split between the groups was much to the liking of Guérin and his cronies who ran Romans, coexisting with Paumier's men while opposing them. Guérin's group detested Laprade, and hated the Huguenots. The feeling was more than reciprocated, and at any moment the memory of the St. Bartholomew's Day massacre (organized by the elitist clique) might be revived.

Under these conditions there was a shuffling of alliances,

resulting in what we might term a "holy alliance" against the outlaws. Paumier pulled the strings and remained rather "above it all." He avidly and shrewdly directed and observed the process.

By late February 1579, the peasant leagues, furious at Laprade's massacre, moved to retaliate. At the command of Captain Paumier (in this instance our sources dub him *captain-general* of the lower Dauphiné forces), the communities of the Valloire and Valence regions were ordered to assemble promptly, armed and numerous, *so as to lay siege to the thief Laprade and his accomplices, to put an end to his thievery, and to deliver the province from oppression* (P 66). It is noteworthy that in so doing the *communities,* expressly implicated, and their captain-general, Paumier, acted on their own initiative in place of royal authority. Represented by Maugiron, royal authority was in a gravely weakened state. *Neither the edict of pacification, nor Monsieur de Maugiorn, had been able to stop Laprade's thievery,* Eustache Piémond points out with perhaps ironical regret.

The leaguers were to gather at Romans, headquarters for Paumier and the whole lower Dauphiné region, on March 1, 1579. On the appointed day 4,000 league members presented themselves, good soldiers of the people, *led there and commanded by their chiefs and captains.* From there they all *went to Château-double quite unprovided* (with hastily improvised weapons) *as if Laprade should surrender at the mere sight of them* (P 66). The league's action (organized by Paumier) presented Maugiron and the bourgeois consuls of Romans with a most embarrassing *fait accompli.* Three days after the league expedition (March 3), Romans's consuls at last decided, after much hesitation, to join in the fight against the outlaws.

Many factors prodded Romans's notables to move in that direction. First of all, they were encouraged by Paumier's friends who had recently joined the town council as supernumerary members; they also sensed that Maugiron himself—in other words the crown's man—was about to take over at Château-double to avoid having a revolution on his hands. It seemed better to side with Paumier, no matter how much they hated him, *in obedience to His Majesty.*[42] To top things off, the league militia, camping beneath Châteaudouble's high walls, *awaited the aid and assistance* of Romans's town government. In any case, there was not much danger in the decision, since the town fathers, hedging all bets, pointed out that Laprade had finally *been disowned by those of the supposedly Reformed religion* (in fact they had only half-disowned him; had the outlaw defeated the league, Lesdiguières would not have hesitated to take up with him again). No matter what the circumstances, Romans's governing body continued in its tangled argument. It could do no harm to get rid of Laprade, enemy not only of the countryfolk, but the townsfolk and merchants as well. They resolved to go all out and call forth *the best troop that can be assembled of the good men of this town* [Romans] *on foot as well as horseback, with all necessary provisions.* Two captains were "elected" by the consuls: a certain Beauregard for the cavalry (he was also the local pillar of the mock "abbey" of Maugouvert-Bongouvert, a thoroughly bourgeois invention), and, more important, for the infantry, Laroche, a Romans ropemaker and craftsman.[43] It was not a chance appointment. Laroche was an influential, active member of the league, yet he represented a sort of third party within Romans, a moderate workingman group. His former friendship with Paumier had turned to hatred. A year later, Laroche went over to the patricians at the crucial moment, irrevocably compromising the rebels.

Beauregard and Laroche were fully empowered to select their troops, *to choose and elect the men as they see fit,* then lead them toward the outlaw's stronghold. The ropemaker swiftly put together a detachment and hustled toward Châteaudouble. Between the two groups of league volunteers, Paumier's and Laroche's, there must have been a good many men from Romans.[44] At some point the two cannons abandoned in Romans by Gordes, the former lieutenant-governor (who had died in 1578), had been brought to Châteaudouble by them.[45]

The next step toward cementing the "holy alliance" was quickly taken: Maugiron himself joined the siege against Laprade.[46] As the modern cliché would have it, he appeared by popular demand. The reasons he gave for going to Châteaudouble were humanitarian and may well have been true. As lieutenant-governor of the entire province in the name of the crown, he thought Laprade would cut his helter-skelter attackers to pieces if the royal army or "regular troops" did not take the situation in hand. Since Laprade was an ally, albeit insubordinate, of Lesdiguières's, Maugiron, an ultra-Catholic, would not have appeared in a favorable light if the outlaw did rout the league army. The lieutenant-general *foresaw that if people other than this common people did not become involved, everything would be confused, and* (Laprade) *would cause such carnage as would never be forgotten* (A 38). Our leaguers had nothing against Maugiron a priori. They had hoped he would come to their aid with his professional soldiers, and that the nobles would follow suit since they were supposedly the military class. Thus "the people" were happy when Maugiron arrived, and they showed it. *They begged Maugiron to come with them, and that he bring what nobles and soldiers he had at his disposal, for the taking of the said castle and the said Laprade* (A 38).

"Holy alliance" notwithstanding, at Châteaudouble "allies were watched over as closely as enemies." Maugiron was no genius, but he had common sense. He planned to take charge of the movement to keep it from turning into civil war. As for the leagues, their motives were not so simple either. Châteaudouble was only a first step. Can we assume that their final goal was nothing less than Grenoble? According to this hypothesis, independently confirmed by two of our sources, they had more in mind than revenge on Laprade; they were after the "key men" in the province: the Grenoble Parlement, the treasurers and other officials whom they accused of skimming tax receipts. *And from there* (once they had taken Châteaudouble) *they wanted to go attack the town of Grenoble so as to overthrow the State and Justice. . . , and to prevent the treasurers from escaping or fleeing.* Their flight would be quite understandable!

The leagues' Grenoble plan was still only a dream, but perhaps not so wild a dream as it might have seemed. Grenoble, a major town, also had its popular, workingman faction, led by Gamot, the rebel attorney; the leagues counted on his party as their Trojan Horse within the provincial capital. They expected a great deal from this *band of mutineer accomplices which had begun to rise up* in Grenoble and—the crowning insult—*revolt against the sovereign authority of the Court of Parlement.*[47]

Paumier's wild hope of taking Grenoble minimized Château-double in his eyes. His thinking was eminently strategic. It also appears that despite his athletic competitiveness, he was not especially fond of battles. The fact is he remained in Romans or returned there very quickly; his home town was his real bastion until greater things called. Was he irresolute? The wait-and-see type? In any event, he left his peasant friends in Romans to act out the roles he had chosen for them, without him. *The said Paumier and his other chief accomplices did not want to stay away from Romans, and let the other leaguers named below stage the farce at Châteaudouble* (A 39).

Maugiron left Grenoble on March 5, 1579, with a few men (P 67). He brought two pieces of cannon which were sent down by river for the first leg of the journey. Paltry artillery, but enough to bring down a stronghold. Once he got to Château-double, accompanied by his adjutant, Monsieur de Saussat, Maugiron found widespread confusion. It was the time for the winter pruning of the grapevines; many of the leaguers were volunteer soldiers, but full-time winegrowers, and their sole concern was to get back to their plants as quickly as possible, trading their arquebuses in for their pruning knives. They had no intention of staying at Châteaudouble for any length of time, only of returning straightaway to their vines (A 39). Furthermore, management of the militia was pathetic, virtually nonexistent. Many of the soldiers had nothing to eat except what meager provisions they had brought in their sacks. Desertions on this account came quickly and in droves. *They had not considered or provided for the things necessary for a siege, having only brought along their sacks full of food, and when these were emptied they decided to go home and abandon everything* (A 39). Paradoxically, it was Laprade who was unwittingly starving out his besiegers. After a few days the whole business came to a sorry end: *In fact the greater part of these good soldiers, having spent two days there* (at Châteaudouble) *began to disband, to go off by night.*[48] The league leaders did not even take the trouble to block off their charges' flight. In short, it was chaos.

Although it had been awaited like the second coming, Maugiron's arrival only seemed to make matters worse. Some of the "dove" league members were afraid they would incur the lieutenant-governor's wrath for having followed the "hawks," the extremist faction. The "hawks" were also considering leaving town to escape Maugiron's displeasure. Diplomatically, *since he feared an outbreak,* Maugiron soothed all the concerned parties (P 67). The siege would go on. The lieutenant-governor also took skillfull control of material problems. *He brought order to everything, so much so that provisions and ammunition were in good supply* (A 39).

Towns like Romans, where the traditional ruling class had been challenged but continued to govern, were reassured by Maugiron's presence in Châteaudouble. Since he was maintaining law and order, they felt free to give their full support to the fight against Laprade. The same went for towns like Vienne and larger villages like St. Antoine run by timid or slow-moving lesser notables, who had refused to cooperate with the leagues up to that point. Maugiron had sanctioned the people's initiative, so these towns followed suit, sending reinforcements. A tax of 333 *écus* (more than 9 *livres* or 3 *écus* per soldier) for each company of 100 armed men was levied on the towns and villages.[49]

On March 10, 1579, a grand gathering of Dauphiné's communities—the towns and larger villages represented by their consuls or delegates—was held in Romans.[50] The "holy alliance" was thus institutionalized. It was decided that no effort should be spared for the capture of Châteaudouble. At that same time, the communities did not lose sight of their prime institutional objective: the end of tax exemptions for the privileged ranks. The whole province thrilled with a jubilant feeling of locomotion. This was the *rising of the people,* in the true and profound sense of the term.

It was a honeymoon period: there was a coalition between the league and the royal, provincial, municipal authorities, and it seemed predestined. The Parlement of Grenoble put its shoulder to the wheel. It once again dispatched Thomé to Romans to encourage the townsfolk to do as Maugiron bade them, their consuls' differences over Paumier notwithstanding.[51]

Behind the walls of Châteaudouble, Laprade no longer had a chance. Half-abandoned by the Huguenots, he was now at the mercy of Maugiron's artillery. The outlaw gave up, disheartened, as the first cannon shots were fired around March 15, 1579. *With no help in sight, Laprade surrendered the town* (really a village) *and the castle of Châteaudouble to Monsieur de Maugiron* (in exchange for) *his life and those of his men with all their arms and baggage* (P 69). He headed east across the Alps and took refuge in the Marquisate of Saluce. There he availed himself of several connections with Protestant sympathizers. But not for long; the maréchal de Bellegarde, who was friendly with the Dauphiné Huguenots, took him in, gave him a command . . . and had him knifed to death some months later in punishment for an unknown crime.[52] *A fitting end for a thief,* Eustache Piémond philosophically concludes.[53]

The town of Châteaudouble also paid for the crime of having harbored an outlaw band, however unwillingly. As a security measure *Maugiron had the castle* (of Châteaudouble) *dismantled and razed, and made great holes in the walls of the town* (the adjoining village).[54]

Laprade's defeat struck a final blow against the provincial outlaws. Shortly before Châteaudouble, Roussas fell; it had been Captain Laroche's headquarters and the second bandit stronghold in the district.[55] The victory at Roussas was credited to Jacques Colas (see above, Chapter III).

Châteaudouble, and to a lesser extent Roussas, serve to illustrate in how many complicated and opposing directions the various social and political groups in Dauphiné were pulled, both mentally and physically. Let us enumerate the various tendencies or shades of difference: Huguenots in the southeast, divided into factions for and against Lesdiguières;[56] peasant leagues; urban workingmen's leagues, which might include Huguenot or pro-Huguenot elements, as in Romans, or be staunchly Catholic, as in the southern regions around Montélimar, and in either case be divided—Romans furnishes the perfect example—into moderates (Laroche) and hardliners (Paumier). In addition, within the jointly urban and rural leagues the peasants had their own goals and could take the movement in unforeseen directions, against the outlaws, for instance, and later against the seigneurs. Finally, "above the salt" there were the bourgeois patricians and the nobles. The two groups had distinct views on tax questions, but eventually rallied around the highest administrative power in the region, namely the Parlement of Grenoble and the lieutenant-governor of Dauphiné, in this case Maugiron, who controlled one part of the province's armed forces. In 1579 Paumier ably navigated around all these groups, although he seemed to lose his touch the following year. He was playing a loaded game: first he negotiated with the Huguenots, even the outlaw elements. Then, pressured by his peasant allies, he attacked the outlaws. Finally, he let the directors of his faction conclude a fragile pact with the royal and provincial authorities and the bourgeois patricians who were his natural enemies, personally and polit- ically speaking. They then patched together an offensive against Laprade at the last possible moment, or, as the Scripture has it, the eleventh hour.

The fall of Châteaudouble would have had no significance for Maugiron and the notables unless they saw it as an integral part of a return to their idea of normalcy, with the peasants and the league remembering their place after having moved out of line for a few months.

For a while it seemed that Maugiron had achieved just that. He summoned the principal leaders and captains of the urban and peasant leagues to his temporary lodgings beneath the ruined walls of Châteaudouble and delivered a nice little speech (P 69). In essence, *he thanked them for their good will, the zeal they had exhibited in exposing their lives and property for the good of the country.* The breach had not been mended, however; the initial differences remained. Despite the united forces' victory over Laprade, Maugiron did not forget that the initiative for the siege had come from the people, the peasants, with no official sanction. Therefore the orator added, *in the future do not set out for the battlefield without the will and command of the King.* The lieutenant-governor's speech alternately praised and rebuked: your undertaking of the siege, he said to the rural folk, *was too audacious and noxious. Still it is forgiven, provided you never do it again* (except with the express permission of crown authorities). *I grant you leave to return to your homes, to live in peace in obedience to your superiors, as God ordains.*[57]

The league leaders were not exactly cowed. One or several of them, whose names have not come down to us, took the floor to answer Maugiron. Polite but firm, they gave in on form but not content: *We did not take up arms against the King's authority, but in his service. We wanted to see the edict of pacification obeyed* (P 69–70). They seemed to suggest that their pacifist intentions were thwarted by the local garrisons, as well as by Laprade and his thieving gang, and they felt they had to do something about it.

In the end the league activists, still armed, reached a compromise with Maugiron. He was pliant as a velvet glove in their presence (though the iron hand would soon be in evidence). They asked the lieutenant-governor to support the demands made in their *Cahier;* they asked him to help them, men of the third estate, to reapportion a part of their tax burden to the nobility and the clergy, as would be in keeping with Dauphiné's traditional privilege. Jean de Bourg was close at hand . . .

With his back to the wall, Maugiron promised (vaguely) to defend plans of this nature at the forthcoming session of the Estates in Grenoble. The last word (P 70) fell to him: *Remain in peace, love one another, and wait until the next Estates.*

A son of Dauphiné, Maugiron could speak the Franco-Provençal dialect of the region and knew how to talk to the people. His eloquence banished ill will for a time, if not for very long. He would also try it out on the citizens of Romans. The lieutenant-governor had Thomé, the Parlement of Grenoble's habitual envoy, accompany him to the seat of protest activity.

Maugiron complained in general terms to the town council of the *rumors and new stirrings* that had taken place in Romans shortly before the siege of Châteaudouble.[58] He then specifically reproached Paumier's faction of rebel craftsmen for having *seized the keys and taken away responsibility* (P 70) from the captains who were designated keepers of the keys to the city—the keys that let the village leaguers come right into Romans!

As always, the townsfolk of Romans were singled out for their extremist, radical tendencies. They had dared what even the Valence league had not attempted, Maugiron hinted. "You replaced the keepers of the keys,"—an insult upon injury.

The lieutenant-governor's visit implicitly acknowledged the existence of a "dual power" situation in Romans. On one side there was "Captain" Paumier, "governor" of the workingmen, who claimed to be master of the town and in fact commanded the ramparts, gates, certain quarters of Romans, and the extraordinary-supernumerary portion of the town council.

Opposing him were high officials: the consuls, Romans's court of justice, and judge Guérin. Guérin and the consuls took moral refuge in their bastions, the town hall and the neighborhood of the Cordelier's friary. And rightly so: invited to respond to Maugiron at the town hall, in the name of the full town council, Guérin rather ingratiatingly asked the lieutenant-governor of his province to excuse the wrong that may have been done him, the displeasure we may have caused (in all truth, the judge and his friends had done no *wrong,* having upheld law and order in the streets and the hearts of the townsfolk as best they could). Nothing major had transpired so far, but the session ended on a more substantial political note. The entire town council of Romans, *solemnly raising their hands to God,* swore an oath of loyalty to the king and Maugiron. They vowed never to take arms against the superior authorities of the realm and the province.[59]

As for Paumier, Maugiron met with him and hypocritically *entrusted him with the honor of the town and obedience to the King* (P 70). Paumier just as brazenly swore to everything asked of him. Then, with his supple conscience as guide, he hastened to add, following the example of his colleagues in Châteaudouble, that the league was only promoting *the just pursuit of the privileges the people wish to enjoy in accord with the king's wishes.* He was of course referring to the tax privilege Dauphiné still believed was its right and which the commoners freely interpreted to mean the nobility and clergy should pay a share of taxes. We are not told what else, if anything, the two men discussed. But Paumier did not give an inch on the main point. He was firm yet flexible, the happy combination that would see him through the remainder of 1579. He defended Jean de Bourg's petition of grievance. Four months later he displayed the same qualities in his meeting with Catherine de'Medici. The following year would not be so auspicious for him.

The accord between Maugiron and Paumier was bound to be superficial, all the more so since trouble was brewing in Grenoble. If you leave your place you lose it, the proverb tells us; the provincial capital had conveniently forgotten Maugiron while he was attending to his duty in Châteaudouble, along with the regular troops usually stationed in Grenoble. The consuls of the provincial capital were conservative men—in any case not radicals like Paumier—but they had quickly taken over the town, temporarily free of armed forces. By March 15, 1579, they had the population armed; men were required *henceforth to take and habitually wear the sword, and keep their arms ready in case of need.*[60] On March 19 they formed a militia of 300 men under the command of four prominent citizens. On March 27 the town was alive with rumors of Maugiron's return, but the consuls and the town council were not backing down. By a defiant majority they refused to have any troops of professional soldiers stationed in Grenoble (a freedom they had known in the past) or in the immediate vicinity. Valence had made the same outrageous declaration on February 5. Grenoble's consuls, however, were afraid Maugiron might say he needed soldiers to help bring his cannons back into town, then keep them inside the walls. They therefore *offered, if need be, to go themselves and accompany into Grenoble the artillery brought back from Châteaudouble, at their own expense.*[61] All this was done in the name of the *Union*— a league just as urban as it was rural. It included the authorities, legal or otherwise, of several large towns: Valence, Romans, Grenoble. It coalesced a part of the bourgeoisie and the workingmen, although a marked split between the two was already apparent in Romans.

Back in Grenoble, Maugiron was dismayed to see what had become of his "good town": *upon his arrival, he found that those of the Union in the said town were guarding it with a drum in great number and outfit, which angered him* (P 71). The following day he convened the consuls, and called a town meeting (of the council? the townsfolk? we are not told). It was held in front of the palace (the Parlement building, perhaps?). The indefatigable Maugiron addressed the crowd in flowery terms and warned of the *danger that can come about when a people takes arms against the authority of its natural prince.* Maguiron apparently did not take his subjects' protestations of loyalty to the crown very seriously; perhaps he was right. After arguing for king and country, he tried Parlement. What he said in substance was: "You just shouldn't do such things" in a town like Grenoble, the seat of Parlement, which was the king's council (P 71). Grenoble's bourgeoisie had in fact attacked the Parlement judges, once members of the third estate, who had acceded to the tax-free nobility. But no matter what the variations, Maugiron was ostensibly making the same speech for the third time. He had already practiced it in Châteaudouble and Romans. The professional soldier was getting to be a veteran stumper, not unlike a political candidate of our own day. It is quite possible that Maugiron was not as thick-witted as his enemies claimed.

He did not have much luck in Grenoble, a populous and restive town. The citizens' designated representative gave him an unequivocally negative answer. It clearly called for Grenoble to continue in the league (which the events of the following winter were to compromise). The representative declared: *The town of Grenoble is of the Union with Vienne, Valence, Romans, and others, to free themselves of garrisons and to live in peace, following the edict of His Majesty.* The rest of his speech affirmed the two essential demands Grenoble shared with the other Dauphiné towns: *to guard their towns themselves . . . as good patriots.* This was not "French" but purely local or regional allegiance. They also wanted to pursue *their just remonstrances contained in the Cahiers of the people* (P 71). Simply stated, they wanted the dreaded garrisons out of town; they wanted the nobility and clergy to pay a share of taxes. This was a rather moderate platform; the reference to de Bourg and his *Cahiers* was the common denominator.

Maugiron saw that the townsfolk were determined, and he realized that it was useless to protest. So he gave in, and with a tremendous loss of face *he offered his assistance* to the people of Grenoble. There was now a glimmer of hope for the forthcoming provincial Estates, for a general reconciliation of the various social groups so at odds, *that at the conclusion of the next Estates, the three orders would embrace and acknowledge each other as well they should* (P 72). Maugiron's ultimate solution to the grave struggles assailing Dauphiné and its class structure was a fraternal embrace. *Embrace each other, good people, love one another,* was his message to the crowd at Grenoble, at Châteaudouble.

Maugiron's natural prudence, the waiting game he played, led him to attempt adapting to a situation which was rapidly becoming unstable, which was at once open and strained, almost revolutionary in places, especially Romans and its surrounding countryside.

In Romans, despite the show of rapprochement Guérin and Paumier had made, the workingmen remained on guard. Paumier's following numbered up to a thousand or more active protesters ready to hit the streets. Guérin, always well informed, mentions 750 leaguers in Romans at the beginning of 1580 (A 171); the figure indicates a rather high rate of mobilization, considering that the population of adult males could not have been much over 2,000. It was a real revolution.

The capture of Châteaudouble had made the leaguers' hearts swell with pride. Guérin was always careful to note the rebels' behavior; he reports (A 40) *they returned to Romans so puffed up with vainglory one hardly dared look at them.* Just imagine the incredible parade through the streets of Romans, the victors in glorious rags. They had eliminated one of the region's most dangerous outlaws, a superb feat. The local bourgeoisie had only to wait its turn. Swelled with vanity, the militia had the audacity to march *through town* with the two cannons which by right belonged *to the town*. They had brought them back from Château-double along with their wagons and baggage: *They dared say that these cannons belonged to them.*

Moreover, the agitation was turning against the seigneurs. As we shall see, this tendency emerged in theoretical manifestos. Far more disquieting signs, however, could be detected in everyday behavior. The league adherents in Romans and elsewhere, upon their return from Châteaudouble (A 40) *threatened the gentlemen, who had houses a bit too fine, with overturning them.* This time Guérin's report makes note of what the rebels *said*. It should be remembered, however, that the nobility, or at least several gentlemen who could be said to represent it, had helped turn Laprade, the peasant's enemy, out of Châteaudouble. Gratitude is obviously an unknown quantity in politics. Social classes, including the lower ones, can act like cold-hearted monsters: *the league members and peasants did not acknowledge the good the nobles had done them at the said Châteaudouble* (A 40).

Verbal or more than verbal abuse against the nobility and even against the extant system of landholding was swiftly spreading around Romans: *in the said town and the surrounding villages the meanest lout thought himself as great a lord as his own seigneur* (A 40). These few sentences of Guérin's are precious: one of those rare instances when real peasant talk is recorded.

Antinoble feeling was also current, though much less outspoken and with no violent outbreaks, to the south, around Montéli-mar, even though the league there was theoretically much less ambitious than in Romans. When the people and the consuls of the village of Marsanne wanted to elect a "deputy" of their own during the summer of 1580, Louis d'Eurre d'Oncieu, their seigneur (noble landlord), ex-lieutenant-governor of Provence, connected to the best families of both Dauphiné and Provence, curtly brought them to order: *I do not think,* he wrote to the consuls, *that you should wish to follow the style of the League* (of villages) *which is to seize what belongs to your superiors; keep better council, and under my judgment and command; and do not be convinced by perverse illusions which are against all provisions of law.*[62] Louis d'Eurre's letter addressed the consuls and the community government, that is to say, the literate elite (town scribe, etc.), an elite which officially represented the village, but was in fact bourgeois, with the distinguishing feature that a few of its members could read and copy a letter, in the king's French to boot. In this case it was really the community, then, bottom *and top,* exposed in an attempt at questioning the power and property of their "superior," in other words the seigneur. Indeed, Marsanne and other nearby villages, branded extremist, were miffed at Colas and the moderate management of the regional league. Colas was worried about the overly antinoble tendencies of these villages which were supposed to be under his control: *a lot of scoundrels,* he said, *were threatening so many good gentlemen.* The Montélimar leader even considered, it seems, an *inhuman massacre* of these village communities forming the "left wing" of his own league.[63] Colas had built his political career on antinoble slogans, but evidently he was much less radical on that point than many of his adherents.

The terms Louis d'Eurre used to rebuke the consuls are interesting: *perverse* illusions, against all provision of *law,* against your *superiors,* the *commands* . . . With very few changes, these are the identical terms the Huguenot nobility in the lower Rhône and the Cévennes region around Nîmes had used in 1562 to admonish the Protestant peasants who were citing Scripture in defense of their total rejection of the seigneurial system— the landlords' rents, dues, and shares—along with their refusal of the tithe.[64]

In Romans the craftsmen's protest against the nobles in the judiciary, in trade, and in the consulate, had remained nonviolent. But the fight against the seigneurs which had begun in a disjointed fashion in the surrounding countryside during the spring of 1579 was more reckless. There was killing, sometimes preceded by torture.[65] Quite another story compared to the essentially symbolic class struggle in Romans (which was to change quite drastically at the very last moment). Guérin notes in his inimitable style the resulting divergence between town and country (A 42). *As for the villagers,* he wrote, *they committed an infinity of excesses, murders and burning even more atrocious than those* (the protesters) *of the town of Romans.* In the barony of Clérieu, a huge domain near Romans, the seigneur's administration was first attacked: in other words his political-judiciary representative (judge), his military force (steward), and his bureaucracy (registrar). Clérieu had a tiny administration, probably a single registrar: *In the said barony of Clérieu they were so wretched as to kill the judge, the steward, and the registrar exercising their functions, and cruelly made them die a slow death* (A 42). Following the torture and death of these unfortunates, the protest reached such a pitch that the nobles themselves were attacked, tracked down in their manor houses by the peasants for a variety of reasons: fear of noble plotting, lingering grudges, hatred of the new nobles and their tax exemption. The peasants' intention to destroy or at least damage the entire seigneurial system was explicit.

The agitation culminated in the burning of the noble landlord of Dorbain's castle, followed by his murder on April 19, 1579 (A 42). It is instructive to compare the two accounts we have of this bloody episode. The one from Guérin's pen is ferociously antipeasant, pronoble. The other, written by Piémond, is indulgent toward the rural folk and opposed to nobles of Dorbain's type if not noblemen in general.

A gentleman (Guérin reports without ever naming Dorbain), *having some particular peasant enemy, was assaulted by a number of peasants in his house, whence he defended himself and killed some of them.*

The anonymity of the characters in this description is immediately striking. Can it be explained by the fact that the report was intended for Catherine de'Medici or the ruling element of the royal court? At all events Guérin did not bother with trifles like proper names ("Dorbain," for instance). Perhaps he thought that such details would be of no interest to the national leaders. Or was he afraid that providing them might harm his antipeasant argument? If Guérin's account is to be believed, Dorbain's troubles arose from peasant grudges.

Piémond, however, goes over the problems and nicely states

the questions: *toward the end of the month of June 1579* (not quite correctly, since the events took place in late April; Guérin is better on dates than Piémond)[66] *rumor had it that Monsieur Dorbain was gathering noble gentlemen at his house, including certain new nobles, and that they were planning to carry out some vengeance. This occasioned a great gathering of peasants from all the villages who went to his house.*

From the beginning, then, Piémond laid the blame on the new nobles: through their recent exemption from taxes, their parvenu arrogance, they had earned the hatred of the third estate who were fighting for fiscal justice. Simultaneously, Piémond pointed a finger at the nobles' thirst for revenge, rather than peasant resentment, as the cause of the episode.

Guérin, as we have seen, gave a highly condensed version of the incident so that it would fit in with his general tenet that the peasants were to blame, which was only partly true. In one sentence he summed up the villagers' assault and Dorbain's legitimate self-defense: to save his hide, he had to kill a few of his assailants.

Piémond gave a far more detailed account, no doubt closer to the truth, also highly damaging to the cause of Dorbain and his noble or recently ennobled accomplices. *Warned of their* (the peasants') *coming,* Piémond reports, *Dorbain quickly removed himself* (from his house). *The troops, seeing that he was not there, went back to their own place, and gave notice to the other communities.*

Note that Piémond uses the term "communities," which implies not only the participation of individual peasants but also of collective units of administration, perhaps even regular, consular governments; the term also implies the participation of armed volunteers who constituted the peasant league.

How did the naïve but honest Piémond view what our Tartuffe of a Guérin called Dorbain's legitimate self-defense? *The same night,* the notary records, *Dorbain, aware that the troops had left, returned to his house with his men. There they decided to defend themselves in the said house if the troops came back* (P 74).

Up to this point nothing was out of the ordinary. But the plot was thickening, with trouble in store for Dorbain's reputation and the lives of a few tenant farmers.

When he arrived home, Dorbain sent for three of his neighbors, poor laborers who customarily worked for him in his house.

When they arrived, he questioned them:

—*Who are these people who came to my house? Where are they from? The three laborers replied that there were so many of them* (the intruders) *that they* (the laborers) *did not recognize them.*

But Dorbain, knowing that they (the laborers) *had seen several gentlemen gathered in the said place* (his house) *and that they knew the secrets of that house, had them led out of the house and beaten, leaving them for dead.*

One of them got away, mortally wounded. He died two days later, but before (dying) *he revealed everything that had happened and that during their murder they had recognized Monsieur Dubois and certain of Monsieur Dorbain's other neighbors* (P 75).

Guérin's abbreviated sentence would merit a long exegesis: *Monsieur Dorbain defended himself and killed some of them.* In fact Dorbain had persuaded friends (such as his accomplice Dubois) or hired killers to murder two of his farmworkers in cold blood, fearing that the laborers would divulge his guilty secrets. Peasant indignation could only have flared at the news. The leaguers' first call on Dorbain had been for defense purposes; now it was revenge they had in mind.

From here on Guérin and Piémond relate the same facts. Still, the notary's account is more detailed. Piémond had nothing to hide, but Guérin offered little or no information which did not advance his antipeasant thesis.

In any case it appears that when the laborer's deathbed account of the murder got out, the communities and volunteers of the league once again took action. *Alerted, the people gathered to take revenge on this insult* (P 75). *They gathered at the sound of the tocsin* (A 42). *Eight or nine hundred strong, they went back, intending to lay siege to Dorbain's house* (P 75).

Dorbain heard the news and did not wait to hear more. He fled. Thwarted, his enemies settled for burning down his house after they had looted it; they ate all the food and drank all the wine they could find (P 75). *This gentleman* (Dorbain), *seeing the great strength* (of the peasant force) *and that their number unreasonably grew from hour to hour, found the means to escape and so doing saved his life; but not his property or his house, which was looted, and then burned to the ground* (A 42). After Dorbain it was Dubois's turn to pay for his part in the murder of the three laborers; his house was also burned. (The peasants') *fury, not yet appeased* (Guérin writes) *they then went to burn the house of another gentleman of the neighborhood, and then they set out to do the same to that of another gentleman* (A 42).

Although he was now lord of a gutted manor, Dorbain had reason to believe his life had been spared. Nothing was less certain, however, and *it must be mentioned that subsequently* (Guérin reports), *on April 19, 1580, he* (Dorbain) *was killed by these peasants with an arquebus when he went to survey his ruined house* (A 42).

Brisk as a police reporter, Guérin mentions the murders, which he writes off as rural agitation, in order to paint the situation the blacker for the benefit of his highly placed Parisian readership. In so doing, the judge, as usual, is at once dispassionate (as to the facts) and partial (as to motivation). He neglects to report that although Dorbain was murdered, his criminal action against the three laborers may have been at the bottom of the affair. Moreover, Guérin fails to mention that Dorbain did not have a clean record when all these events transpired. Piémond, on the other hand, is more than willing to give us all the facts, even though he gets the date of Dorbain's death wrong. He accuses the gentleman of patricide: *The said Monsieur Dorbain was commonly said to be mutinous and factious, and as such he was killed by some who returned* (to his house) *from Romans, the very place where it was rumored he had killed his father* (P 75).

In brief, Guérin's version sticks close to the facts and the chronology of events. Hypocrite that he is, he cannot help but tell the truth somewhere. But the wily Guérin manipulates and abridges his narrative. Piémond, who cannot always be trusted to remember dates, is certainly more authentic than the judge when it comes to weighing the peasants' motives for attacking Dorbain and his fellow nobles. The Parlement of Grenoble would later implicitly support Piémond's version against Guérin's, even though the Parlement had little use for the village leagues. When the judges of the High Court meted out punishment to the participants in the Carnival in Romans and their country allies, they harshly rebuked the peasants for several incidents such as "the looting of the Gaste manor at Payrins on February 18, 1579, and the murder of the judge, steward, and registrar of the barony of Clérieu, at Veaune in April 1579."[67] Yet they carefully refrained from speaking out or taking corrective steps "against the looting and burning of the houses of Dorbain and Dubois" or against Dorbain's murder, despite the fact that the nobility and its privileges—which they themselves enjoyed—were dear to their hearts. By glossing over the unlawful attack on Dorbain they implicitly ratified Piémond's specific accusations against him (which Guérin neglected to mention). The judge camouflaged the ambush Dorbain had prepared for the laborers. By omission he hints at the ambush he himself would arrange for Paumier.

On the whole, the nobles, including those directly threatened by the springtime uprisings, were preparing for the worst. In June 1579 the count of Tournon (who would later outdo himself in the quelling of the revolt) assembled an army of 400 men, ready for action.[68] The peasants' fears were justified.

As the terrible burnings and murders of spring 1579 took place, the province's notables had one slight but undeniable consolation: the bloody, incendiary, radical peasant agitation was confined to the region around Romans: *we are happy that elsewhere* (in the rest of Dauphiné) *the peasants have contained themselves,* wrote Basset, high clerk of the Estates, in a letter dated May 12, 1579. He recommended in it that the consuls of all towns take heed to foresee any new troubles and to arrest such barbarous factions.[69] Once again Romans and its country districts were right in the eye of the hurricane.

Were the seigneur and his manor the real objects of the peasants' fury, or did it go beyond that to include the whole network of rents and services owed a noble landlord? It would seem that the rural mutineers had no qualms about attacking the very act by which each villager acknowledged his individual dues, an act aptly called *acknowledgement.* The attack consisted of burning the register containing a record of the acknowledgements, which was called a land register or *terrier* in the legal language inherited from northern France. The village offensive degenerated or bloomed into an attack against these registers, gradually expanding to involve murder and other trespasses. Peasants who were acting on Paumier's orders or claiming to be his associates, according to Guérin, *killed Captain Monluel, land-agent for the Count du Bouchage, who was seeing to the renewal of the Count's acknowledgements in the village of Auterive; they seized his land registers and burned them, after stealing his purse and those of his assistants, as well as their cloaks, swords, and other possessions* (A 42).

The burning of the *terriers* was most significant: the land register represented the intrusion of the written word and modern method of calculation into the casual archaicism of the seigneurial system. The peasants considered them efficient, therefore highly dangerous. Their adverse reaction to the land registers was unfortunately not taken seriously by those in power. Only under the special circumstances of the peasant war in 1579 did Guérin mention one such violent attack, yet they must have been frequent. In Savoy during the late seventeenth century, there were fierce attacks against the same sort of registers. The private papers of noble families note these riots in horrific terms; only by using private archives as a source did Jean Nicolas, a Savoy historian, discover the protests against the *terriers*.[70] Judicial records in southeastern France do not stoop so low, however, as to give us accounts of these "petty" incidents. Even so, the case of the *terriers* evidences a double, contradictory process of modernization at work: for the landlords, a growing bureaucracy; for the peasants, growing protest.

Rural unrest with its antinoble slant was aggravated by a freak change in the weather that would have had little importance under more normal circumstances. *On April 16, 1579, a bitter cold northern wind blew, unnatural for the season* (P 72). The next day, April 17, it turned to snow. A killer frost hit the vines and the walnut trees, already running with sap, which were so typical of Dauphiné. It looked bad for the fall harvest of grapes and walnuts (pressed for their oil), *which caused the jug of wine, worth only 14 deniers during Holy Week, to go up to 36 deniers at Eastertide* (after the frost) *and at the harvest time to 48 deniers.* The price of a pound of walnut oil *soared from 6 liards to 4 sols.* We can see that speculators—those who had stocks of wine to sell—were counting on a bad harvest; they started raising the price of wine in the spring.

Wine lovers who had no vines of their own were hard pressed on account of this accident to the grapes. A blacksmith, a *hearty drinker,* furious at the price of wine, declared: *If I had hold of God who made the vines freeze, I would stroke his head as I do the iron in my forge.* Four hours later the blasphemous blacksmith died of a bloody flux.

Such was the atmosphere—urban agitation, peasant uprising, a minor agricultural calamity—surrounding the opening of the Estates in Grenoble on an unseasonably frosty day, April 19, 1579. The representatives of the third estate or "the people"[71] were to display a most militant ardor. The commoners' vehemence in 1579 (to be echoed in 1789) threw the two dominant orders off balance and inspired in them a variety of contradictory reactions. The clergy, wooed by de Bourg,[72] was ready to make partial concessions: despite the tax exemption it claimed, it agreed to paying the *taille* on property it had recently bought from commoners. The remainder of property owned by the third estate would be somewhat less heavily taxed as a result.

The nobility, on the other hand, proved hard-headed if not downright unyielding. Their quarrel with the third estate was based on commoners' land bought up by gentlemen, which resulted in a larger share of taxes for commoners, and tax exemptions for the new nobles, which had the same result. Particularly in the villages, the peasants seethed under this added burden.

The nobles fought like the devil in defense of these two points: *the nobility strongly prevented the payment of any taxes for property newly acquired from the commoners;* and elsewhere *the new nobles prevented everything they could* (P 73). The new nobles' willingness to fight to the end was not surprising: having so recently pulled themselves up from the third estate, and its fiscal inconveniences, they had no intention of being taxed anew. So they turned against those they had left behind.

Even the third estate did not present a united front. There were the moderate bourgeois patricians, delegates to the Estates, who were firmly opposed to tax privileges for the nobility and clergy, but equally determined not to tolerate the peasant uprisings; and then there were the radical leaders like Paumier who claimed the allegiance of the plebeian elements. By May 12, the third estate delegates, law-abiding and deliberate men, sent their constituents a conciliatory proclamation. They declared they were aggrieved *at the excesses and horrible executions lately committed in the villages surrounding the town of Romans.* They energetically denounced *the murder committed on the persons of the judge, the steward, and the registrar* (of the baron) of Clérieu in particular. They condemned the burning of castles, *the houses of Messieurs Dorbain, Dubois, and de Gaste,* among other outrages. The notables who gave this lecture congratulated themselves on the fact that rural disorder had not spread beyond the Romans area, which was as usual in the vanguard of extremist protest. Were they deluding themselves? Betraying their constituents? No matter what, they saw the relatively narrow scope of disorder as positive proof that the *Cahier* would win out in the end as the vehicle of the third estate's complaints and demands.[73] Finally, they reiterated that at least minimal harmony had to be guaranteed by the quadruple and supreme authority of the king, his lieutenant-governor, the Parlement, and Justice; in other words His Majesty himself, Maugiron, and the lords of the court and other magistrates. This supposedly peacemaking text was countersigned by Basset, representing the consuls of the various Dauphiné communities—mainly urban—which had sent deputies to the Estates. And of course Dauphiné's "Ten Towns" were among them.

We can thus distinguish clearly at least the outline of three nonsilent minority groups within the third estate; urban oligarchies, urban workingmen, and peasant elements, in this case out of control. They had looted castles in the name of vengeance or hatred. Craftsmen and peasants had united, after a fashion. By contrast, the rift between the urban elite and workingmen was rapidly widening, despite their mutual dislike of tax exemptions for the nobility and clergy.

The tensions and fissures within the third estate are readily explicable. Rural fighting was becoming more radical, wilder. It did not suit everyone's purpose. After all, Dauphiné's "Ten Towns" themselves lived off income from rural property and more generally off a share of crops, which directly or indirectly reverted to the townsfolk as a whole, through gifts from notables or the money they spent. It was obviously not in the towns' interest for peasant uprisings to destroy the whole system supporting rural prestations: tithes, seigneurial dues, even farm rents.

Among the peasantry there was also alarm at the bloodthirsty deeds done in the name of the league by its most determined elements. Judge Guérin took advantage of this situation, which bred internal dissent; as usual he had quickly sniffed it out. Through a letter which won over *certain of the mutineers* (A 42) he was able to calm some of the leaguers and save a castle from burning.

In Romans proper the moderate elements of the *Union* or league did not look favorably on the acts of arson; they could see the smoke from atop the town ramparts. The split within the craftsman party began to develop in early summer 1579. *A subtle way was found* (by Guérin and friends, no doubt) *to make a soldier of the said town* (of Romans), *called Laroche, enemies with Paumier and hateful to him.* Laroche was a ropemaker, therefore "in textiles" just as Paumier was a draper. The two men had become comrades; one was even godfather to the other's child. *Laroche and Paumier, from their youth, had been good friends and had been to war together.* They were co-founders of the local *Union*, and had both participated in it. As late as January 1579, Paumier, when elected King of the Arquebus, had named Laroche his "servant" or *second.*[74] The link between the two men embodied the alliance between the plebeian league (Paumier) and the semicraftsman elements in the more bourgeois quarters (Laroche), a link severed during an upheaval which prefigured the bloody Carnival of 1580.

Laroche had been leaning more and more toward the patrician party, moderating his stands. He was letting Guérin get his hooks into him. Paumier, however, though on a par with Laroche socially,[75] remained an extremist or at any rate clearly at odds with the town fathers. The reason for the split between the two craftsman leaders was that Laroche, alarmed at the peasants' violence, had made certain remarks which Paumier did not find to his liking.

If the mutineers, Laroche said, *continue to do such violence, so many of them will be hanged that the streets will stink from it* (A 43).

This annoyed Paumier; he quite rightly feared he would be among the first cartload the "gentlefolk" sent to the gallows. Furious, he threatened Laroche. Perhaps he considered having him killed. A group of moderate leaguers, also members (secretly) of the law and order party, helped Jean Serve's enemy weather the storm and save his neck: *Laroche resisted by means of a good number of friends he had in town, and gentlefolk who lent him support* (A 43). Laroche was just what the patricians required: a discreet (though not secret) agent who would give them a foothold in the enemy camp. They helped Laroche leave town, quietly, for ten days or so. Then things settled down. The ropemaker, still on bad terms with the craftsman hardliners, was able to return to Romans. He went about his usual activities until the next, decisive confrontation.

The split within Romans's popular faction during the spring of 1579 typified a general dissociation between urban moderates and radicals. Was the breach any less marked in rural areas, where country notables and insurgent peasants were concerned? All this was a far cry from the holy alliance, when gentlemen and peasants fraternally embraced after the fall of Châteaudouble . . . Now the popular factions were losing both their noble allies and their internal harmony or coherence. The nobility *began to grow more angry and furious with the people than ever* (P 75). The leaders of the league disowned those of their members who had burned Dorbain's manor. This left the arsonists cold, even though they had been threatened with the strictest disciplinary measures (never applied). It was the perfect time for the directors of the league to remind all members of the purely pacifist, defensive goals it had originally intended for its activities. Their aims were protection against enemies and *in all humility* (P 76) to demand and obtain satisfaction of the requests made in Jean de Bourg's petition of grievance.

Just as the *principal chiefs of the Union*, as Piémond called them, were splitting up on account of peasant unrest, urban agitation was taking on importance in Romans. First of all, it pitted the ample number of men in Paumier's group against the consular oligarchy (and when I say men I mean men; women are strangely absent from this urban movement). The debate centered around money issues—thievery as it was called—attributed to the officials of the municipal administration. It was said they stole from the poor and from taxpayers on the orders of the rich. Guérin denied these allegations, but Piémond says they were correct (P 88); the people's claims were not necessarily false. They involved considerable sums, at any rate. *The beginning of their outburst*, Guérin wrote (A 40), *in the said town was against the consuls and the administration of Romans, whom they accused of having stolen more than twenty thousand écus.*[76] Twenty thousand écus, or 60,000 *livres*, was a large figure for the times. The "mutineers" asked that the money be restituted *to liquidate the debts of the community of Romans*. The debts were large ones: financiers or *fat purses* in Grenoble or Lyons held some of the letters of credit on them. The popular faction had its newly appointed friends on the town council designate auditors who proceeded, with total disrespect for the notables controlling or manipulating the budget up to that point, to go over the books with a fine-toothed comb. They harassed the clique of former consuls, who were interrelated and on friendly terms with each other. Guérin, a canny sociologist, defined the group of local "mafiosi" as consisting *for the most part of bourgeois notables and merchants of Romans, who had almost all been consuls in the space of twenty years* (A 41). Those twenty years would take us back to 1560, the beginning of the Wars of Religion which had plunged the town into financial crisis—in turn riling the lower classes, who consequently turned against excess taxation and prevarication in the town hall.

The newly appointed auditors tried to pick a fight with the former consuls, who were asked for the *interest on interest* on missing or supposedly missing funds. The eventual result was an impasse which persisted for several months. The auditors, unable to get their adversaries to meet their debts, still managed to rule out the "closing" of the accounts. In this way they made insinuations, perhaps well-founded, about the former consul and the patricians in general. In retaliation the most incendiary elements of the popular faction considered pillaging or sacking the property of the law and order partisans *who had grown rich at the expense of the poor*; the most lenient plan was to have them make restitution. These looming threats, and particularly restitution, were at the bottom of the deathly masquerade that opened the Carnival in Romans in 1580. On this point Piémond confirms Guérin.

In addition to pressure from the urban workingmen, there was the peasant or village impetus. Paumier's role as an acknowledged leader of both movements was one factor behind their double-barrelled strength. Antoine Guérin sensed the danger a coalition between town and country radicals represented; another of its targets was municipal and financial administration, as the leaguers rallied around slogans on the order of "Down with the crooks!" *The mutineers were not satisfied*, the judge opined, *with having held all of those of the town in this evil deliberation; they further held the villagers in this same hope of receiving much money by means of the said revisions of accounts.* Thus, the "mutineers," as the judge is wont to call them, none too affectionately, could put together *a common pretext and use the villagers to execute their evil intentions* (A 41). Once again the idea was that village debts would be paid off by the money coming from financial restitution by big city "swindlers."[77]

The popular faction was not content with simply challenging the handling of town funds. The rebels harassing local accountants and ex-consuls also attacked the representatives of justice—forcing criminal trials to be turned over to them; freeing prisoners on their own authority; breaking the doors and windows of the office of the court clerk in Romans (A 41). Such violent behavior amounted to a challenge against the urban version of the seigneurial judge, or the Estate of Justice as it would eventually be called.[78] It was a weighty structure indeed. French royalty had not trod lightly in Dauphiné in general and Romans in particular. The chapter of St. Barnard had long since been stripped of the legal role it once played as powerful lord or co-landlord of the town. The priests' loss was the king's gain; since the end of the Middle Ages, he had gradually become co-seigneur, then seigneur—the sovereign justiciary within the walls of our town. The king's supreme if not always affable power was embodied by the king's agent; in our case, the magistrate was Antoine Guérin. Attacking the local administration of justice,[79] interfering with trials, stealing prisoners, breaking windows in the court building were actions tantamount to attacking one of the cornerstones of social order with a pickaxe—the royal, seigneurial, and social order, in fact. Judge Antoine Guérin was the acknowledged leader of the consular faction which had not completely surrendered to popular agitation. Guérin dominated his faction authoritatively. He aspired to be the real master of the town, the *deus ex machina* of its citizens. He was connected to the bourgeoisie, town government, and the judiciary. He had a finger in every pie and licked his sometimes bloodied chops over the fact.

The attack on justice was very much in tune with the beginnings of the Dauphiné revolt. The peasants at Marsas, who initiated the movement, had risen up *against* the royal court in Romans, actually against Guérin. The judge had ordered the execution of some of their relatives, perhaps at the time of the St. Bartholomew's Day massacre, and had made sure the sentences were carried out. In Romans proper certain facts were not mentioned in public but surfaced in everyone's memory: memories of the local St. Bartholomew's Day massacre in 1572. "Someone," anonymously, had had the town prison filled with smoke; the ten or so Huguenots providentially in custody that day were then slain by masked men. This anonymous, murderous "someone,"[80] predictably, was Guérin himself, specializing in Carnival masks, in camouflaging, asphyxiating smoke . . . It is understandable that under these conditions some of Romans's Protestants, seven or eight years after the slaughter of their brethren, had decided, however hesitantly, to support Paumier against Guérin. The judge was a Huguenot-killer, a form Huguenot or at least sympathizer himself, so he knew what he was up against. The Carnival was chock-full of renegades from both religious persuasions.

Given the "dual power" situation in Romans, there was no question of the protesters ousting the real, bourgeois masters of the town—namely Guérin, of course—and then the consuls, or those of the consuls who sided with Guérin as members of the ruling oligarchy. In fact, it is probable that Paumier had something in the back of his mind, that is, a reserve strategy, kept under wraps for the moment. Knowing that he could not win on his own strength, Paumier was counting on the eventual and probable success of the mountain general, the Huguenot chief Lesdiguières. Paumier consistently curried his favor, even when the leaguers were scuffling with some of the Huguenots' allies. Paumier recognized Lesdiguières's immense talent as a soldier; he reckoned the Huguenot army would one day come down from the highlands around Die and Gap to flatten the Catholic or so-called Catholic leaders like Maugiron. A coalition would be set up in Romans that would include the bourgeois Huguenots and the Catholic but anti-Guérin craftsmen and plowmen. They would run Guérin out of town or kill him.

Paumier's calculation was not completely unfounded.[81] Lesdiguières did take control of Dauphiné in 1590 with the aid of a Catholic splinter group, in the name of Henri IV. But Paumier was not to profit from this victory; he had been dead for ten years. One wonders, furthermore, whether Lesdiguières would have shared the fruits of his victory with the Romans leader had he survived. Lesdiguières, a future High Constable, sometimes had use of the unruly populace but he was hardly fond of the people. Moreover, he would be a tardy convert to Catholicism!

While awaiting the victory of the highland Protestants, Romans had to organize in order to survive. The workingmen were in no position to banish their adversaries. Would the future belong to the one who could hold out longest? A battle of nerves seemed the only answer. It was an efficient enough tactic for the time being, but dangerous and inadequate in the long run when dealing with a diabolical enemy like Antoine Guérin. In comparison, Paumier came out of it all the perfect picture of innocence.

The urban leaguers therefore attempted to get control of those subordinate posts that the very nature of community life made indispensable and plentiful and which were accessible even to the poorest and least outstanding citizens. The offices of tax collector or of administrator of direct and indirect municipal taxes were examples. *They put the most militant and mutinous craftsmen they could find in charge of community business* (A 41).

Popular activism was also directed toward the town's military and paramilitary organization. Romans had long had a sort of militia called *compagnons de la ville*;[82] there was also the more or less convivial fraternal order of the Abbey of Town Archers and Crossbowmen. Each year this "abbey"—which did have its religious ceremonies, yet secular and scarcely monastic ones— held a "popinjay shoot" at a site the town reserved for the purpose. The winner was proclaimed *King of the Crossbow*, a title which quite naturally changed into King of the Arquebus as the use of firearms became widespread during the second half of the sixteenth century. (Paumier, as we have seen, was king in 1579; his marksmanship won him a popular following and gave him an authority independent of any regular governmental institution.)

The militia's tasks, however, were more than mere folklore, especially since the Wars of Religion had broken out. Precautions had to be taken against marauding outlaws, mercenaries, or soldiers on the march, or else their sporadic wrongdoings had to be dealt with after the fact. The town's walls and gates had to be guarded against those stricken with plague, outsiders, and so on. The captain-general and the captains of the various gates and quarters of Romans respectively commanded the body and the neighborhood detachments of this rather less than impressive urban militia. They were supposedly named by the consuls or the town council, whether directly or indirectly.[83]

But in 1579 the ranks were seething with insubordination. The parttime soldiers were workingmen and loyal to their class even when they shouldered the arquebus. They tried to strip their captains of their rank and in more than one instance managed to have them replaced:[84] *they banded together directly against their captains, whom they wanted to relieve of responsibility* (A 41). By February 1580, however, it appears town hall (Guérin) control of the militia had been restored.

In 1579 the common folk indulged in *so many pieces of impudence that whoever tried to record them would waste much time* (A 42). Still, it would be wrong to picture the town as totally in the hands of the seditionists. In April 1579 Henri III sent a mollifying letter to Romans's consuls;[85] he knew they had refrained from getting too deeply involved in the "diverse movements" of the four preceding months. The king congratulated the town fathers on the capture of Châteaudouble (even though they had in fact entered the fray at the eleventh hour). He forgave them for the troubles and disorder in their town and promised that *the memory of all the disorder occurring in Romans will remain forever dead and buried.*

What is more, in May the triumvirate of Maugiron, Thomé, and Guérin, invested with the authority of the king, Parlement, and local justice, respectively, attempted to regain control of and stabilize the situation. Thomé, perhaps at Guérin's behest, ordered a curfew. He forbade swearing and fighting. Above all he required the inhabitants, particularly the innkeepers, to inform judge Guérin of the presence of any outsiders: they were *to make a declaration to the said judge within an hour of the strangers' arrival,* and to *seize their firearms,* even when the outsiders were relatives of their hosts.[86] The idea was of course to prevent town leaguers from joining forces with their friends (or relatives) from the villages, smaller towns, and other large towns in the region. The inns were where the mobile, therefore suspicious, elements of the population intersected.

At the same time Guérin, responsible for the patricians' uncertain fate, was evincing confidence and mastery of the situation. He packed the town council with his own men, some twenty persons he shamelessly gave himself the permission, by law, to coopt. He further had the public gallery demolished, since Romans's citizens, including protesters and brawlers, had used it to sit in on the council's sessions and deliberations. Guérin's excuse was that the gallery was ancient and about to collapse under the weight of the visitors. He unsuccessfully attempted to cut the town council off from the public by having it meet in virtually closed sessions. Guérin was testifying to Paumier's relative defeat; the craftsman leader had not been able to get control of the consular system. In spring 1579 protests had achieved the changing of the gatekeeper-captains and had won extraordinary-supernumerary seats on the council for the entire year for certain rebel leaders (Serve, Brunat, Fleur, Robin), but they had not been able to bend the town's key institution, to wit, the consular system, to their purposes. The consuls from the two upper ranks (Bernard Guigou and Jean Thomé), appointed after the "events" of early 1579, were necessarily partial to the reigning oligarchy; they belonged to it. The consul from the third rank was Pierre Philippot. In November 1579[87] he strongly favored taking the hard line against the bakers' tax strike; although a member of the craftsman rank, he was on Guérin's side. So was Antoine Vine, consul from the fourth, peasant rank; both men remained members of the council *after* Guérin's purge of it, which coincided with the consular elections following the tragic events of February 1580. Romans's 1579 revolution was thus merely peripheral as far as the institutions of town government were concerned; its sole accomplishments were the replacement of the militia men and the placement of the extraordinary-supernumerary council members.[88] To a certain extent dual power existed, but power did not change hands.

However small-scale and disorganized the events in Romans might seem, they were to have an effect on national politics. In early July 1579, *the news reached Romans that the Queen Mother of the king* (Catherine de'Medici) *was on her way to the country of Dauphiné* (A 43). In fact Catherine had begun a long southward journey in September 1578. Plump to a fault, she was still quick-witted in her sixties. She was skeptical and ill-educated (*she never knew what a dogma was*, an Italian ambassador said of her), a born peacemaker but profoundly reactionary, steeped in the nobility's tax privileges. Catherine brought her talent as a tenacious negotiator and her celebrated charm to bear on the southern regions. She was an old hand at settling wars, but success was not just around the corner in the southern provinces, torn as they were with religious conflict and class struggles.

The Queen Mother had followed a circuitous route. First visiting the southwest, she had stopped in Nérac, today in the department of Lot-et-Garonne. During the same month that the first fires of the Carnival protest had flared in Romans, Catherine concluded a peace agreement between the crown and her son-in-law Henri de Navarre and his Huguenot followers. In exchange for their promise of good behavior she granted them the rather meager gift of fourteen safeholds for a period of six months (three of them in Guyenne and eleven in Languedoc, mainly in the Cévennes).[89]

Meanwhile, the Queen Mother held interviews with Soffrey de Calignon, envoy of Dauphiné's Protestants. She made various concessions to him (December 1578) which Henri III would approve a month later.[90] Through Calignon, contact was established[91] with Lesdiguières and the Huguenot bastion in the southern Dauphiné Alps.[92]

Leaving Nérac, Catherine stopped briefly in Carcasonne. A few days later she accepted the ambivalent homage of Montpellier's townfolk, the majority of whom were Huguenot. Two rows of arquebusers flanked them as they paid homage; muzzles brushed against the royal visitor's carriage.

At Aix-en-Provence Catherine became fully aware of the "social" difficulties that would soon be hers to deal with in Dauphiné. The sting is in the tail, she would be inspired to say. In 1578 and 1579 civil war ripped through various regions of Provence, sometimes set off by social struggle and the peasant movement, much as in the mountain and plainlands of Dauphiné. The Queen Mother's official hosts at Aix acquainted her with the scope of the conflict in Provence. The *Carcistes* or *Marabouts*, ultra-Catholic partisans of the Count of Carcès, were locked in fratricidal struggle with the *Razats* (shaved ones, literally), which included Huguenots and moderate Catholics, and the *Communes*, the communities' protest movement with urban working-class and peasant branches. The *Razats* coalition was like the league that had formed in Dauphiné around Jean de Bourg and Paumier. In addition it included a few nobles. Feelings ran quite high; there was even a peasant uprising recorded in the village of Callas in 1579.[93]

Besides these upheavals there was much resentment of taxes in Provence, specifically in Aiz and Marseille, just as there was in Dauphiné and all the provinces that had their own Estates, in both the north and south of the realm. There was a trial of the *taille* in Provence as well as Dauphiné, even though the former had apportioned taxes much more equitably than Grenoble or Valence did.

In Aix and Avignon Catherine did her best to reconcile the *Carcistes*, *Razats*, and community factions. She succeeded, after a fashion, then headed north again, only to face still tougher problems.[94]

The Queen Mother's visit to Dauphiné began on Thursday, July 16, 1579. Coming from Avignon, she entered the southern limit of Dauphiné and made her way to Montélimar, the first large town. There she was met by a delegation of Dauphiné's military, civil, and religious authorities. Waiting for her were Maugiron, the lieutenant-governor, with a suite of nobles, a *good troop of his friends, all fellow gentlemen*; then the Bishop of Grenoble, Guillaume de St. Marcel d'Avançon, who was strongly opposed to the Protestants and ill-disposed toward the leagues. The welcoming committee also included a few officials of the Parlement of Grenoble.

Shortly after her arrival in Montélimar Catherine met Jacques Colas, the local head of the popular league, who was also an enemy of the Protestants (on this point he differed with Paumier and the other leaguers to his north, who favored joint action with the Huguenots).

The Queen Mother did not mince her words on the subject

of Colas. She regarded him as a mad *presumptuous soul*, the avowed enemy of the local nobility; he and his men, the other leaguers, and Dauphiné's entire third estate wanted to saddle the nobility with taxes, Catherine said. She was scandalized: despite her wish to establish peace and unity among the classes, she had an iron-clad belief in maintaining the nobility's privileges. This she clearly indicated to the "principals of the leagues and communes of Valence" who had come to greet her. She gave them a piece of her mind: *Commoners*, she said, *pay your taxes; do not try to subject the nobility to taxation; cease to expel my royal garrisons from your towns; behave peaceably one and all.* In four phrases she summed up the lecture she also gave to the good people of Valence and Montélimar before continuing her journey.[95]

The next leg of her trip led to Valence, where her welcome was superficially warm but in actuality wary: *the fighters from Valence*, Catherine wrote,[96] meaning the commoner militia, *did not even appear before me. They feared that with* (the complicity of) *the Nobility I would seize the town. They kept a heavy watch all night long. . . .*

The Queen arrived in Romans on July 18, 1579. Guérin's men had control of the town hall, but Paumier's still held the streets and the ramparts, and his faction had decided to refuse Catherine entry (A 43). Since the keys to the town gates had slipped through Guérin's fingers and now belonged to the craftsman rebels, their refusal was plausible. They went so far as to summon their friends from the surrounding villages to help them mount a guard on the gates. Then the craftsmen's militant spirit receded as they realized they had misjudged their strength. In an about-face, they decided to give the Queen Mother the best reception possible under the circumstances. *Those of the town of Romans*, Catherine wrote on July 18, 1579, *appeared before me in good number. Their captain, known as Paumier, a merchant draper,*[97] *made me a short address of welcome.* As Catherine herself testified, it appears that the chief of Romans's league movement was then at the height of his popularity and influence in the region: *I must tell you*, the Queen Mother reported, *that the said Paumier has such great great influence and authority over these Leagues that his least word will set those of this town and the surrounding region on the march. . . . I would greatly like to speak with him*. The meeting was hastily set up. *Why are you against the authority of the King, my son?* she asked. The workingman leader responded with a little speech that has come down to us thanks to similar accounts in two independent sources.[98] *I am the King's servant*, he exclaimed, *but the people have elected me to save the poor folk afflicted by the tyranny of war, and to pursue humbly the just re-monstrances contained in their Cahier*. That is Piémond's version; here is Guérin's: *I was elected chief by the third estate to ask* (ac-ceptance for) *what was contained in the articles* (the petition of grievances) *carried to Grenoble*. Both accounts are essential; they show that Paumier, who probably spoke French (he discourses in French about *Cahiers* written in French), solidly supported de Bourg on the main point made by the commoners in the said *Cahiers*: namely, that the nobility should pay taxes. Guérin also notes (A 46) that Paumier *was so overweening that he did not want to kneel before the Queen notwithstanding that all the gentlemen present* (her suite) *cried loudly to him several times: On your knees!* Guérin then describes one of Romans's patricians respectfully kneeling before Catherine. And a few weeks later the maréchal de Bel-legarde (P 84) would have no qualms about kneeling in front of the Queen Mother, but then it is true he had a great deal to ask forgiveness for.

In the end Catherine gave Paumier a piece of her mind (yet another!). It had no effect on him, yet she did not label him a *madman* or *factious* like Colas or de Bourg; perhaps she even found him relatively moderate.

The Queen Mother momentarily achieved a double restitu-tion. Paumier's men gave the keys to the city back to Guérin's forces, who were, after all, the legal administrators, and con-suls, of the town. The two cannons Gordes had abandoned in Romans and which the leaguers had appropriated were sent to Lyons, to the regret of Paumier's faction. Whereupon Her Maj-esty left Romans for Grenoble, where she was to spend several months. While there, she would evade the commoners' demands for equal taxation, and she would arrange the temporary im-prisonment of Gamot, the passionate, Swiss-style defender of the urban and rural commoners.

VI

Strikes and Debts

Catherine's visit had momentarily subdued Romans's populace, but only in part. Even while she was still in town, around July 18 to July 20, 3,000 peasants illegally entered Romans with Paumier's help. They gathered in the streets and at crossroads after dark, concealing drawn swords under their cloaks. Like Valence's notables, the town patricians were very nervous about the situation, and so was the Queen Mother's entourage.

After Catherine's departure, things went from bad to worse; an atmosphere of violent peasant insurgence spread through the surrounding countryside. The tax and a part of the tithes (light as they were) had already been rejected for the harvest of 1579; for the coming year, 1580, the peasants were talking about an outright strike against the tithes in their entirety and against seigneurial obligations. Guérin's statement on this subject is another of those precious, exceedingly rare instances of actual peasant speech being quoted. The peasants heaped the nobility and gentlefolk (urban patricians, in other words) *with nasty and annoying words* (A 150). Along with their obligations to the seigneurs, the country people challenged the debts they owed wealthy citydwellers; city process-servers were pelted with country stones. In Romans bands of pro-Paumier hoodlums roamed the city during the summer and fall of 1579. They intimidated the gentlefolk, freed a prisoner council member that Jean Thomé was leading to jail, and threatened to slit Thomé's throat. The urban power elite and local judiciary were once again threatened simultaneously. The patricians even feared they would be the collective victim of fifty-five assassination attempts; it seems Paumier's friends had drawn up a hit list! Romans's marketplace or town square was the meeting ground for the peasants and craftsmen, the place where they elected their captains. During the first week of September 1579, there was talk of taking over Grenoble, since the leagues already controlled Romans, Valence, Montélimar . . .[1]

The unrest seemed all the more dangerous because each of the opposing parties persisted in picking any number of fights with the other: at the height of Paumier's activity, for example, Romans's food sector also called an excise strike. The case of the angry butchers and bakers should first be put in contemporary perspective. From 1576 to 1580, the key issue seems to have been the *tributs*, indirect taxes fed into the municipal treasury which could neither do without them nor make do with the percentage of the royal *taille* or direct tax which was its due. The largest share of the *tributs* seems to have come from the butchers: even though meat was sold in several different shops, the trade was under tight municipal control. It was part of Romans's "socialist" sector. The consulate refused to tolerate any competition in the meat trade except when it was time for bidding on the annual contract between the town and the butchers. Competition flourished most of the time, however (although the distinguished economists of the nineteenth century did not always realize grain prices fluctuated during the sixteenth century; despite groping attempts at regulation, the host of small marketers/producers and buyers/consumers gave nearly free play to the laws of supply and demand). Thus a group of professional slaughterers bid each year for the right to the town's butcher trade. It included buying the animals (mostly sheep, occasionally cattle); the butchers slaughtered, cut, and sold the meat at prices established in their contracts, from which they were not supposed to deviate. They agreed to pay the town a certain sum out of the profits they made in the effort, calculated per head of livestock killed. By 1545 the butcher trade furnished the town with its most lucrative *tributs*.[2] It brought in 369 *florins* per year, compared to 180 from *pontonnage* (duties the town levied on merchandise coming across the Isère bridge), 220 *florins* on wine brought into the city, and so on.

Naturally, one of the main causes of friction between the butchers and the town government was this kickback due on each head of livestock slaughtered. The town's tax collectors wanted to keep it high; the butchers, low.

The disagreement had been cemented three years earlier, on September 9, 1576. That day the sound of the trumpet and the bell in the Jacquemart tower advised all Romans's heads of households of a general assembly. In fact, it was nothing more than an enlarged version of the town council: four consuls, forty regular members of the council, and sixty "extraordinary" participants. It gave dissenters an opportunity to express their misgivings, if only by their presence.[3] The majority of those in attendance were workingmen, including the urban peasants, of course. The only people at the meeting who were addressed as "Monsieur" (a nobleman) or "Maître" (a bourgeois patrician) were the twenty members of the council who came from the upper social categories (nobility, bourgeoisie, merchants). Among the sixty "extraordinary" persons in attendance there was a single additional "Monsieur"; the rest included a number of characters (all craftsmen) who three years later were to become known agitators. Present were Jean Robert-Brunat, a close relative of the famed rebel draper Guillaume; François Robin the draper; and two relatively well-off butchers, Geoffroy Fleur (a future leader) and François Drevet. Not one of them said a word, according to the rather summary record of the meeting, but even their silence was significant, given the active, outspoken role they were soon to play. At the assembly of 1576, the consuls declared "that the town has 50,000 or 60,000 *livres* in debts. It is *therefore* necessary to increase the *tributs* to *pay the interest on these debts.* That is why we have convened this general assembly of heads of household." (Proof positive that the town government, though ruled by the local "dons," had to have a certain consensus among the craftsmen before piling more taxes on them.) "The *tributs* will therefore be augmented," the consuls continued. "Butchers will pay *four times more*, or 12 *sous* per steer (up from 4 *sous*), 8 *sous* per calf, 2 per sheep (instead of a half-*sou*), 4 per hog, 2 per goat . . . ." For flour weighed on the communal scale the percentage was sextupled, reaching 1 *sol* per setier (and occasioning a loud protest from Antoine Coste, who had provisionally bought the scale to help the town out financially). The bakers' and pastry-cooks' *tribut* was only doubled, going up to 1 *sou* per wheel (of a cart), in other words 2 *sous* per cart. On the communal scale which the merchants were required to use, the *tribut* tripled. It quadrupled on wine brought into Romans. These measures were approved by the enlarged council or general assembly with no apparent opposition. Nevertheless, two days later (September 11, 1576), the butchers and bakers unobtrusively requested that they be allowed to raise their prices to make up for the increase in *tributs*. They knew their arithmetic.[4]

Provocation or what was felt to be provocation played a capital role in triggering protest in Romans. Provincial taxes were considered intolerably high, and at the local level the increase in indirect taxes the craftsmen or shopkeepers paid was also seen as a provocation.

The general assembly of 1576 would belatedly give rise to the butchers' and bakers' protest in 1579. September 1576 was an interesting month in several ways. Politically, it was the date the *national* Estates opened in Blois, in other words, the start of Jean de Bourg's first campaign; we have already examined how important the *Cahiers* were, ideologically speaking, to the protests of 1579. Economically, 1576 was at the crest of a formidable wave of price increases which had begun a decade earlier.[5] Let us say that the price of a *quartel* of wheat remained stable at 100 to 150 *deniers* from 1549 to 1564. Between 1566 and 1576 it was 200 *deniers* and up, as high as 310 *deniers* in 1574 (a year of drastic shortages). This inflation was part of a general trend over the entire sixteenth century. During the ten years under study (1566–1576), it also corresponded to long-delayed monetary influences resulting from the importation of precious metal from Central and South America. Inflation was the real cause of the rise in *tributs* the consuls pushed through in 1576. But it can truly be said that there was also a price to pay for the increase; the social effects of inflation were felt through the secondary price increases it engendered in those sectors subject to indirect taxes. Discontented butchers and bakers found company in the drapers and the weavers (a fearsome alliance between the cloth and the food sectors); that was another of the secondary effects. Soon the craftsmen would reach the breaking point.

The extent of the craftsmen and tradesmen's discontent could already be gauged in February 1577, a few months after the arbitrary increase of the *tributs*. A revealing incident: that same month judge Antoine Velheu, scion of one of Romans's great consular families (which was to lose one member to the rural revolts in 1579), presided over a case involving the draper Jean Serve, known as Paumier.[6] Paumier, the future leader of the uprising that would kill a Velheu . . . the draper had boldly insulted Jean Bourgeois, a member of the oligarchy and agent of the consuls. Bourgeois had been instructed to remove a fence around the Huguenot church and cemetery in Romans, officially reopened for burials following the edict of pacification (probably what was known as the peace of Beaulieu or "Peace of Monsieur" concluded on May 7, 1576, and favorable toward the Huguenots).[7] The entire affair is rather obscure, and it is difficult to say whether Paumier was for or against the Huguenots, or what the town government's position was. All we can state for certain is that the Huguenots were quietly on the scene both at the Estates General and in Romans, where they added heat to an already inflammatory situation. The Paumier-Bourgeois case was nothing more than an insignificant anecdote except that it revealed the magical way (in both the positive and negative senses) in which Paumier, a war hero and local leader, could already sway public opinion in the working-class neighborhood around the Protestant church. Out of twelve persons who had witnessed the altercation, not one was willing to testify against Paumier. The consuls thought they were keeping much too silent, and all twelve spent ten days as guests of the town jail.

The Carnival month of February 1577 was loaded with tension, if it was not downright explosive. In the same docket as Paumier's case, Judge Velheu heard that of a certain Adamet Boyer, weaver, who had refused to hand over his *taille* to the consuls' designated notable agent. This prompted one of the consuls to try confiscating some of Boyer's cloth, but the weaver fended him off with a pitchfork, seconded by his friend Jean Vallier, known as Pataud ("the lout"). Velheu had Boyer put in jail, but he had to be let out on bail because he was a corporal in the town militia. With the corporal in jail, who would dispatch men to their watches? The third incident within a week, finally, involved Antoine Coste, the local tycoon. He was insulted by Antoine Fresne, baker, known as Pain Blanc (or "white bread"); this was not just any baker, but a leader of the 1579 tax strike, one of those executed in 1580 following the Carnival in Romans. Pain Blanc was not afraid to tell Coste:

—*Those who are in the town hall* (the consuls and town council) *are nothing but thieves, who feast on the town's money in the town hall. If the consul* (in charge of my neighborhood) *comes to ask for my taille I will beat him.*

The incident was judged to be of such gravity that the consuls assisted Velheu with his inquest.

Thus, as early as Carnival time in 1577 the combustible material which would ignite during the Carnivals of 1579 and 1580 was already piling up: anger at abusive taxation, and corruption in the town hall and its coterie.[8] And there was already group action on the part of the weavers, drapers, butchers, and lower staff of the urban militia (that is, the corporals): they formed a hostile bloc in opposition to the power elite, in support of leaders like Paumier and Pain Blanc who were in a position to mobilize the lower classes, although the fight was as yet lacking in cohesion.

In 1579 things were even clearer. An understanding of the craftsmen's protest, soon to develop into a tax strike, is provided by the essential text[9] to which the draper Guillaume Robert-Brunat proudly affixed his handsome signature *for the people* before sending it off to *Our Lords of the Parlement* on May 16, 1579. At the time "Captain Brunat, Paumier's adviser" (P 89), functioned as a kind of tribune for the people, accepted by the craftsmen and tolerated by Guérin. Brunat is one more person to raise the question of the town's *debts*; his view of them may have been paranoid, but the important thing is that it was shared by his popular supporters and is very different from the picture the "dons" painted in 1576. The town's debts, Brunat held, were not a product of hard times, but simply the result of former consuls' misconduct (going back twenty years[10] from 1579). He found their behavior patently immoral. "Formerly (before 1579)," Brunat writes, "the consuls *had handled* (the) *funds from the inhabitants and peasants of Romans,*" money they got from the regular levying of taxes and *tributs*. But instead of funneling the said funds into the effective payment of the town's usual expenditures, which would imply deposits to the Crown Treasury or payment of standard municipal expenses, the said consuls kept the money in their own pockets and used it for personal purposes. The consuls may well have been dishonest, but the fault was not entirely theirs; Romans's incredibly archaic accounting practices were also to blame. Instead of a *centralized* accounting system (Montpellier, for instance, used one at the time) each of the consuls was assigned a quarter of the town's gross receipts, and a quarter of expenditures to manage, as his own personal empire. A consul might collect taxes in one neighborhood, and out of that money pay an employee in another quarter—a tangled web, and one that encouraged deceit.[11]

In Brunat's simplified view things were clear, all too clear. The consuls in 1578 and the preceding years *are indebted for considerable sums.* As proof, Brunat cited the audit of municipal funds effected by Romans's protesters in the spring of 1579. The consuls, he added, had handled town monies to their own profit, each in his own quarter. As a result, the community of

Romans, defrauded of its income, had had to *incur new expenses, to borrow money* to *substitute for the sums which the said consuls* (unscrupulously) *had removed.* The community had of course been obliged *to pay the interest on the said loans.* This is another version of the problem of the "20,000 *écus*" of town debt[12] the protesters alluded to in 1579 when they attacked the consular-bourgeois-merchant management of town funds over the preceding twenty years.[13] From their point of view the problem was not monetary inflation but municipal corruption.

The "criminal" ex-consuls, if one is to believe Brunat and the popular uproar, went even farther than that. With unparalleled perversity, the local political bosses lent the community money to cover the deficit caused by their own mishandling of funds. In other words, they lent the town its own money, then made the town pay interest on it at the exorbitant rates of that period (10 percent and up). They even demanded interest on the initial interest when a payment was the least bit late! *In this manner the debts of the said community were greatly augmented,* and none of it would have happened if the consuls had been honest or at least had repaid what they took. The result was a sort of financial suction pump: each year the new consuls neglected to make the previous year's consuls pay; the former consuls then lent their successors the money they had stolen from the town, with the whole process generating 50,000 *livres* or more of debt for Romans.

Brunat proposed as corrective measures (1) that the ex-consuls should repay the principal *and interest* of their heretofore concealed debts to the town; and (2) that the most recent consuls who omitted having their predecessors pay up should themselves be required to pay the back interest on such sums!

Frightened by the ferment in Romans and desirous of making at least an appearance of amends, the Parlement half-heartedly accepted Brunat's petition. They theoretically agreed to a number of audits and reimbursements.[14] But they made judge Guérin their executor, which was as much as saying things would not go beyond a certain point.

Brunat's action leveled accusations at Romans's entire consular oligarchy; it was a virtual declaration of war.

According to the election registers the oligarchy included a certain number of families of recent consuls: those of Bernardin *Guigou,* Jean *Thomé,* Jean de *Solignac* (a noble and squire), Messieurs de *Manissieu* (nobles), Antoine *Coste,* Jérôme *Velheu,* Jean *de Gillier,* Gaspard *Jomaron,* and of course the pre-eminent, parvenu family of judge Antoine Guérin. Large figures followed the names of these consular families in Romans's *taille* roll of 1583. While the lower classes paid an average 2 or 3 *écus* tax, the chiefs of these ten families paid a minimum of 10 *écus* and an average of 18 to 20 *écus* tax, [15] or six to ten times the 1583 average.

The workingmen had no chance of wresting power from the oligarchy. The best they could hope for was that Lesdiguières's Huguenots, were they to win, would put the town council in the hands of the local Protestant bourgeoisie, which had allied itself with the craftsmen, but only for tactical purposes. In fact, Brunat the draper and Fleur the butcher had set rather modest goals for their causes: they did not even challenge the division of the council into four categories (dignitaries, merchants, craftsmen, peasants) based on the social "ranks." They did not attack the value system, only its institutions. Their ambition was simply to fill the ranks of the town council with additional members who were none other than the leaders of the craftsman class. Thus on March 23, 1579,[16] Jean Serve, known as Paumier, draper; Guillaume Robert-Brunat, draper; and François Robin, craftsman of unknown profession (but who like the two others would be convicted after the Carnival of 1580), sat in the council meeting as "extraordinary" members. They in no way changed the majority, but they did influence discussion and decision-making; in point of fact their very presence (it was not their "place") was enough to make judge Guérin break out in a cold sweat.

And they were appointed for a full year.[17] On November 22, 1579, at the general assembly (in fact only an enlarged version of the town council), sixty-eight persons were present. Besides the four consuls and forty-odd members of the four social ranks, there were twenty-two extraordinary council members, including, at the end of the list, the familiar names of our local protesters: Jean Serve-Paumier, Guillaume Robert-Brunat, Geoffroy Fleur, Jacques Jacques, François Robin, and Jean Jacques. On December 5, 1579, only three consuls and eleven council members were in attendance at the regular session of the council; Paumier was one of them. The questions under discussion were important ones: the wheat monopoly, complaints about grain leaving town, the butchers and bakers' strike on indirect taxes. Paumier, Fleur, and Jacques Jacques were respectively present at the meetings on December 11, 14, and 26. On January 11 and 14, 1580, Guillaume Robert-Brunat and Geoffroy Fleur attended council meetings on the town debts. On February 10 and 12, in the middle of Carnival and the eve of the fatal *passage d'armes,* Jean Serve-Paumier (clad at the time in a bear skin) sat on the council along with Jacques Jacques and Antoine Nicodel, two other protesters, representing the craftsman rank. The order of the day touched on such questions as the closing of the town gates guarded by neighborhood militia captains (often friendly toward the peasants), and the never-ending problem of the town debt. Over an entire year—until the bloody quelling of the revolt in mid-February 1580—the leaders of the popular faction were able to take part in the council, providing them with all sorts of information and means of applying pressure on problems such as taxes, aid to the poor, choice of delegates to the Estates, audit of town finances, provisioning of grain, and, of course, the fabled municipal debt.[18]

These extraordinary council members were meant to deal a heavy blow to the town treasury and property. They were supposed to collect from the rich, the ex-consuls, the powerful, so that the town's flagrant debts (55,000 or 60,000 *livres* in all) could be paid off. Perhaps it would not be revolutionary, but it would amount to undermining established wealth (paying back 60,000 *livres* would be no small undertaking, and Romans's rich men were by no means rolling in money, and only well-off compared to the local lower classes and poor). The thought of being forced to make restitution made the bourgeoisie's hair stand on end. The poor people's Carnival in 1580 was a folk dance with the theme: "rich men, give the town back your dishonest gains" (P 86). It was a jumble of drums, little bells, swords, brooms, rakes, flails, and shrouds. Those in power, and above all, Guerin, interpreted and overinterpreted it to mean "the poor want to take all our earthly goods and our women, too; they want to kill us, perhaps even eat our flesh." The question of debts and usury in moneylending, of the *rentes constituées* (the tolerated private and public money-lending system) that dominated the entire social scene in the sixteenth century was thus a very far-reaching one, much more so than we in the twentieth century might suspect. It sent threatening feelers into the furthest reaches of the collective unconscious of the poor, of course, but also and even more disturbingly into the fantasies that haunted the rich, prey as they were to Fear.

Let us note that the approach Brunat and his draper friends used was analogous to de Bourg's. Romans's rhetoric in 1579 literally copied Dauphiné's 1576 rhetoric. Jean de Bourg had proposed that the unbearable debts of Dauphiné towns be collectively paid off by the Grenoble financiers largely responsible for the existence of those debts; they were to make restitution to the people.[19] In 1579 Brunat plagiarized de Bourg on a more modest scale, proposing the same thing within the limited context of Romans: have the local oligarchy pay up to clear the town debt. Quite simply, the two challenges were not on the same scale. De Bourg went beyond the regional financiers to attack the privileged orders as a whole—nobility and clergy. From this point of view he prefigured Dauphiné's militant action in 1789. Romans's protesters, however, allowed themselves only the bourgeois patricians of their little city as targets.

A discussion of debts brings us back to the problem of indirect taxes which had been irking the craftsmen ever since the "fatal" resolutions of 1576. To liquidate the town debt, the bourgeois consuls had decided that year to double, triple, or quadruple the *tributs* due from the craftsmen. Well then, the craftsmen said to themselves, we'll give them a run for their money. Brunat, their leader, proposed in 1579 that funds for repayment of the town debt be extracted directly from the tainted pockets of the local oligarchy. As a logical corollary, Geoffroy Fleur declared a butchers and bakers' strike on the increase in the *tributs*, since Brunat's thesis excluded them as necessary to the repayment of the town's debts!

The butchers involved in the strike were fully integrated into the economic "establishment," since the town had the monopoly on the butcher trade; they were essentially protesting against Romans's political and fiscal institutions. It was a logical attitude, and it would be ridiculous to accuse them of political narrow-mindedness. The annual contract for the butcher trade was dated April 7, 1579, and was then renewed on February 12, 1580, just before the conclusion of the revolt. The first of these contracts bears the signatures of the consuls (lessors) and the handsome flourish of Geoffroy Fleur (lessee); he was one of those who went to the gallows in the wake of the 1580 Carnival. The other lessees included members of the powerful Terrot family, butchers (and bakers); they were no doubt illiterate. One of them, Claude, was convicted in March 1580. When the contract was renewed on February 12, 1580, the same personages were in attendance with the exception of Fleur, who was accounted for but absent; he was busy directing the popular faction's Carnival and probably had no desire to rub elbows with the bourgeois consuls.

At the signing of these two contracts, which were supposed to run from Lent to Lent, the butchers pledged to provide beef, mutton, and veal for sale. They would pay the required *tribut* at the increased 1576 rate. They would sell beef at 15 *deniers* a pound, with other animals including fresh pork at 18 *deniers*. They would supply meat to the sick during Lent at the rate of 22 *deniers* a pound. They would sell no diseased livestock. They would save the fat from the animals they slaughtered for the town merchants at 3 *deniers* per pound of candles. The consuls in turn guaranteed them a monopoly on slaughtering in Romans; as security, they pledged the communities' goods. The butchers pledged their goods and their persons, and everyone seemed satisfied with the deal.

Was there already trouble by late June 1579, even before Catherine de'Medici's visit to Romans? It is quite likely. On July 2, Guérin and the two members of the town council appointed to supervise the butcher trade called on the town *tribut* collector to pay the 192 *écus* he owed the consuls. This collector protested that he owed only 100 *écus*.[20] By June 27, 1579, a check showed that Geoffroy Fleur was 16 *écus* 50 *sols* in arrears. He had probably started a one-man strike.

On September 10, 1579,[21] Catherine de'Medici's July visit was fading in Romans's memory; the promises of harmony were forgotten, the strike was rapidly evolving. It coincided with strong peasant and urban agitation based in Romans's market-place, where captains of the people were being elected and leaders chosen, so that the league could take over Grenoble.[22] In this atmosphere of near insurrection the butchers and bakers felt ready to reject en masse the huge increases in the *tribut* the 1576 resolution had instituted. The furious consuls must have said to themselves "What about the prices they charge for meat and bread!" Hadn't they gone up in proportion to the general inflation of the past ten years? Yet the craftsmen-tradesmen of the food sector called their strike not only on the increase in the *tributs* but on the *tribut* as a whole. It will come as no surprise that the notables' satirical treatment of the lower ranks during the next Carnival (1580) concerned food prices. In September 1579 the consuls lamented that they could no longer pay the town's bills (without the fat *tribut* from the butchers and bakers) for debts, the schoolteachers' wages, repairs to the walls, bridges, fountains, clocks, the town hall; according to the archaic accounting system, each consul would directly parcel out a portion of the receipts from the *tributs* for just those purposes. The consuls therefore humbly entreated judge Guérin to give the necessary legal commands to the defaulters. The judge was more than glad to: he bade them to submit. In vain. Was Guérin losing his ability to call the shots?

On October 17 and 30, 1579, new summonses were addressed to the butchers—at least fifteen of them, signers or co-signers of the previous spring's contract, were refusing to pay the *tribut*. Once again, some of the great names of the future Carnival agitation and post-Carnival repression appear: Claude Terrot and especially the record-holding butcher François Drevet (he had slaughtered 324 sheep).

In view of the October 1579 documents, it appears that the strike was essentially held during the summer, between the feast days of St. John (Midsummer's Day) and St. Michael. In one case, though, it had begun before Midsummer's Day, in the late spring. Each butcher owed an average of 7 *écus* back tax in October (adding up to a hundred or so *écus* or 300 *livres*—not a negligible sum for a town the size of Romans). At that time 300 *livres* was the entire income of a good-sized grain tithe-hold in the open country. During the three summer months each of these butchers had killed 201 sheep, 1.5 steers, 3.2 calves, and 4.7 *brancos*, which would put Romans's annual consumption of meat—with 15 butchers over 11 months, allowing for Lent—at a *minimum* of 11,055 sheep, 82 steers, 176 calves, 148 cows, and 258 *brancos*. We can estimate that each inhabitant, excluding infants, ate his or her two sheep per year and a "tenth part of beef," a rather hearty average (historically, more meat was consumed in the towns than in the countryside). These statistics point up how important the butchers and their profession were in Romans in the sixteenth century. Some of them could read and write, others were illiterate, but what they had in common were solid family ties: out of the fifteen butchers taking part in the strike, three had the family name *Olivier*, two were *du Conseils*, two *Thibauds*, and four *Terrots*. All of them worked under the same municipal contract; they were also bound into even closer associations of two butchers operating together. Often one of them recorded the slaughter of a half-cow or a halfcalf, which of course implies he was working in tandem with a colleague.

United and prosperous, they were a formidable group for Romans's consuls to confront, the more so since the fifteen mustered around a hard core of five (including Drevet, a du Conseil, and two Thibauds); these five butchers stated they would only pay *tributs* at the low pre-1576 rate. The others more prudently pledged to pay their quota "when the others do" or "another day."

In November 1579 the bakers followed their butcher friends and colleagues into the strike.[23] They too took it upon themselves to reject the 1576 increase, although, like the butchers, they had paid increased *tributs* in 1577 and 1578; now the political scene had changed. Among the recalcitrant bakers was another Claude Terrot, probably belonging to the protesting branch of the Terrot family that dominated both the butcher and baker trades. In all, we have record of nine "bread men" taking part in the strike. They rejected both the tax on each setier of bread and that on the scale-weight of flour. Eight of them wanted a return to the favorable pre-1576 rate of 6 *deniers* per setier (instead of 2 *sous* or 24 *deniers*, the increased rate). One more moderate baker said he would pay the increased rate *if the others do*. Their essential demand was a return to the "old practice" (prior to 1576). In this the bakers were far more inclined to look to the past than was Jean de Bourg.

November and December 1579 went by, and the strike continued. The consuls did not know which way to turn. They invited judge Guérin to intervene anew. And in his bold, authoritative handwriting he reiterated his promulgation that Romans's butchers and bakers should return to their regular habits as taxpayers.[24] Again in vain.

January 1580: with Carnival time approaching, delegations of strikers converged on the town hall. Bakers and pastry-cooks were first led by the potter-baker Mathelin des Mures (his oven was used to fire pots in addition to baking bread); he would be hanged later that winter. The bread men told the consuls they did not intend to be sacrificial offerings to inflation. They wanted *all* the town's taxpayers (*including* bourgeois property owners) to pay increased indirect taxes on *all* products (not just bread, grains, and flour). Until something was done about it, the baker-pastry cooks would refuse to pay the increased *tributs*. That very day the butchers made a similar request; their demands and arguments were roughly the same.

It is established that the butchers and bakers would be among the principal leaders and participants in the Carnival tragedy within a matter of days. They would also make a heavy contribution to the hangings in the final act of the 1580 Carnival: it was all up for Fleur, Mathelin de Mures . . . once Guérin took things in hand. By February 26, even before the hangings the judge fined the strike leaders, declaring them guilty as such: Des Mures, Fleur, Pain Blanc's wife (at last we hear of a woman participating!), Claude Terrot, Guillaumin Gazon, and others. As for the consuls, they forcefully emphasized the link between the tax strikes in the food sector and the painful problem of urban debt in February 1580, just as they had in September 1579. "Because of the strike on *tributs* our treasury is at rock bottom, we will not be able to pay our creditors," they cried. If they could have, Fleur and des Mures would have answered from the gallows: "You thieves, you're the ones who should pay the town's debts, all you'd have to do would be to shell out the town's money that you made off with!"[25]

The butchers and bakers' strikes were very far from being the sole cause or motive behind the events of February 1580; protest was widespread, varied, and intense throughout the entire region during the fall of 1579 and the ensuing winter. In early November a bad omen gave the inhabitants of Romans a fright: *On Monday November 9 1579,* Piémond wrote, *at nightfall, there was a terrible spell of lightning, thunder, and heavy rain. It was already wintertime. In Croix-la-Valleu, near Romans, three men from that town, coming from Valence, had repaired to Romans when the lightning and thunder began. Two of them made the sign of the cross. The third mocked them, saying 'You are much afraid, but the devil will have none of you. You pray him too prettily.' At the very moment he said these words, lightning struck! And the blasphemer fell stone dead, but without hurting the two others, who were only badly shaken. They say that the man who was hit was of the* (Protestant) *religion, and that in the past he had helped break down and destroy the church of St. Barnard* (in Romans). Piémond sententiously concludes: *all this is an example that it is wrong to mock those who shield themselves with the sign of the cross, and who always pray to God* (P 85).

The inclement weather was insignificant compared to the tax strike, but ironically it had a far greater immediate impact as far as taxes went; it influenced direct contributions from the bulk of the urban and rural communities. At the beginning of November, in Grenoble, *it was decided that the communities which had refused to pay the taille of 15 écus 5 sols per hearth be made to pay it; and furthermore the taille of 2 écus and 40 sols for affairs of the province* (P 86). But *the poor people found themselves on the brink of famine because it had been a bad year for crops.* The heavy rainfalls of October 1579 had in effect damaged the seed crop, and this was rightly or wrongly interpreted to mean that the next year's harvest would be bad. The recent grape harvest ought to have brought money flowing into the villages as wine was made and sold, which should have helped pay taxes, but instead it was a money-losing harvest because of the frost that had hit the vines the previous spring. Thus "the people," through their delegates to the Estates, replied that for the moment they could not pay taxes. Beyond the usual complaining, the antinoble demand for fiscal equality once again popped up like a jack-in-the-box: *When the King accedes to our petition* (of grievance), the community delegates said, *we hope that each one, rightfully, will do his part* (that the privileged orders would pay tax). *And after that we will pay the levy* (the double *taille*).

Faced with this twin challenge from the lower classes, the Parlement of Grenoble's instant reaction as defender of existing laws and of tax exemptions was a repressive one: *the Parlement had all those of the communities who were in Grenoble put in jail* in order to force them to pay the taxes their constituents owed. But the people stood firm, going so far as to talk of insurrection: *they did not want to obey, the people sooner whispered of rising up;* whereupon the Parlement had the prisoners released. Obviously force would not work, so milder measures were attempted: on December 4, 1579, the provincial Estates, meeting in Grenoble, displayed a more flexible attitude than the Parlement. They dispatched Monsieur Montanier, "village delegate," to Valloire (P 86, note 1). He was supposed to work his way into the villagers' hearts as well as their pocketbooks; he gave them to understand that the *taille* of 2 *écus* 40 *sols* per hearth was solely intended for provincial defense spending. This Montanier had a double-barrelled role: his office had been created to defend village interests; he was also transmitting the government's message and sweetening the medicine.

The peasants might have quieted down if fear had not taken over. Once more it was the Valloire region, always ripe for agitation, that acted as the sounding board: *at this same time, the communities of Valloire had been advised that Monsieur de Tournon was gathering his cavalry and infantrymen.* The scene was the town of Tournon just across the Isère from the Valloire; the peasants of Valloire were alarmed at the bloodthirsty lord of Tournon's call to arms. They were protesters; Tournon had little use for them, and vice-versa. They clearly remembered *the threats he had made to them, saying he would ride over their bodies* (P 86). Camped on their left bank of the Isère, *the Valloiriens thus went armed to the banks of the Rhône;* they hoped to prevent M. de Tournon from crossing the river and taking vengeance on their territory. It was a false alarm: Tournon, a good Catholic, was simply planning to take a Huguenot town on the right bank of the Rhône, in Vivarais (now the department of Ardèche).

It was one thing after another: as soon as Tournon was forgotten, Merle and Mende struck terror in the peasants' hearts. At Christmas, 1579, Captain Merle ("Blackbird"), a villainous outlaw who worked for the Huguenots, took the Catholic town of Mende in Lozère. To make his job easier, Merle attacked Mende while the whole town was at midnight Mass; the tolling of an enormous bell, called the None-Such, muffled the noise of the captain's attack. Some Christmas: the murders committed in Mende rang in a new outbreak of fighting between the two religious groups, involving all of southern France.[26] At the same time, for good measure, it seemed that civil conflict was imminent. The omens were not good: *In January 1580, the day of St. Paul's conversion* (January 15) *was beautiful and clear. And then a great northern wind blew, meaning, according to the old proverb: war . . . the harshest war the people would ever know* (P 87). During the same month—January 1580—*we heard in Dauphiné that the Nobility was readying several regiments of foot guards to exterminate the Third Estate. The people were greatly astonished, hearing of what was being hatched . . . .*

The third estate was now showing what it was made of. Taking the offensive, the league movement vastly extended itself by jumping the Rhône, from left to right bank, east to west, from Dauphiné to Vivarais. The shift took place down near Valence, south of Tournon's sphere of influence and out of reach of any antipeasant measures he might have taken.

On February 3, Guérin somewhat frantically wrote his old friend and accomplice Hautefort, the first officer of the Parlement of Grenoble, about the "rising of the people in Vivarais for the past few days:"[27] *a great number of the people of both religions started a campaign to break, as they say, all levies and taxes on the people.* . . . In truth, the rejection of taxes and threats of killing tax collectors, all propagated by roaming agitators like one Fournier around Privas, had been going on nonstop since October 1579 in Vivarais.[28]

As was traditional, the "bi-religious" peasant movement addressed itself to the problem of military occupation of the province with a rational furor. Garrisons were implanted in Vivarais towns and castles, exactly as in Dauphiné. The demand for *peace* was likewise fundamental on both sides of the Rhône: *they are in the Vivarais league,* wrote Charles Gelas de Leberon, bishop of Valence, on February 2, 1580 (Candlemas day), fearing for his town and his episcopal chair; *they have begun a campaign to constrain all those who refuse to observe the peace.*[29] In Vivarais, which was part of Languedoc and where nobles did pay taxes, tax exemption was not the key to popular discontent as it was in Dauphiné.

Dauphiné's leaguers had chosen leaders from the craftsman class and the bourgeoisie. The Vivarais protesters, less advanced and still caught in the nets of a strong seigneurial system, coaxed some local nobles, perhaps a bit roughly at times, to head up their movement; M. de St. Serge was one, M. de Pierregourd, another. This became customary in the province.[30] *A gentleman leads them,* the bishop wrote, *they made him their chief by force; I believe he is called St. Serge.* The Vivarais leaguers were many and well organized as Carnival time rolled around.

From Valence's ramparts on the left bank, the band of leaguers from the province across the Rhône could be clearly seen: *about three hours after noon,* the bishop continued, *we discovered* (across the river) *on the plain between Granges and Crussol a troop of arquebusers who must have numbered about five hundred, marching in order to the beat of the drum.* Drums were always a feature of league outings; this one would quickly turn serious: in the late afternoon or early evening, the castle of Crussol, an old fortress perched atop a mighty rock opposite Valence, was burned by the rustic militia. Successively occupied by the Huguenots (1573), then Catholic supporters of the crown (1579–1580), Crussol was wiped off the map; it would never again shelter peasants in the name of a noble landlord gone to war.[31]

The Vivarais leaguers had their distinguishing characteristics (noble leadership, minimized urban influence, goals which appear rather limited, almost entirely aimed toward achieving peace, and scarcely "social" in nature). Their action would continue into the seventeenth century, retaining these traits. In 1579 and 1580 Vivarais was more moderate than Dauphiné, but there was still a connection between the Huguenots and the restive peasants in both provinces, as judge Guérin nervously pointed out. It was more or less a tactical alliance, in opposition to the established Church and authority deriving from the crown. Several persons, the judge observed from the other, equally troubled side of the Rhône, *are astonished that the start of such undertakings* (the Vivarais league action) *took place in Catholic territory and in places* (Crussol) which were *for the King.*[32]

At the time the Carnival in Romans ignited, the entire mid-Rhône valley was feeling the heat. In Valence it was a banked fire: Jacques Colas, the league chieftan from Montélimar, overwhelmed by his troops, felt *the umbrage and defiance of the people* in Valence, Guérin reports. *Seeing which, Jacques Colas retired to Montélimar, much saddened.*[33] The town's bishop, unlike Colas, did not have the option of leaving Valence and heading home. He had to remain in his episcopal see and support the "gentlefolk" (bourgeois patricians) against the "common folk" of craftsmen and plowmen, who had been stirred up, represented, or led for a time by Bonniol the miller, "Colonel" Fortunat de Dornes, and Guillaume Savinas, a member of the town council. On February

26, 1579, Savinas had invited the remainder of Maugiron's troops to leave Valence.[34] On March 19 of that year an assembly of the "common folk" of Valence (authorized, perhaps unwillingly, by the consuls) had elected Fortunat de Dornes, a man-at-arms, colonel and "superintendent" in charge of defense—the people's defense—of the city.[35] On April 30, 1579, Bonniol the miller (in real life François Chevalier, leader of the people) and one Sanglard had tried to let fighters from Vienne, in other words, armed peasant league members, into Valence. The patricians found the very thought unbearable, and so did a splinter group of the "common folk." Among the latter was a certain Antoine Moet who denounced the actions of his ex-comrade Bonniol before the town council.[36] There was thus a split between hardliners such as Bonniol and moderates like Moet, as there was between Paumier and Laroche in Romans. The test of loyalties came as it so often did when a decision had to be made about peasant troops, who were the allies of the most radical elements in town; letting them into the town might well lead to looting.

Early in February 1580 the situation in Valence was far from settled. While keeping an eye on the Vivarais side of the Rhône where the embers of Crussol still glinted, the town's bishop, Charles Gelas de Leberon, sadly noted that *this poor misguided people* (Valence's popular faction) *has taken to opposing* (the notables) *at the instigation of the Turbulents* (Protestants), *who are still rather more numerous than I would care to have them in this town.* Charles Gelas even feared the worst: *they were on the verge of causing me much pain, myself and the Good* (the "gentlefolk") *who are on my side.*[37] The prelate did manage to calm things down in the seat of his diocese after he administered a few remonstrances to the most extreme hotheads. Valence then stayed relatively calm during the Carnival of 1580.

In Romans everything came together, then fell apart. As Maugiron would write to the king on February 12, 1580,[38] *still I fear only for Romans. For Valence is governed by a good man, your loyal servant the Bishop of that place. But the division in Romans is so troubling, so frightening. . . .*

Romans always meant more than just the town itself. There were also the dependent villages to the north that had been consistently protesting for a year or more. It meant Marsas, Chantemerle, and the Valloire region in the background.

In Marsas, February 1580 was an exact repeat of February 1579. The soldiers' misdeeds gave the village an excuse for holding half-folk, half-defensive gatherings at Candlemas, 1580. These were real military gatherings, if a letter of Guérin's is to be believed: *Last Tuesday the feast of our Lady* (Candlemas) *our surrounding villages gathered at Marsas armed and with drums, under 15 or 16 banners, however with no disorder.* Fifteen or sixteen banners meant about 1500 men from several parishes meeting in one of the district's towns.[39]

As for Valloire, so troubled throughout the fall and winter of 1579 and always ready to take up arms against a real or imagined enemy, Catholic or noble, the district again sent certain of its most determined inhabitants to Romans: *on Candlemas day* (February 2, 1580) *there came to this town several men from Valloire to attend the Assembly.... They had a great desire to see this gathering quickly under way,* (their language was) *full of threats and outbursts according to their mood which I* (Guérin) *tried with all my might to stem.*[40]

While the judge was unleashing the full flood of his eloquence in the hope of calming the Valloire intruders (who in any case would soon scatter due to a mistake in the arrangements for a meeting), another curious phenomenon presented itself, this time from within the town walls: Paumier donned his bear costume.

VII

ᏫᏫᏫᏫᏫᏫ

Antoine Guérin,
Master of Ceremonies

In 1580, as in 1579, it all started up again in Romans with Candlemas (February 2) and St. Blaise's Day (February 3). In town and country, these two feast days marked the beginning of a deeply troubled Carnival period.

By late January, Romans was in a flurry of preparations for Carnival. Around January 30 and 31, in keeping with their folk tradition, the local drapers, *deciding to hold festivities, had horsemen go through town to announce their parade and invite the people to arm and outfit themselves as was the custom* (A 152). They were not merely repeating a ritual; this was also the first anniversary of Romans's year of semi-independence from state domination; the first anniversary of a system of dual power, with Guérin at the center and Paumier on the fringes. The craftsman leader did not shy away from center stage during the Candlemas festivities; when the parading drapers acted like noble cavaliers on horseback, *it should be noted that one of the horsemen was the said Paumier* (A 152). The funereal, military beat of drums resounded for the next few days: *they then began to march with drums and arms through the town.*

Dressed up as the Candlemas bear (whose early February emergence predicted how much longer winter would last), Paumier frequented the town hall with his friends (the records of council proceedings for January–February 1580 mention his attendance at meetings).[1] *Paumier, wearing a robe of bear skin, went to the town hall and took a rank and seat which were not due him and which he had never before taken* (A 153). The judge interpreted this intrusion as the symptom of a demand for power—an illegitimate demand, to be sure. All this *made those who saw farthest ahead think what they had always suspected, that he* (Paumier) *must have elaborate schemes* (A 153). With his usual exaggeration and tale-telling, Guérin attributed what seem to be inflated pan-Dauphiné ambitions to Paumier: *moreover, the said Paumier proclaimed that he wanted everyone to know there was not a man in Dauphiné who could dictate to him.* One of the more serious allegations made by the judge was that there was a secret understanding between Paumier's camp and the Huguenots. According to Guérin, the bear skin may have been a cover-up for a Huguenot plot. *Therefore, the gentlefolk* (of Romans) *decided to keep a closer watch on Paumier and his adherents, most of whom, even the chiefs of the leagues, as said before, were of the* (Protestant) *Religion, which troubled them* (the gentlefolk) *more than anything else* (A 153). Actually, the league leaders were not Huguenots at all, but it is true that they had consorted with Huguenot emissaries. Jean Guigou had done so the previous year, but then he scurried back to Guérin's camp.

February 2 was Candlemas, the day the bear was supposed to poke his head out. February 3 was St. Blaise's Day, the feast day for the grain flailers and the carders whose tools had ripped apart the martyred saint's body. *With the coming of the said Day* (St. Blaise's). *there were a good six hundred of the said trade armed and outfitted* (A 152). Six hundred drapers in Romans? Guérin's figure is too high, yet there were certainly 600 heads of household in the crafts and trades, and hundreds of men, craftsmen or simple workers, who were employed in the carding and weaving trades and their workshops. Drapers, carders, and others, the self-employed, small employers and their employees, must certainly have added up to 600 adult males in the workingmen's armed parade. Was this a political, military event meant to intimidate the bourgeoisie? Guérin suggested as much. He was not entirely wrong, even if he simplified reality to the point of caricature, as usual: *this,* he wrote, *made the hearts of Paumier and his adherents so greatly swell with pride that he was then assured of being able to carry out his plan, set for the near future.* The plan was of course the total overthrow of the notables; Guérin rather gratuitously made Paumier the author of such a scheme. Not that the draper was innocent, but it seems unlikely that he would attempt anything of the kind on his own—that is, without direct aid from Lesdiguières and the Huguenots.

St. Blaise's Day was replete with the traditional activities. It began on February 3, but the events continued through the next few days. The men in the drapers' parade *ran the sheep, holding a Reynage like the year before.* There was a footrace for some of the participants in the parade, particularly the young ones. The winner was heralded as the fastest man in town, assuming the judging was fair. The prize was a sheep, perhaps a castrated ram. Sometimes they ran the poor beast and killed it by throwing sickles at it.[2] Finally, there was a *reynage*—a parade of the imaginary Carnival royalty elected for the occasion, probably ending in a banquet. The "Sheep King" may well have had a costumed suite including a chancellor, a prior, and so on. Most probably, the Sheep King was one of the leaders or outstanding personalities of the popular faction, but we know nothing about him. Guérin's use of the term "like the year before" in connection with the *reynage* is significant: despite the ring of swords and thud of boots, everything was still in keeping with the annual Carnival custom and, for the moment, was nonviolent.

So customary was it that when Guérin wrote a dispatch updating events the same day (February 3), he was not at all worried by the St. Blaise's Day parade.[3] He was more concerned about the trouble in Valence that had driven Jacques Colas to seek refuge in Montélimar, and about the chronic, recurrent troubles caused by the peasants in Marsas and the Valloire district. In contrast, the Romans drapers' parade seemed harmless. The judge later reinterpreted it in light of subsequent developments, including his own plot.

The Sheep *reynage* remained simply a part of the popular festivities celebrating Candlemas and especially St. Blaise's Day. On February 3 and for days afterward, there was dancing in the streets of Romans, specifically in the working-class quarters. These street dances were called *branles*, literally *shakes* (the word might be comparable to our *reel*). *They held street dances all through town*, Guérin noted. But what kind? There seem to have been several. Some groups of dancers went at it with *Swiss drums, bells on their feet, and drawn swords* (A 152), an example of the sword dance (perhaps featuring simulated killing?) found in countless regions of Dauphiné, Germany, and Italy.[4] Bells on the feet were reminiscent of the medieval fool or jester's bells; they call to mind the famous Rabelaisian episode of the "stealing of the church bells" in *Gargantua*. And in Romans there were bells on the feet as the town danced out its folly. The pandemonium of "Swiss drums" accompanying the bells and swords had a political meaning: they evoked the sturdy Swiss brand of democracy the "seditionists" were accused of wanting to introduce in Dauphiné. This type of drumming represents a triple code composed of sound, time (the calendar of feasts), and social factors, found among many peoples in many different parts of the world. In this instance the drums beat out the division of time (annual feasts) and of a society (Romans's).

A second group of St. Blaise's Day revelers danced to a different drum: *others did* (dances) *of another sort, some carrying rakes, others brooms, yet others flails for threshing wheat* (A 152) . . . *dressed in death shrouds.*

"Brooms and rakes," wrote J. Roman, who edited Guérin's manuscript, "probably meant that the gentlefolk were to be unseated; flails meant beatings, and the shroud meant burial."[5] Not that Romans's reasoning is wrong: a few months before, in Grenoble, an attorney turned protester, Gamot, had been arrested *for having carried the rake, exciting the people,* Catherine de'Medici tells us. And in a famous passage from *For Whom the Bell Tolls*, Hemingway described how Red peasants exterminated notables with flails. During the nineteenth century, Dauphiné peasants still chased their wayward daughters homeward with brooms . . .

Aggression was not the only meaning of the flail dance. Flails, rakes, and brooms were also part of the traditional dance performed at the end of the wheat-growing cycle. In Romans and the surrounding villages, the flail was still used for separating grain from the straw and chaff. (This was no longer true in the lower Rhône valley, where Mediterranean methods were in use: there, horses, oxen, and serrated rollers did the threshing in the summertime.) Around Romans, however, wheat was hand-threshed during the winter by teams of flailers. Hence, the St. Blaise Carnival was a threshing rite: the untied sheaves were beaten, and the grain, straw, and chaff were swept apart from each other. It was the end or death of the cereal cycle, a prelude to the rebirth that spring's sowing would represent. St. Blaise's place in Dauphiné's Carnival tradition was as the patron of the spring sowing of grains.

The flail bearers, enacting the death of an annual cycle—the sowing, sprouting, harvesting, and finally, the beating of the grain "to death"—were also the dancers of death itself. They carried flails for threshing wheat *dressed in shrouds with others who cried that before three days were out the flesh of Christians would sell for six deniers the pound.*

The dancing procession of grain-threshing techniques was at the same time, then, a classic Carnival funeral procession. The cloak worn by Romans's undertakers, we learn further along in Guérin's text, *is the cloak of the crier of the confrérie of the Holy Spirit, of the colors red and blue, which is worn in the presence of the dead about to be buried* (A 160). The *confrérie* or confraternity of the Holy Spirit mentioned by the judge was an offshoot of an earlier, agrarian organization of the villages and market towns of southeastern France. Its chapel was in the church of St. Foy near Romans's working-class district. The fellowship constituted the core which evolved into the municipal community (that is, government entities) during the Middle Ages.[6] The membership was in charge of distributing provisions and alms to the poor. Furthermore, it was composed of both living and *dead* members! By paying special dues during his lifetime, a member could continue to belong to the association for some years after his death. At fellowship dinners, dead members were represented by the poor. In this way, thanks to the confraternity of the Holy Spirit (whose special patron was St. Blaise),[7] craftsmen and paupers found the means of mixing publicly and fraternally, as part of the St. Blaise's Day celebrations.

The day's ceremonies shrouded certain cannibalistic fantasies that ultimately emerged. Crying *flesh of Christians, six deniers the pound,* the parading members of St. Blaise's fellowship made a half-serious, half-jesting threat against the notables; in the same vein they offered the crowd the flesh of corpses to eat. That was the fellowship's idea of black humor, since they were the ones in charge of burying the dead: eating the dead would therefore produce living flesh anew.[8]

The popular rites of St. Blaise's Day operated on three levels: *warriors* (of the strictly Carnival variety) brandished swords during their dance; *peasants* beat flails and brandished wheat-threshing rakes or brooms; and the confraternity of St. Blaise, in charge of *religious* ceremonies, flaunted the pall.

These three primitive treatments—agrarian, martial, sacred —of the *initial* Carnival theme of death are essential. The later and secondary role of St. Blaise as protector of the carders whose combs tore him to death, was comparatively minor during the February 3, 1580, festivities, even though the parade was supposedly held by the carders and drapers' St. Blaise fellowship, backed by the Holy Spirit confraternity which corresponded to the primitive core group of plowmen. Lest we forget, agricultural workers made up 36 percent of Romans's population around 1580.

The drapers were weaving a shroud for the old world, a shroud they waved like an undertaker's pall. The agricultural workers and craftsman's pantomimes on St. Blaise's Day were pure folklore. But they rapidly turned political as they continued throughout the week following the saint's feast day. Guérin described the process (A 152): *they held street dances through the town . . . and all these dances were to no other end than to announce that they wanted to kill everything.*[9] The judge, one might protest, was a notoriously unreliable witness on this point. But Piémond, far more impartial, also flatly stated that the dances went beyond mere tradition. Piémond in effect declared (P 88) that the people of Romans's league or Union, on the occasion of the various "kingdoms" they organized for the Carnival period between St. Blaise's Day and Mardi gras, *held several great feasts, street dances, and masquerades and during the whole week in their street dances proclaimed that the rich of their town had grown rich at the expense of the poor people....*

The insinuations made by the poor men's Carnival were chilling. *Fearing that restitution would have to be made, some of the notables and merchants were angered, and although some of them belonged to the Union* (league) *they still tried to put down the most factious among the members of the craftsmen's group, and to that end, in cooperation with some who were against the Third Estate, they held another "kingdom" in the town hall on the Monday before Lent* (P 89).

We will bypass this other *reynage* for the moment which the rich began organizing by Tuesday, February 9. But let us now focus on how the St. Blaise dances displayed a plurality of meaning (*polysemy,* linguistically speaking) characteristic of folk behavior and festivities. The craftsmen's demand that the rich *make restitution* implied a class struggle; it also harked back to the Carnival theme of *collection,* the redistribution of older people's worldly goods to the young, the rich men's wealth to the needy. After the Carnival in Romans, generation after generation of young Dauphinois from the seventeenth century through the nineteenth century would go to Carnival dances and masquerades, entering houses and begging for eggs and presents of food or money from their settled elders, married couples, and other heads of household.

The St. Blaise street dances and masquerades demanding *restitution* seem to have gone on sporadically and varied in intensity from Wednesday, February 3, 1580 (St. Blaise's Day) until Saturday February 13—ten days in all (P 88).

The workingmen were not alone in their merrymaking. On February 6, a Saturday, or on Sunday February 7, a second "kingdom" arrived in the streets of Romans. *In the meantime, a good group from the neighborhood of the Jacquemart gate resolved to hold a "reynage" of their own, and to run a rooster* (A 153).

This good group, as the term indicates, was made up of moderate leaguers or "gentlefolk" from the relatively prosperous Jacquemart quarter. The league "doves" had progressively quarreled or become disenchanted with the "hardliners" who still acknowledged Paumier as their supreme leader.

An impending break was not, however, a sure indication that

the Rooster *reynage* would be political in tone—at least on the surface. In fact, their merrymaking seemed like the spontaneous folk outbursts; the winner (prearranged?) of the rooster race was a young man named Laigle ("the eagle"), a popular fellow in the Jacquemart quarter, a neighborhood dandy. The Jacquemart Carnival overflowed with references to virility: overtly masculine, their "eagle," dressed up in the feathers or the erectile crest of the Chanticleer, could not stop crowing. The Jacquemart king, a strutting, rapacious individual, ruled for two days (Monday and Tuesday, February 8 and 9, 1580). *Laigle held his feasting for two days with all the gaiety and entertainments he could contrive so that during his reign, which lasted only the said two days, there was talk of nothing but masks, dances, the hunt, and other entertainments* (A 153). So the Jacquemart quarter, clustered around its tall, narrow clocktower, buzzed with masquerades, banquets, balls, and street dances for forty-eight hours. The rites of the hunt, characteristic of Carnival's most primitive core, were also a feature.[10] Apparently, the atmosphere was not unduly charged with fighting among the different factions. In fact, a great show was made of feigned cordiality. Paumier, either out of sheer gullibility or because he fancied himself a Machiavelli, pretended not to be alarmed at Laigle's kingly doings and the Rooster *reynage*. *Neither Paumier nor his fellows seemed to show any displeasure or suspicion* (A 151). King Laigle's feasting climaxed on February 9; there was probably a spirited parade accompanied by a few sporting jousts (A 155, 162). The festivities culminated in a *supper;* the most notable guest at this exceptional banquet was Paumier himself, who had come as a neighbor: a good sport, he paid court to his rival, the ruler of the Jacquemart roost. It seems unlikely that Paumier could have predicted he would soon be murdered by this Carnival monarch and his friends and that the Rooster King would become the darling of Romans's upper-class ladies as a result. However, the craftsman leader was accompanied by some contemptible-looking individuals, according to his enemy, Guérin: *a short time afterwards* (Tuesday, February 9), *Paumier returned with some shady characters,* and *headed for the supper the Eagle King was having who had held festivities that day* (A 155).

It is noteworthy that here Guérin put down *le roi de l'Aigle* (the Eagle King) instead of the patronymic *Laigle,* emphasizing how he finally viewed the events: as a kind of folk tale.

Laigle's feast was quite an affair, but politics and war were not far off. On the eve of the Rooster King's feast day (February 9, 1580), the Huguenots failed at an attempt to take Grenoble (February 8). Full of resentment, their troops then fell back on secondary sites around the Dauphiné capital, such as Vieille, St. Quentin, and La Motte-Verdier. These insignificant skirmishes—viewed in perspective—led up to the equally inconsequential *guerre des amoureux,* a minor military conflict between Catholics and Protestants that moderately troubled southern France in 1580. In Dauphiné, however, these clashes were particularly significant. If Catholic paranoia at the time is credited—and it was not always unwarranted—the Protestant activities were part of a larger plan drawn up at a Huguenot gathering in the town of Anduze (in Cévennes), which called for renewed and united efforts on both banks of the Rhône. Lesdiguières and his friends were supposedly involved; so were the peasant leagues in Vivarais and the entire Romans region. East of the Rhône, for instance, the Huguenot captain Bouvier had just taken charge of 500 well-armed peasants and with their help captured several castles. To parry the threat the lieutenant-governor of Lyonnais, François de Mandelot, gathered his meager forces in a military and political coalition with Maugiron's men and the Parlement of Grenoble. Mandelot tried to win the delegates of Dauphiné's Estates to his cause (six representatives of the clergy, six nobles, and twelve members of the third estate). A few companies of Catholic or crown soldiers and some hundred noble gentlemen organized and marched. This made the third estate commoners in both town and country exceedingly nervous. They did not necessarily believe that those who spoke in their behalf at the Grenoble Estates were properly representing their interests (P 94).

Maugiron was especially uneasy about Romans. The walled city had just gone through a series of profound crises and had not completely recovered. No other town in the province had been so troubled, for they had been better controlled, by their bishops, (as in Valence), or by the notables.

While Carnival was intensifying in Romans, Maugiron's own brother was acting on the lieutenant-governor's behalf in Romans (he had been sent there secretly) with judge Guérin and a few other "gentlefolk" as auxiliary go-betweens. *I did so much,* Maugiron wrote to the king on February 12, 1580,[11] *that I won over certain of the gentlefolk and Catholics* (in Romans), *who watch over the behavior of each and all in order to counterbalance the secret schemes and communication of those of the* (Protestant) *Religion.* Maugiron's maneuvering had played a part in the apparently innocent organization of the Eagle-Rooster *reynage* (in the local political scene the organizers of that "kingdom" occupied a sort of neutral ground where Guérin would not fear to tread).

Maugiron's influence on the next *reynage* was even clearer: the bourgeois patricians had clear title to the Partridge Kingdom.[12]

On Tuesday, February 9, 1580, the day of the Jacquemart king's final festivities, *certain of the most notable of the town, while talking together in the town square* (marketplace), *put forward holding a reynage* (A 153). They decided to *run a partridge;* in other words, to hold yet another footrace; the winner of this one would take home a partridge. This Partridge Kingdom originated *in the neighborhood of the town square and the bridge.* In form, it would be a folk gathering, in content, political; its epicenter was the most bourgeois part of town surrounding the marketplace or "great square" and contiguous to the bridge linking Romans with its suburb on the opposite bank, Bourg-de-Péage.

Perhaps all the organizers of the Partridge *reynage* had in mind was a flattering imitation of their friends and neighbors who had crowned the Eagle-Rooster. Guérin was one of the organizers and that is what he innocently and no doubt truthfully maintained. But it is only a part of the truth. Piémond sometimes confused his dates, but since he sympathized with the leaguers he was accurate when it came to the bourgeoisie's bloodthirsty intentions. He plainly states that the Partridge Kingdom was the rich men's suppressive retort to the craftsmen's antipatrician folk demonstrations, which they considered to have menacing undertones. Had not the workingmen started it all with their Sheep *reynage* and subversive dancing? In a few days they would do it once again with the Hare and the Capon Kingdoms. Given the circumstances, the Partridge *reynage* was an authentic urban folk ritual, but one incubating a murderous plot against the poor, a massacre with a lighthearted beginning.[13]

The Partridge "plotters" identified themselves by wearing a slip of paper in their hats. Each bore a virtually cabalistic number the illiterate masses could not read, thus distinguishing Romans's upper crust from the *hoi polloi*. *With the decision quickly made, it was said that those who would take part in it* (the Partridge *reynage*) *would have a slip of paper with a number, to recognize each other. And in fact, the said slips were thereupon made and delivered to those present; and afterwards to those who wanted to be in it; then they put them in their hats* (A 154).

These bits of paper posted in the patricians' headgear were an intentional contrast to the lack of insignia that usually characterized the peasant league members, who, for the most part, could not read. *They* (the leaguers) *had had three hundred wooden horns* (trumpets) *made to sound off to each other from parish to parish, and for their insignia they wore no cord on their hats,* Lyonne had noted in 1579 (A 43 note 1).

Some sixty members of Romans's patrician bourgeoisie were in the town square on Tuesday, February 9, with their little slips of paper. The figure of sixty, as opposed to six hundred men parading with the drapers and other craftsmen, is very much in line with the proportion of patrician families in Romans. According to the tax rolls, there were obviously many fewer gentlefolk than craftsman or plowman households.

In his narration, Guérin repeatedly tries to convince us of the purely sporting nature of the *reynage*; what he tells us about the game is interesting. *They* (the sixty participants) *thought of nothing but getting ready to run well,* (in the race that would open the kingdom's festivities) *to become King, and to feast together* (A 153). Thus the rich men's carnival was just like any other in appearance. First there was a race with an animal as grand prize (the partridge, in this instance); next, the proclamation of the winner as a Carnival King; and finally, the "feasting" and the various festivities it entailed.

It was not just a matter of feasting, however: the Partridge looked like a sham. From the very start the Sheep partisans were suspicious.

Paumier himself, advised that slips of paper had appeared in his opponents' hats, went to have a look at the town square and size up the situation. He immediately got wind of a scheme against him, *thinking that this was some undertaking against those of his faction* (A 154). He nonetheless decided to wait. A friend who was with him, "one of the most seditious," was less inclined to patience when he saw the Partridge beginning its run. *He put his hand to his sword; taking it half out of its sheath, he began to wax most angry* (A 154). He cursed liberally and offered to fight it out with Paumier's foes:

—*This is too much waiting*, he said to Paumier. *If they decide to strike, we are done for. Do you want me to fight them?*

Paumier once more displayed his pacifist, perhaps temporizing, nature. He calmed his bodyguard and blithely went off to dine with the Eagle-Rooster that very evening; he had just been invited to the banquet by his "friendly" enemies (sooner enemies) from the Jacquemart quarter.

On February 10 nothing of any note happened in Romans. The Partridge Kingdom simply continued its preparations (for the footrace) and its plotting (for bloodshed). On Thursday, February 11, the Partridge race was run in the friary square. The open space in front of the Cordeliers friary was a favorite meeting place for the gentlefolk, men and ladies alike. The common folk as well turned out to see their young masters compete. *Thursday . . . those who had prepared for the partridge race did not fail to go to the Friary square where a great number of the Ladies and the people were gathered to see the entertainment* (A 155). The reference to ladies, in other words, women of the bourgeoisie, is interesting. We know they customarily graced royal entrances into Romans and the rich men's parades. However, this is the first time women appear in Guérin's narrative. All evidence suggests that the orientation of the poor men's Carnival was resolutely masculine.[14] Women must have played some role, but such a minor one it was not worthy of mention. In contrast, women were an integral part of the rich men's Carnival. The feminine influence is seen in the choice of an emblematic animal (partridge is a feminine word in French), and above all in the number of lovely ladies who attended the Partridge race.

We have no technical information on how the footrace was conducted. Did the participants run after the grounded partridge, stoning it to death? Was the winner given the bird as a prize at the end of the race? In any case, the political side of the event was rigged from start to finish. A good number of young men—perhaps a few dozen—between the ages of eighteen and thirty-six, all members of upper-class families, had signed up for the event. Within full sight of the ladies they fixed the race so that Laroche would come in an easy first and be named the Partridge King. Was justice blind? Laroche the ropemaker had quarreled with his friend Paumier and the hardliners in Romans's popular faction. He had become the cosseted protégé of the patrician jurists, merchants, and property owners: they felt no compunction about promoting a craftsman as their chief when it meant driving a wedge into the working class. Consequently, the strongest runners slowed their pace to let Laroche win his partridge. *Fortune had it*, Guérin says with a straight face, *that the greatest enemy, at least declared, of the said Paumier, who is Laroche, was King.*[15] The expression "at least declared" is noteworthy. If we read between the lines, we see that Paumier's greatest *undeclared* enemy was none other than Guérin.

Fixing games like this was a common practice in urban sporting and folk events. Carcassonne's archery and shooting match, for example, was always won by the town consuls; the best shots in town would let one of the consuls kill the snake or eagle effigy, even if he were a dotard *incapable of taking aim at any target whatever,* so nearsighted that he pointed the gun at his own face.[16] Laroche's skill as a runner (at a flabby forty, perhaps?) was debatable; his victory was prearranged. The craftsmen reacted to it in various ways and were suspicious: the occasion *allowed Paumier and those of a feather to presume that it all had been handmade and decided in advance* (A 155).

Paumier rather belatedly began to wonder if there was not

more to the situation than was obvious, and therefore took some dissuasive measures against the patricians. Employing self-styled neutral persons as his "go-betweens" (A 155), he sent warning to the patricians. He most cordially recommended that they cancel the feasting scheduled for Monday, February 15 (or *lundi gras,* the day before Mardi Gras), which was to celebrate the "kingdom" decided on the day of the partridge run, Thursday, February 11. The craftsman leader and his men *tried, by the mediation of certain of those from outside his party who had been involved in its affairs, to postpone the said kingdom* (A 155). Paumier's unsolicited suggestion fell on deaf ears. The patricians were not about to be intimidated, and went on with their plans. They deserve some credit for taking a stand, for the popular faction's warning was not to be taken lightly. It came with the barely veiled threat that the surrounding villagers would put pressure on Romans; they were Paumier's faithful followers and likely to lend assistance to the craftsmen in time of need. It is important to remember that Romans was literally surrounded by the countryside, a situation the patricians found very disquieting, hemmed in as they were by commoners in the working-class quarters and peasants in the country parishes.

Roughly speaking, the message Paumier transmitted to the notables was "if you insist on organizing the Partridge festivities, *you will put doubt into my men's minds which could cause you harm and you will rue it, for* (my men) *are neighbors of the town"* (A 155). A few days later Guérin attempted to justify the murder of the craftsmen leaders (which he described as a defensive measure) after the fact; he accused Paumier (by then a dead man) of *having taken it upon himself to bring a great number of villagers* (into Romans) *to help with his endeavors.*[17] The charge may be exaggerated, but it was not a fabrication. It had happened on a smaller scale the year before, in 1579. And a century later, it happened again, in Aix-en-Provence.

But let us return to our subject, the Partridge King. The young patricians and their elders refused to cancel the feasting, despite pressure from the lower classes. Our narrator, Guérin, was a Catholic imbued with the Augustinian notion of predestination; remnants of the Calvinist indoctrination he had renounced may also have lurked beneath his born-again Catholicism. He therefore explained his friends' tenacity as inspired by divine intervention, all-powerful and dictated from on high: *Since it is impossible to avoid what God has preordained . . . God, I say, put into the hearts of these gentlefolk so great a resolve that they decided to continue with the said reynage. And in fact, it was said that it would be held the Monday of the beginning of Lent. . . .* (A 155).

Let us note the expression "the Monday of the beginning of Lent," in other words, *lundi gras,* the day before Mardi Gras; the latter was called *carême-entrant* or *carême-prenant* (beginning of Lent) in Provençal and Franco-Provençal. Guérin's use of the term to designate Monday, February 15, 1580, was a departure from his usual style. He always referred to the solar calendar, for example "February 3" (the Sheep Kingdom) or "February 9" (the partridge run). Starting on Wednesday, February 10, or Thursday, February 11, however, he changed over to the lunar calendar. the dates of *lundi gras* and Mardi Gras (which fell on February 15 and 16 in 1580) were actually calculated according to the moon, as is Easter, the primary date in the whole Mardi Gras–Lenten period. Mardi Gras comes forty days before Easter which falls on the Sunday following the first full moon after the vernal equinox. All of Carnival went along with this shift from solar to lunar time. From February 2 (Candlemas day, when the bear came out of his den to check the sun) until Mardi Gras, the Tuesday after the new moon, it was a transition period. Halfway through it the judge bore witness to the change and modified his vocabulary accordingly.

The transition came on Tuesday, February 9, the end of solar reckoning in the judge's text. It coincided with the supreme and truly Carnival rite of inversion or role reversal. At the time, the Partridge King, monarch of the patricians, had proclaimed himself ruler of all Romans for a few days. He then decreed that the town was to turn itself into a *pays de Cocagne* or land of Cockaigne, a favorite theme in contemporary Provençal folktales.[18] In this imaginary land, wine flowed like water, sugar-coated strawberries were sold off at the price last week's herring usually fetched . . . Laroche, the Partridge King, thus had his mock *Grand Conseil* or high court promulgate an ordinance dated Tuesday, February 9, 1580, the very first day of the Partridge Kingdom's existence. It is obvious that the mock ordinance was at the very heart of the patricians' intentions.

The decree regulated prices for *foodsellers, publicans, and innkeepers,* with the humorous injunction that the new prices be heeded. This would have turned the entire world of food and drink upside down. Scarce foodstuffs were listed as cheap and vice-versa. "Henceforth" the highest prices would be for hay, straw, oats, all animal feed, as well as for bad or wormy wine, salted eel, rotten herring, and fatback. (Pork, inversely, was prized, recalling certain well-known aspects of Carnival's Rabelaisian celebration of the hog and sausages of every variety.) All the prices quoted were around, or slightly more than, one *livre tournois.*

At the opposite end of the scale, according to the rules of inversion, delicacies were to sell for a few *deniers* or *sous,* next to nothing: turkey studded with cinnamon and cloves, pheasant or ruffled grouse, partridge, hen, hare, roast snipe, ringdove à l'orange, fatted veal, mutton, trout, carp, pike, wine from Cornas or Tournon, hypocras, strawberries with rosewater and sugar . . .

Supposedly Laroche himself promulgated the satirical price list. But Guérin was giving the directives, as always. The judge was used to handing down ordinances to innkeepers; he wrote more than one during his long career as the town's high magistrate,[19] and it was he who dictated the lines of the comic price list to Laroche. The inversion of value placed on food mocked the "poor" who wanted to be the patricians' equals, even change places with them, like rotten herring substituted for strawberries.

There was more behind Guérin's ludicrous price list than simple and short-lived political satire; it coincided with the delicate, central nerve impulse of Carnival which sent time flowing backwards, and rendered everything topsy-turvy. This impulse was rooted in a cultural tradition active long after

1580. The theme of role reversal was commonplace in folk imagery from the end of the Middle Ages through the first half of the nineteenth century:[20] engravings or pamphlets show, for instance, a man straddling an upside-down donkey and being beaten by his wife. In some pictures mice eat cats. A wolf watches over sheep; they devour him. Children spank parents. The father, not the mother, wipes a baby's bottom. The cart goes before the horse; travelers pull a stagecoach. Hens mount roosters; roosters lay eggs. The king goes on foot. The sick man cares for the doctor. The client advises the lawyer. The general sweeps the barracks courtyard. The fisherman gets caught. Rabbits trap a hunter. The goose puts the cook in a pot. The turkey roasts the farmer. A wheelbarrow stows a sack on a man's back. A maiden serenades at a man's window. Tigers in the zoo kill their keeper who was trying to eat them.

Statistically speaking, exchanges in character between animals (cat eaten by mice) or man and animals (farmer roasted by turkey) are far more frequent than changes in natural order, or what culture perceived as natural. The Carnival in Romans was no exception to the rule: the February 9 price list reversed the roles of animals as delectable or as everyday fare for humans, or else substituted animal for human food (hay, straw, oats). Guérin the playwright, however, master of ceremonies and of role reversal, displayed a fertile imagination. He added exchanges between all kinds of dead animals, from rare game birds to pot roast. The overwhelming majority of folk imagery, on the other hand, shows live animals exchanging characteristics. Once again the Carnival in Romans was typical but nevertheless unique.

A weighty symbolism was at work here: among the meat and fowl on Guérin's list were a number of the totem animals of Romans's five *reynages:* sheep, rooster, partridge, hare, capon.

We should not confuse inversion with subversion. It is true that the line between them became somewhat blurred now and then during the commoners' Carnival: for instance, the corpses of the rich were seen as fare for cannibals (*flesh of Christians, six deniers the pound*), and there may have been the stray impulse to change the distribution of money and women, discharging poor

housewives from their functions and replacing them with rich
ladies (A 171). Simply daydreaming this version of things
would have been both an inversion and socially subversive. But
when Guérin and Laroche, in the name of the patrician Carnival, proclaimed the February 9 price list, their primary aim
was using absurdity to illustrate "an *order* in which Nature and
society are soundly unchangeable or untouchable as to facts
and as opposed to myths." They put forth "an upside down
vision, the better to dissipate subversion through amusement."[21]
Granted, this vision unwittingly substantiated through its hys-
teria exactly what it was ridiculing. But what counted for the
political outcome was what went on in the judge's mind, since
he was masterminding the patricians' show. In his case there
can be no doubt: the price list had only one meaning. Stripped
of its Carnival ballyhoo and in view of the way things turned
out, it can be summed up in a simple motto: *order, authority,
royalty.* If men exchanged roles during Carnival it was only to
reaffirm the strength and permanence of the social hierarchy.[22]

The "gentlefolk," then, had named their Partridge ruler.
King Laroche set up shop in the Cordeliers friary, his temporary
palace, conveniently situated for his subjects' intrigues. From
Friday, February 12 on, each royal festivity was more ostenta-
tious than the last. Lacking sergeants-at-arms and police companies (the craftsmen had usurped those functions in Romans),
the wealthy "establishment" created a royal court and an army,
both still in keeping with the atmosphere of "healthy" jesting
appropriate to Carnival (A 155, 156). *On the Friday* (February
12), *Saturday, and Sunday after the said race, which had been held on
Thursday, there was talk of nothing but laughter and amusement. You
would have seen but couriers, ambassadors, sergeants and quartermasters
all over town.* A number of Romans's solid citizens (or country
noblemen who had come to town covertly) costumed themselves
as officers, mounted orderlies, courtiers of every variety, all in
the service of their Carnival monarch. Dusty couriers on horseback and ambassadors oversaw the tragi-comic creation of a
sovereign principality within Romans's walls, where they went
to pay homage. Sergeants and quartermasters designated lodgings for the princely entourage of the Partridge King, who had

just "entered" his good town for the first time; they also designated the house where the various detachments of the "royal" army would be quartered. In fact, all this preparation was psychological and intoxicating, masterfully orchestrated by Guérin. He wanted to make Romans's recalcitrant elements experience it all—that is, surround them with a real or imaginary military atmosphere. The proceedings were not original; the townspeople were familiar with such preparations in custom if not in fact. Romans had an old and joyous tradition of royal processions dating back at least to François I. There was also a newer, more somber tradition of military contingents and all that they imply, carefully cultivated since 1560, the beginning of the Wars of Religion. In February 1580 these traditions were intertwined with the facetious behavior camouflaging or justifying a serious operation: *the couriers carried packages; the ambassadors came to the King's lodgings* (in the friary) *and asked for an audience; the sergeants and quartermasters marked the doors of houses. In short, everything was done for pleasure and to give pleasure to those watching.* The streets were lined with gaping, delighted spectators, dumbfounded by the comings and goings of ambassadors and quartermasters in their town.

Starting with Guérin, the Partridge entourage took their imitation of royalty (in this case French royalty) very seriously indeed. HRH Laroche, while orderlies rode through town on Friday February 12 and Saturday February 13, went everywhere with a mock palace marshal who was in turn flanked by a troop of archers. The Valois kings' system of laws actually provided for just such a palace marshal, a commanding officer whose duty was to run the royal household in an orderly fashion wherever it might be. Within the limits of his courtly functions this marshal decided civil claims and offenses concerning the courtiers, the inhabitants of the town in which they were staying, and the merchants attached to the court.[23] In fact the satirical price list mentioned above was strictly enforced by the palace marshal; he checked on the publicans, innkeepers, and shopkeepers attending to the court (A 156). This coincided with a minor deployment of police forces in the streets of Romans on February 10 and 11: *the palace marshal marched through town with his archers to punish those who would flout their ordinances, which they* (the Partridge partisans) *had made on the price of food.* In this respect, the Carnival in Romans might be described as a meticulous imitation of the rites of royalty within the framework of the midwinter cycle of neopagan festivities.

The presence of the palace marshal's archers probably implies the involvement of the confraternity of archers and arquebusers which held the annual popinjay shoot; in 1580, despite the fact Paumier had won the title the previous year, the patricians seem to have taken it over.

The marshal and his archers policed food suppliers, and in Romans there was no police force without the support of the judiciary. On that crucial Sunday, February 14, Dame Justice made a splendid entrance into Romans: *On Sunday, like an omen of the punishment the seditionists would receive from justice, the* (Partridge) *King's Grand Conseil arrived in the said town, made up of presiding officers, magistrates, attorney, court clerks, process-servers, solicitors, and litigants* (A 158). One could hardly ask for a better description of the real *Grand Conseil* the French kings had evolved. Distinct from the *Conseil d'État* or royal council since 1497, the *Grand Conseil* was a sort of Supreme Court hearing national cases which "the provincial and Parisian Parlements lack the necessary impartiality to judge."[24] The crafty Guérin knew his law well; when he set up his make-believe royal judiciary he was acting with full knowledge of the case. The people of Romans, however, had no notion of what the *Grand Conseil* was all about. They probably connected the judge's parade with the pomp and circumstance of the Parlement of Grenoble (itself the descendant of the *Grand Conseil* Dauphiné had had before its annexation to the crown). Indeed, this august body had on occasion honored Romans with its presence; the dignitaries had made a solemn "entrance" bedecked with special caps, fur-lined cloaks, and other finery. In the Carnival parade the "solicitors and litigants" may have made quite a show, acting out their squabbles and enlivening the judicial farce. Yet under its circus exterior this was serious business, and Guérin meant it that way.

It was customary for the magistrates and officers of a High

Court to come and welcome their king (or queen) when he (or she) was in transit or in residence in their province. On such an occasion, the sovereign had no qualms about lecturing the distinguished jurists who had come to pay their respects, or even reprimanding them. To this day, the President of France receives delegations from the various branches of government, and when Catherine de'Medici came to Dauphiné in 1579 she received the Parlement: *certain of the officers of your Parlement of the province,* she wrote to Henri III (July 18, 1579), *came* (to meet her) *in Montélimar where yesterday afternoon before leaving I had Maugiron gather them together in my chamber, and I thoroughly acquainted them with all the reasons for my journey.*[25]

After Guérin's mock *Grand Conseil* made its triumphant entrance, it ceremoniously headed for the Cordeliers, where the comic magistrates bowed to the Partridge King. Laroche greeted his company, disposed of practical matters *(he ordered his quartermasters to lodge them),* then lectured them, half joking, half in earnest, about real problems: *he very expressly ordered them* (the members of the *Grand Conseil*) *to do justice so that his people would not have occasion to complain and that they* (the magistrates) *should make them* (the people) *all rich, for he* (Laroche) *spoke in these terms only to the gentlefolk, and to the others who would not do their duty he spoke only of hanging* (A 158).

Laroche the Carnival King practiced selective justice. His brand of justice opened the doors to the Cockaigne castle with its fountains flowing with good red wine, moats filled with hypocras, walls made of tarts and sweetmeats, fatted veal pâtés, sausages, grilled meats, and blood pudding.[26] Yet only the gentlefolk and those loyal to them could enter. Laroche dispensed favors where they were least needed. As for the members of the popular faction, they could go hang, and some of them quite literally did.

Sunday, February 14, saw not only a magisterial entrance, but also some opposing *reynages* or "counterkingdoms." Either the people had organized them as a retort to the rich or they had just materialized spontaneously. We will return to these *reynages,* of the Capon and the Hare.

However, if we are to have an overview of the patricians'

Carnival and the processions and the parades it entailed, we should also take a look at what happened on Monday, February 15. *Lundi gras* was the day of the Partridge banquet which was to crown and surpass all the feasting begun on Thursday, February 11. *In the morning of the said Monday, the said Partridge King, having returned to his lodging in the Friary, where the banquet was to be held, left the said place to go to Mass attended by his bodyguards* (A 159). This corps of "bodyguards" no longer consisted of make-believe policemen, like the palace marshal's archers, but of real armed soldiers recruited for the occasion from among the rich or prosperous youth of the town: *his guard was made up of forty fine young men, helmeted arquebusers.* They also wore real breastplates made out of solid metal from the St. Etienne forges. These soldiers carried pikes, the long Swiss kind, some fourteen to fifteen feet long. They formed into ranks commanded by their *chiefs and members;* in other words, their officers and junior officers—captains and subordinate staff or corporals in the bourgeois portion of the town militia. The forty young men had outfitted themselves at their own or their families' expense, or with the help of grants from a few rich supporters of the gentlefolks' cause. Who knows if Maugiron himself did not surreptitiously contribute in order to bring arms into Romans for his friends and Guérin's? Whether from within town or without, instruments of destruction were brought out on *lundi gras.* Both sides polished their weapons, preparing for the best, or the worst. Would they really be used, and if so, what good would the craftsmen's old-fashioned swords be against the gentlefolks' arquebuses?

The forty well-armed soldiers were not the patricians' only strength. Just behind them in the parade marched twenty "Swiss guards," armed and outfitted *with handsome uniforms made to order* (A 159). The uniforms in question are evidence that Guérin and his group had aesthetic conceptions, unlike the "boorish" workingmen; their urban aesthetic appears more than once in Guérin's account (A 160).

In 1580 Romans had mixed feelings about Switzerland. As the Carnival began, even judge Guérin was plagued by nightmares of antinoble slaughter, direct democracy, and commoner communities armed for their own defense. The St. Blaise's Day street dance had been performed to the sound of wooden trumpets and skin drums. But as Mardi Gras drew nearer, the stereotype was reversed; there was an "image change." What the gentlefolk now hoped to suggest by disguising themselves as the citizens of Berne or Basle was the magic power of a formidable Swiss infantry in the streets of Romans. The Swiss army was a traditional ally of the king of France, thus a natural ally of King Laroche, since the Partridge ruler, defending his interests against the popular faction, claimed to be the loyal subject of Henri III.

Immediately following the military parade came a civilian one, impeccably organized by judge Guérin. He knew his protocol far better than King Laroche, who was just a ropemaker. First, with feathers in their caps, came the *crown officials* (probably including the *Grand Conseil* justices who had already paraded the day before); then King Laroche's *chancellor* (the craftsmen's kingdom also had its chancellor, none other than Guillaume Robert-Brunat the draper, and its presiding judicial officer, Geoffroy Fleur the butcher) (A 170). Next came the members of the mock high clergy, *chaplains, bishop, archbishop* (A 159); they recall the prelates of the Feast of Fools. And bringing up the rear, appropriately, marched the "come as you are" delegation of third estate bureaucrats and merchants, *about eighty of the most notable bourgeois, merchants, and citizens of the said town*. For Romans's 1580 Carnival, like Basle's in 1579, everyone prepared as elaborate a costume as his means permitted: *these notables had left no beautiful thing behind in their houses in order to look their best and do honor to their King* (A 160).

The patricians came to a halt at the town's largest church, St. Barnard, and the parade ended with an authentic Mass. Carnival was, after all, a Catholic phenomenon. Paradoxically, it was also a mock Mass, since it was performed by the pseudoprelates fresh from the parade (a sacrilege in terms of orthodox theology). Scattered throughout the Mass were burlesque inventions:[27] *there was music all during the Mass. Ambassadors arrived from everywhere, even the Grand Turk who sent four men dressed in Turkish fashion with turbans and scimitars; after having shown their letters* (of credit), *to His Majesty* (Laroche), *they sat down on a thick carpet they had brought along for the purpose and stayed there on the floor until the end of Mass* (A 160).

Turbans, scimitars, oriental rugs, a scene worthy of Mamamouchi in *The Bourgeois Gentleman*. (Molière, of course, drew on the southern French folklore of his own day for his Turkish scene; it was a richly oriental lode.) Like the Swiss, the Turks were allies of François I, then of the French monarchy in general; they were thus the natural friends of King Laroche. Make-believe arrivals of foreign ambassadors had launched the Partridge festivities the Friday before. On *lundi gras* the entrance of even more pretend diplomats was a logical conclusion to the celebrations. Furthermore, a real Turk, and a gallant one at that, had frequented the Romans region in the late fifteenth century; the local elite had preserved his memory in their traditions.

At any rate, the socially metaphorical parade of governing bodies and the Estates or local *ranks* was typical of Renaissance urban folk tradition. By the second half of the fifteenth century processions of the sort in Paris could include tens of thousands of people, each marching with the confraternity of the corporative guild to which he belonged.

During the decade which began with the Carnival in Romans, Jean Bodin considered urban sociology in the Latin edition of his *De la république* (1586); he elucidated his theory by describing a long procession, a sort of enormous human centipede; a spectator peering down from the town square's belfry would see its interlocking linear segments as the image of the city's social structure.[28] Admittedly, Bodin took a liberal stand: he was perfectly willing to have each town's master of ceremonies determine in what order its citizens would march, given the almost infinite variations in local custom and law. However, Bodin just happened to have a model society on hand, one that seemed to him the very guide a master of ceremonies could turn to if he had questions. The model town was governed, not surprisingly, by a monarch. At the head of the procession, which eventually included the entire (male) population of the urban community, walked the king. He was not included in any group of citizens and was indeed outside the general "order" of the community. Bodin naturally put the clergy after the monarch, then the sacred order of the "Senate," as he called it (he was overflowing with Roman lore). This august body was nothing more than the aldermen or consuls at the pinnacle of municipal government. Next came the military: the head of the army, *imperator* or master of soldiers, leading his dukes, counts, marquis, landgraves, burgraves, barons, vassals, and all the rest of the military, whether they be nobles required by birth to do service, career soldiers, recruits, or simply wearing a uniform for the occasion. (Thus, depending on local circumstances, there might be a professional army, a noble fighting group, or a simple urban militia like the one in Romans, sometimes all three. Also interesting is Bodin's curious amalgam of the ranks of the army and his use of aristocratic titles effectively derived from military grades.)

Behind the soldier the toga-clad legal profession walked at a stately pace: the curia of judges, fittingly honored by their subalterns: orators, jurisconsults, lawyers, litigants, practicioners, attorneys, scribes, scriveners, notaries, messengers, ushers, extras of every description, town criers, secretary-assistants, jailers—the whole herd crowding into forum or courthouse. Next in line were the doctors, pharmacists, knights of the high-colonic, the lancet, the mortar. Then the horde of pedants, the self-appointed know-it-alls, and with them teachers, professors of canon and civil law, medicine, physicists, mathematicians, dialecticians, historians (but of course!), poets, grammarians. Then the merchants, dealers, customs officers, silversmiths, banker-moneychangers, broker-go-betweens, and other profiteers. Next, purveyors to the belly, skeleton, and outer shell of the town: bakers, butchers, fishmongers, fishermen, hash-slingers, cooks' boys, master chefs; peasants and herdsmen living in town; architects, armorers, carpenters, quarrymen, metallurgists, coiners, goldsmiths, jewelers, metal-founders, glassmakers and ornamental glassblowers, public bath keepers, ceramists, makers of trumpets and hunting horns, ivory-carvers, candlemakers. There were also the clothmakers: silkworkers, weavers of wool, goat, and camelhair, linen, hemp, and so on.

They worked in the production of cloth, rope, baskets, clothing, rugs, tapestries, sails, papyrus, paper and parchment. They were followed by curriers, tanners, fullers, wool-scourers, tailors, dressmakers, shoemakers. Then came the printers, their position in line dictated by the newness of their profession; they deserved a better place in the parade, Bodin thought, since theirs is such a worthy trade. Nearing the tail end of the line we come across a column of undistinguished personages, panderers to the sensual pleasures, including sculptors and other makers of more or less undraped statues; painters, paintsellers, flute players, histrions, mimes, market-day wrestlers and other "gladiators"; coachmen, actors, comedy players, lackeys, pimps, procurers. Bodin must have been tempted to put the acting and gaming categories at the very end of the parade; he disliked them because he found they disturbed the order of things. They ought to come, he thought, after the slew of sordid but useful trades concerned with the evacuation of the impure or dealings with the Vagabond: steambath owners, barbers, sailors, innkeepers, stablemen, undertakers, guards, henchmen.

Laroche's parade in Romans was in some ways analogous to its near contemporary: Bodin's dreamlike procession. In Romans, too, the king, the high clergy, the army, high officials of the crown, the patrician bourgeoisie, and the rich merchants led the way, taking the most important, in fact the only, places in the Partridge parade on *lundi gras*. But there the likeness ends: Bodin's soldiers were real generals, or at least they were generals in the half-real, half-imaginary paradigm he proposes. In Romans, on the other hand, not everything was make-believe, admittedly, but everything was carried to extremes. Only the merchants and bourgeois patricians, or part of their number, appeared in their real-life roles of merchant and patrician, if a bit dressed up. As for the "king" and the "high clergy," the high crown officials, they were quite simply solid, beaming citizens of Romans who had put on miters or crowns, thus elevating themselves in the social hierarchy. They wholeheartedly entered into their new, inflated, heavenly roles, but they were full of self-aggrandizement and this boded repression for the populace. They were bolstered by the collective organization embodied in Romans's laymen's abbey of Malgouvert (misrule), to which we will return.

The second difference was that in the *Grand Conseil* parade Romans's craftsmen and tradesmen did not play the authentic role of the professional rank and file of an ordered society that they were assigned in everyday life and in Bodin's procession. Quite to the contrary, they kept to themselves and would have nothing to do with the pageant in the town square. Instead they held impromptu neighborhood Carnivals on the edge of town, refusing to comply with the Carnival hierarchy which placed the king at the head and the lowliest commoner at the tail of the parades; within their own rituals they bowed to the archaic values of Earth, Death, and War, swaying to the dance of swordplay.

Besides, Jean Bodin had taken care to warn his readers: my procession of all the ranks and all the professions carries the risk, he wrote,[29] of conflicts of priority and the possibility of popular revolts. Let us not overdo, he added, except in case of dire need, ceremonies of this kind.

Exactly: by the Sunday before Mardi Gras, as Romans was well into the Partridge King's feasting, the wildcat Carnival celebrations in working-class neighborhoods were causing trouble.

Our two sources agreed completely on the reappearance of popular protest on or around February 14, though, as usual, Guérin and Piémond differed on the details. That Sunday the people's kingdoms either started up again or merely continued: the craftsmen and farmworkers were involved, or course, and some of the town's Huguenots. *In the town of Romans,* Piémond wrote, *the Sunday before the beginning of Lent were held two kingdoms so they might all rejoice together, one of which was held* (the first) *by the great friends, allies, confederates, and comrades of Captain Paumier, general of the League, whom they had made governor of the said town* (P 88). At this first "kingdom," *they ran a hare, a bad omen.* The second sabbath *reynage* Piémond described was put on by *another number of the people of the Union,* in other words the league, also supporters of Paumier: *there a small bird was run.* The "small bird" was a capon[30] or neutered rooster.

The second kingdom was thus called "Capon" but was also referred to as the "slingshot" *reynage*. The contest leading up to the Capon coronation probably required each participant to try to kill the unfortunate fowl with a slingshot, thus winning the day's prize. We know the slingshot was used by Romans's politically restless, discontented youth. The French word for sling was *fronde,* which later took on the meaning of national revolt after giving a name to the Paris uprising in 1648. Did it have a similar significance during the Carnival? It is not unlikely. Once again it is hard to separate athletics, folklore, and politics.[31] The two working-class *reynages* held that Sunday began with the usual chase or shooting of the hare and capon, and progressed into *feasting, street dances and masquerades;* the frolics and politics of the preceding week were continued. As always there was a twin purpose: pure and simple enjoyment, first of all, but social, political, municipal protest as well, clearly illustrated in Piémond's text, as we have already seen: *in their street dances and masquerades they said the rich of their town had grown rich at the expense of the poor people....Fearing that restitution would have to be made, some of the notables and merchants were angered . . .* and so on (P 88).

According to Piémond, the Partridge Kingdom may even have been organized (by Guérin, the rich, and Laroche) in reaction to the Sunday hare and capon incidents: *some of the notable bourgeois and merchants were angered* (by the Hare and Capon *reynages*), *so they tried to put down the most factious* (among their workingman opponents), *and to that end . . . they held another Kingdom in the town hall, which made it the third that was held the Monday of the beginning of Lent (lundi gras); all the richest men were there . . . and a partridge was run, which was not a bad omen like a hare* (P 89). As to the chain of cause and effect, Piémond was in error: the partridge run did not take place on Sunday or on Monday February 15, but on Tuesday, February 9, well before the hare or any capon whatever had come on the scene.

The notary's analysis, however, is very interesting concerning his interpretation of the three *reynages* or "fighting kingdoms" that were irrevocably dividing the population of Romans by Sunday, February 14, and *lundi gras.* Two short months after the conclusion of the Carnival tragedy, in April 1580, Piémond wrote about raids which the various contending factions, Catholics, Protestants, and what was left of the leaguers, were carrying out in the countryside: *we were pillaged by three sorts of men of war, namely the Huguenots and leaguers in the same party, and by the Catholics; that,* the notary added, *was the* (premonitory) *meaning of the three kingdoms of Romans* (P 105).

This text, corroborated by other evidence, described the Hare Kingdom (like its Sheep predecessor) as representing one of Romans's craftsman quarters and contingents, partially supported by the small but influential local group of Protestants. The Huguenots accounted for less than a tenth of the town's population, roughly speaking; as we shall later see, they did not get too involved in Carnival; nonetheless they did participate, supported as they were by that far-off, yet formidable figure, Lesdiguières.

The Capon Kingdom corresponded to another neighborhood, another group of craftsmen and field and vineyard workers (36 percent of Romans's population was active in agriculture!). They were also Paumier-supporting leaguers, but not Huguenots; they remained within the Catholic fold. The very fact they were leaguers, however, implicated them in certain compromises with the Protestants of which Catholic "purists" like Maugiron and the Parlement officials strongly disapproved. The aristocratic Partridge Kingdom, finally, favored the official Catholic party which Maugiron was leading in a fierce struggle with Lesdiguières and his Huguenot followers. Piémond simplified all this into a triple equation:

$$
\left[
\begin{array}{l}
Hare & = Huguenots \\
Capon & = Leaguers \\
Partridge & = Catholics
\end{array}
\right.
$$

We have no details on the Hare Kingdom's technical, political, or religious functioning, with its underlying Huguenot schemes, but we can assume there actually was some type of race with the hare, an animal better adapted to the purpose than the partridge (or at least a partridge with clipped wings).

The Capon Kingdom, on the other hand, has been well described by judge Guérin. He informs us (A 158) that it came into being on *dimanche gras,* the Sunday before Lent, February 14, 1580. He called it Paumier's reply or counterfire in the face of the Partridge Kingdom's *Grand Conseil* parade, which had itself been organized as a rejoinder to Paumier and his men: *the said Paumier and his accomplices, seeing all these things* (the threatening parade held by the patricians) *and foreseeing what would happen to him* (his own murder by the Partridge clan) *and yet without there being any premeditation* (of murder) *on the part of the Partridge he resolved to spoil the sport and came up with the racing of a capon for the major part of the plowmen and handicraftsmen* (literally "mechanical folk" in the language of the time) *of the said town.*

Here, interpretations of the events differ. Piémond's account (quoted above) explains the Partridge *reynage* as a counteroffensive to the Capon (a factual error). Guérin, however, said that the Capon was an irritated reaction against the Partridge; his version stressed the patricians' responsibility for the bloody events to come, contrary to the official viewpoint (meaning the judge's version of the affair). Is his analysis completely correct? The two kingdoms, Partridge and Capon, could also have sprung up spontaneously in the two opposing camps and in the town's different neighborhoods. Once in position that Sunday, Capon and Partridge reacted against each other. No matter what its source, an explosive situation had been created.

The Hare Kingdom was partially Huguenot, since it was held by craftsmen (a number of them had Calvinist leanings). The Capon was more a peasant kingdom and therefore remained Catholic; it primarily attracted the farm and vineyard laborers residing in the Romans neighborhood where it originated—as Guérin says, *the major part of the plowmen of the said town,* plus a few craftsmen.

Thus on Sunday, February 14, the workingmen in the Capon Kingdom *gathered in the number of more than two hundred.* After the capon run or shoot, after they had "made their king," as the expression went, *they walked through the town with their weapons* (A 159). Here Guérin's style is ambiguous, as is often the case. A "walk" has a peaceful ring to it, but still, weapons were carried.

Was it an act of aggression? At all events, there was no longer a ritual welter of flails, rakes, brooms, and little bells which had set the tone for the symbolically murderous parades on St. Blaise's Day a short time before.

On Sunday, February 14, then, an encounter was being planned for the following day, *lundi gras*. A decisive one? Nothing pointed in that direction. *Sunday*, the judge noted, the two hundred strollers *decided to hold their feasting on Monday, the day the Partridge's feast was to take place.* Guérin, like the master he was, furnished the Capon revelers with his own aggressive intentions. He claimed they wanted nothing better *than to pick a groundless quarrel* (with the rich). But the patricians had decided to stand firm, and informed of their adversaries' ill will, *the gentlefolk decided to go all the same* (to their own Partridge feasting, including the parade of dignitaries described above). *In this way, if they were attacked* (by Paumier's band) *they would defend themselves* (A 159).

That same Sunday, when all paths seemed to intersect, there was a historic reunion between Laroche and Paumier. It was to be their next-to-last meeting. Whether by chance or design, the new "King" of the gentlefolk (and Guérin's straw man) met the rebel leader of the Sheep Kingdom in the town square, each of them brought there by the lively political events. Was Laroche wearing his Partridge regalia? Somewhat hypocritically he kindly invited Paumier to the "triumph" to be held the next day, *lundi gras*. (Keep in mind that the craftsman leader had attended the banquet put on by the Eagle-Rooster King, who was soon to demonstrate a most peculiar brand of friendship toward Paumier.)

This time Laroche's offer fell flat. Paumier courteously declined his invitation, and Laroche left the scene. Then the league captain explained the reasons for his refusal to some conciliatory parties who were trying to make amends between the Partridge and Capon kingdoms:

—*You will never find me*, Paumier told them, *in a place where my enemy* (Laroche) *is feasting, if I can help it.*

If he comes to the place where I am, I will not leave on account of him. But I will never go to a place where I know him to be.

Paumier's three-point statement was as clear as a syllogism. This and a few analogous episodes shed light on Paumier's personality. A moderate, self-possessed leader, he was quick to reject provocation in any form, whether someone was picking a fight with him or setting a trap for him. The dialogue also informs us that the feasting in question was the conclusion of the "triumph" that closed a *reynage* (in this case, the Partridge Kingdom).

The meeting between Laroche and Paumier led up to a second, more significant encounter. It may have been unintentional, but it was certainly unfriendly. It caused the Capon and Partridge camps to meet in the streets with a 100 to 150 demonstrators each. This dangerous episode took place on *lundi gras* as the Partridge King's Mass, described above, let out. The Mass was half-holy, half-farce; half-Christian, half-Turk. At the most profound levels of social intercourse, tragedy and comedy often intermingle. We have seen how Laroche and his courtiers, in a grand and orderly parade, proceeded to St. Barnard on Monday morning. *When Mass had been said, His Majesty* (Laroche) *retired to his lodgings* (went back to the friary) *with the aforesaid company* (the various military and civilian groups represented in his parade), *and with the four Turks, who walked before him.*[32] To get to the friary Laroche had to cross the entire town from south to northeast, as if taking possession of Romans.

The four Turks who led the procession and walked immediately in front of King Laroche were the first to cross the path of the Capon parade. *On their way they encountered that mob of people called the Capon Kingdom, also called the Fronde* (A 160). Romans's streets were narrow; the two parades came within inches of touching. The atmosphere was charged. In the first row of the Capon parade was a mounted apparition of death, disturbing and insulting: *riding a donkey, he was dressed up in the cloak of the crier of the confrérie of the Holy Spirit, a cloak of the two colors red and blue* (mourning colors), *the same that was worn in the presence of the dead about to be buried* (A 160).

A donkey leading a funeral parade is easily explained. In the folk tradition of the Rhône region, both Occitan and Franco-Provençal had an *assouade,* the ritual donkey ride endured by a husband whose wife beat him.[33] If the husband was not available, a near neighbor was entreated to replace him, the better to ridicule the unhappy spouse. Putting a donkey at the head of the "poor men's" procession was an insult to the rich men's masculinity. It suggested they did not wear the pants and that in this inverted world of Carnival their wives might well administer thrashings and then move on to better husbands, poorer men, perhaps, but more virile ones. Finally, in a profusion of symbols, it was an insinuation that the patrician's nearest neighbor was the funeral crier, that he would take an unwholesome pleasure in laying them out and putting them six feet under.

Once again, funeral rites came to the forefront in a workingmen's parade. The red and blue cloaks of the herald and the crowd behind him *were worn purposely to give evidence of the massacre they hoped to commit the following day* (Mardi gras), *the day they had chosen for the execution of their unfortunate and criminal undertaking* (A 160).

We can dispense with the judge's accusations of plotting. In fact it was Guérin himself who harbored hostile intentions toward the men of the Capon Kingdom. It was the pot calling the kettle heaven knows what. Yet there is no denying the "poor men" had enacted a large-scale, symbolic funeral procession; on this point the judge was not at all mistaken. It was in the traditional Carnival spirit, half-joking, half-serious. There was an important folk practice around this time of year: the Carnival effigy, sometimes even a live person, disguised as a Carnival character (bear, etc.) was tried, convicted, and buried after a sham execution, drowning, or burning. In Romans in 1580, things were even more complicated; there were in effect *two Carnivals, that of the plebeians and that of the notables, themselves divided through and through*[34]—the rituals of life and death, fertility and killing, skillfully intertwined in the microcosm of the seething town. By Sunday, as we have seen, the Partridge King's *Grand Conseil* was threatening to mete out justice to the opposing Carnival, with the ultimate goal of hanging those who refused "to do their duty." That was the Carnival theme of the forthcoming *trial*, logically followed by execution. It was all performed in the Partridge Kingdoms's best style (in fact, real enough hangings were soon to come). But on *lundi gras* the workingmen gave the patricians a symbolic run for their money.

From the beginning—Candlemas and St. Blaise's Day—the people's Carnival had focused on rituals celebrating death and calling for the burial or cannibalistic disposal of Evil, of the Old, the Corrupt, the Putrid. Thus, on *lundi gras* their black humor—it never went any farther—informed the patricians that the poor would bury them without benefit of a real trial, just as the Carnival dummy was buried or beheaded. *The popular faction was so rebellious,* Guérin added (A 160), *that some of them, intending to mock the price list of provisions which was mentioned above, continued to cry as formerly* (on St. Blaise's Day, February 3):

Flesh of Christians, four deniers the pound!

Words so wicked and rebellious, Guérin noted, *I nearly neglected to mention them. But because they were heard by so many people, even strangers to our town, I did not dare conceal it.*

Once more the theme of cannibalism surfaces, although flesh had now been marked down from six *deniers* to four. Of course, it was nothing but a joke, if a sick one, based on fantasies of eating human flesh. Romans's citizens certainly would not have eaten the liver of some patrician they had just slaughtered. Likewise the "blood drinkers" of the French Revolution were with few exceptions only metaphorical.

All the same, the cannibal theme is a gripping one. It may be linked to the symptoms that psychohistory probes, and surely is related to certain specific rituals,[35] peculiar to Carnival and riots and their cannibalistic inclinations (Agen in 1635 and Montpellier in 1380 are examples).

Guérin gives us a scathing commentary on the Capon Kingdom's blasphemous slogan *Flesh of Christians, four deniers the pound!* He says it deserved a specific riposte from the patricians' Carnival, a cleansing effort supported by God in person. In Romans, one Carnival always seemed to produce a prophylactic counter-Carnival: *I believe that God,* the judge stated, *at once punished them for these wicked words, more than for any of the rest of their evildoing* (A 160).

But wasn't the Christian deity a bit out of place in this affair? In their intimidating folk display, Guérin and Laroche had gone so far as to head up their after-Mass parade with four Turks, rather bizarre disciples of Christ, in fact, diabolical characters.

It is true that the judge had more than one trick up his sleeve: at this point in his narrative he set aside his customary eulogizing of the Catholic religion and tapped his schoolboy stock of Renaissance classical learning. He no longer labeled the Capon revelers as simple blasphemers against the baptised and therefore against the sacrament of baptism. No, he heedlessly painted them as *Scythians* bringing their native savagery to bear on that veritable Athens of the Alps, the good town of Romans. Did Guérin take himself for Demosthenes? *The Scythians and the greatest barbarians in the world,* he wrote, *could not have done so much evil as they* (the Capon supporters) *had decided and resolved to do* (A 160). Admittedly, the Athenian digression in the judge's narrative is quite brief. The Partridge faction quickly lost its identity as Greek (that is, the opposite of Scythian) and once again became Catholic, even ultra-Catholic. To be exact, Guérin referred to it as "the Mass party." A specific allusion, it recalls the serious/farcical and Turkish/Christian rite that had been celebrated that *lundi gras* morning for the crowd of gentlefolk in their splendid dress.

We left the two kingdoms just after that Mass, when Partridge and Capon had just rubbed elbows, though hardly in a friendly fashion, in one of Romans's narrow streets—an unpleasant but brief encounter. They went their separate, opposite ways. The Partridge group thus returned to the friary, King Laroche's palace, to sit down to the midday meal ("dinner"). The grand feast, for the 140 royal followers, so-called high officials, pseudocareer soldiers (though they were fully armed with real weapons), was worthy of Carnival in every way. *To come back to our subject,* the King Laroche *went to dine with the Mass party* (the Partridge Kingdom) *where there were a good seven times twenty plates piled high with everything that could be got* (A 161).

After the dinner (with 140 seated guests, as Guérin indicates), came the dancing, not in the friary but in the town hall. The "beginning of Lent" ball in Romans was traditionally organized by the "abbey" of Bongouvert, alias Malgouvert or Maugouvert (Good government or Misrule), a jolly fellowship controlled by the young and older patricians and dependent on the consuls. It was also under the omnipresent watchful eye of judge Guérin, who oversaw folk ceremonies along with everything else in town. The members of this counterfeit abbey were laymen, yet their confraternity remained half-religious (contributed sums for the rebuilding of the town's religious premises and for the wages of Lenten preachers). Its duties, at once farcical and official, were to police weddings, *charivaris,* pre-Lenten dances, the *chambrières'* dance, and to put up the Maypole, a tall post topped with the branch or trunk of a verdant pine tree. The abbey fellows set the Maypole in the town's main square, its marketplace, in honor of maidens and courtship, in conjunction with the month of May and Pentecost celebrations. These direct descendants of the ancient rites of spring were preceded by the ball Maugouvert held each *lundi* and Mardi Gras, celebrating romance, maidens and young women, courtship and marriage. Rife with patricians, the Partridge Kingdom was on very good terms with Maugouvert, as the Parlement of Grenoble's subsequent inquest made clear.[36] From the time of the footrace on Thursday (February 11), the patricians' *reynage* had accorded an important place to the second, or fair sex, in contrast to the Sheep, Capon, and Hare kingdoms, which, if not blatantly misogynist, were not geared toward women. The Partridge King happily demonstrated his fondness for the ladies: *Laroche, after dinner, went to the town hall where the ball was set up with a good number of the ladies and damsels of the said town.* The words "ladies" and "damsels" indicate that the women attending the ball were for the most part members of the patrician bourgeoisie.

The bourgeois center of Romans, then, on this day of revelry reached romantic heights. Men and women sought each other out, formed or reestablished ties. At the same time, the Partridge's military plot solidified, strengthened to the rhythm of the dance, though it was not a virile one like the sword dance so dear to the lower class and the Sheep Kingdom. It was time for a redefinition of differences and loyalties. But first, a touch of Carnival gallantry and diplomacy was in order.

The Eagle seems to have taken the first steps toward a rapprochement; the Partridge suffered a sweet trespass gladly. *During the ball,* Guérin reports, *there arrived some heralds* [37] *from the*

Eagle king (A 161). "Herald" meant an army officer (in this case a Carnival version); once again we find an obsessive imitation of the rituals of Dauphinois or French royalty. The envoy wore a crown and had the fleur-de-lys embroidered on his outer clothing, specifically on his chest and stomach. He carried a special rod. By virtue of the power invested in him, a herald transmitted his royal superior's summonses or challenges to a duel to fellow monarchs, friendly or hostile. He also supervised tournaments. The Eagle's herald, in Romans, *brought a challenge to the Partridge King* (Laroche), *in which he* (the Eagle) *complained about what was going on within the borders and confines of his own kingdom; he* (Laroche) *had not deigned to send envoys to him nor invite him to his feast* (A 161). The Partridge's various parades had indeed proceeded through the immediate area of the Rooster-Eagle's territory (the Jacquemart quarter) without making the requisite show of friendship. The Eagle was thus attempting negotiations across a border, in this case the frontier between the marginally bourgeois Jacquemart quarter and the more elite neighborhood around the town square and the Isère bridge. The procedure normally involved a chivalrous combat at a frontier or the gate to a town, with friendly competition and détente as its goals; all of this made good neighbors, even within a town. The Eagle pretended to believe there had been some misunderstanding between him and the Partridge (indeed, the Eagle's partisans had at times demonstrated support for the league, if moderately, while the Partridge's subjects had by and large stayed clear of the peasant league). "Has Laroche haughtily ignored me," the Eagle asked, speaking roughly and dramatically, "because of some resentment of me?" If so, "I offer him the combat of my person against his own."[38] The prospect of a sham battle between two males brought to mind mating combats and displays, a sure sign of spring. The rest of the Eagle's message was positively flirtatious: "If Laroche has acted that way *out of scorn, let him know that the Eagle in his flight could take the Partridge at will,*[39] *even if she were protected and half covered by a rock.*" Guérin himself pointed out the double pun obviously intended for his lofty Parisian audience; it was simply wordplay on *Laroche* (the name means "rock") and his union, mystical or otherwise, with the Partridge (feminine in French).[40] Thus, the emblematically feminine wild bird had two suitors. First was the Rooster-Eagle, Romans's super-male, half barnyard sovereign and bird of prey, able both to puff out his reddish comb and to hurtle through the skies toward his delectable prey. The second suitor was Laroche, symbolically half-engaged in a loving embrace with his darling partridge, a scene his rival threatened to interrupt. The theme of two rivals vying for the heart of a lovely lady was typical of Carnival. On or around Mardi Gras it was a frequent theme in the street theater common to all of central and northern Italy, which was very close to Dauphiné culturally as well as geographically.[41] But at winter's end, and in the spring, this theme also gave rise to tournaments; by the last third of the sixteenth century they had taken the form of tilts at the ring, and so on. The result of such contests was that the loved one bestowed her symbolic or real favors on the winner. Everything had been done in chivalrous fashion and sealed an *entente cordiale* between the participants, who were more likely sporting competitors than enemies. That is exactly what happened in Romans the afternoon of *lundi gras. Peace was made quickly* (between the Eagle and Laroche), *for there was no great dispute; the better to swear and insure this peace, it was said that they* (the two monarchs) *would meet an hour later, on horseback and carrying the lance, to tilt at a ring, which was done* (A 161).

A tilt at the ring did not have the quasi-warlike character of the older tournaments. The competing horsemen rode at full gallop and tried to tip a ring atop a vertical support or pole onto their lances. They might also try to pin a *faquin*, meaning a dummy or simply a "turk's head" (the term has come to mean "scapegoat" in French) or some other effigy of a head which was placed on the ground; the horsemen were supposed to hit it or knock it over. Whatever the object, games of this sort were part of armed rituals that had been so typical of Carnival's earlier incarnations. Such games also appeared during the various spring festivities a few weeks after Carnival. Thus, the ritualized jousts foreshadowed, then were part of, the reawakening of spring and of rebellion, even fostering it, almost like magic. At the same time, the jousts worked in the interest of social and geographical integration. The wedding of the Duke of Savoy's children in 1608 involved celebrations costing a million *écus* in gold (150,000 just for fruit preserves and torches), including a tilt at the Carnival dummy followed by a huge folk ballet: Savoy hunters, sailors from Nice, country-men from Val d'Aoste and countrywomen of the Piedmont performed, each speaking his or her own language (French, Italian, Provençal). It was a reaffirmation of Savoy's unity, multiprovincial and multilingual though the duchy might be. Likewise, in Romans, the Partridge parade was a ritual defi-nition of the bourgeois quarter around the town square and the bridge, tracing its limits as far as the Cordeliers friary. And later that day the two kings, Eagle and Partridge, held a tilt at the ring to reseal the coalition between their two half-friendly, half-rival neighborhoods.

The play battles over rings, effigies, or neighborhood borders actually concerned the stirrings of sexuality, of fertility, grow-ing toward the end of winter and in full bloom by Easter, the lovely month of May, and culminating on Midsummer's Day. In 1620, the Queen of France, Anne of Austria, stood on the Place Royale in Paris (today Place des Vosges) looking at her young husband, Louis XIII. A tear in her eye, a smile on her lips, it thrilled her to watch him charge and thread a series of rings onto his lance . . . awaiting, as she had been for some time now, the day he would make her a mother. More generally speaking, be it in Savoy, Dauphiné, or Île-de-France, the ladies, both humble and grand, were the passionate stakes in these jousts celebrating the marriage of a princess, the amorous ex-ploits of a king, the pleasures of an imaginary land. The *lundi gras* tilt at the ring in Romans was no exception to the rule. It was referred to in metaphors punning the idylls of the Partridge with her Rock (Laroche) or her Eagle. The tilt was followed by an elaborate ball where the ladies of Romans displayed their beauty. The ball began with a masquerade during which eager Carnival characters escorted a resplendent queen. *After these two kings had tilted at the ring,* Guérin informs us, *the Partridge King led the Eagle King to sup with a part of his entourage and his troop; and once they had supped they went to the ball, where there came a mask* (masquerade); *after that there was another, very beautiful one with four kings leading a queen, who was so sumptuously dressed that she was all aglitter. . . .*

Night comes early in February; it had fallen on the Partridge's social whirl. Was the masquerade lit by tapers? By torchlight? Whether or not it was brightly lit, the royal feasting was on an ambitious scale. There were two kings in attendance, and two additional make-believe kings appeared from the merry ranks, for a total of four. Lest we forget, there were already three kings of the people: Sheep, Hare, and Capon. Not to mention Paumier, the regal Bear and uncrowned king of the league. A town of 7,000 with eight kings: the ratio was disproportionate. There was bound to be trouble.

At the beginning of the dark yet festive night of *lundi gras,* in the last moments before the final fray, an overview of the situation seems justified.

We should first consider the bestiary our Carnival has assembled, animal by animal. The craftsmen and plowmen took the bear, sheep, hare, capon, donkey (in that order); the patricians, the rooster, eagle, partridge. Diagrammed, this gives:

		eagle	partridge
(Upper) Patricians		rooster	

			capon	
(Lower) Craftsmen and plowmen	bear	sheep	hare	
				donkey

The contrasts are striking: the patricians chose airborne or at least winged animals. The three birds embody the dominant classes: upper as compared to lower, airborne as compared to earthbound. The popular faction included only one bird in its collections: the capon, a castrated, domesticated creature—in short, a weakling. The capon's counterpart in the patricians' bestiary was the rooster, bristling up, flapping his wings, calling to his harem with his masculine crowing, all actions the capon's state in life precludes. The patricians' animals are sexed, distinguishable. It hardly needs to be pointed out that the rooster, in age-old imagery, represents a sort of walking, feathered phallus; but the eagle and the partridge as well were linked in flight on the afternoon of *lundi gras.*

The poor men's animals, on the other hand, were castrated (the capon, perhaps the sheep) or bad omens (the hare) or symbolically mismatched and neutral from the sexual point of view (bear, sheep, hare, capon, donkey). In other words, there was no chance they would mate, even symbolically as the eagle and partridge were rumored to do (but would not have in nature). The bear alone might embody a savage masculinity, but in classic Carnival symbolism he represents violation in general; he does not affirm the union of a chosen couple, wedded or not.

Thus the animals chosen by each camp were a faithful representation of the dual Carnival and its consistent symbolic system: the wild and earthy orientation of the commoners' St. Blaise's Day *reynage,* with its particularly significant emblematic animals; and the nuptial, airborne orientation of the patricians' *lundi gras.*

Symbols aside, the shifts in alliance and power plays that accompanied Carnival should be examined. The Eagle and the Partridge had a complex, fickle relationship: pseudotiff, flirtation, ring tilt, "mating flight"—all of it ending in a solid rapprochement. It was a dramatic illustration of the way certain groups within Romans realigned their positions. The Eagle-Rooster's subjects were former league members who had "gone astray." They had originally supported the urban and peasant Union's efforts toward peace and had opposed taxes and outlaws, and so on. Then they broke off from the league and its Romans (hardliner) variant because of the violent and "seditionist" tendencies attributed to it: *the said Eagle King showed with his troop that although most of them had formerly been of the said "League" they did not like nor did they support the mutineers* (A 161).

Besides, as was often the case under the *ancien régime,* per-

sonal, or rather family, quarrels added one more divisive element to an already deteriorating political scene. Among the
leaguers who had rallied to the Eagle, now joined to the Partridge for better or worse, were some men who, at the outset,
were among the most unruly of the troop of seditionists (Paumier's men).
But a family incident (A 162) had subdued them: some of their
relatives had been attacked and wounded by comrades of theirs,
even though they were all members of the pro-Paumier, pro-
league faction. Fighting does not always make friends of men.
Those responsible for the incidents had been imprisoned on
charges of attempted murder. The dominant faction within the
league had wanted to free the captives, despite the fact that
their incarceration was warranted. Paumier's men took advantage of the position of strength they still occupied in Romans—
if not for long—to release the prisoners. This flagrant travesty
of justice irritated the league members who were related to the
victims of the attack. They therefore rallied to the Eagle and
the Partridge, and *having gone over to the gentlefolk, effectively showed*
they did not at all like (Paumier's supporters); *and they caused much*
astonishment to the said troop of seditionists, wrote Guérin. (Let us
reiterate that in Guérin's vocabulary *seditionist* meant a hardline
leaguer or supporter of Paumier.)

The first two weeks of February should certainly be depicted
as full of Carnival commotion, festivities, kingdoms, and gatherings, in the midst of an uninterrupted stream of peasants,
merchants, and mule-drivers who had come to Romans on
business and for news. Even during the holidays it was business
as usual. People came to town to sell wheat (large-scale farmers, merchants, mule-drivers) or to buy it (small farmers, consumers, all those who did not produce enough for their own
needs). In December 1579, for instance,[42] 240 setiers of wheat
came into Romans through the Jacquemart gate, another 28
through the St. Nicholas gate. (These two were the "agricultural" gates to the town; at the north end of Romans, they led
to the grain-growing open country on the northern bank of
Isère.) Simultaneously, sixty-four small buyers from the sur-

rounding country parishes bought 166 setiers of the wheat in small lots of two or three setiers, each of which they would take back home to their mills and ovens. A few larger mule-drivers may have exported the wheat even farther from Romans (although in any case it did not go terribly far); they thus bought up wheat on the Romans market in rather heavier "loads" of ten to twenty setiers. The setier which was then calculated at 112 *livres* weighed 56 kilograms, or slightly more than 123 pounds; thus they loaded a maximum of one ton of grain.

On February 5, 1580, when the commoners' festivities were already well under way, seventy-one rural buyers are mentioned as coming into the town to "take out" the wheat that had been brought in. On February 9, as the *reynages* became more frenzied, there were sixty-three buyers purchasing their modest stores of grain ... and taking an active part in the merrymaking as well as supporting the people's complaints and demands. (The monopoly requiring transportation in such small quantities by mule rather than carts, which were more efficient for transporting grain, automatically multiplied the number of wheat-buying tourists in Romans.) The list could go on: on February 20 there were about a hundred visitors buying 220 setiers of grain that had come in the same day through the Jacquemart gate, and so on. From December 21 until February 12, 3,763 setiers came into Romans; 4,619 went out—a slight deficit. The harvest year 1579–1580 had produced an adequate supply of grain, thus allowing the town to draw on its stores for exportation. After all, the recent harvest had provided a substantial stock, and the people's purchasing power was in good shape since they had been able to pay taxes that year. However, the result of all this was apprehension on all sides (which heightened resentment during Carnival time). The urban lower classes felt it: they nervously watched Romans's supply of wheat leaving town.[43] The bourgeoisie, too, was afraid: might they not be attacked by all these peasants coming to town to buy grain? Mardi Gras drew near, though no one realized what it would bring. Guérin had his plan, his personal lightning rod—or perhaps simply the rod he would not spare the people.

Romans, February 15, 1580, the evening before Mardi Gras: as night fell on the quiet Dauphiné city, it became alive with suspense. Knives hit the whetstone. At the tables the patricians had laid in the Cordeliers friary, the night began with a huge spread, with sausages and lard. It ended in blood and tears. Mardi Gras day would go by like a nightmare, and might as well have gone straight into the mourning of Ash Wednesday.

With few exceptions, contemporary witnesses are rather close-mouthed about what went on in Romans on February 15 and 16. Just-Louis de Tournon, the governor of Vivarais, in a letter to Catherine de'Medici dated February 18, sheds only a feeble light on Romans's darkest night. He speaks of *some commotion and small execution* (sic) *carried out of late by the most outstanding of the town of Romans against some of the league of that town, and the principal leaders of the latter* (the league leaders). In another letter sent to Henri III the same day, Tournon attributes the events to irreconcilable differences between the elite and the league: *the most outstanding of the said town were no longer able to bear the many mockeries and indignities to which they had long been subjected by those of the league; in the end* (the "most outstanding") *were forced to attack* (the leaguers) *and crush them.*[44] Tournon noted that several noble gentlemen, including one of his own officers, Monsieur de Veaulnes, had come to the aid of Romans's bourgeois patricians. *With this assistance, they* (the "most outstanding") *killed some small number of men, the principal leaders of the said League as well as others of the most seditious.* All that was left to do was thank the Almighty for defeating the leaguers: *strength, thanks to God, remained on the side of the Outstanding of the town with the help of the neighboring noble gentlemen who subsequently joined them. . . . The said place* (Romans) *remains henceforth under your obedience* (obedient to royal commands) *and in favor of the Nobility of the region.* A happy ending, Tournon informed the king: just consider that the town of Romans *was for a time one of the most seditious of Your Realm.*

On one point the count's letter is invaluable: it confirms the collusion between Romans's bourgeois patricians and the noble gentlemen from the surrounding countryside. Other than that, it adds little to the details furnished around February 18 by a certain Sibeuf, a league partisan wounded in the fighting. Three tumultuous days later (according to one account), Sibeuf managed to escape over the walls of Romans and head for the country north of Isère, where he informed the peasant communities of what had happened. *The powerful of Romans were killing the people, which frightened the people* (P 89), whereupon they took up arms. Exit Sibeuf. Piémond, the notary, and judge Guérin gave a more detailed account in their narratives; we shall now return to them.

According to Piémond, the primary responsibility for the massacre fell on the "rich men" of the Partridge Kingdom, whose supporters, writes the notary, *retired toward Night* (Monday evening, February 15, 1580) *to the town hall* (to hold their feasting) *and to ready themselves, not for dancing, but to do away with the protesters.* In other words, they were preparing a coup against Paumier and his men, whom Piémond dubs "the Capon faction." From the start, Piémond accuses the notables of having planned the bloodshed. And he continues: *after they* (those of the Partridge) *had supped, they made ready the ball; a mask then came there,* meaning the masked parade of the "four kings and a queen" Guérin has already mentioned. The splendorous and dazzling masquerade seems to have attracted a horde of spectators, perhaps ever eager admirers, from the town's entire geographical and political spectrum. The prospect of gazing on the masked ball brought *the people flocking,* even *certain of Paumier's faction* (P 89). Precisely at this point on *lundi gras* day, perhaps toward nine or ten o'clock in the evening, began the fighting Piémond claims was deliberately set in motion by the Partridge, flanked by the Eagle-Rooster: *the men of the Partridge, being closely watched by those of* (Paumier's) *faction who were there to watch the masquerade, all came out* (of the ballroom). *They began to charge.* They massacred all the Capon-Paumier supporters they could lay their hands on: *some were killed, others wounded.* Those of the Partridge *repeated this attack all over town, from guard house to guard house* (P 89). Another armed group also left the ballroom in the town hall and headed straight for Paumier's house: *they go to Captain Paumier's door,* Piémond reports; *hailed by certain persons of his acquaintance, Paumier comes down to his door, knowing nothing of disturbances. He is killed by a pistol shot* (P 89). On this account, some of the leader's friends who chanced to be present or came running when they heard the commotion, *were killed or massacred in the fury* (by the Partridge "commando"). *Some escaped...* (P 89).

Guérin relates the events that took place between Monday evening and the following night in more detail and more deceitfully. Let us take another look at the last part of the judge's text quoted above: *After the tilt at the ring, the Partridge king led the Eagle king to sup with a part of his entourage and his troop* (A 162). It appears from the context that this supper took place in the Cordeliers friary. *Once they had supped, they went to the ball* (held in the town hall). The whole town was dancing and singing, so their princely stroll turned into a parade from the friary to the town hall, with a short detour toward the Isère bridge. It was a proper folk procession: the two kings, Eagle and Partridge at the head, followed by their respective entourages. Next came a group of masks, or masquerading revelers, then a second; we have already met the second masked group—*very beautiful, with four kings and a queen, who was so sumptuously dressed that she was all aglitter.* By this time the head of the procession, led by Laroche and the Eagle-Rooster, had reached the ballroom, already bustling with fiddlers and Romans's fine ladies and damsels. As for the tail end, it was still in the streets, not very far from the bridge, when the attack—according to Guérin's version, radically different from Piémond's—occurred. The judge informs us it was not started by the Partridge Kingdom, but by the Capon King's followers who had, as we know, come to watch the masked spectacle. Exhilarated by the sight of the exquisite queen, her jewels, her train, her finery, and her entourage, the Capon men are alleged to have moved a bit too quickly to the offensive, in the hope of pillaging the queen, raping her, or rummaging beneath dresses, bodices, whatever . . . This *was cause,* Guérin states (A 162), *that a troop of seditionists* (the Capon faction), *not having the patience to wait for the appointed hour of their plot* (against the Partridge), *which was not until six in the morning; and seeing what seemed to them an easy way to a rich booty, flung themselves upon the latter* (the queen and her following) *with their drum sounding the alarm* (A 162)—the same drumbeats that punctuated so many events in Romans and the surrounding countryside.

Guérin's version is, clearly, diametrically opposed to Piémond's, if not in terms of facts, at least in terms of the intentions attributed to each of the factions. The judge, reporting to Catherine de' Medici and the court bureaucrats, wanted above all to convince them, rightly or wrongly, of the existence of a Capon conspiracy against the Partridge: he says an attack was set for Mardi Gras morning at six, just before dawn. But the time was moved up to *lundi gras* night due to the wantonness and thirst for lucre the masquerade had inspired in Paumier's followers. Unable to restrain their base instincts, they were sent into a sudden frenzy at the idea that they could assault the lovely Partridge ladies, their swains, the damsels at the ball. Under these conditions, the "gentlefolk" were put in a state of legitimate self-defense; they did not fail to resist. When the Capon bullies wounded some of the young patricians who were at the rear of the Partridge procession, the rich youths then turned the tables and *bore up* on their attackers, as Guérin has it. *Whereupon Paumier's men* (A 162), *seeing they had been found out, decided to force the guard house at the bridge, which they were near.* (This guard duty was performed by a splinter group of the urban militia which remained faithful to the municipal government, Guérin's party.) *But they were so ill-received* (by the guard house soldiers) that they were forced to retreat to their neighborhood, not without having been soundly thrashed.

Once again the importance of the warring bands' respective bases of operation comes into play: according to Guérin's analysis (full of half-truths), once the Capon men had been "thrashed" by their opponents, they went to recover their strength and their morale in the working-class Le Chapelier quarter which had always been their bastion and one they considered impregnable.

At this point Guérin and Piémond concur on the Partridge troop's exit from the ball. The judge, a rather biased narrator since he himself masterminded the operation, reports that the armed men rushing out from the dance floor were acting in self-defense. Piémond, however, says it was a punitive act of aggression. *Meanwhile,* the judge continues, *the rumor reached the town hall* (where the ball was in progress) *that it had come to blows* (there had been a skirmish at the rear of the parade) *and that the murderers were coming for them. . . .*

Note the reversal of the sequence of events: in Piémond's version, the exit of the Partridge partygoers (armed soldiers) provoked the skirmish with the paraders, while Guérin maintains it was exactly the opposite. Let us continue with his version: *. . . and that the murderers were coming for them, which so frightened the women and angered the gentlefolk gathered there, that having gone out with the arms of which they found themselves possessed and fortuitously* (sic!), *but quite by the will of God having formed three troops able and ready to do combat if the occasion required* (these three troops exceeded thirty-six men in all), *one troop went straight to Paumier's house . . .* (A 163).

Next comes Guérin's version of Paumier's death; before we examine it, however, a few thoughts on the text up to this point are in order.

First of all, the *fortuitous* character of the organization of three armed detachments, speedily assembled by the patricians, is ludicrous. The three troops, each made up of a minimum of twelve men, had access to the Carnival weapons (which were not toys) the Partridge Kingdom had been brandishing for the past few days. They may also have raided the urban militia's arsenal, kept at the town hall where the fatal ball was held. But there was nothing *fortuitous* about the mobilization of the three troops: as a letter of Maugiron's indicates, it had all been arranged secretly several days earlier.[45] A striking fact is that Guérin had scarcely put down the ridiculous term *fortuitously* when he changed his mind and instead attributed it to *the will of God;* He alone was responsible for the patrician shock troop's exit from the ball and for their victory. Guérin did his best, however, to second Divine Providence. Or was God no one but Guérin himself, a *deus ex machina?*

The second train of thought we should pursue concerns women. As Guérin relates the causes of the fighting, he twice seems to say *"cherchez la femme."* First he describes the Carnival queen, attired like a lifesized relic, *so sumptuously dressed that she was all aglitter.* He declares it was the sight of this walking icon, female and queenly, that sparked the premature attack by Paumier's group at nightfall, and he maintains that the men suddenly realized the possibilities offered by the situation to pillage and plunder other of the upper-class ladies.

The second mention of the so-called weaker sex in this part of Guérin's account concerns the commotion outside and the rumor, true or false, of imminent murders (inevitably preceded by rape) in the town hall. This *frightened the women* in the ballroom and spread panic, which in turn caused the patricians' defensive, then punitive, retaliation. They decided to put a stop to things once and for all.

Was the judge completely in error in alleging that feminine panic primed the fighting? On the contrary, there was probably some truth in what he wrote. The young men of the lower classes in southern French towns were no angels ("young" meaning anywhere from the ages of sixteen to thirty-six). In various articles,[46] Jacques Rossiaud has described the bands of young males, journeymen or apprentices, that wandered the darkened streets of the small cities in the lower Rhône basin; they literally "chased skirts" and practiced gang rape. There were a great many of these juvenile delinquents, representing a large share of their age group. They fell heir to the tradition—however diluted—of the fourteenth-century's raging *charivaris;* whenever there was a wedding, young and violent practical jokers broke into the church, "smashed crucifixes, insulted the priest, beat the newlyweds," then looted the couple's new home. Sometimes they dragged the young couple down to the river for a dunking or took them to the local brothel as a finale to the nuptial festivities. Such brutish behavior, tamed but not really eliminated with the passage of time, did not mean the lower classes were entirely unromantic. Nonetheless, their good conduct did not even approach the more polished, tender, and ritualized courtly behavior that flourished among the young patricians of both sexes—members of the abbey of Maugouvert, in the bourgeois milieu of Romans, Lyons, and elsewhere.

These institutions buzzed with sweet nothings, and the woman, lady, damsel, or "novice" in the "abbey" was an object of adoration rather than humiliation.

Enlightened attitudes toward women came and went, but the lower classes maintained the medieval tradition of male chauvinism and brutality toward the second sex. There is some excuse for them; the urban world they lived in was a frustrating one. Many young women had married men twice their age, and were therefore off limits to the younger men. One might raise the objection that the frustrated young men could always have satisfied their instincts, for lack of a better solution, in various houses of prostitution: public brothels officially established by the town, or privately owned baths that had "beds everywhere, bathing facilities nowhere to be seen," where plump girls boldly frolicked; there were also "small private bordellos kept by madams," or finally, the girls who were in business for themselves.[47] However, these were but a poor remedy at best and were challenged by an as yet quiescent puritanism, for in the late sixteenth century the Reformation and Counter-Reformation threatened the very existence of prostitution. Brothels were often shut down; then the young plebeians' aggressive instincts shifted toward the rich men's wives or daughters, particularly when Carnival permitted an outburst of sexual joy or madness, culminating in Mardi Gras. This outburst is what the youth "abbeys" tried as best they could to discipline, to channel into courtly behavior, the feminine reign of pseudokingdoms, and also into flirtation paving the way to marriage (the object of the Mardi Gras ball). Despite such control valves, lapses were always a possibility, especially during periods of popular revolt. If there was panic among the patrician ladies at the Partridge ball and the damsels in the queen's entourage in the street, it was not entirely feigned, nor was it unjustified; the Capon men probably planned to take a few liberties—fondling, pinching, and so forth—perh'ps even rape some women. The women's panic was not, however, what produced the patricians' conspiracy; Guérin had arranged that well in advance of *lundi gras*. But it did hasten the execution of the plans, which had probably been set for later, say, Mardi Gras at six in the morning, if we assume that Guérin's report attributes the judge's own intentions to his adversaries, the members of the Capon Kingdom.

The Partridge men's surprise attack, which they feared would be forestalled, was thus precipitated by a distressed, panicky crowd reaction suddenly sweeping through the ballroom, principally among the women.

Paumier's murder once more affords us the opportunity of comparing the testimony of our two witnesses, judge Guérin and Piémond the notary. According to Piémond, Paumier, who knew nothing of the disturbances, was seen coming down from his room on the second floor to the door of his house. He had been called there by an acquaintance of his (a traitor?). When he crossed his doorstep he was shot dead by a pistol, by one of the men from the Partridge ball commando group. Piémond's version exculpates Paumier, and makes Guérin ultimately responsible for the life of the craftsman leader.

Guérin's version, however, tries to gloss over certain facts (although they are indisputable, considering the homespun, disinterested character of Piémond's account). Be that as it may, one of the three troops of a dozen men each mustered in the ballroom (Guérin writes) *went straight to Paumier's house* (perhaps they knew what they were up to). *They found him outside, accompanied by eight or nine of his accomplices* ("accomplices": such vocabulary dooms the men it designates. Some of Guérin's phrases really leave much to be desired . . .). So Paumier was outside with his *accomplices* (Guérin's version) and not "inside his house knowing nothing of the disturbance" (Piémond's version, with which, by the way, Guérin could not have been acquainted). Using one of those linguistic tricks at which he was so adept, Guérin suggests at the outset that his main opponent, already out in the street and surrounded by *accomplices*, was not entirely blameless in the affair.

The detachment of young patricians from the ball who had set out fully armed for Guérin's house was commanded by Laroche himself, the Partridge King. (Naturally Guérin did not bloody his hands himself, but let his friends or faithful retainers do the dirty work. We have already witnessed his cunning, secretly murderous attitude during the St. Bartholomew's Day massacres in Romans in 1572.) Laroche, Guérin tells us, then planted himself before Paumier's doorway and there, like a latter-day Cicero, made a speech to his former friend, now his close enemy, *amicably demonstrating to him that he was wrong to have them* (the Partridge paraders) *attacked while they were entertaining themselves* (holding Carnival festivities), and that it was contrary to the promise that he (Paumier) had made, which was *that all would live in peace and friendship with each other* (A 163). The real neo-Cicero, however, was the judge, who wrote the speech and had Laroche deliver it, the better to indict Paumier (by then he was a corpse) of having planned the imagined or real attack against the Partridge Queen's masquerade. This accusation is about all that matters in the slim and trumped-up brief brandished by Guérin. At the same time, the smooth-tongued judge mentions—by means of Laroche's supposed speech—the vague promise Paumier had made to Catherine de'Medici that all would live together harmoniously. This promise had been lightheartedly violated by the unhappy times and unyielding men ... the more so since the said promise had been made on the condition that the Queen Mother would accept the third estate's egalitarian *Cahiers*. She never did.

Things were happening fast; it was not the time for speeches. The Laroche-Guérin faction moved to act and carry out their *blitzkreig* in Romans. The episode that followed was the symmetrical inversion of what had happened a few days earlier—on Tuesday, February 9. On that day one of Paumier's men had tried to wrest command from his leader and fling himself, sword and all, on Guérin's men. Paumier swiftly calmed the potential attacker. Now it was the same thing all over again, but vice versa. Laroche was "overwhelmed" by his supporters. But he gave in a bit too easily: "a young man of the said troop (Laroche's) noticed the arrival of people *à la fille audit Paumier*." Here there is a problem with the original text; should *à la fille* be read as *à la file,* people "moving in file," given the instability of sixteenth-century orthography; or could it literally mean *à la fille,* friends of Paumier's daughter (we know he had a daughter)? In any case, *the young man, seeing that these people were gathered and could do much ill, said loudly: "Enough talk," and approaching the said Paumier who had a halberd in his hand, struck him a blow in the face with a boar-spear; then suddenly Paumier was hit by two pistol shots and stabbed several times* (A 163). The boar-spear slew the wild beast, the bear Paumier had been, now dead as if in the wild. But then all of Laroche's troop rushed in with pistols and swords. With help from his men, the Partridge King had eliminated the Candlemas Bear. Guérin's account is damning for his own faction this time, since he acknowledges that his men had murdered Paumier, without provocation, once the initial boar-spear blow had been struck.

Paumier was dead, his followers discomfitted. *Some of them fled,* Piémond writes. And Guérin, more exact, remarks that the brutal passing of the popular leader *so frightened the accomplices* (encore) *of the said Paumier who were there present that they began to flee and abscond, some over the walls with ropes they had readied, others swimming across the Isère* (A 163). Panic had first spread through the ranks of the patrician women, the excuse for the Partridge men's attack, with the result that the poor men or popular faction panicked; the rout thus produced finally put an end to the intolerable distress the Capon partisans had kept suspended, like a dark cloud, over Romans's power elite. Guérin, in effect, welcomes the beneficial consequences of Paumier's slaying in cold blood. Stunned by their leader's death, *all the others of the said league,* the judge relates, *partially lost the will to defend themselves.* It is true Guérin wanted above all to persuade us that the booby trap Paumier had fallen into was intended to defuse the craftsmen's coup which was supposed to take place the following day, around six in the morning. On this point, the judge is far from convincing: There is no reason why we should not believe the craftsmen might have been devising a military plot, set for dawn on Mardi Gras; but neither is there proof of one. This reasonable doubt removes any immediate justification for the Guérin faction's bloody act as a preventive measure. As the judge's otherwise unruffled editor J. Romans writes, "The disarray which followed Paumier's death, and the lack of energy or resistance on the part of the leaguers, lead one to think . . . that their plot against the lives of the gentlefolk of Romans, if indeed there was one, was not at that time ready to be executed" (A 163 note 1).

VIII

Mardi Gras 1580 or,
God on Our Side

Paumier's death and the popular faction's disarray brought an end to Carnival, properly speaking. On the other hand, the blood-soaked Mardi gras of 1580 may well have expressed the essence of the institution, founded on conflict, expulsions, and murders (usually symbolic, yet quite real in 1580): ". . . for within the hollow crown . . . of a king/ Keeps death his court," Shakespeare wrote, and that includes Carnival kings.

From this point on, the various parties simply tried to get even. If the situation could not be described as civil war, it was at any rate more intense than simple street fighting in a town of 7,000 inhabitants. Laroche's tiny troop had just cut Paumier down and scattered his inner circle, but did not remain tiny for long. The Partridge troops' prime objective was to gain control of the St. Nicholas gate and the quarter of the same name on the far eastern edge of town, just inside the walls. This was the poorest and one of the most agrarian neighborhoods in Romans. The average per capita tax paid there was only 2 *écus* (in the *taille* roll of 1583, which was broken down by quarters).[1] There were no taxpayers who could be called wealthy (those who paid 12 *écus* or more). St. Nicholas was the home of many plowmen (again, in the French Midi the word simply meant an agricultural worker or farmer, including the very small-scale ones). The 1583 *taille* roll is far from exhaustive concerning

social and professional categories, yet it lists twenty-five plowmen in the St. Nicholas quarter. They were far from rich, with
their tax averaging 1.5 *écus* per family. Further, the same *taille*
roll shows fifty taxpayers who were craftsmen, including thirteen carders who paid an average tax rate of 2 *écus*, and who
often rented their living quarters and workshops. There were
eleven middle-level drapers, eight of them paying only 2 *écus*
each and the other three little more; four weavers who paid 1
and 2 *écus* each; a handful of butchers and bakers, not much
better off than their craftsman neighbors; and there was even
a bookseller (paying a paltry 2 *écus* tax) in this plebeian quarter.
It was nonetheless the home of Romans's primary school, which
did not help the neighborhood's socioeconomic standing, although it did give the town an intellectual cachet. This was,
then, a predominantly craftsman and urban farmworker milieu,
and a poor one. It did not produce the leaders of the town's
league movement. However, the St. Nicholas neighborhood and
social milieu were likely to furnish the grass roots support for
the popular faction, and no doubt participants for the Sheep,
Hare, and Capon *reynages* as well.

Guérin and Laroche therefore considered control of the St.
Nicholas quarter essential to the total domination of the city
and elimination of Paumier's followers. Otherwise, the neighborhood would have posed a threat to the Friary, Jacquemart,
and St. Barnard quarters where the bourgeoisie was based.
Paumier's corpse was still warm when Laroche's sergeants-at-
arms and shock troops, armed to the hilt, rushed toward the St.
Nicholas gate and the one beyond it, the Bistour gate in the
eastern ramparts. *This troop*, Guérin writes, *went from there* (the
site of Paumier's murder) *to the St. Nicholas and Bistour gates.*
After some combat, partially due to confusion on the part of those standing
guard, being gentlefolk, and in part due to ill will (resistance from the
neighborhood leaguers), *the said gates were seized*, and placed
under the name and authority of the king (in fact under Guérin's
authority; "the king" was a handy catch-phrase). *After establish-*
ing guards there, they returned to the said square (the town square or
marketplace near St. Barnard's church), which was *the favorite*
meeting place of the gentlefolk (bourgeoisie).

Back in the town square, the rapidly swelling ranks of the Guérin-Laroche faction were in their element. The bourgeois craftsman quarters in the town center extended from the Friary to the Jacquemart tower and the church of St. Barnard, and encompassed the town hall and square; very few plowmen lived there, and the numerous craftsmen who did were in constant contact with the notables, whose houses were either grouped together or spread out in these neighborhoods. The Friary quarter in the northwestern part of this large central sector had an *average* tax share of more than 3.2 *écus* per capita, a very high figure, relatively speaking. The 1583 *taille* roll census (far from complete, to be sure) reveals only two plowmen, two carders, and two drapers in the Friary quarter; a meager showing. Insignificant in number and wealth, they paid only 1 or 2 *écus* tax each. Most of the craftsmen and tradesmen in these neighborhoods catered to the needs of the privileged classes: in the Friary neighborhood there were no fewer than three butchers, paying 2, 3, and 4 *écus,* and then shoemakers, each at about 2 *écus,* except for one rated at 5.5 *écus* (a fondness for new shoes, a privilege restricted to prosperous citizens, was a sign of an emerging "consumer society" at the end of the sixteenth century). The quarter had two innkeepers (one of whom operated the Red Hat at 2 and 3 *écus*; two goldsmiths, one of whom, Jean Arnaud, paid 16 *écus* 57 *sous*, putting him in Romans's top tax bracket (in 1583 that meant anyone paying more than 12 *écus* tax). The other goldsmith, Jean Malbruny, paid only 3 *écus* 26 *sous;* a relative of his, an armorer with the same name, also lived in the Friary neighborhood and paid 2 *écus* 40 *sols.*

Wealthy bourgeois families, perhaps patrician, dominated the Friary quarter; among them were the Velheus (Monsieur Charles Velheu paid 14 *écus* tax) and the Thomés. Four Thomés are listed, including *Jean Thomé the elder,* probably the aforementioned Parlement official, who shared his wealth with both Grenoble and Romans (paying 12 *écus* in his home town); *Jean Thomé senior,* son of Mathelin Thomé (3 *écus* 40 *sols*); *Jean Thomé the younger,* also a son of Mathelin (5 *écus* 20 *sols*); and finally a Philibert Thomé (4.5 *écus*). Two members of the Guigou clan, one of the town's great consular families, were also residents

LA VIL
EN

Based on *Cosmographie universelle de Munster enrichie et augmentée par François de Belleforest*, 1575. Bibliothèque de l'Arsenal, Paris. Photo Lalance.

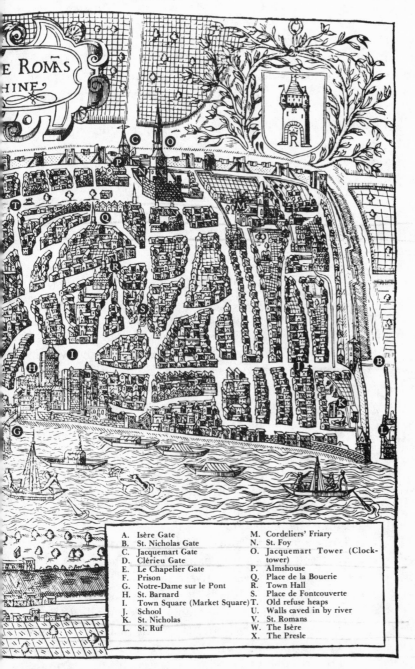

E ROMĀS
HINE

A. Isère Gate	M. Cordeliers' Friary
B. St. Nicholas Gate	N. St. Foy
C. Jacquemart Gate	O. Jacquemart Tower (Clock-tower)
D. Clérieu Gate	
E. Le Chapelier Gate	P. Almshouse
F. Prison	Q. Place de la Bouerie
G. Notre-Dame sur le Pont	R. Town Hall
H. St. Barnard	S. Place de Fontcouverte
I. Town Square (Market Square)	T. Old refuse heaps
J. School	U. Walls caved in by river
K. St. Nicholas	V. St. Romans
L. St. Ruf	W. The Isère
	X. The Presle

and contributed 19 and 7 *écus,* respectively. So was Jean Peloux, the consistorial advocate, and last but not least Romans's most substantial taxpayer, Captain Antoine Coste, one of the nota-bles' most important leaders, who easily outdistanced everyone in town at 96 *écus* 30 *sous.* He undoubtedly owned a great deal of real estate.

Another name stands out in the *taille* roll for different rea-sons: Jean Robert-Brunat was a close relative of one of the leaders of the popular faction, Guillaume Robert-Brunat. Jean was quite well-to-do, paying a healthy 9 *écus* 40 *sous* tax, indi-cating that the leaders of the popular movement were cousins or even closer relatives of rather wealthy families, cloth mer-chants and others, who lived in the respectable Friary neigh-borhood.

The Friary quarter centered around the Protestant Church (perhaps closed down in 1580) and the Morin wharf, which was situated at the southern edge of the quarter and to the west of St. Nicholas, in the east-central part of town. Laroche and his men could count on this area as their "bastion." Distin-guished citizens, including judge Antoine Guérin himself, were among its residents. Guérin had had the foresight, however, to have himself legally exempted from taxes; his judgeship earned him the privilege. In the same quarter we find another note-worthy homeowner, Antoine Garagnol, the vice-bailiff of the bailiwick of St. Marcellin, whose jurisdiction included Ro-mans. Besides being Guérin's father-in-law, Garagnol was a very prosperous citizen and paid 20 *écus* 42 *sous* tax. There were also a few really rich families: Antoine Bonnaud senior paid 40 *écus* 2 *sous* tax. His nephew, Antoine Bonnaud, paid 10 *écus* 20 *sols* (*sol* is an alternate spelling for *sou*).

The Protestant church and Morin wharf quarter was another with very few agricultural workers as residents. The 1583 *taille* roll lists only two plowmen, respectively taxed at 1 and 2 *écus.* One of them did not even own the house in which he lived. The scarcity of farmworkers was due not only to the faintly bour-geois flavor of the neighborhood, but also to the fact that it was far from any of the town gates. Transporting crops for any distance through the narrow and winding streets in the heart of an old town made no sense. However, this semifashionable

neighborhood did have a number of craftsmen—even protester—residents. It was the home of four drapers, a low figure
for the town, paying 2 *écus* each in tax, three shearers (also at
2 *écus*), three dressmakers, three carpenters, and the biggest
group, nine carders (again at 2 *écus* tax).

Like Romans's other neighborhoods, this quarter had its
share of "poor" taxpayers (five or six are designated as such in
the *taille* roll): widows, the elderly, sick, helpless, or simply
destitute, taxed at the very low rate of less than 1 *écu* (for
instance, at 30 or 50 *écus*), "considering their poverty." Those
designated as poor, then, belonged neither to the craftsman nor
the plowman groups, whose ranks taken as a whole might be
said to constitute what we might think of as the poor. The
craftsmen averaged 2 *écus* tax per capita. The *official* poor, therefore, played no significant role in Carnival.

The penultimate sector in the central and bourgeois bastion
was the Jacquemart neighborhood, wedged into the rich or
semirich areas of Romans.[2] A latecomer to the Guérin fold, this
quarter was still of two minds. Its divided loyalties, or lack
thereof, have already been portrayed in its political and Carnival behavior. First leaning toward the popular faction
(pushed by its craftsman core group), it went over to Guérin
and Laroche at the last minute as the result of bitter family
feuds and various other reasons that alienated it from Paumier's
camp. The change of sides came about through a diplomatic or
folk process replete with kingdoms, tilts at the ring, alliances,
feasting, and so on, all intended to convince the Jacquemart
residents that the new bonds between their ranks and the patricians were sturdy ones. Wheeling and dealing was quite
probably part of the shift in alliances: some of the Jacquemart
leaders would be promised consular or other municipal offices.

Like the sociological "superstructures," the substructures
were ambiguous. What the Jacquemart quarter really wanted
was to butter its bread on both sides.

It was not, on the one hand, a particularly wealthy neighborhood. The average share paid by its 295 eligible taxpayers
was only 2.27 *écus*, low for Romans. The low tax rate was in
keeping with certain of the neighborhood's socioprofessional
characteristics. There was a somewhat impecunious core group

of craftsmen who were enthusiastic about the league in 1579; sixteen carders, a high number, eight of them quite poor at less than 1 *écu* tax each, and the other eight slightly better off at 2 or 2.5 *écus*. Then there was an assortment of craftsmen, each the only one of his kind in the neighborhood: a crossbow maker, a dressmaker, a potter, and so on. On the other hand—and this is why a quarter like the Jacquemart was so ambivalent about political protest—there were very few of the drapers who played such an activist role in Romans. Only three very modest drapers (each paying less than 2 *écus* tax) lived in the Jacquemart quarter. What is more, plowmen were few in number (only seven, including one "elder" who paid 5 *écus* 30 *sous*; the rest paid the standard rate of 2 or 2.5 *écus*). This relative deficiency in the agricultural sector was another reason the Jacquemart quarter was less than apt to go along with the hardline protest attitude favored by the heavily agrarian Capon Kingdom. It cannot be too strongly emphasized, and this we shall later study, how deeply rooted the Carnival in Romans was in the practical, political, and mythical life of the surrounding agricultural communities.

Another possible reason for the Jacquemart quarter's conservative tendencies, in keeping with the law and order party's standards, was that craftsmen notwithstanding, it was a rather bourgeois part of town. Some of the oldest, if not the richest families of Romans's patrician bourgeoisie are represented in its *taille* rolls. Jean Odoard, for example, paid 4 *écus* 50 *sous* tax as a resident of the Jacquemart quarter. There were also families with great fortunes in real estate, including some who won renown in the Partridge Kingdom. (Gabriel Loyron, for instance, paid 40 *écus* 21 *sous*; Gaspard Jomaron—one of Guérin's staunchest supporters—38 *écus* tax in 1583.)

We have seen that the strategic Jacquemart sector was bordered on all sides by quarters which the bourgeoisie controlled, though they were not in the majority (that is, the Friary, Protestant church, and Morin wharf quarters to the east and south). To the west and southwest, lay another area under bourgeoisie control, the relatively wealthy Paradis neighborhood;[3] it had 234 eligible taxpayers who contributed an impressive average of 2.71 *écus*. It was the home of some of the well-known and well-off notables, whose names are familiar to us: Jean Jomaron, Laurent de Manissieu (10 *écus* tax), and Jean Guigou (27 *écus*). Then came professional men living in genteel poverty: three notaries (1, 2, and 3 *écus* each) and a painter (quite poor at 1 *écu* 20 *sous*). The Paradis quarter housed six plowmen, a low number in keeping with the "trendy" tone of the neighborhood. They were assessed at the standard 2 *écus* each. A good many craftsmen, quick to rail *against* the bourgeoisie, also lived here (the Paradis quarter was very close to the craftsmen's bastion, the Clérieu neighborhood to the west). Among them were eight carders, paying about 2 *écus* per capita. They were often the tenants of the rich or the noblemen. There were also eight drapers, also in the 2 *écus* bracket. Shearers, weavers, harness-makers were residents . . . and so were the families of some of the most notorious 1579–1580 protesters. Two taxpayers in the Paradis quarters, a man and a woman, bore the common name of Fleur: they were probably related to Geoffroy Fleur, the butcher who was hanged in 1580 after the Carnival "incidents," on the charge that he had been "president" or director of the craftsmen's *reynages*. Another Paradis quarter protester was Michel Barbier, sieur de Chamlong, a rich lawyer and future consul of Romans (1586) who lent his generous support to the peasant leagues in 1580, and became a leader in his native village. After 1580 and its upheavals, he was indicted by the Parlement of Grenoble, then acquitted, which left him free to pursue his very successful career.

We have not completed our tour of Romans's central district and bourgeois "bastion." The working classes were of course in the demographic majority, but the bourgeoisie prevailed to such an extent that Guérin and his men could count on the neighborhoods of the Friary, Protestant church and Morin wharf, Paradis, and Jacquemart.

Let us now return to the endless, bloody night of *lundi gras*. Guérin's armed partisans had already taken control of the outlying St. Nicholas quarter and its gate on Romans's east side. Their tactic was to take the west side of town, still *attacking from guardhouse to guardhouse, weapons in hand* (P 89), the same method

Horace used against the Curiaces. Small, well-disciplined troops took the scattered and poorly entrenched popular forces one after another. It is clear which side was on the offensive and which had planned its attack, at least in terms of *tactics:* the Partridge side. On the other hand, Paumier's faction quite possibly had certain aggressive intentions, *strategically* speaking; but it had neither the time, the means, nor the opportunity to carry them out.

From the St. Nicholas quarter at the far eastern edge of town, Laroche's men attacked the outlying Le Chapelier quarter, also just within the ramparts but directly across town from St. Nicholas. *One of the said troops,* Guérin tells us (A 164), *went to the Chapelier quarter . . . where it ran up against resistance and a few barricades* (A 164). The members of the troop *were thus forced to bloody their hands against the rebels . . . by means of which those who feared for their lives* (among the Paumier faction "rebels") *abandoned the fort to the gentlefolk.* The "fort" in question was most probably the guard house at the Le Chapelier gate in the town's stout ramparts. We shall soon examine the strategic importance of this gate as a link between the urban "seditionists" and the leaguers from nearby village communities.

But first a word or two about the Le Chapelier quarter. The fact that it resisted the judge's troops, however briefly, may be surprising at first glance, since the neighborhood was on the very edge of town and cut off from the rest of Romans by a stream dotted with cloth mills, the Presle. It was also one of the poorest sections of Romans. In 1583 the Le Chapelier quarter had 151 eligible taxpayers at an average of 2.23 *écus* each, a rather low figure. Furthermore, not one person whose name or fortune would show him to be a patrician is found in the 1583 *taille* roll for this neighborhood. The two residents paying the highest taxes contributed 7 *écus* (instead of the 10, 20, 30, 40, even 90 *écus* in other "nicer" quarters). Even the equally poor St. Nicholas quarter on the opposite edge of town had a slightly richer taxpayer, at 12 *écus*. The Le Chapelier neighborhood housed five plowmen, designated as such, paying 2 *écus* each; a carter (who had worked as a domestic servant) at 2 *écus* 6 *sous*; a street porter, two paupers, respectively paying a half *écu* and two-thirds *écu*. There were a few textile workers (a draper, 2 *écus*; two bleachers and three carders at 1 and 2 *écus*, a shearer at 3 *écus*). The overwhelming majority of residents, all paying 1 or 2 *écus* tax (the 1583 *taille* roll lists only family and given names for them, with no indication of profession) was very probably made up of unskilled workers, plowmen, insignificant vineyard owners and employees, as well as other agricultural workers who did not own land and who also worked on embankments as the need arose. We know there must have been winegrowers since a prized wine in Romans was called Chapelier.[4]

The neighborhood, where the young Partridge fighters had had to *bloody their hands*, was considered the link between the urban and rural protesters, between city and country leagues. This is hardly surprising. The wine-growing, rustic residents of the Le Chapelier quarter were very different from the craftsman and bourgeois milieu to the east, in the center of town. It was a sort of country parish within the town walls, empathizing with the rebellious peasants outside and surrounding Romans. The Le Chapelier quarter had the same interest, troubles, complaints, and demands. It was probably also the birthplace of the Capon Kingdom (could there have been a play on the words *chapon*—capon—and *Chapelier*?). Paumier lived almost all the way across town from the Le Chapelier district, not far from the Isère, between the town hall and St. Nicholas; yet the Le Chapelier was his for the asking. His supporters there call to mind the *Lenturlus*[5] in Dijon, bacchanalian winegrowers crowned with trailing grapevines who led a 1632 revolt in the Burgundian capital. Their motto could just as well have applied to the Le Chapelier quarter: *rally round my green plume*. Romans's working-class Carnival had for a fact become more and more agrarian, beginning as a drapers' celebration on St. Blaise's Day in 1579 and concluding with the plowmen's Capon Kingdom on *lundi gras* 1580.

Guérin shuddered at the thought of the town-dwelling farm-workers and their country leaguer friends joining forces, which

is almost what happened during the early and violent hours of
Mardi Gras. Eustache Piémond mentions the abortive union
only through an isolated example we have already examined.
The notary maintains (P 89) that a certain Sibeuf, wounded by
Guérin's men, escaped over the town wall that fatal night,
fleeing Romans and the massacres. He ran to the village of St.
Paul as fast as his wounds allowed; there, he gave out the news
that *the powerful of Romans were killing the people, which frightened the
people. As soon as that was known around Romans, a great number of the
communities* (incorporated villages) *gathered to bring armed relief,
about 1500 men who did not dare to appear at the gates to Romans*
(unfortunately so, Piémond seems to imply), *for if they had gone
promptly to the Clérieu gate, Captain Roux, known as Leguire, who was
inside there, would have let them in.* (We should understand by this
last sentence that Captain Roux, one of Paumier's supporters,
had barricaded himself inside the Clérieu guard house to spare
himself the Partridge troops' wrath; if the peasants had shown
up at the gate and if they and Roux had had enough presence
of mind, he could have let them into town . . . but, fortunately
for the Partridge commando, that did not happen.)

Guérin gives more details than Piémond on this point. He
reports that a troop of "seditionists" started to sound the tocsin
in the ruined church of Saint-Roman-du-Chapelier, just when
Guérin's commando had successfully completed its assault on
the Le Chapelier gate. The sudden clanging sent the victors
racing toward the church, unwittingly leaving the gate they had
just captured wide open. What is more, Paumier's supporters
in the neighborhood had *broken the bolts and locks on the said gate,*
to make it easier for their village friends to come storming into
town, should the occasion arise. Alerted by the mournful tolling of St. Roman's tocsin, the peasants from the rural communities to the north and west of town (most of them very
unruly villages at that) then began to sound their own tocsins
as well. From all around, *the villagers assembled* in the middle of
the night *at the sound of their bells and horns* (wooden trumpets).
The din was heard. A troop of 800 to 900 villagers was able to
muster and march; *in fact, this troop appeared* at Romans's ramparts *and it went as far as a mill adjoining the Clérieu gate, and in the
moats of the said town, to the number of 800 to 900* (villagers) *at the*

least. Some twenty of them came into town through the Chapelier gate (which had been left open) *and more than thirty paces within* (the town). *They would have gone on . . .* had they not been seized *with fright, upon hearing the fighting that was going on* (in Romans) *and finding no one there that they knew, although they had been promised someone would meet them* (A 164). They were so frightened *that they went out again. They abandoned the said gate* (Le Chapelier) *and the moats, and they retreated* (through the fields) *in such disorder and confusion that if twenty cavalrymen had attacked* (the villagers) *the horsemen would have made such a wreck of them that they would never have forgotten it.* Guérin would have shed no tears if the moats of his town had held with a few slaughtered peasants, a good lesson to the surviving riff-raff. But there was no massacre, and the judge resorted to a refrain expressing his habitual (and quite sincere) piety. *It must be true,* he writes, *that God did this act* (that He spared the villagers). Their day was soon to come, however: six weeks later (March 26 through 28) 1500 to 1800 men were killed at one fell swoop in Moirans.

The Le Chapelier connection[6] between the countryfolk and towndwellers was thus paved with the best of intentions on both sides, but never realized. The theater of Romans's little war was shifting more to the east and northeast, toward the Clérieu gate and its quarter. Quite a theater it was, too, torchlit on the bloody night of *lundi* to Mardi gras. *It should not be omitted,* Guérin writes, *that on the said Monday there were many torches carried by little children who took no more note of the fighting than if it had been a game. That was much to the advantage of the gentlefolk, and frightened those who hated the light above all* (A 168). Again, we should bear in mind that Mardi Gras comes forty days before Easter, at the new moon, meaning a dark night. That would have encouraged the less than gentle folk in all their evil designs. Had these torchbearing children been recruited to illuminate the street fighting? They left a trail of fire and murder in their wake; they made it possible for the Partridge troops to have their battleground lit bright as day. The result was the deaths of a few Paumier supporters who otherwise would have been able to hide in convenient nooks and crannies. It was like a tragic Caravaggio.

Yet there was no Machiavellian plot behind the torches.

They were not premeditated; they were simply a folk tradition. Called *brands,* they had their place in the Catholic pre-Lenten celebrations, in the children's kingdom. Every year at Carnival time youngsters paraded with these torches, symbolically intended to kill rats, the insect pests preying on fruit trees, and the field mice that harmed harvests and egg production. The ritual guaranteed a good harvest of apples and hemp for the next fall, and eggs and chicks for Easter. It was a rite of purification and fertility. On the mythical level,[7] *all* of Carnival was geared toward insuring fertility over the months to come.

Guérin's reflections on the Le Chapelier fighting and the symbolism at work in Romans feature a deadly interplay of light and shadow. The shadows were thick with people in blackface and masks; their agrarian stamp on the festivities was evident in the noisy frolicking beginning with St. Blaise's Day, and the Sheep and Capon Kingdoms. Then, in contrast, came the high-toned parade of birds (eagle, partridge, rooster); the rich men's kingdoms acted out the gradation of superior states and ranks. It closely represented the celestial hierarchy: heaven and earth, night and day. The shining, Christian, purifying, and fertile flame of the torches, in the dark night before Mardi gras dawned, naturally had its place in the scheme of our Carnival. Against the black, macabre, demoniac masquerades of the poor was the heavenly light of the torches. Tatters and fancy dress, beasts and birds, castration and sexuality, all did battle in the class struggles of this Mardi gras, eventually coming together on the mythical level, and in their respective ways, earthly or lofty, joining in the extermination of parasites and insuring fertility for the coming season. The Partridge King had killed the Carnival bear. Now Guérin, like St. George, would slay the dragon.

The abortive battle of Clérieu, on the town ramparts, was Romans's last domestic struggle during the small hours of Mardi Gras. It gave a starring role to a character Guérin's faction considered essential. He kept a close eye on the little Dauphiné city from beginning to end of Carnival. His attitude

was all the more commendable since He had many other problems to tend to and bigger ones at that, what with all of France
caught up in religious strife. Not until after 1600 would the
nation truly regain its composure.

At the start of the February events in Romans, God (yes, it
is Him we are talking about) was mainly occupied with the
leaguers (according to Guérin) who opposed the patricians. In
other words, he had kept a watch over *the people* and the *gentlefolk*,
as the judge called them. He had made the drapers, carders,
and others who had plotted the 1579 St. Blaise's Day festivities
lose their hearts and minds (A 33), but He had also ordained in his
infinite wisdom and Divine Providence that the rebels would be
punished as early as that same spring (A 36). He had aroused
some village dwellers: although they were leaguers, they forestalled the outlaw Laprade (A 37). He had divested Laprade
of his common sense (A 40). He had given the gentlefolk to
understand that He would not let these wicked doings go too
far—which inspired the gentlefolk to temporize for a little
while (A 46). Now, during the Chapelier fighting, He had just
spared (only He knows why) the dreaded troop of 800 peasant
leaguers: they were vainly attempting to come to the aid of
their urban, Paumier-supporting friends. A few days earlier,
God had been outraged by the dreadful cursing one of Paumier's comrades had indulged in. In the same vein, He had
decided to punish the Sheep and Capon subjects for their cannibalistic chants of *Flesh of Christians, six deniers* the pound (A
152, 154, 160). He had taken note that the gentlefolk refrained
from such obscene language.

The fact was that since the end of 1579, God had stopped
being interested solely in the leaguers (for quite a while they
were the object of His solicitude, since He wanted to rub their
noses in their own evildoings). Now He was more concerned
with the gentlefolk. He had advised moderation, a *wait-and-see*
policy, with Jean Thomé as his mouthpiece. Then the snail-like
Thomé had been replaced by the hard-shelled, claw-equipped
Guérin. At this new juncture, God, the almighty joker, did not
find it beneath his dignity to enter directly into the buffoonery.
He had thought up a Carnival trick beforehand; it would allow

the Partridge partisans to trick, to overthrow, their Capon opponents; now He whispered the plan to Guérin (A 151). With a little help from His subordinates, God was preparing to deploy His terrible swift sword to the benefit of the gentlefolk. As a result, Guérin's use of the word *people* changed: he first used it to designate the *seditionist* leaguers who had come *unbridled* in February 1579 (A 34). Toward the end, however, the term *people* crossed over to the other side, into the heavenly host of the gentlefolk. From there on it designated God's chosen people, latter-day Israelites: faithful to their God and to their king, they were about to put their plan into action and enjoy revenge. At the close of 1579, God chose to act directly on the patricians' *hearts,* an organ He viewed as an empty container. He filled them with a seething zeal, bent on exterminating unrest. The Clérieu confrontation was the *opportunity* God devised to grant the gentlefolk victory (A 161). Once this fatal step had been taken, the battle won and the town liberated, God was requested not to stop His efforts there. It was hoped He would keep the gentlefolk under His wing and shield them from their wicked opponents (A 170). He had answered the fervent prayers of the bourgeoisie, and Guérin personally. Worshipful thanks, honor and glory were due Him for the success of the judge's friends (A 171). Guérin's narrative is truly uplifting.[8]

The paradox is that the history of the Carnival in Romans provides us, thanks to Guérin, with a day-by-day account of God's reactions. And yet we know almost nothing of Paumier's thoughts and feelings; he was an antihero without style or substance, but still the acknowledged leader of the people. It must be admitted that very few faces emerge from the crowd in our records. Romans was richer in situations than in characters to study, richer in sociology than psychology.

Let us bear in mind that the judge's God is specifically contemporary as well as universal. He came after Calvin and before Malebranche. The townsfolk of Romans saw Him as acting personally, not through the Virgin or the saints. He was thus a child of his time, revised and corrected by Calvin, before the strong comeback of a baroque, virginal, sanctified Catholicism. We should not forget that Guérin was all the more fanatically Catholic for having undergone the influence of Calvinism, as his neighbors did, for a time.[9] It was not something he was proud of.

But Guérin's God, despite his modern, Calvinist side, was still archaic in other ways: in 1580 He was not above intervening in the course of history, even the history of a small city like Romans. A century later, to the contrary, Malebranche's deity was more like a listless constitutional monarch in heaven, a forerunner of Louis-Philippe, perhaps. He refrained from changing the course of human events with His arbitrary lightning bolts. He delegated authority, let the laws of Nature and Society handle everything. He had created them, after all, for just that purpose.

would an American historian think to talk of God so sarcastically?

The references to God were fundamental to the judge's writings and the gentlefolk's thinking. It was probably much the same with their opponents in the popular faction. Yves-Marie Bercé has compiled a statistical index of words appearing in the manifestos and other texts of the Croquants in Périgord (1595). As we have seen, the Croquants were quite similar in spirit to the Dauphiné leaguers. Bercé's study shows that the word *God* is used more than any other in these writings. The Croquants' God was on permanent call in their judicial revolt (He would charge a high fee). No doubt it was much the same with the oral pronouncements of the discontented Dauphiné peasants and townsfolk, with Paumier in the lead. Death made Paumier the Christ of the revolt, except that he failed to rise again after three days.

We can only guess at the elementary Christianity or Deism of the rebels; they left no writings like the ones Bercé used for his study. The leaguers were more men of action than of words. What is more, they were often illiterate. All we know about their thoughts and feelings has come down to us in the overly learned voice of third estate jurists from de Bourg (1576) to Delagrange (1600). (See Chapter XIV.)

The Clérieu battle, no matter how heaven intended it, was played out on earth, against the background of ramparts and ramshackle houses. What can we say about the Clérieu quarter, the site of the leaguers' last stand in Romans?

In the main, it was the home of craftsmen, some of whom were prosperous. The 1583 *taille* roll shows 257 taxpayers living there, with an average tax assessment of 2.61 *écus*, quite a substantial sum. It was neither agrarian, nor basically poor, far from it, in fact; only five of its residents were designated as plowmen (one was poor, paying only 1.5 *écus*, the other four were of modest means, at the standard 2 *écus*). On the other hand, there were fifteen carders; a good number. They were a beggarly lot, paying 1 or 2 *écus*. Then there were seven drapers, two at 2 *écus*, two at 3, and, remarkably enough, two who paid 6 and 7 *écus*, thus part of the elite of prosperous and enterprising drapers. They were even above the level of the two top drapers in the protest movement, Paumier and Brunat. We also find two weavers, two dressmakers (2 *écus*). It was really a textile district. Four bleachers and three millers appear, paying 1, 2, and 3 *écus* (the mills were on the Presle, a stream cutting through Romans on the west. The residents of the Clérieu quarter, then, were predominantly processors (especially in the production of textiles), while the Chapelier quarter was primarily one of producers (of farm crops and wine).

Another characteristic of the neighborhood was that it housed no members of Romans's oldest families, nor any of the richest: not one resident was in the 12 *écu*-and-up tax bracket (as in the central part of town). There was one exception: the heirs of the deceased council member Velheu were taxed at "nothing" (they may have been exempted from taxes).

It is easy to see how this working-class quarter—rather prosperous but with no "white collar" patrician residents—had become, under the late Paumier's direction, the craftsmen's last bastion, at loggerheads with the bourgeoisie. (Paumier himself, however, did not live here but farther east, close to the Isère.) Two weeks earlier, Clérieu may well have been the cradle of the Sheep Kingdom, so to speak.

It is equally easy to see how, despite this, the "gentlefolk" had a certain influence in Clérieu, working as they did against their most powerful opponents in the league, trying to sway the most prosperous craftsmen, not all of whom supported Paumier. In fact, when the confrontation began, the Paumier and Guérin factions, if not united, were at least barricaded together inside the guard house at the Clérieu gate.

And with good reason, for the Clérieu quarter and its gate were in a strategic position; hence the bitter dispute. The neighborhood stretched from the gate (to the north) to St. Barnard's, and as far as the Isère bridge (to the south). It flanked the entire western half of town: taking Clérieu meant taking Romans.[10]

Two of the night-owl Partridge detachments hastened to the Clérieu gate: *these two troops, small in number yet great in courage* (A 165) *saw that God was granting them so great an opportunity, which was to place the town once again in obedience to the king, and recover its honor . . . they set out for the Clérieu gate, where a great number of the said seditionists* (the Capon men) *had retreated pell-mell with the gentlefolk of the neighborhood . . . all together they were barricaded.* In other words, while Guérin's supporters had firm control of the Isère bridge guard house, and the Le Chapelier guard house was occupied (at least initially) by Paumier's faction, the little Clérieu gate had been captured by neither but contained both capon and partridge. Men from the two opposing groups were thrown together in the "fort." A few sparks must have flown, but at heart the leaguers were not much more resolute than the Partridge commando fighters when they assembled a few hours earlier. In short, they did not really want to fight, and were still relying on a waiting game. When two more opposing groups arrived on the scene, the situation became even more complicated. From within the town came more Guérin supporters, fresh from their victory in the Le Chapelier quarter. On the outside, peasant leaguers, alerted by the sound of the tocsin, were still prowling beneath the ramparts. At any moment they might try to force their way into town through the Clérieu gate, since they had not gotten through the one at Le Chapelier.

Why, we may ask, didn't the urban league adherents in the

Clérieu guard house intimidate or override the Guérin supporters sharing their cramped quarters and then throw open the fabled gates and let in the flood of peasants?

Guérin was afraid they might, he was plagued by the quite plausible fear that the peasants would break in, pillage, and conquer the town.[11] *It was to be feared,* he writes (A 165) *whether by peaceful means or by force, that they* (the proleaguers in the guard house) *might open* (the Clérieu gate) *despite the number of gentlefolk in the fort with them, thus letting in the enemy* (the peasants) *which was at the said door.* Eustache Piémond goes along with Antoine Guérin: if the 1,500 armed men assembled from the peasant communities, the notary writes, had *dared to appear at the gates to Romans...if they had gone promptly to the Clérieu gate* (P 89) *Captain Roux* (known as Leguire) *who was inside there* (barricaded and commanding the leaguers) *would have let them in* (to town).

A frontal attack by Laroche's men, then, would have been dangerous, for the Paumier supporters inside the guard house might have felt cornered and, in desperation, opened the gate under their control. The unthinkable union between town and country would then be accomplished. Rather than having it come to that, Guérin thought, the leaguers inside the guardhouse should be persuaded to surrender. Relating the events that followed, the judge was able in retrospect to cast himself in a favorable light as he officially reported to the authorities.

Soon a bargaining session was underway at the Clérieu guardhouse, and the patricians had a distinct advantage over the craftsmen. The judge unleashed a flow of eloquence: he had not, it seems, exposed himself to the physical danger of the initial combat; he was too cunning for that. But now, by taper or torchlight, as the fighting died down, he left his lofty perch, and came through the cold night to reap the harvest of his scheming, to taste victory. This *was the occasion,* he records (A 165) as his tone becomes more and more autobiographical and admiring, *on which Monsieur the judge, assisted by some who were with him, and of the most prominent, began to parley with them* (the delegates of the Paumier supporters within the guard house). He *began by asking them why they wanted to hold out against their king and their town.* Guérin had mentally escalated the fight: the town is now seen as <u>united against the attacking peasants, who</u> are depicted as <u>the dangerous element</u>. The urban rebels were thus automatically excluded from the urban community, even if they did represent a strong minority, if not a majority, among the lower classes.

You can see the risk, the judge continued, addressing the group of leaguers as one man, *you can see the risk you are running, if you hold out; what you risk either from those who are inside* (Guérin supporters, that is, us) *if you "persist in being forced* (if we have to attack you); *or from those outside* (the peasants) *if they enter* (if you let them into town). Here the judge implicitly suggests that "they will loot and pillage everywhere, even your own property and families, and you will be responsible for it all." The judge gets his second wind: *you will be doing a great injustice, not only to yourselves but to your posterity; you will be the cause of your own ruin and that of your fellow townsfolk.* (The threat against *posterity* was a real one: several Paumier supporters convicted after the fact for their role in the 1579–1580 "incidents" were not only hanged for it, but their property was also confiscated and their children forbidden to reclaim it.)

Enough of the iron hand; the judge now reached somewhat hypocritically for his velvet glove: *he promised and swore to them* (the rebel delegates) *that no harm would come to them and that he would take them all under his protection* (A 166).

Guérin's words were treacherous music to the ears of the small group of leaguers; their morale had taken a serious fall with Paumier's death. *The judge's word backed up by one* (one of his highiy placed assistants) *who was with him had such vigor that either they took fright, seeing men arrive from the other side* (Guérin's supporters) *who had just taken and now held the Jacquemart gate; or else,* (they were afraid) *that if they tried to misbehave, the gentlefolk barricaded with them would take them in the back; they agreed to retreat* (leave the "fort") *and obey the said judge provided their lives were spared. And indeed, all at once, they all went out, broke down the said barricades, and left the said* (Clérieu) *gate.* One of Guérin's squadrons immediately took control of the gate, just as some of their cohorts had taken over the Jacquemart gate minutes before (east of the Clérieu gate). It would be an easy gate for Guérin's men to hold: the Jacquemart quarter was solidly in their camp.

In summary, the last battalion of Paumier's supporters, afraid of being caught in the crossfire, sandwiched between enemies inside and outside the town walls, gave up the fight before they ever began it. They lost a battle never waged, and with it, the urban war.

For the peasants, Paumier's faithful friends, still prowling around the ramparts, this was the signal to scatter: (then) *retreated all the peasants, who had come to enter the said town and pillage it in the disorder* (A 166). The hand of God had guided Romans to "safety."[12]

Piémond's version of these events bears out what Guérin tells us. Still, it is less favorable regarding the judge than Guerin's own account. The notary points out (P 89) that Captain Roux, known as Leguire, commander of the Paumier supporters at the Clérieu gate, did not give himself up to Guérin but to *Monsieur de Combovin, who kept him from harm*. So the judge had not won everyone over, especially his fiercest opponents; they preferred to surrender to Guérin's adjutant. Subsequent developments would show grounds for this circumspect surrender.

IX

❦❦❦❦❦❦❦❦❦❦

A Slaughter of Peasants

On Mardi Gras, February 16, Carnival died an early death. Over the next few months, unrest in the villages came to a bloody halt. As for the town of Romans, after the three days that it shook Dauphiné, it gradually ceased to be the center of the storm. Armed conflict had slowly escalated; now it leveled off. Carnival had made Guérin a symbol, cosmic and malevolent, for a few days. Now he returned to normal, a county seat politician, albeit a particularly vicious one. The storm center moved on toward the Dauphiné hills and plains to the north, toward the peasant uprisings in the Valloire, and the repression of the peasant movements in the Biévre district.

Romans had become peripheral, and yet much would be done before the town returned to normal. It was necessary to upbraid, punish, examine, hang, whip, draw and quarter, force confessions, and confiscate property. In all fairness, it should be pointed out that the repression in Romans resulted in only twenty to thirty deaths (this number includes those who were hanged after the event), while more than a thousand rural leaguers were slain a few months later; Romans's low percentage of deaths, however, was relative, considering that the vast majority of Dauphiné's population lived in the country.

Guérin, the reigning spirit of repression in Romans, first ensured that the hastily banked fires would not flare up again. The last Paumier partisan in the Clérieu gate guard house had barely surrendered when the judge sent off letters calling for help to various provincial authorities likely to support Romans's small number of elite, now surrounded by the threatening populace. Three missives went out, one to Maugiron, the lieutenant-governor; the second to the Parlement of Grenoble; and the third to the nearest regional magistrate in the bailiwick that included Romans, Antoine Garagnol, the vice-bailiff or *vibailly* of St. Marcellin, who was related to the judge by marriage. We should take note of the fact that Guérin did not solicit the aid of the representatives to the Estates or "Three Estates" of Dauphiné, although they represented an essential regional authority in addition to Maugiron, the Parlement, and the vice-bailiff. The Estates, and especially the third estate, were not automatically predisposed toward the judge's ultrarepressive aims (in this they differed from the other authorities). Nor did they favor polite ignorance of his bloody initiatives during Carnival. Rightly or wrongly, they probably saw the judge and his enemy Paumier for two firebrands. Maugiron, the Parlement, and the *vibailly,* on the other hand, were only too willing to do as the judge wished.

Guérin therefore *sent to Monsieur de Maugiron begging him to favor the said town with force* (begging him to send reinforcements) *to resist the said enemies* (Paumier's men). *He also sent to Messieurs of the Court of Parlement* (of Grenoble). . . . *Finally he sent out three messengers variously on foot and horseback with letters for Monsieur the vice-bailiff of St. Marcellin, to advise him also of everything* (A 166).

Even so, these epistolary measures left much to be desired. Mail was slow, and the Parlement and Maugiron weighed down by bureaucracy. Several days passed before any results were seen. In the meantime, the indefatigable Guérin sent a Romans nobleman on an emergency mission to summon local country gentry. The rural nobility was still furious with the peasants and leaguers who had burnt castles and challenged the recently ennobled, and had decided to align themselves with the hard-line faction of Romans's bourgeoisie, evidence of the unity of a certain elite group of nobles and patricians. During the first few hours of Mardi Gras, *a gentleman living in the said town who had witnessed all the acts* (the crushing defeat of the Capon faction)

carried out on the said night, and who bore the marks of it on his hand
was sent out *through the bridge gate to advise certain neighboring
gentlemen.* They were quick *to arrive* in Romans *the next day* (Mardi
Gras) *about eight in the morning, in the number of twelve hundred seven
or eight soldiers* (the figure seems much too high for a town of
7,000 at the most) (A 167). In any case, other sources inform
us that the seigneurs of Montelier, Charpey, Brette, and Bay-
anne, as well as 200 soldiers under the command of Antoine
de Solignac, seigneur de Veaulne, had made their entrance into
town (which they then policed) by Mardi Gras morning. Solig-
nac-Veaulne's presence in Romans was significant; he was connected both to Romans's oligarchy and the great noble families
on both banks of the Rhône, respectively represented by Maugiron and the Count of Tournon. The troop of a few hundred
noblemen and mercenaries immediately began to regale itself
in the local inns at the town's expense. Since they had come to
Romans at Guérin's request, the town had agreed to supply
them with lodging, board, and horse feed until regular detachments arrived from Maugiron. Some 105 gentlemen sent by the
lieutenant-governor did ride into town on Friday, February 19,
about two hours after noon (A 166). Meanwhile, the town had
remained completely closed off (P 89). The new troops were
welcomed by the "population" (with Paumier supporters ab-
staining or changing camps) *with all the gaiety that can be expressed.*
This post-Carnival gaiety may well have been in compensation
for the Mardi Gras that had not taken place, obliterated as it
was by the Capon massacre. At all events, the bourgeoisie and
perhaps certain nonbourgeois and "lower class" elements of
the population were relieved that there was less chance of
looting peasants entering Romans, now that they had been *so
gladly freed one and all from the tyranny of peasants and leaguers* (A
167).

Maugiron's detachment was joined by some hundred nobles
who had come from St. Etienne-de-St.-Geoirs in Bièvre, where
repression of peasant *jacqueries* was mounting. *That shows,* as
Eustache Piémond puts it (P 90), *that those of Romans* (Guérin's
party) *were in the same league with the nobility.* This antipeasant
force, many of whom had been recently ennobled, was not

content just to deal severely with the town, now in a virtual
state of military occupation; it further *made some expeditions into
the villages,* and *killed the peasants like swine for which reason some
of them* (peasants) *fled into the woods to wait until the terror was
past* (P 90).

In Romans, the local authorities were more than ever under
Guérin's control. He was now at the height of his power. In the
relative calm immediately following the eventful Mardi Gras,
the authorities recalled their deep-seated fear and oversaw
repressive measures. They took advantage of the dazed condition of the lower classes, now experiencing the "hangover"
that follows large-scale popular uprisings, especially when
they fail.

Guérin's party exploited the situation to the full; they purged
the limited council and the so-called general council as well
(in fact it was not open to the public at all). The Paumier-
supporting or "extraordinary" members of these bodies were
disgraced or incarcerated. Some were killed, a few tortured
beforehand. The town had been placed under the rule of an ad
hoc, extraordinary, illegal council set up by Guérin. Romans
was sealed off, a self-blockade originated inside the walled city
by the ruling elements.

From now on, with calm restored in best bourgeois fashion,
the sham councils and the pseudogeneral council could have
private discussions of the great "massacre" that had failed to
take place on Mardi Gras—meaning Captain Paumier's alleg-
edly intended extermination of the town's "honorable citizens."
The deceased craftsman leader, no longer able to defend his
behavior, was thus accused of having plotted to bring a great
number of his rural allies into Romans to obviously murderous
ends. Unfortunately, the documents on litigious proceedings in
Romans, organized by the Parlement of Grenoble in 1580, have
disappeared. Without them historians cannot judge the accusations posthumously made against Paumier. Exaggerated as
they were, they may have contained an element of truth, although we cannot say what.

During the last two weeks of February, the revolutionary—
or rather counterrevolutionary—council formed by Guérin was
far from inactive. At its urging, the town's regular governing
bodies, which had been thoroughly purged, voted on a variety
of measures: all the gates to Romans were sealed, except for
two—the Jacquemart and Isère bridge gates—which were left
open as if by chance but in reality because they were tightly
controlled by the notables. Paumier's accomplices were dis-
armed and locked up. Bed and board were granted the 140
noblemen who had come from Bièvre and Valloire to reinforce
the Maugiron and Veaulne contingents and to lend Romans's
elite a hand against the common people. Despite the exorbitant
cost of keeping them, the 140 nobles were requested to remain
in Romans until the threat of popular revolt had completely
disappeared. The Count of Tournon's assistance was also accepted. From his district on the west bank of the Rhône he had
offered his good and loyal services to the town, in the name of
solidarity among the elite, bourgeois patricians as well as nobles. The council also instituted a tax on bread; local bakers,
moreover, would be fined if they charged a price above the
maximum limit set by the judge. The members of Paumier's
faction were forbidden to move out of their houses and opt for
exile: *Any house unfurnished will be refurnished.*

And then, starting on February 22, 1580, the Clérieu and St.
Nicholas gates were slowly and carefully reopened. They were
much more dangerous from the notables' point of view than the
Jacquemart and Isère bridge gates. Clérieu and St. Nicholas
were opened only between six and seven in the morning so that
winegrowers and plowmen—it was plowing time—could leave
to work in their fields, at least those farmworkers not considered
likely to flee Romans. Naturally the notables or their followers,
transformed into neighborhood captains, as well as their subordinates or *members,* were urgently dispatched to do guard duty
at the gates: in the evening the plowmen were under orders to
come back into town through the Jacquemart gate, making it
easier to check on them.[1]

These simple police measures tapered off rather quickly.
Repression, however, began to grow increasingly severe at the

beginning of March. On March 2 a special court of justice, a temporary detail of the Parlement of Grenoble, came to Romans. It began its job of interrogation, and sentencing, to torture and death by hanging. The incarcerated Paumier supporters, whom Guérin had spared the fury of his own faction, did not have a chance. They were given a bad time of it before they died.

All this took place in a town in dire financial straits. One of Romans's leading citizens, Gaspard Jomaron, was imprisoned for debts in February 1580, because of the large sum a financier, de Blayne, claimed was due him out of town revenues. On February 18, the consuls tried as best they could to obtain Jomaron's freedom.[2] As for the indirect consumer taxes or *tributs* levied on the local butcher and baker trades, they had been neither adequately collected, as a consequence of the urban economic crisis, nor posted in the town account books since the beginning of 1579.[3] The butchers and bakers had paid no taxes for more than six months.

With destitution threatening, the wildest rumors spread in Romans from February to April 1580, encouraged by Antoine Guérin. The "rebel's" plan, the judge declared in his speeches to the town council and his official report to the national authorities, had been *to begin on Mardi Gras to kill the nobility, the judiciary, and even Messieurs of the Court of Parlement, the clergy, all the notable bourgeois and merchants of the town of Romans, and afterwards even kill their own women, and marry the wives of the said notables whom they had killed and whose property they had seized and divided up, and after all this bring the Huguenots into the said town* (A 171).

Of course we cannot give credit to these rumors, quite to the contrary: they were aimed at discrediting the popular movement Paumier had led, justifying strong repressive measures. The three-part program imputed to Paumier's men—murder, economic and sexual revenge—was actually rooted in the collective imagination. These themes were in keeping with the era's idea of popular uprisings. They were an integral part of its outlook, as was the image of the *man with a knife in his teeth* which coincided with a certain European view of Bolshevism during the 1920s.

No matter what these rumors tell us about Romans during the early spring, the town had relinquished its position as the center of class struggle in Dauphiné after February 1580. Romans did become the home of a deadly judicial repression, furnishing us with material for a sociological study. But this aspect aside, the town was bogged down for a long time in dull, municipal affairs, with only a bit of tragedy to liven it up.

The main subject of discussion in Romans's town hall from spring until autumn 1580 was the election of a new town government, at Guérin's instigation. Under the judge's aegis, Romans became a one-man town.[4] The council proceedings also mention that back *tributs* or indirect taxes (on the butcher trade, wine, weighing of merchandise, bridge toll, and so on) were still difficult to collect; the proceedings refer to the former consuls' audit of the town books. They discuss sending a delegation to the upcoming provincial Estates. This was a hardship mission, since the Protestants and former leaguers were intercepting travelers on both banks of the Isère. The proceedings also record the admission of a few new inhabitants to the town. Indeed, it seems Romans experienced a temporary demographic upswing after the 1579–1580 incidents, only to have it wiped out by the plague of 1586. There was also the chronic problem of the poor, exacerbated by the fact that the townsfolk themselves were too impoverished to give to the indigents (or so they claimed), and so called a collective halt to almsgiving—to the point that the municipal representatives in charge of the poor had to consider a last resort of letting them beg openly in the streets. The town elders also saw fit to award a gratuity of a few dozen *écus* to judge Guérin for his good and costly services during the crisis. In fact, Guérin had his men on the council propose this "reward." The town government further took care of back pay as best it could, which was not very well: wages for the bridgekeepers, the recent veterans of Guérin's counter-revolution, and the schoolteachers. The town's creviced walls were repaired at great expense and in haste; a neighboring château (Peyrins) was torn down for if it remained standing it would likely become an outlaw hideout. Most important, the taxpayers were recalcitrant and the town went into debt to pay its taxes and to provide for the military contingents, Monsieur de Veaulne's for instance, that were protecting Romans from a new revolt. The soldiers took advantage of the situation to forage for provisions and livestock in the neighboring country-side. Financial necessities—urban debts so outstanding that the town's largest creditors, from Lyons and elsewhere, threw Ro-mans's consuls in jail—would become more and more pressing during the summer of 1580. At the same time the Duke of Mayenne's state forces made their way through Dauphiné, com-ing from the northeast; they demanded money, hay, wheat, oats, wine, and cartage for their cannon. In return, they would "liberate" Romans from the Protestant, formerly league-di-rected threat, but the price was high.

During the same period the last exploits of the peasant league were played out, though not in Romans this time. Quashed in that town, the league movement was still active in some smaller towns and especially in the country to the north. The disaster in Romans had attracted a great deal of attention. The peasants took to the woods, if not to continue the fight, to escape the repressive measures they too would experience. In 1580 more than 2,000 of them, armed with arquebuses and with Huguenots among their company, were sighted at Beauvoir (near St. Mar-cellin); there were also similar reports from Roybon, Moirans, and other places in the rebellious, rural Valloire region.

The rural movement was fairly autonomous in relation to Romans's league effort which had ended so unhappily. From the beginning of February onward, the Valloire countryside had also revolted against excessive, unjustly apportioned taxa-tion, and the nobles' tax exemption. In secret, Huguenot agents fanned this brush fire into flame, motivated by Gentillet, Les-diguières's adviser and a specialist in popular revolts on the Swiss model. Peasants and craftsmen from the villages gave vent to their resentment of all the privileges enjoyed by the nobility and clergy, not only tax exemption. The smoldering castles and slaughtered noblemen of the preceding year were fresh in their minds. They remembered having sent the Queen Mother word of their desperation through the intercession of the town consuls, during the summer of 1579. And as the Dauphinois historian Chorier put it, *he who speaks of desperation to his sovereign threatens him* . . . In short, at the beginning of February 1580, 4,000 peasants were up in arms. They were scrutinizing the democratic and antinoble example of Switzerland, *where only good citizens are acknowledged as noble.*[5] A few small-town jurists, lawyers and notaries, headed up the peasant army.

Valloire's populace was more stunned than demoralized by the catastrophe befalling the people of Romans, which nevertheless caused a certain ebbing of the popular movement. By early March, Maugiron was able to break up the sedition, highly active though it was. At a gathering of consuls held in Goncelin, which he flooded with talk of conciliation, the lieutenant-governor stopped the revolt from spreading to the Grésivaudan communities. Then, bolstered by reinforcements under the command of Mandelot, summoned to his aid from Lyons, he felt able to crush the Valloire insurgents. The peasant troops had used up their meager stores of gunpowder and food during the first few weeks of fighting. The help their Protestant ally Lesdiguières sent them from his mountaintop was late in coming. What is more, the troops had split up. The 500 most seasoned soldiers, armed with arquebuses, were now entrenched at Beauvoir, where they built a fort. There they fell under the command of Captain Bouvier, an old Huguenot highwayman. As for the bulk of the rural league forces, already demoralized because of their lack of ammunition, they were camped at Moirans, at the base of the Préalpes, with no time to build fortifications. There were now fewer than 2,000 *harassed and frightened men* (P 101) in Moirans. More than half of them would be killed there on March 26, 1580, by the small royal armed forces (1,000 horsemen and 3,500 footsoldiers) raised in part from Lyons and led by Maugiron and Mandelot. It was a bloodbath, at least by the relatively humane standards of the times, as compared to our own. At all events it was a slaughter of villagers, comparable with the mass murders that put an end to the Jacquerie of 1358 and the peasant war in Germany in 1525. At Moirans, Piémond recounts, *the people* (the armed leaguers) *were already most harassed and frightened. All at once a regiment* (of Maugiron's army) *which was behind a badly guarded barricade* (the leaguers'), *approached it, knocked it down and came in, crying* *"The town is ours." The people* (the leaguers) *did not have the courage to defend themselves, so that they were all killed and slaughtered. Some of them, however, were saved by fleeing. There remained nine hundred* (lying dead); *besides them two hundred were taken prisoners; Lapierre* (the leaguers' captain) *and several others were hanged; of the prisoners, most of them were killed in cold blood* (by Maugiron's men). *I have heard tell that Monsieur de Tournon* (the great antileaguer noble from the west bank of the Rhône) *killed seventeen of them with one sword, the most deplorable and scandalous and harmful thing that has ever come about in Dauphiné, with so many widows and orphans left* (P 102). Chorier relates (II, 699) that one of the leading gentlemen in Maugiron's army "carried his hate so far it became infamy": drunk with anger, he hanged a former valet of his with his own hands from a walnut tree. The example set by friends and relatives had drawn the poor servant into the league.

The victorious troops had *carte blanche* to pillage, and the natives had no hope of ever recovering their possessions. Since the victors were not from Dauphiné, they carted their spoils out of the province.

The massacre at Moirans illustrates certain familiar problems: a peasant guerrilla troop, even an aggressive one, fares badly in a direct encounter with a regular army storming a town, or in pitched battle. Even so, this spectacular, bloody episode did not mark the end of the village league. The peasant partisans still had a firm hold on their last bastion, the fort in Beauvoir near St. Marcellin. They were reinforced by an elite cadre of Huguenot soldiers, which Maugiron's army, brave but not foolhardy, refused to fight. With Beauvoir as a base, the leaguers engaged in random looting and guerrilla warfare. They made off with horses, wheat, and money from Guérin-supporting Romans merchants. They seized munitions and supplies from the Maugiron-Mandelot army in sweet retaliation. They also attacked their former friends who had become renegades—from the country or small towns—and all the turncoats who had bargained for their pardon from the provincial authorities. In short, the rebels, joined by the Huguenots, *come and go unchecked in the country of Vienne by means of the fort they have made at* (Beauvoir) *St. Marcellin, which is causing and will hereafter cause the total ruin and desolation of the said country, if it is not promptly attended to by His Majesty* (Henri III) (A 171).

The problem was that Henri III was unpredictable: in May and June 1580 measures of clemency recently formulated in Paris brought a (partial) end to the spring's severe judicial measures. They had been particularly energetic in Romans, a bit less so in Vienne. The new atmosphere of pardon induced a certain number of peasants to quit the league-Huguenot party and quietly return to their homes (P 109). Yet a sturdy core group of unreconciled leaguers kept on. In May and June 1580, true to their antilandlord traditions, they attacked, captured, and pillaged one after another the castles of Faverges in the Viennois and La Forteresse near St. Etienne-de-Geoirs, in Bièvre.[6] Another group of leaguers began operations in Valloire, where they found ample cooperation: gentlemen and priests were raided, pillaged, taken prisoner by the rebels. On July 6, 1580, they still numbered 140, including thirty horsemen. They descended on the town of St. Antoine, where they had well-placed accomplices. They made off with the furnishings and the inhabitants of the local abbey, killing a ninety-year-old monk who was unfit to travel and taking a few cattle; on their return trip they were the ones to be killed or scattered, ambushed by Captain de Beaucressant's royal detachment (P 112). On July 18, St. Antoine was once again alive with rumors of another attack by the league-Huguenot troops from the Beauvoir fort. A noble, Monsieur de la Cardette, was in fact killed by this band—and thus one more was added to the dead roll. *No one dares leave the house anymore,* Piémond wrote of his home village. (P 113).

At the end of July, the Duke of Mayenne's Catholic and royal army arrived in Lyons. At last! Seven or eight thousand footsoldiers, 2,000 horsemen, 500 pioneers, eighteen pieces of cannon (P 155). There were six regiments in all, plus the legendary Swiss guards, real ones this time. A "healthy" fear began to spread through Dauphiné. Yet the leaguers in the hill country around Vienne, even St. Antoine, were backed by Lesdiguières in his Huguenot keep in the southern Alps. The league forces did not put down their arms, nor did they lose heart. They carried on as if nothing were amiss. For example, one Lambert or de Lambert, a St. Antoine lawyer, had been playing both ends against the middle since February, consorting with Maugiron, Lesdiguières, and fire. As early as February 1580 (after Paumier's fall), Lambert had promised Maugiron he would behave and had offered the lieutenant-governor the full compliance of his town, as did the representatives of Valloire's incorporated communities.[7] But four months later the shameless Lambert was in touch with Lesdiguières about a defensive and offensive alliance between the mountain Protestants and the league partisans in the Vienne countryside.[8] With Mayenne on the horizon, these negotiations were confirmed by the Protestant assembly at Die, held in August 1580: the terms of the agreement called for the leaguers to *take to the fields* and seize certain places and town ramparts as soon as the Protestants were able to bring their *reiter* (German cavalry) and *lansquenet* (German footsoldier) reinforcements into the province. For their part, the Huguenots pledged not to stop the Mass from being celebrated in any of the Vienne region's non-Protestant localities which might rally to their call to arms. The most extremist ministers did not agree, but Lesdiguières, always a good politician, settled things in favor of tolerance. The point was to ensure the Huguenots' best chance of survival, if not success, when facing the difficult challenge from the national Catholic troops now just to the northwest.

Unfortunately for the leaguers, they were no match at all for Mayenne's "steamroller" of an army, in open country or even in a stronghold. Lesdiguières knew it: he took inexpugnable refuge in the mountains, where his enemies would have a hard time transporting their artillery. He let his peasant allies fall to Mayenne's troops in the hill and plain country, which were so hard to defend against a regular army. Lesdiguières apparently had not taken the peasants very much to heart, perhaps because of their revolt against the seignorial system.

Mayenne, however, was holding all the right cards. He dis-

pensed both honey and vinegar with an unexpected flexibility.
Honey: even before making his entry into Dauphiné, he once
again promised amnesty to those *guilty in the popular risings.*[9]
Vinegar: Mayenne threatened those who would dare resist him
with execution and total military destruction. This time the
leaguers were in real trouble. In August–September 1580 Mayenne advanced through Dauphiné along the Isère. Once again,
his adversaries committed their chronic tactical error. Instead
of scattering through the woods and fields, they agreed to fight
in a fortified place, in a quick siege, a nearly pitched battle. A
portion of Mayenne's army was detached against them: this
"portion" numbered 4,000 men under Maugiron's command.
On September 9, 1580, the 4,000 soldiers surrounded the Beauvoir fort; it fell under fire from Maugiron's cannon. All of the
surrounding countryside was crawling with crown and professional soldiers: *in short, this is destitution, we have no wine* (the
soldiers drank it) . . . *the pilferers* (pillaging soldiers) *are looting
a league in every direction, a horrible thing . . . .*

Caught in a vise, the peasants in the Beauvoir fort could do
nothing but surrender. *Captain Ferrant, the commander of the fort,
surrendered with his life spared; nonetheless, several ill-willed leaguers
who had kept to the woods were secretly killed* (by Mayenne and
Maugiron's soldiers); *others were held for ransom* (P 116). A week
later, the Huguenot captains Bouvier and Dallières, who were
holding the castle of Pont-en-Royans and the village of St.
Quentin not far from Beauvoir, also gave up. The Catholic
soldiers had a difficult time taking Pont-en-Royans, however,
since the Catholic occupants had been very well treated by
Lesdiguières and were devoted to their Huguenot ex-occupants,
even though they had once clashed with Bouvier.[10] After Dallières and Bouvier surrendered, several peasants in their band
were killed in cold blood by Mayenne's men; other, luckier
soldiers were treated according to the rules of war and were
even allowed to remain armed: *those who were thus armed were led
to near St. Quentin; the others were almost all prisoners. Some* (of the
prisoners) *were held for ransom, others were secretly killed among the
tents. Sibeuf, of Romans, was killed there* (Sibeuf had fled Romans
to warn the villagers on Mardi Gras). *There was a soldier who, for*

an écu, killed a peasant from the quarter (village) *of Montrigaud at the request of a gentleman. It was a time of taking revenge.* (The Duke of Mayenne) *kept the women from being forced and protected them. There was a Spaniard who had forced a maiden. He was hanged the same day from a tree. . . .*

Such was the definitive end of the peasant war in Dauphiné (1579–1580). Yet Mayenne had not seen the end of the fighting. His victory over the demoralized band of villagers had come too easily. Later on November 5, 1580, after a dreadful siege, he took the Dauphiné and Protestant town of La Mure, which was held by a woman, "Red Petticoat." But it was a pyrrhic victory. La Mure was only the foretaste of the insurmountable problems Mayenne was to face, and which would once again doom the Catholic campaign to win back Dauphiné. Mayenne was very ambitious, but when he tried to take Lesdiguières's mountain bastion, he overreached himself.

The Catholic campaign, however, does not concern the village revolt, now ended. The only thing that remained was for provincial authorities to take revenge. Piémond had seen his fill of horrors: in December 1580, he writes, Mayenne's men and other professional soldiers *were here and there overrunning the villages, even up to the gates of Lyons and Vienne, murdering and pillaging all the villages and any towns that were not walled . . . it was a settling up of their hatred for the League . . . to pillage a poor villager, who had no defense but to raise his hands to Heaven* (P 124). The now-extinct league movement had originated in hope of stemming just such excesses. By November 1580, moreover, the inhabitants of Valence, in an enthusiastic display of antileague spirit, attacked neighboring Huguenots, killing some sixty of them. The people of Valence *had been suspected of being in league with the Huguenots, they showed the opposite* (was true) (P 122).

As late as May 1581 a few former league guerrilla fighters who had become highway robbers were sent to the gallows: *On May 6, 1581, six merchants from Montélimar who were coming back from the St. Marcellin market fairs were assailed by ten furious robbers; the merchants, who were no cowards, defended themselves fiercely; the robbers were forced to flee. Three merchants were wounded. On this occasion Le Grison* ("graybeard," "gray hair") *of Serres, a scoundrel who had led the leaguers in the woods, was taken and hanged* (June 3, 1581). . . . *The roads were a bit freer* (P 126).

That was the end of it. At most, there remained the vague fear that the Huguenots might once more make use of the people's resentment, as they had done in 1579–1580, thanks to Paumier and his friends. *I do not doubt that the Huguenots have various plans, and that they will try everything they can, with the help of the people's discontent,*[11] Bellièvre-Hautefor wrote to the secretary of state, Louis de Revol, on March 15, 1581.

The fears were unfounded: during the 1580s, soldiers fleeced the poor people of the province at will; there were no reprisals. Romans's Carnival, and the subsequent disasters, had given them a distaste for insurrection.

X

❧❧❧❧❧❧❧❧

"Magpies and crows have pecked out our eyes..."

—François Villon, "Villon's Epitaph
or Ballad of the Hanged Men"

This distaste for insurrection derived from, among other things, the judiciary repression that had followed the Romans incident of February 1580. It is worth our consideration, for it casts a harsh, cruel light on the militant leaders of the popular faction, as seen through the sentences dealt them. For the duration the walled city of Romans was transformed into a garden of earthly horrors.

The minor carnage on *lundi gras* and Mardi Gras called for justice, but each faction had a different view of who the guilty parties might be. Should Paumier's supporters, who had disturbed the bourgeois peace, be prosecuted? Or should it be Guérin's men, who had killed members of "the people"? The third estate leaguers, including the moderate elements, inclined toward the second solution. Eustache Piémond, a leaguer at heart, is categorical on this subject: the people of the Valloire communities, *who were for the people,* sent a delegation to Maugiron by the end of February 1580, to ask him to do justice against those who had quelled unrest in Romans, to the point of killing common people. Two delegates of the Valloire deputation to the lieutenant-governor, Montchenu and Lestang, were nobles, perhaps recent ones, and moderates (P 90). They were nonetheless representatives of the local people: one was the bailiff of the Vienne district, the other had been a deputy from the Vienne district's nobility to the Estates General in 1576, evidence that the nobles were far from united in the murderous antipeasant madness. Maugiron told these ambassadors from the village that justice would indeed be done, except it would favor Guérin and be against the "people."

Such was the revamped atmosphere in Romans on February 27, 1580, when six magistrates from the Parlement of Grenoble arrived. They were to form a special court where they would try the defeated leaguers, both dead and surviving. Along with them came the presiding judge Buffévent and the attorney general Ruzé (P 91). *Three companies of footsoldiers escorted them,* in addition to nobles. Their entrance into Romans was a serious version of the traditional military and judiciary parades characteristic of Carnival. The court session, however, was a scandalously long Carnival—bitter and bloody once again—drawn out through Lent. It topped off the exhibition of the more spectacular forms of authority that had begun with the patricians' supposedly comic *Grand Conseil* procession on *lundi gras.* The special court went right to work. It tackled big game, or big names, first. Proceedings against the three supreme commanders of the urban league—Paumier, Brunat, and Fleur— began immediately. Since he was already dead, Paumier was hanged in effigy and by the feet. His corpse was *too putrefied to be strung up,* reports Guérin. Brunat and Fleur, taken alive, were naturally condemned to capital punishment, unfortunately with some embellishments: Paumier's portrait was traced on the ground, the two convicted leaders were dragged over it, then tortured, before being hanged. All this was done during the first half of March 1580: speedy justice. Other Romans craftsmen were also tried, dead or alive, during the first two weeks of the special court session.

Justice, so-called, had been carried out. From March 30 onward, the Parlement magistrates could attack a new "catch" of suspects: that day marked the beginning of the trial of some fifteen craftsmen and plowmen implicated in the Carnival incidents as early as a February 1579 *ad hoc* memorandum of judge Guérin's. The new group was sentenced to the gallows; many of them, fortunately, defaulted.

The Parlement magistrates wasted no time. They simultaneously started proceedings against the directors of and participants in the peasant uprisings in the villages. It was felt that the rural attacks against seignorial stewards like Monluel, Velheu, and a few others, had been more violent and crueler than the Romans incidents. Events in Romans before February 1580 had been mere psychodrama, without bloodshed. On the rural scene as well, those sentenced to the gallows numbered in the dozens: the majority, however, fled. The villagers found it easier to avoid being caught than did the city militants, who were trapped by the walls of their town.

Finally, in April 1580, the special court decided to take more general measures: it prohibited all *reynages*, Capon, Partridge, Sheep, Maugouvert, and so on, which had served as a framework for both the popular and antipopular movements. Perhaps Romans feared that, with the folk celebrations during May, protest action would revive. The prohibitions did not keep the bourgeois abbey of Maugouvert-Bongouvert, however, from growing in importance over the next few decades.

Repression gradually became less severe as the weeks went by. On April 14, 1580, the first sign of the new tendency toward leniency appeared when a certain number of suspects who had fortunately not been hanged during the initial fury of February and March were now set free. They were given minor sentences: forbidden to bear arms, denied participation in the town assemblies, and so on.

On April 25, after further proceedings against the villagers in the surrounding districts, the court decided that its work in Romans was done. It moved on to similar tasks in Vienne. The Carnival incidents were already falling into perspective. At any rate, Vienne was less guilty than Romans. Repression there took less time and was less incisive. On June 10, 1580, the court declared it had done all it had to do; with its usual pomp it headed back to Grenoble to nestle once more in the bosom of the Parlement.[1]

The dossiers of the proceedings of this special court afford us an overall study of the leaders and participants in Romans's workingmen's Carnival, as well as a more fragmentary and sketchy overview of the country protesters who took part in or led the peasant war in Dauphiné.

Before taking a closer look at the protest militants who were prosecuted, I would like to settle an interlocutory question. It concerns the Huguenots: Guérin accused them of involvement in the workingmen's plots, so-called, in his town. On this count the judge was not completely wrong. The infidel Lesdiguières, from high in his Alpine stronghold, was not above fishing in the troubled waters of Romans, through his intermediaries. But what about Romans's own Huguenots? Did the local Protestants play a quiet role, and if so, what role, in the Carnival in Romans? An earlier document provides some elements of an answer. On August 24, 1572 (St. Bartholomew's Day), judge Guérin ordered the town's Protestant families to be taxed, that is to say, fined. A few days later the judge organized a little massacre of imprisoned Huguenots, complete with smokescreen and masks.[2] So that the said fine could be collected, a list of Romans's Huguenots was drawn up with the amount demanded roughly proportional to each family's wealth.[3] The list contains the names of 128 heads of household, or less than 10 percent of Romans's population. The great majority (90 percent or more) of the local citizens, then, had remained Catholic or returned to the faith. The town's romance with Protestantism had never gotten beyond the flirtation stage during the early 1560s.

Romans's so-called elite was touched by the Huguenot reform, but not to any great extent. The rich Huguenots in 1572 were taxed at 15 or 20 *livres* and up, as opposed to 3,5, or 10 *livres* for the craftsmen and other less wealthy Protestants.[4] The list of the Huguenot rich includes some of the most prestigious names of Romans's upper crust consular families: Sire Jean de Villiers, a future consul, and, it appears, a future re-convert to Catholicism; Jean Guigou, who followed the same path; Sires Jean, Mathelin, and Antoine Thomé; Antoine Bouyraud; Jean Magnat; Gaspard Syvet; and so on. In 1580 these "well-bred" names appeared in the ranks of the law and order party. They were to form a moderate group, in league (but not in love) with the hardliner judge Guérin. At least one of them, Jean Guigou, had for a time entered into a tactical alliance with the people during the spring of 1579. Then he reverted to his former position as a Guérin man.

The Protestants whose professions are indicated on the 1572 list (a minority, unfortunately) also include a good number expressly designated as craftsmen or shopkeepers: a merchant, a notary, but also four drapers, a bleacher, a ropemaker, two masons, a cabinetmaker, a hosier, and so on. In the nearby town of Vienne, from 1560 onward, the Huguenot townsfolk were mainly craftsmen and only secondarily bourgeois, while farmers and winegrowers accounted for a tiny proportion; no doubt it was much the same in Romans.

This was the general case for all of Protestant southern France during the initial phase;[5] yet it does not necessarily mean that Huguenot craftsmen were the leaders of the urban protest movement in Romans. There was a single Protestant among those prosecuted in the aftermath of the 1580 Carnival: Antoine Nicodel, farrier, who had been fined 10 *livres* in 1572. The other personages who were hanged or simply sentenced in 1580 were not on the 1572 list, although their age (they were well into their thirties or forties) would have made them eligible for the fine had they been Huguenots at that time. It was only to be expected that the 1579 protesters did not include Protestant craftsmen from the 1572 list: the St. Bartholomew's Day massacre, and the climate of fear it created, spurred a massive migration of Huguenots from Romans to Geneva in 1572, one of the largest from any town in the French Midi.[6] It seemed best to get as far away as possible from the lethal Guérin. The other course was to renounce Calvinism, leaving behind the Bible and its "fountains of spring water" for Catholicism and its "pitted cisterns." Renunciation and exodus, combined with the small numbers of Protestants to begin with, ensured that not many of "those of the Religion" took part in the craftsman unrest of 1579–1580. In fact, the framework for that unrest was provided by the Catholic confraternities, the St.

Blaise and the Holy Spirit, that had proved the *bête noire* of
the Protestant dictatorship in Romans in 1562, so much that the
Huguenots banned such organizations for the interim.

In summary, the Huguenot bourgeoisie briefly courted Paumier, then changed sides to become the moderate faction of
anti-league leaders. The Huguenot craftsman ranks were decimated by violent death or exodus and thus only contributed a
marginal proportion of the participants in the unrest. At the
most, a few Huguenots were among the ranks of one of the
workingmen's kingdoms, the Hare. We must not, of course,
exclude the possibility that some solid Huguenot resentment of
judge Guérin was still festering as a result of the St. Bartholomew's Day massacre; it fed anti-Guérin feeling in 1579 in
Romans and even more in the surrounding villages (A 30). Nor
should we exclude the possibility that Paumier and his friends,
although Catholic, were scheming with Lesdiguières. But that
is far from saying that the people of Romans were completely
manipulated by the Protestants. The important fact remains:
the Carnival in Romans was primarily an internal affair among
Catholics, setting Guérin, a militant Catholic leader, against
the craftsmen and their confraternities. Under the banner of
their patron saint, these organizations democratically entered
the fight against the elitist dons. Lowly Catholics battled
mighty Catholics. Let us now turn our full attention to the
overwhelmingly Catholic "troublemakers" from the lower
groups.

A statistical study of the men prosecuted, hanged, tortured, and
whipped in March and April 1580, and those who defaulted on
their sentences as well, is meaningless except in relation to the
larger background of Romans's social structures in general.

Let us review the four "ranks" or orders laid out in the *taille*
roll of 1578[7] and according to which the town's society was
divided. Among the taxpayers of the *first rank,* only one really
sided with Paumier's men against his own class: Michel Barbier, known as Champlong. Barbier was in the cartload of
convicts that never reached the gallows in 1580; in fact they
defaulted, having wisely decided to flee even before the repres-

sive trials began. A few months after being sentenced *in absentia*, Barbier was acquitted. In 1586, Barbier was consul of Romans; he died that year, not on the gallows but in bed. Like a few thousands of his compatriots, he succumbed to the plague of 1586.

Could Michel Barbier really be called a citizen of Romans in 1579–1580? Later on, when he had become a prominent lawyer, then consul, there could be no doubt of it. But in 1579 such a statement was premature; Barbier was no more than a very rich village notable. He owned a house in Romans, probably only for a short time. He paid only 1 *écu* tax on his Romans dwelling. In 1580 Barbier was representative of a group of well-off *village* notables who effectively became leaders in the *peasant* revolt, but he was not implicated in the *urban* revolt, strictly speaking, nor was he in any way typical of the leadership of that revolt.

On the whole, the members of the first rank—bourgeois patricians who lived like aristocrats off the income from land, bureaucratic office, rents—were not implicated in the urban unrest. Quite the contrary: with Guérin in the lead (an easy first as far as manipulators went, if not in financial status), this group represented a counterrevolutionary element, or, more precisely, the antiprotester group par excellence.

Now with regard to the second category, the other half of the upper ranks, it included merchants, notaries, and other members of the commercial bourgeoisie; it was well-to-do, certainly not a craftsman group at any rate. Analysis of this rank reveals absolutely no leaders, or even participants, in the protest movement. Not one of those sentenced in 1580 is listed in the *taille* roll of 1578 as a member of the second *estat*.[8] Much like the first rank, this group apparently constituted the backbone of the law and order party.[9]

We now come to the third group of taxpayers, the craftsmen. As our narrative sources indicate (though history written on "popular risings" does not always bear this out, since each case is different), it was the craftsman rank that supplied the real leaders of the revolt. Out of twenty-six persons prosecuted between February and April 1580 for Romans's *urban* incidents, there was a single member of the elite (Michel Barbier); only seven members of the sizable plowman group were involved; but there were eighteen members of the craftsman rank, composing 69.2 percent of the protest group as a whole. Five of the eighteen craftsmen were drapers, by far the most common profession. This confirms Guérin's statements on the preponderance of drapers, members of the St. Blaise confraternity, involved in triggering the revolt and providing its political and practical leadership. One of the rebel drapers, of course, was Jean Serve, known as Paumier, the supreme commander of the Romans and regional campaigns. Paumier paid 2.2 *écus* tax, indicating a certain minimal prosperity; the average for craftsmen as a group in 1578–1579 was 1.2 *écus*. There were other drapers as well, such as Guillaume Robert-Brunat, Paumier's next-in-command, tortured and hanged in February–March 1580; in 1578, he paid 1.2 *écus* tax, or the exact average for the craftsman rank, but more than the mode or most frequently recurring figure for that rank, 0.8 *écu*. We also find the draper Jean Besson, known as Massacre, an important figure in the protest, sentenced in 1580 to forfeit his property, pay a 239 *écu* fine, be flogged, and do ten years service in the royal slave-galleys, followed by banishment from the realm. In 1580 he paid 1.2 *écus* tax. François Robin, draper, was active in the revolt, but not as important as Serve, Brunat, or Besson-Massacre. He was only sentenced to confiscation of his property and a 35 *écu* fine. Jean Jacques, draper, was sentenced in his absence to hanging and a 129 *écus* fine. He was the poorest of the rebel drapers, paying only 0.8 *écu* tax. It was hardly a living, but it was not dire poverty either; on our 1578 scale, real poverty probably meant 0.1 or 0.2 *écu* tax.

After the drapers, the next most important craftsman leaders and agitators were two butchers. Geoffroy Fleur was called the chancellor of the league; he was tortured and hanged after his Carnival failed. In 1579–1580 he was a member of the triumvirate, with Paumier and Brunat, that ruled the hardliner league faction in Romans. He was able to integrate the butchers' sectarian tax strike into the broader movement of craftsman activism. In 1578 he paid 2.4 *écus* tax, a relatively large sum. His colleague and comrade-in-arms, François Drevet, then in misfortune, was in the group of rebels more lightly sentenced in March 1580. Their punishment consisted of attending the executions of their guiltier "accomplices," being flogged, forbidden to bear arms, and forfeiting their property. Drevet was quite well off before the incidents of 1579–1580, as were most butchers. He paid 2.8 *écus* tax, which placed him slightly above the average for Romans's taxpayers; Drevet paid even more than Geoffrey Fleur. He was the second wealthiest man in terms of taxable income in the group of post-Carnival convicts. Only Captain Roux, known as Lesguire, paid more— 3.8 *écus*.

Drapers, then butchers, formed the core group of activist protest leaders. But the squad of men sentenced after Carnival also included representatives of other professions. A baker, Antoine Fresne, nicknamed Pain Blanc ("White Bread") was accused of treason and in addition to his "trespasses" in Romans proper, was charged with having handed over the keys to St. Marcellin to the smaller town's rebel inhabitants. He was sentenced to the gallows.

Then there was a shoemaker, Jacques Jacques, who also paid 0.8 *écu* tax. He was sentenced to be whipped until blood was drawn, to ten years in the slave-galleys, then perpetual banishment from the realm. There was also a potter *cum* baker, Mathelin des Mures, once again taxed at the craftsman mode of 0.8 *écu*. He went to the gallows; his property paid off his 160 *écus* fine and was then confiscated. We also find a carpenter, Pierre Lambert, known as Le Gros ("Fat Man"), yet again paying 0.8 *écu*. His sentence: he was flogged, forbidden to bear arms, and stripped of his property. Next comes a farrier or shoesmith, Antoine Nicodel. He paid 1.4 *écus*. Nicodel, a Huguenot, had strayed from his anvil and hammer; he had filled an important function in the revolt and was executed for it. Six more craftsmen appear on the list of those sentenced: one of them may have been an innkeeper and publican (*hôte*). We are given no data on their specific professions.

The invaluable *taille* roll of 1578 allows us to pinpoint the financial status of the eighteen craftsmen involved in the 1580 judiciary proceedings, especially in relation to their own group. None of them was really rich, paying 10 *écus* or more in tax, as was the case for twenty members of the two upper ranks. (Consider the great wealth—comparatively speaking—of Gabriel Loyron, 18.6 *écus*, and Captain Antoine Coste, 41.4 *écus*, respectively representing the landed, merchant bourgeoisie.) Comparisons notwithstanding, we should be careful not to jump to the conclusion that the eighteen craftsmen in question were poor men. Their tax share was in fact average, more often than not slightly higher than average, for their rank. Again, we should keep in mind as a guideline that while the average tax in Romans was 1.48 *écus* in 1578, the average for the craftsman rank was a bit lower—1.2 *écus*—and the statistical mode for craftsmen was 0.8 *écus;* the same figure holds true as the mode for all of Romans in 1578. Excepting the restricted group of prosecuted rebels we shall presently examine, an overall study of the craftsman group shows that the 637 members of this rank included 106 heads of household, or 16.6 percent, paying *less* than the 0.8 *écu* mode; 257, or 40.3 percent, conforming *exactly* to the mode; and finally 274, or 43 percent, paying more than the 0.8 *écu* mode, representing the more prosperous craftsmen.

Tax	18 Prosecuted Craftsmen (1580)		637 Craftsmen Taxed in the Third Rank	
	# of persons	%	# of persons	%
less than 0.8 *écu*	0	0	106	16.6
0.8 *écu* (mode)	7	38.9	257	40.3
more than 0.8 *écu*	11	61.1	274	43
total	18	100	637	100

The statistical comparison quickly informs us that the restricted group of prosecuted craftsmen was on the average slightly more prosperous or less impecunious than Romans's craftsman rank as a whole. None of them paid less than the 0.8 *écu* mode. Yet when we apply the same criteria to the entire craftsman group, the percentage paying less than the mode is no longer 0 percent, but a substantial 16.6 percent. Working our way down through the table, we see that the percentage paying the mode, 0.8 *écu*, is about the same for the prosecuted craftsmen and their group as a whole: 38.9 percent and 40.3 percent respectively. Next we find that eleven of the eighteen craftsman ringleaders, or 61.1 percent, come in above the mode, while only 274 out of the 637 persons classified as craftsmen in the 1578 *taille* roll did so, or 43 percent. The sampling of prosecuted craftsmen was on the whole somewhat more prosperous, then, than the overall sampling of the third or craftsman rank.

Are we thus to assume that the restricted sampling of those prosecuted was mainly composed of well-to-do craftsmen? The answer is an unqualified no. While the convicted craftsmen were far from destitute, they were average for their group and did not cross the fateful threshold of 3.8 *écus* which would have put them in a bracket with the most prosperous members of their group, who were rather wealthy men. The vast majority (97.2 percent) of craftsmen were not tried by the special court in 1580, and out of all 637 members of the craftsman rank, fifteen, or 2.4 percent, paid more than 3.8 *écus* tax, compared to 0 percent of the "guilty" craftsmen.

In conclusion, it may help us to picture Romans's craftsman order as divided into four subgroups, ranked according to what might be termed a financial "upward trend." The chart below refers to a lower group (less than 0.8 *écu*), a lower-middle group (0.8 *écu*), an upper-middle stratum (0.8 to 3.8 *écus*) and an upper level (more than 3.8 *écus*). The results are as follows:

	Lower	Lower-Middle	Upper-Middle	Upper
A) Craftsmen as group	16.6%	40.3%	40.7%	2.4%
B) Prosecuted craftsmen	0%	38.9%	61.1%	0%
C) B compared to A	–	#	+	–

It is apparent that the craftsmen protesters, or at least the protest leaders, were neither destitute nor rich in relation to their own group. They came from the most representative section of their rank, the lower-middle section corresponding to the fiscal mode. The most influential leaders—Paumier, Brunat, Fleur, and the like—were slightly better off than the average, or minimally prosperous; they represented the upper-middle subgroup.

The documents relating to the judicial repression of February–March 1580 provide us with a sharper, more detailed picture of the upper-middle group defined above than tax records alone would give. Let us begin at the top with the craftsman leader, Paumier.[10] The suit for damages brought after his death and the confiscation of his property by the daughter of his first marriage and his widowed second wife informs us of his background and his modest yet undeniable property. In 1560–1562, twenty years prior to the Carnival incidents, when the future craftsman leader was between twenty and thirty years old, he married twice in rapid succession, both times quite well as we have seen. His first marriage on February 27, 1560, was to Antoinette Thomé, daughter of the late Jean Thomé, a local merchant, member of an old Romans family prominent both in town and in the Parlement of Grenoble. Antoinette brought with her a dowry of 160 *écus* or roughly the value of 2.2 hectares in vineyards.[11] She died shortly after the marriage, perhaps in childbirth, leaving a daughter who, survived to adulthood, outliving her father as well and suing for her mother's dowry after his death. On November 20, 1562, the young widower was remarried to Marguerite Loyron, who came from an established bourgeois family. In the spring of 1580, after the death of Serve-Paumier, Marguerite's personal property, accumulated through her dowry, inheritances, and so on, was assessed at 280 *écus*, or the equivalent of nearly 4 hectares in vineyards. During his lifetime, then, Paumier reigned over the equivalent of 6 hectares in vineyards brought him by his two wives. Taking his own income as a draper into account, he must have been worth around 10 hectares in vineyards. He also owned land and a barn in Peyrins, a village near Romans, worth 15 *écus* in all, or 2 hectares in vineyards. Many men were richer, but many were far worse off, too: this was basic middle-class comfort. Young Jean Serve (who was perhaps twenty or twenty-five years old in 1560) overcame his rural, no doubt peasant origins (he was born in Montmirail). An attractive, athletic, ambitious master draper, his two marriages were brilliant, potentially dynasty-making. Moreover, no matter how upper-crust the Thomés were, and how briefly Jean Serve had been their son-in-law, they remained strangely accommodating toward him to the end.

It is true that Paumier did not entirely fulfill the promise of upward mobility hinted at by his two marriages. He nonetheless achieved relative prosperity between 1560 and 1580, although he did not move on to the next highest rank of merchants; a difficult task for a draper, who was still considered a manual laborer. Paumier's real specialty was as a leader of athletic, paramilitary, confraternity, and folk gatherings. This earned him the admiration of his craftsman colleagues, but lost him just as much in influence and respect with the bourgeoisie. Even before the craftsman revolt, Paumier had clashed with Guérin, another social climber, but much more determined and ruthless. The easygoing draper lost his life in his next clash with the judge. Before he died, however, he proved that the middle class and even quite prosperous sections of Romans's craftsman rank might well assume local power, or at least a portion of it. Small businessmen against powerful patricians . . . To the end, Paumier made full use of the St. Blaise confraternity—as a vehicle for the protest. The confraternity included under one heading craftsman organizations, the carders' popular mythology, and folk traditions involved with the fertility of coming harvests.

Paumier's death was not everyone's loss. Ruthlessly continuing his search for revenge, Guérin went so far as to arrange to be given some of Jean Serve-Paumier's former property. In 1580 the judge bought 100 *écus* worth of the land the town had confiscated as part of Paumier's estate. The judge gave the 100 *écus* to his new friend and accomplice Jean Guigou, solicitor of fines from those sentenced as a result of their Carnival activities. But the municipal government, in a decision of the greater town council, returned half that sum, or 50 *écus*, to the judge "in consideration of the services he has rendered to the town,"[12] meaning that half the property the judge had bought was now his. Paumier thus made a double contribution, mainly through his downfall and through his property, to the fortunes of his enemy. Over the next two centuries, the judge's family rose to astounding heights; his descendants included the philosopher d'Alembert, a famous cardinal, and a charming and clever abbess. The powerful Guérin clan, with the noble "de Tencin" appended, had a curious coat of arms: it showed an apple tree (in French, *pommier,* a variant of *Paumier*) with branches laden with fruit. The pun was in the worst of taste, but it leaves no question as to the origin of the family's fortune. When he was ennobled in 1585 for outstanding conduct and service to the realm, Guérin personally designed his coat of arms: "in gold with a *Pommier arraché* (uprooted apple tree—Paumier) sinople . . ."[13] Guérin arranged Paumier's death; he walked off with top honors as a public servant. The prodigious success of his descendants was based on Paumier's death. Once power was secured in Romans, even by dishonest means, it was not easily dislodged.

Let us move on to another protester who was prosecuted, then hanged: Guillaume Robert-Brunat, draper, Paumier's right-hand man. Taxed at 1.4 *écus*, Brunat was just above the average for Romans's craftsmen (1.2 *écus*) and just below the average for the town (1.5 *écus*). His financial status was not particularly outstanding, but Brunat's social position made him a man of consequence among his fellows. Brunat was "chancellor of the league," and the network of relationships he had with other protest leaders in both town and country was extensive. The admissions he made under torture in jail (dubious under those conditions) led to numerous arrests in the Romans region in March and April 1580. What is more, Brunat was a long-time freelance worker in the town's financial and fiscal affairs. The local bourgeoisie, even Guérin, had respect for the draper in 1579; Brunat was influential, he was trusted. In May of that year he was apparently in the consuls' confidence.[14] The judge, too, considered using Brunat in his position as a "tribune for the people" to influence the lower classes to the benefit of the elite. Guérin was not gratified on this count.

In addition to being hanged, Brunat was also sentenced to a 400 *écu* fine, demonstrating that for a craftsman his estate was substantial, or that his business had a considerable turnover. He was not rich in land, vineyards, or excellent marriages like Paumier. He rented his house rather than owned it.[15] Yet he bought substantial quantities of wool, as much as 300 kilograms at a time, and made it into cloth, perhaps with the help of his wife and children, and one or two servants or apprentices. Then he placed the cloth with a dyer, who applied the desired color, and returned it. There was not a great deal of profit involved: Brunat was in debt when he died; he owed wool merchants and dyers 170 *écus.*

Geoffroy Fleur the butcher, known as "the president of the league," was the third member of the triumvirate. Married in 1561, Fleur must have been at least forty years old during the incidents of 1579–1580. He was well off for a member of his rank, paying 2.4 *écus* tax, a bit more than Paumier, twice the average for the craftsman group. A brief look at his real property, sold by public auction after his execution, confirms that he was minimally prosperous. Fleur had owned property in Peyrins and Pisançon, just outside Romans, some 6 *sétérées* in all, worth 150 *écus;* he also owned winegrowing properties, one valued at 18 *écus,* four *sétérées* of land worth 62 *écus,* and two other vineyards worth 82 and 20 *écus* each. The butcher owned a house in Romans, not far from the Chapelier quarter valued at 152 *écus,* plus a stable and barnyard in another part of town which went for 51 *écus.* Thus, the recorded extent of his real property was worth some 534 *écus,* or 7.5 hectares in vineyards. It was a very solid position in a society where many of the common people had to be content with less than 1 hectare. Geoffroy Fleur's fortune in real estate was modest, then, but not insignificant. Next to drapers, butchers were the most active profession in the protest movement; they had never been regarded as poor craftsmen. Furthermore, Fleur had dealings (not always satisfactory) with the leading businessmen in town: between 1567 and 1580 he left a debt of 30 *écus* outstanding to Jean Magnat, merchant and future consul.[16]

In comparison to the three members of the triumvirate—Serve-Paumier, Fleur, and Brunat—two other craftsmen executed in 1580 were somewhat less comfortably off: Mathelin des Mures, the potter-baker, and Antoine Nicodel, farrier, married in 1570 and 1571, respectively. We can thus assign them a hypothetical age of thirty-five. Their very modest but not poor status is indicated by their tax shares of 0.8 (des Mures) and 1.4 *écus* (Nicodel), the craftsman mode and average, respectively. Still, they were better off than the truly indigent taxpayers who contributed a mere 0.2 *écu*. Their widows' private property (from dowries, and so on) amounted to about 50 or 60 *écus* each, or less than the equivalent of 1 hectare in vineyards. One of the two men (Nicodel) also owned a tiny plot of land. We know that Mathelin des Mures was in favor with the consuls (not for long) in July 1579, since they entrusted him to ride as a messenger to the country parishes.[17] In his spare time, des Mures also collected the archbishop of Vienne's seignorial dues in Romans. It did not earn him much; after his death the income from this source was evaluated at only 4 *écus*! All in all, we can conclude, he was a man of middling means. This was also true of the other prosecuted craftsman, Simon Tisserand, of whose tax share we have no record but whose property was sold at public auction. He was a *peyrolier*, a manufacturer of copper goods, kitchenware, cheese pots, and so on, by trade, and was hanged for his role in the 1580 revolt. He was probably about forty years old at the time (he had married in 1565). On the Jacquemart square, next to the St. Foy almshouse, he owned a shop valued at 16 *écus* (or 0.22 hectares in vineyards). His widow was able to claim 47 *écus* in dowry property (equivalent to 0.65 hectare). Claude Terrot the butcher, known as Bas-Jarret, hanged in effigy (he defaulted), was perhaps the most substantial of this group.[18] He was sentenced to a fine of 129 *écus*. He owned land in the Chapelier quarter and in Peyrins, valued at 168 *écus* (or 1.3 hectares in vineyards).

Such is the essential data on the prosecuted craftsmen, including five drapers, three butchers, a baker, a baker-potter, a shoemaker, a carpenter, a farrier. In short, they were a rather representative sampling of the various skilled manual professions.

Whether of comfortable or modest means, all the prosecuted craftsmen were above the poverty level, let us say 0.7 *écu* in tax. But from another point of view they were far below the level of the craftsman elite. The 1578 *taille* roll shows fifteen taxpayers in the third group assessed at more than 3.8 *écus* (the prosecuted group's "spread" was from 0.8 to 3.8 *écus*). Not one of these well-to-do individuals compromised himself in the popular movement. Although they technically belonged to the craftsman rank, they adopted a prudent wait-and-see attitude in dealing with their own group's grievances. In fact, they considered themselves closer to the merchant order, the second rank. A significant fact is that a certain number of craftsmen, rich or simply of average means, were indifferently referred to as "merchant" or "draper." The ambiguous designation shows that transitions were possible, if difficult. Paumier's faction was at the strategic center and heart of the craftsman group, but it did not control the higher reaches of the rank, enthralled by the difficult climb toward merchant status.

Let us now consider those participants in the revolt who were *agricultural* workers living within the town of Romans. Their milieu was one of plowmen, sharecroppers, carters, workers in the fields and vineyards. The statements we are able to make about them are not very different from those in our study of the craftsmen. The prosecuted farmers did not come from the prosperous or upper sections of local agriculture; we might envision the epitome of the well-to-do farmer as manager of a seignorial domain, and he would naturally be a conservative. None of the plowmen in question paid more than 1.6 *écus* tax. The prosecuted men did not, however, belong to the poorest class of farmworkers; not one of them paid less than 0.8 *écu*. The seven convicted protesters from the fourth or plowman *estat* were Jean Chapreyssot, Jean Morat known as Ragousse, Etienne Romestan called Gosson, Louis Fayol, Jean Lisle, Guillaume Lisle, and Jean Troyassier. Falling within a very restricted fiscal spread (they all paid between 0.8 and 1.6 *écus* tax in 1578), they were exactly within the *average* of their huge group of 478 plowman heads of household in Romans. While the average farmer paid a tax share of 1 *écu* (the average for Romans was 1.5), the average among the convicted plowmen was 1.1 *écus*.

Farmers who were well-off or even rich paid more than 1.6 *écus* and as much as 12 *écus* in tax. There were forty-five of them, or 9.9 percent of the 478 members of their category; they were not involved in the protest movement,[19] and like their well-to-do craftsman counterparts they naturally leaned toward the two upper groups of merchants and patricians.

At the opposite end of the agricultural scale were the poor farmworkers, paying less than 0.8 *écu* in tax (between 0 and 0.6 *écu*); there were 143, compared to 290 in the middle group which included all those convicted after the protest, or compared to the forty-five prosperous members of their rank who were not involved in the protest. The poorest plowmen probably supported the various *reynages* that constituted the people's Carnival in Romans, but they did not contribute a single leader to the movement. If and when they participated they were followers.

For the most part, farmworkers became involved in the revolt through their original confraternities, especially the Holy Spirit, in this way meshing gears, so to speak, with the events of 1578–1579. The middle group of very small-scale landowner-farmers or winegrowers living in town was certainly implicated in the protest. However, the convicted farmworkers took orders rather than gave them. The main leaders of Romans's lower classes did not grow wheat or wine: they worked with cloth or sold meat at their stalls. They were not urban peasants but drapers and butchers like Paumier, Brunat, and Fleur.

The preceding monographs on the repression[20]—if they have been overlong, I beg indulgence—permit me to frame more concretely certain questions intrinsic to the study of popular revolts.

Boris Porchnev sees urban revolts as expressing the resentment, grievance, and desires of a *plebeian* group of craftsmen and possibly peasants or farmers residing within town walls. On the other hand, Roland Mousnier, more or less seconded by his students, views such revolts as manipulated by the notables, nobles, and bureaucrats who secretly stirred up popular unrest,[21] thus striving to thwart the increasingly centralized monarchy that threatened to engulf them.

As far as Romans in 1580 is concerned, Porchnev is right— or perhaps Rosa Luxemburg, since she theorized on the spontaneity of the masses. The leaders and eventual judiciary victims of Romans's movement included only one patrician— Michel Barbier-Champlong—an outsider with very minor holdings in the town, where he had played no public role. Barbier's campaigns were waged in the main in the countryside outside Romans. As statistics on the remaining protest leaders make clear, the heart and mind of the revolt were in the craftsman milieu, with farmers on the fringe. The fact that Paumier and his friends maintained contacts with agents from Lesdiguières and the Protestant nobility high in the Alps does not mean the commoner leaders were puppets of this nobility. In Romans, the craftsmen ran their own show.

Conceding this point to Porchnev means we must examine the craftsmen's and farmworkers' role in sixteenth-century Romans.

First of all, it was a large one. In 1578, out of 1,932 *écus* tax paid by the town of Romans, 764 *écus*, or 39.5 percent of the total tax, came from the craftsman category, called the third rank. And 497 *écus* came from the farmers, or 25.7 percent. In all, these two groups of manual laborers, skilled and unskilled, paid 65.5 percent or two-thirds of all taxes in Romans. They represented, however, 85.5 percent of all taxpayers.[22]

No matter what injustices were involved in the apportionment of taxes, it was accomplished by means of the updated land rolls and the assessment of each taxpayer's real property. Thus, it roughly corresponded to economic reality. Romans was neither an administrative, nor a judicial, nor a military center; production was therefore essential, as in any industrial city today. The difference between the sixteenth century and our own is that the main products then came from the crafts, farming, and winegrowing. Small-scale, family-based manufacture and farming were of the utmost economic importance. Under normal conditions, these local economic giants were virtually nonexistent in political terms. But everything changed when there were revolts. In Paris, for example, the League brought the diverse swarm of workers in the legal profession to the forefront. In Romans the drapers, the butchers, the winegrowers were suddenly at center stage. Their massive intrusion forced the craftiest and most fearsome leaders of the ruling class, like Guérin, into double-dealing with them before making an example of their defeat.

The rise of the commonfolk was only temporary. The craftsmen and farmworkers were inclined toward dramatic, even violent politics, and the casting of the various roles, particularly the leading roles, was not taken lightly. The craftsmen were in control. The urban peasantry, an undeniably important group, played second fiddle. The average Romans farmer was, it is true, poorer than the craftsman, and at the very bottom of the social scale.

Within the two protesting ranks the rich and even merely prosperous members of the craftsman and peasant groups were out of step with the rebel faction: the Jacquemart craftsmen's pro-Guérin attitude was typical in this respect. The rich or prosperous elements either passively or directly supported the two dominant groups (landlords and merchants). They "sold out" their own group of manual skilled workers.

The most prosperous craftsmen and farmers were repelled, then, by the ruling core group of the revolt. Also excluded though in a different way was the opposite extreme: the poorest and most destitute taxpayers assessed at less than 0.8 *écu*. Eustache Piémond (P 88) accuses Romans's wealthy citizens of having "grown rich at the expense of the poor people." He does *not* say that the poor people instigated the revolt, however; he describes it as led by Paumier's friends. In fact the *real* poor, the indigent, misfits, and beggars, may have taken part in the St. Blaise, Capon, Hare, and other Carnival demonstrations. Romans manufactured its own poor; it also received free imports from the countryside.[23] But at no time did the poor assume leadership of the movement. It always remained under the control of the confraternity leaders, more generally speaking, under the control of the lower middle class of craftsmen, with plowmen on the side, corresponding to those who paid 1 or more often 2 *écus* or more tax in 1578.

By the same token, women from the two lower groups never appear in the accounts of Carnival incidents or the proceedings of the judicial repression, Not one of them was hanged, tortured, or sentenced (although this is not necessarily a sign that judge Guérin was especially indulgent toward women). They did in fact play a role in the struggles, but a very subdued one. The Carnival in Romans seems not to have had its equivalent of the *tricoteuses* in 1793 or *pétroleuses* of the 1871 Commune, nor of the female *capitainesses* in Valence's 1645 uprising, or Montpellier's pre-Fronde *branlaires*. The young were relatively subdued as well: the leaders of the popular movement were not young men, as far as we know, but already mature citizens between the ages of thirty and fifty. The enemy camp, the more bourgeois Eagle-Rooster and Partridge kingdoms, were more likely to let women and young men take a more active role as witnessed with the ladies, damsels, the novices and young warriors of the mock abbey of Bongouvert.

So much for the urban leaders of the revolt. As for the rural leaders in Romans's adjacent or more remote country parishes, they represent a cross section of the *ruling* elements in the village communities. Out of fourteen prosecuted leaders, we learn the professions of thirteen through the proceedings against them. Only one of them, Captain Cussinel, belonged to the lesser rural nobility (he was not a poor man, as the community of St. Antoine owed him 600 *livres*). Two lived in castles. They were not noble landlords but stewards, perhaps patrician bourgeois.

There were two court clerks, the approximate though somewhat more prestigious equivalent of a modern-day town secretary; a lawyer, a notary; and besides these prominent or legal personages there were two innkeepers, a miller, a "bourgeois" (all we are told), and two plowmen. Day laborers as well certainly must have participated in the rural uprisings. They were not leaders, but may have overruled the leaders when violence broke out.

There is no specific information for the region that can compare to the facts we have about the town of Callas (Var). During a revolt in 1580 against a very unpopular seigneur, the local government included, council proceedings show, a proseigneur faction, another faction in favor of the same landlord's son, and a rebel opposed to the landlord and all his kin.[24] We do, however, know enough about Dauphiné to warrant the assumption that the rural revolt was directed by the communities' regular councils, and also by the folk organizations and gatherings which consolidated rural youth. Both government and folk organizations and gatherings were sometimes overruled or overwhelmed by the unchecked elements within the parishes' lower group, day laborers or misfits. A remarkable fact is the total absence of the lower clergy in the leadership of our peasant war.[25] In this respect it was very different from the *Pitauts* uprising in southwest France in 1548 and the Normandy *Nus-pieds* in 1639, where parish priests incited peasants to attack crown soldiers or *gabeleurs*. Had the influence of Dauphiné's lower clergy declined as a result of Huguenot gains in the region, even in those parts of it remaining Catholic? Or could it be that the lessons of civil war had turned the parish priests into opponents of disorder? Once burned, twice shy . . .

In brief, a comparison between the two types of leadership in Dauphiné is enlightening: the urban example of rebel craftsmen against the bourgeoisie reflected a *splintered* urban community. The rural leadership *consolidated* the rural community in more or less united movement against the nobles.[26] Castle stewards and registrars were obvious targets and victims of the rural revolt (in the barony of Clérieu, for example), because they were seen as accomplices of the noble landlords, of Romans's elitist clique. But other registrars, other stewards farther afield from Romans, even lesser nobles, in Moras, Beaurepaire, or St. Vallier, for instance, became leaders of the revolt. For personal or local reasons they shared the peasants' grievances and their friendship. The most extraordinary case in point was the nobleman André de Bouvier, a half-outlaw, half-mercenary Huguenot soldier, a born enemy of the peasants when they rose up at the very beginning of the rural war in 1578. Yet he went on to become their chief—no more, no less—at the Beauvoir fort in 1580 when they had lost all hope and had no alternative but to join Lesdiguières's Protestant guerrillas.[27] An eleventh-hour leader, Bouvier shortly thereafter reversed his position and betrayed his peasant friends.

These are isolated examples. For the most part the activists and leaders in the urban and rural popular movement were identified, even stripped to the bone, by the judicial repression that decimated their ranks, enabling us to locate them in all certainty among the influential or middle-class elements in the villages, and to a far greater extent in the corresponding strata of the urban craftsman rank. The preponderance of craftsmen in the protest leadership was only normal: on occasion, rebels in the Romans region had asked a judiciary official to serve as their chief, but they were flatly refused.[28] Consequently, they relied on leaders who were members of the common people, principally small tradesmen or craftsmen. The large proportion of Romans's farmworker inhabitants—more than two-thirds of the population—did not imitate their rural counterparts who elected to follow notaries or town secretaries. Instead they gathered around the banners of their craftsman chiefs, while the urban common folk's "entertainment committees" made use of their agrarian folk traditions for the Carnival festivities.

XI

❦❦❦❦❦❦❦❦❦❦❦❦

Paradigms, Confraternities, Kingdoms

The special court dossiers allow us to focus on the sociology of the revolt, but we must go on from there. More broadly speaking, the Carnival of 1580 was the meeting point of an urban movement and powerful rural pressure. We shall now examine these two aspects in all their complexity and, as much as possible, in the light of comparative history.

In the Occitan and Franco-Provençal-speaking Midi, struggles involving the social factions or classes *within a town* can be classed according to two paradigms, which for the sake of convenience we might call the Karl Marx and Ibn Khaldun paradigms.[1] The Ibn Khaldun paradigm refers and conforms to the fourteenth-century Arab historian's analysis of factions in conflict as rival family clans within the wealthy ruling class. An instance in southern France would be the clash between the nobility of the sword and of the robe in Arles in 1644.[2] In this paradigm, each of the clans—one firmly in power, the other forming the opposition—tries to rally a popular following to its cause. The Karl Marx paradigm, of course, is a true class struggle between craftsmen, peasants, and plebeians on the one hand, and the notable bourgeois, even nobles, on the other. Again, Arles provides an example, with a revolt in 1637 in that town. Needless to say, the two paradigms represent extremes,

and in the vast middle ground of cases a simple conflict between
two powerful clans degenerated into a combat between the
ruling oligarchy and sections of the masses, each supporting
one of the rival clans. The Aix-en-Provence revolts of 1649–
1651 were an example of this intermediary type, providing the
people with a symbolic if temporary sense of purpose.[3]

The 1579–1580 episode in Romans is a nearly perfect example of class struggle. A few others, most of which are not so
clear-cut, are to be found among the various urban uprisings
that occurred in the Provençal or Franco-Provençal-speaking
areas, in Acquitaine and other provinces, from 1579 to 1720.
Through their confraternities, craftsmen took on the elite of
merchants and traders, jurists and towndwelling landowners.
In Romans and a few other cases like Arles and Aix, there was
also some group participation on the part of towndwelling
peasants. And what about the marginal elements, drifters, beggars, or *lumpenproletariat?* In Romans they accounted for a small
percentage of the population, but played no part in the popular
movement—although that was not always true of such revolts.
Also missing were the lower-class women, a group which
played a large and active role in the starvation riots of the next
few centuries. A substantial number of Romans's patrician
ladies did figure in the elitist Carnival, but only as sex objects,
admiring, admired, and desired.

René Pillorget's study of Provence has statistically demonstrated that clashes between the upper and lower sections of an
urban community are one of the most frequent forms of collective action.[4] By 1579 Romans shared this common feature.
What is more, the grievances formulated in the town's protest
are standard. Like the Florence *Ciompi* of 1378, Romans craftsmen took a lively interest in taxes and indirect levies, especially
municipal ones, and corporate debts, all instrumental in their
oppression. There were no demands for wage increases per se,
however; Pillorget, Castan, and Bercé have shown that this
holds true for all of the French Midi from 1570 to 1789. The
Lyons printers' strike in the sixteenth century was an isolated
example, typical of a new and dynamic profession; it was many
years before it found any imitators. In addition, the specific or

cultural gravity of the journeymen, the craftsman group's wage-earning workers, seems to have been slight in comparison to that of the self-employed master craftsmen, who were in fact small businessmen. In the context of the demands of the craftsmen as a group, a wage protest would have been devoid of meaning, although strikes against indirect taxes were liberally indulged in, especially by master craftsmen.

If we look at the protesters' demand for local power, we find a few concrete results. The neighborhood captains were removed and replaced in a manner more to the people's liking. The drapers Jean Serve-Paumier and Guillaume Robert-Brunat, Fleur the butcher, Jean Jacques the shoemaker, François Robin, and other leaders of the urban league regularly took part in town council meetings, of both the restricted and general councils. They had been admitted as "extraordinary-supernumerary" members after the February–March 1579 incidents, and there they remained until Mardi Gras 1580, the day of their death, flight, or arrest. Even so, the majority of Romans's council members were guardians of the ultimately triumphant *ancien régime* "system." Nor did the craftsmen infiltrate that top quartet, the consuls, or unseat Guérin from his judgeship-for-life. The Fronde-related Ormée protest in Bordeaux in 1649, also involving many craftsmen, was more successful, taking over every important municipal function.

Finally, Romans's urban micro-revolution approaches the British historian E. P. Thompson's analysis of the origins of popular movements. He discusses a plebeian group of self-employed craftsmen and shopkeepers in England up to and including the eighteenth century. Journeymen and wage-earning workers played only a minor role within this group. Thompson, like Albert Soboul, styles the plebeian-craftsmen-shopkeepers as "sansculottes"; they were a group always to be found in traditional towns. Naturally an industrial, manufacturing town like Romans had a more important craftsman/plebeian group than did Arles, a farming center where the main participants in the revolt were day laborers, peasants, and brawl-loving nobles. Romans's plebeians demanded a revision of the municipal *norms* relative to taxes, debts, and the composition of the town council. They wanted a return to more equitable norms, and they wanted the traditional community values upheld; the elite, and especially the judge, had violated them. Yet Romans's common folk did not come close to proposing new, egalitarian values. These were already in an embryonic state of development, but the ideologue formulating them was Jean de Bourg, the leader of Vienne's bourgeoisie, not a craftsman. In fact, no one before Jean-Jacques Rousseau clearly defined the ideas of individual liberty and popular sovereignty; the philosopher courageously defended the common people of Geneva against that town's lesser council, typically coopted and oligarchic. By 1600, however, Dauphiné had already made certain efforts in that direction.

As for sovereignty, Romans was far less bold than Auriol, a Provence market village where in 1599, well before Rousseau, the common people requested that their consuls be elected by popular vote.[5] This would have meant a return to a custom and a town democracy that may have existed in the Middle Ages. It would have meant abolishing the principle of cooptation, an almost universal practice in southern France of the late sixteenth century. It would have meant an end to the growth of the local oligarchy, a consequence of Renaissance expansion and the increasing power of the crown bureaucracy.

But Auriol was only a large village, mainly rural, not a real town like Romans, where the principle of cooptation was barely challenged. The town's elite had been schooled in French, even Latin, and securely lorded it over the common people who spoke an Occitan patois, with often no French at all.[6] Romans's protesters only minimally and temporarily encroached upon the near-stranglehold the elite had had on municipal power since 1542.

Yet the protesters represented a potential danger to this elite, which partially explains the violence of the final counteroffensive. It was feared that Paumier would bring his peasant allies into town to attack the rich. Guérin's subsequent repressive measures allayed such fears. They had not been unfounded: during a heated urban revolt in Aix in 1630, peasants from the surrounding villages invaded the town, mercilessly pillaging the homes of a few detested members of the town oligarchy.[7]

Another obsession fueling Guérin's deadly revenge on the protesters: he accused them of wanting to divide up the rich men's property, then their women, considered younger and more attractive than the poor men's wives. His sexual fantasy was perhaps based on fact—gang rape was common in Renaissance streets and town hall registers. As for the protesters' wanting to divide up property, it was probably a libelous representation of Paumier and Robert-Brunat's real intentions. As protest leaders go, they were reasonable men. It is likely, however, that Guérin's charge corresponded to some of the less cool-headed rebels' vague yet plausible motivations or objectives. We encounter a trend toward division of property in Provence around 1609, in Rouergue about 1627, possibly in Vivarais in 1679. Such protests proclaimed their desire to *put all the rich in caves . . . divide up their property. . . . The time has come for the earthen pot to break the brazen pot . . .*[8] Articulating such fantasies, however, was a far cry from carrying them out, and at least under the *ancien régime* it never came to that. In Romans, as elsewhere, it was still only a nebulous vision, shared by a very few. Only the revolt of Münzer's apocalyptic religious fanatics in 1534 went so far as to act on such impulses.

Romans's common people did not, then, justify their grievances with apocalyptic reasoning, nor Protestant, biblical, or millennarian reasoning, as did the sixteenth-century Anabaptists in Germany, the disciples of Thomas Münzer in 1524, or the Englishman Winstanley in 1650. Admittedly, urban craftsmen in lower Dauphiné were avid supporters of the Huguenot Reformation during the 1550s and 1560s, but almost all of them broke away after 1570.[9] The Massacre of St. Bartholomew upset them, especially in Romans, where Guérin had Huguenot leaders stifled or eliminated; the survivors preferred to head for Geneva. And then the high-handedness of the nobles or the power-hungry or both, like Lesdiguières, who made Dauphiné's Protestant movement into their own private affair, distressed many ordinary people. The extraordinarily interesting thing about the uprising was not a Protestant ideology—this was nonexistent or inactive as far as Romans was concerned—but its rich use of symbolic[10] and folk codes underlying and justifying the hostilities, on both sides.[11]

By folk codes I mean *folklore* in the most general sense of the term: popular traditions. They were part and parcel of Carnival in Romans. Their chief mode of expression was through *confraternities*, whether plebeian or bourgeois. These organizations assembled each of the various social groups and planned festive and other activities. We will briefly discuss four of the confraternities: St. Matthew and Maugouvert-Bongouvert for the elite; St. Blaise and the Holy Spirit for the craftsmen and towndwelling peasants. There were more than a dozen additional confraternities or groupings of the same type in Romans and Catholic and sociable organizations promoted by the church. During their brief reign in the early 1560s the Huguenots tried, to no avail, to abolish the confraternities and take over their property.[12]

Romans's St. Matthew confraternity was a select organization. It had a chapel in the Friary, the favorite meeting place of the elite and the law and order party. The members were supposedly all master merchants; there were some fifty or sixty of them toward 1578–1580, only about thirty in 1516. Like a proper elite corps, the confraternity did not expand. Among the officers and principal members in 1578–1580 were Captain Beauregard and Captain Antoine Coste; Jean, Félix, and Ennemond Guigou; Sire Jean Bernard; Ennemond Bourgeois-Mortnet; Captain Mornet; Ennemond Ricol, secretary of the town hall, and others. Excepting the rather special case of Jean Guigou, we can say that these worthy personages also controlled Romans's government and the law and order party, not to mention the mock abbey of Maugouvert-Bongouvert, the upper class's other "club."

Matthew (his saint's day is September 21) was a natural patron for the merchants; the money men. The apostle began his career as a publican, a specialist in financial and tax matters. This confraternity was more specifically oriented toward salt merchants or *sauniers*. Salt was the big national business of the time. It came up the Rhône on barges from the Camargue salt flats, to Valence, where Romans dealers took it over. They functioned as *gabeleurs* (working for the state *gabelle* or salt monopoly). Members of the St. Matthew confraternity paid relatively high dues: 10, 20, or 30 *sous* each, that is, two, four, or six times the dues of the St. Blaise confraternity. St. Matthew's functions were characteristic of a religious confraternity. The members had low Mass said, with communion, on September 21, then a high Mass on September 22. They also distributed alms to the poor.[13] There were other, underlying roles as well: St. Matthew, as Vienne's merchant confraternity, the Purification of Our Lady, functioned as a "garden or seminary where the town consuls and notables gather." It was a marriage of town hall and parish church.[14] From 1580 onward, the confraternities of penitents, originated by judge Guérin in person, would play a similar role in Romans.

Even more important to our study than St. Matthew was the so-called abbey of Maugouvert, or Bongouvert. Its active presence in Romans's Carnival, in the Partridge parade, is attested by a text of the Parlement of Grenoble.[15] Romans's own archives acquaint us with this curious institution.[16]

The mock abbey of Maugouvert—found in many other towns, large and small, along the Rhône or in Dauphiné—had "young males" as its members. They were all bachelors and roughly eighteen to thirty-eight years old, and were designated either as *monks* (full members) or *novices*. Their chief, called an *abbot,* who almost invariably became a consul later, may have been closer to forty. There was also a treasurer, virtually appointed for life. Maugouvert's roles were Christian, diverse, dionysiac. They had to do with Lent (paying Lenten preachers) and Carnival, but also spring (fertility of crops), power (political and municipal), and love (sexual and conjugal). At Mardi Gras time, the abbey organized the annual servant girls' ball, involving a stage and five or six fiddlers, paid for out of the Carnival "collections" taken up in town by the Maugouvert monks. All the dances and masquerades during Christmas and Carnival were to be under Maugouvert-Bongouvert's supervision, if possible.[17] The mock abbey also controlled the captain and the military parade of the "Native Sons," an upper-class youth group which in case of necessity policed military and

antiplebeian parades on feast days, as in 1580. The comic tone
the abbey texts in the town archives affect is thus a cover-up for
a serious and even lethal organization, with strong ties to local
authority, underlined by the way Maugouvert spent its money.
The abbey's revenues came from a tax it imposed on weddings,
especially those involving outsiders[18] who were charged 1 to 2
percent of the value of the dowry, plus 60 *sous* " . . . due from
those who wed a woman born outside the town." Priority spending of this income was first of all for repairs to the town hall
(we find endless bills for cartage of stone or sand, for masonry
work, and so on). The heads of the abbey were all young or
more mature patricians, whose names we also encounter in the
lists of consuls, the St. Matthew confraternity, and so on. They
included the Guigous; the Bernards; Captain Beauregard, a
good fellow and officer in the King's army, not just the local
militia; Pierre Bourgeois-Mornet, Maugouvert's treasurer for
life and descendant of an old Romans family, already part of
the town's financial elite at the beginning of the sixteenth century.[19] We have already observed that Bongouvert and St. Matthew often overlapped in terms of leaders. During the 1580s
Bourgeois-Mornet even held concurrent terms as consul and
treasurer of the abbey.

Maugouvert reached the height of its symbolic power in May.
The maypole was emblematic of a trinity: spring, power, and
love. Attached to the pole was a verdant box tree, the symbol
of perpetual fertility and of the Easter feast of Palm Sunday.
(In France green boughs, not palms are distributed on that
day—*translator*.) A pine sapling, also green, was tied to the top
of the maypole, reinforcing the symbolism. Thus trimmed, the
maypole embodied the annual renewal of the crop cycle in a
magic and semisacred fashion. But it was also a political tree.
To this day, a similar pole is planted in front of the homes of
newly elected municipal officials in the Midi. In Romans, toward 1577–1580, Maugouvert's annual maypole was erected in
the town square with four coats of arms at its base: the king's,
Maugiron's, the town of Romans's, and the abbey's own arms.

Finally, the month of May was the month of love, and the
elite's matrimonial politics were very much in evidence. During
the festivities Maugouvert-Bongouvert made presents of silver

or taffeta scarves to the lovely and distinguished young ladies of Romans's notable families. Carnival was a time for match-making, but May was made for romantic love.

From love it was a logical step to the policing of weddings. The mock abbey of Bongouvert taxed all weddings taking place in Romans. The "monks" even led a drum-beating *charivari* when outsiders or widowers wed. The church had long dis-couraged second marriages, even refusing them the nuptial ben-ediction. They disturbed a certain balance, which the boisterous *charivari* restored.[20] Each year at Carnival time Maugouvert drew up its tax roll of couples who had wed during the past year. Carnival was the proper time for attending to the conjugal balance sheet because Lent, which it heralded, marked a tem-porary halt to weddings. The pastors of Romans's three par-ishes, whom the Maugouvert monks "paid" with the gift of a hat for the service, gave the abbey a list of recent marriages, yet another link in the indissoluble bond connecting the mock abbey to the town's monocivic and multiparish organization. Maugouvert constituted, then, a phallic and serio-comic May-pole around which Romans's fertility turned, be it for crops, wedded couples, or political and municipal institutions. Mau-gouvert-Bongouvert unleashed the dionysiac fury of the repro-ductive urge, at the same time imposing order on it (Apollonian values, or Durkheim's). Its rites jokingly, sometimes violently, suppressed the anarchic release of inhibitions the Carnival and May festivities represented in Freudian terms. It is not difficult to understand how Maugouvert, its pseudomonks all members of the elite or the middle class, played a large part in the lethal antiplebeian offensive during the Carnival of 1580. For the "bad government" (like the *charivari*) was only a facetious means of reinforcing "good government" (correct observance of the social and nuptial pact). After 1580, even more markedly after 1581, *Bon*gouvert is increasingly favored in the archive documents as the abbey's name, as opposed to Maugouvert. The lessons of public disorder and the Carnival of 1580 had been learned.

Ambrozio Lorenzetti had already expressed those lessons, authoritatively so, in 1337–1339 when he painted his great fresco of the struggles of good and bad government, which is preserved in Sienna's town hall: rural and urban elements form a harmonious unit placed in opposition to the evil forces of disorder within a town, in this first example of European landscape painting.[21]

The two bourgeois or semibourgeois confraternities (St. Matthew and Maugouvert) were counterbalanced by two plebeian organizations, one for craftsmen, the other primarily agricultural: the confraternities of St. Blaise and the Holy Spirit. We have already made the acquaintance of St. Blaise in his Dauphiné incarnation. He was simultaneously *agricultural* (various agrarian rites assured his protection of harvests, flocks, herds); *medical* (he cured illnesses of the throat); *sexual-nuptial* (he saw to it that maidens married); *professional* (torn to pieces by carders' combs, he was the patron saint of carders and drapers; he was thus the natural foil for St. Matthew, the patron of financiers, salt merchants, and so forth).

We learn a great deal about the St. Blaise confraternity of Romans's clothworkers, so active in the 1579 and 1580 Carnivals, from a slightly later dossier in the archives of the *département* of the Drôme (the modern administrative subdivision of France which includes Romans—*translator*).[22]

In 1613, some thirty years after the Carnival in Romans, this confraternity had at least ninety-three members, almost all designated as masters (master drapers), with the occasional *Monsieur* or *Sire*. They were small or very small-scale self-employed businessmen, sometimes forming partnerships. Theirs were family businesses, possibly employing one or more journeymen. They paid minimal dues to their St. Blaise society (5 *sous*). They were economically dependent on the large-scale merchants, who sold them wool, then bought the finished product. Economic dependence did not, however, imply political servility; on the contrary. The merchants, as we have seen, had their own confraternity. The St. Blaise society had corporate functions: each year it held celebrations to welcome new *masters* into the trade (fourteen in 1613). Simple journeymen-drapers, however, were also admitted as members of this relatively democratic confraternity, on what conditions we do not know. St.

Blaise also had other, festive functions: it held a ball on the saint's day, when the new masters were also welcomed, with candlelight, fiddles, and ringing of bells. Could new master drapers have danced their virile rites of initiation on February 3, 1580, at the very same moment sword and bell dances taunted Romans's bourgeoisie? It is highly probable. The St. Blaise confraternity was at the same time a mock abbey like Maugouvert, headed by an abbot (in 1613 it was Vincent Sernons). But as a *trade* abbey it was in conflict with Maugouvert, a supposedly elitist, dominant, citywide abbey.²³ St. Blaise also appointed a captain for its paramilitary February 3 parade, and a king for the crowning feast of its *reynage*, on or about that same day. King, captain, abbot; in other words, the three leading characters in the standard Dauphiné feast day "kingdom."

The other protagonist in Romans's popular movement was the confraternity of the Holy Spirit. St. Matthew was the professional opposite of St. Blaise. On another level, Maugouvert, the overseer of weddings, was in distinct contrast to the Holy Spirit: marriage versus birth and death. As the third member of the Trinity, the Holy Spirit was functionally concerned with the birth, and above all, the spiritual rebirth of the individual, symbolized in the sacrament of confirmation. The gifts of the Holy Spirit were parallel to the gifts of food the confraternity distributed to its members at an annual Pentecost banquet.²⁴ The confraternity also dealt with death, since recently deceased members continued, with the poor as proxy, to dance and dine along with the community of workingmen. Each of us is destined to join the ranks of the dead, but in sixteenth-century Romans every dead man belonged to the ranks of the living, as was only normal in a world with an unshakable belief in ghosts, a world in which damnation or salvation of the immortal soul were matters of immediate concern to each and all. The Holy Spirit confraternity had a religious substratum, then, but lay members. It elected its priors (laymen); it chose its own priests to oversee the religious activities which were supposedly its ultimate purpose. It reaffirmed its internal, symbolic unity through yearly feasting which brought the members together. Uniting Romans's craftsman and even larger peasant masses, it was an organization of medieval descent, embodying the primitive bedrock of the plebeian community. It exalted the archaic and carnal bonding of this group which had maintained the continuity of Romans's people through the ages. These bonds were different from those fostered by Maugouvert, complementary if not contradictory to them. The elite abbey was a ferocious guardian of conjugal order, quick to censure second marriages and battered husbands. The two organizations, elitist and popular, Maugouvert and Holy Spirit, met head-on during Carnival (notably in 1580), then made another date for the lovely month of May. One of them put up a Maypole, the other took charge of the celebration of Pentecost, when the Holy Spirit hovered in the form of tongues of fire above the heads of the apostles and the faithful.[25] From the thirteenth century onward, analogous confraternities of the Holy Spirit, in Marseille, for instance, were hotbeds of urban protest. With possibly revolutionary ambitions for the whole plebeian and craftsman community, they acted under the utopian patronage of the third person of the Holy Trinity, the most collectivist and future-oriented of the three.[26]

All things duly considered, the Dauphiné phenomenon in 1579–1580 is a sort of open-air museum of every form of social organization—"abstract collectives," leagues, ruling and cooperative groups, associations, corporate groups—discovered between 1880 and 1930 by German jurists and sociologists. Their research is infinitely more varied than our contemporaries believe; we too often reduce this great tradition of scholarship to Marx and Weber alone. We cannot see the forest for those two tall trees.

In contact with Romans and more generally speaking with Dauphiné around 1580 we do find *abstract collectives*, defined as the sort "most distant from the empirical individual," namely the churches (Roman Catholic and Calvinist), and then the Paris-based state, represented in the province by its officials and briefly by Catherine de'Medici in 1579. Another prominent role is taken by the charismatic *league* (or *Bund*) uniting the villages and the urban plebeians around a prestigious leader, in our case Jean Serve-Paumier. In Romans proper, we encounter the contrast between associations *(Herrschaft)*, aiming to rule or dominate those outside and, as the expression goes, beneath them, and the "cooperative associations" *(Genossenschaft)* with all members on an equal footing.[27] This domination/ cooperation dichotomy *(Herrschaft/Genossenschaft)* redefines certain distinctions between various groups in Romans society. For instance, there was the abbey of Maugouvert; on the pretext of merrymaking it gathered together the privileged youth of the town, even a few of the well-to-do adults. By means of a tax it policed *all* weddings, with or without *charivaris,* for the rich, not so well-off, and poor, in the urban community. Maugouvert was unquestionably a *Herrschaft* or dominant institution, the expression of the ruling group's hold over certain essential activities. On the other hand, the popular or semipopular confraternities, of trade and otherwise, such as the "Confraternity of Monsieur St. Blaise," as it was then referred to, or the Holy Spirit confraternity, seem much more like cooperative or *Genossenschaft* organizations. They oversaw the activities of a specific group, the drapers and the lower classes in general. They were very little concerned with the ruling or dominant functions on the level of the urban *collective.* One exception, however, was the dominant role master craftsmen had in relation to their wage-earning assistants or "servants": while that was a real enough relationship, however, it found no expression in symbol or folklore, and did not come up during the Carnival in Romans.

Despite the functional divergences between Maugouvert and the St. Blaise or Holy Spirit confraternities, these three organizations and a few others, like the St. Matthew confraternity, can all be classed under the general heading of corporative social associations or groupings *(Verband, Körperschaft).*[28]

A remarkable fact is that the most strictly Carnival-related data we have on the Romans episode of 1580—the satirical price list of foodstuffs—originated in general with Maugouvert and the town's bourgeois institutions. That may seem curious, since such institutions by nature embodied the local power elite and not the common or "folk" elements. However, turning society temporarily upside down implied a knowledge of its normal vertical position, its hierarchy. Rites of inversion emanating from a dominant association or *Herrschaft* had the appropriate function—conservative, integrating, reinforcing the hierarchy—of creating a momentary inversion on feast days, the better to maintain order in the long run, in everyday society outside Carnival. Such inversion was ultimately counterrevolutionary. By contrast, for the February 1580 festivities the purely cooperative or *Genossenschaft* organizations in the workingmen's milieu initiated what were basically political protest actions, involved with combat, aggression—class struggles—even though they were symbolic and folk phenomena as well, intimately connected to Carnival. They made little use of the theme of inversion.

A comparison can be found in a completely different context—the May 1968 incidents in Paris. The Sorbonne students, members of the ruling class whether they liked it or not, and despite their challenge to authority, made use of the Carnival theme of an upside-down world, with rebels in power. The workers who joined them in a general strike, however, limited themselves to what seemed to them a rational course of action, with no folklore about it. Through standard union bargaining procedures, they won a hefty wage increase.

In conjunction with the confraternities, corporate and religious groups, we must also mention the *reynages*. For both of Romans's conflicting groups, Carnival was inseparable from the founding of a certain number of kingdoms or *reynages*, specific folk gatherings and festivities.[29] They appeared in the first uprisings in Valloire in February 1579. (As late as the nineteenth century, many Valloire *reynages* coincided with the feast of the Purification of the Virgin—Candlemas—and other saints' days in February and March.) Such *reynages* are also found in Romans in February 1579 and more important in 1580 with the Sheep, Eagle-Rooster, Hare, Capon, and Partridge kingdoms. Here as elsewhere, they inevitably accompanied saints' days (St. Blaise Day, for example) or at the very least a religious rite (Mass). In the background were the presence of a trade confraternity or mock abbey; a horse or foot race; the killing of an animal which had been the object of a contest of skill, like the decapitation of a rooster, and so forth; the enthroning of kings and queens; appointment of pseudo-officials of the royal court; burlesque events and dances that were sometimes an outrage; a great banquet and ball.

Yet these were merely local examples of a much more widespread and perfectly codified custom. Historians and ethnographers have defined the *reynage* as it was practiced throughout a huge area extending from Limousin to Dauphiné and including Auvergne, the eastern part of Guyenne, and the northern part of Languedoc; the epicenter was perhaps around Le Puy-en-Velay.[30] *Reynages* with all the typical traits first appeared in the second half of the fifteenth century; the first fully relevant text dates from 1498, but the institution was slightly earlier. They developed and became very popular during the sixteenth century. After reaching their high point during the seventeenth century and the Counter-Reformation, around 1600, they gradually waned, though traces and sometimes fine examples of these "kingdoms" were found in the eighteenth, nineteenth, and occasionally even the twentieth century.

Research has revealed the following elements common to all *reynages*:

(a) A *religious core* was essential: the celebration of a saint's day (Saint Blaise) or one of the feasts of the Virgin, for instance. All this was tied to a parish cult, or a communal "votive" feast, a local chapel, holy spring, or some such.

(b) The *election of a king,* queen, and other court officers, ranged from serious to comic. The various royal offices were sometimes more or less fictitious prizes in a race; in other instances they were auctioned off in church. Bidders pledged amounts of money, wheat, or most frequently wax to the chapel or sacristy in question. (The wax was for candles and the parish priest or sacristan was later able to sell the unburnable ends for profit.) Those who bought a "royal" post in this way were called *évergètes,* a dialect word meaning benefactor.[31] The bidders made a costly present of wax to the parish church to win the honor of becoming a "monarch," even a sham one; or else they acted out of piety, or for reasons of local politics. Everywhere, in Limousin or in Romans, a permanent confraternity (a trade association or a village's corporate confraternity) was always responsible for the annual kingdom; it was almost a union affair. A *youth* group was often in charge, but not only the young participated. To this day in Romans *pognes,* a local cake shaped like a crown, commemorates the *reynages.*

(c) *Entertainments* such as hunting or the killing of an animal, foot and horse races, dances, balls, banquets, buffoonery, the celebration of love, occurred in the various provinces, Limousin as well as Dauphiné. The king of the festive realm had a financial function: his role as church benefactor was a way of redistributing wealth into communal religious institutions. But the king also had a religious function—his coronation took place in church, and his reign celebrated a specific saint's day or Sunday. He performed an amorous function in relation to his queen and local maidens and a political function through his imitation of French royalty.[32]

The Carnival in Romans made ready use of the *reynages.* It was rooted in the parish and confraternity-related culture of the time. The notables and other leaders, great or small, plebeian or rich, wanted to *épater les bourgeois* (to unsettle people). They pursued certain finalities, in some cases conservative or radical ones; they attained their goal by donating a modest sum of money or quantity of wax and becoming king for a few days during the Carnival, Easter, or summer festivities. Catholic culture under the *ancien régime* was an admirable blend of sacred and profane, religious and burlesque. In the *reynage* it had created a social tool, allowing the lower classes to express themselves, their mockery, and sometimes even their grievances. Plebeian political tendencies that were repressed during the rest of the year came to light during the festivities. A dangerous group subconscious found a temporary outward structuring in the solemn and formalized institutions of the *reynage.* Here, we might say, Durkheim and Freud join hands: the *reynage* was a synthesis of the primitive and the civilized feast.[33]

XII

❧❧❧❧❧❧❧❧❧❧❧❧

The Winter Festival

Confraternities and kingdoms aside, we must also consider the general question of winter festivals, particularly pre-Lenten feasting in Dauphiné, the French Midi, even Europe as a whole. There is no understanding the February Carnival in Romans without putting it in this wider perspective. We must examine what Carnival was like in the various Provençal[1] and Mediterranean cultures found in France, of course, but also in Savoy; we should consider Swiss Carnivals too, which were Germanic in nature. All these cultures were neighbors or close relatives of Dauphiné's sixteenth-century civilization. We shall concentrate on the following aspects of Carnival: its annual role and Christian/pagan features; seasonal and winter, agricultural and fertility functions; its relation to social conflict; its symbolic or ritual nature.

In terms of form, Dauphiné's Carnival began as a New Year's feast. During the Middle Ages and in some cases as late as the sixteenth century, Dauphiné started the year either on September 25, December 25, or March 25.[2] Carnival was thus one of the periods demarcating the end of one annual cycle and the beginning of the next. Anthropologists (Van Gennep, Leach, and Turner)[3] have provided us with interesting paradigms for festivities related to the beginning or end of a cycle (in this instance an annual one), as opposed to linear or future-oriented time.

Leach draws examples from many cultures—Christian and otherwise—and uses Van Gennep's analyses of rites of passage. He proposes a "pendulum view" of the flow of time in traditional and festive cultures (no matter what their Christian beliefs on historical evolution or the "end of time" might be). Time flowed normally during the year, then ran briefly in reverse during the festive period, returning to its normal flow during the course of the following year or season. This paradigm of alternation harmonizes with the immediate experience of time flow (night and day, life and death, and so forth). The festival thus supposes a first "preliminal" stage (to borrow Van Gennep's terminology), or phase (A), setting it off from time as experienced in normal life, or during the past year. A second or "liminary," (B) phase, is the transitional period during which the threshold into festive or sacred time is crossed, a quick swing of the pendulum, into time running backwards or *role reversal* properly speaking. Finally a third phase (C) is one of *reintegration* or aggregation into profane or ordinary time, which will prevail until the next alternation, and so on.

Leach holds that there is an explicit connection between this three-part time flow and Carnival themes properly speaking, and that there are also three types of ritual behavior encountered on festive occasions: masquerade, role reversal, formalities. The *masquerade* is a striking expression of the breaking away from ordinary or profane time, the entrance into fictive or sacred time. Rites of role reversal signal that the transition period has begun, indicate that the human group serving as the societal base for the festivities is momentarily turned upside down. According to Turner (or Sartre) this is the divine instant of communication between the revelers. The group is "fused" in a mutual state of role reversal. *Formalities,* finally (no fake or mud-daubed noses here, but silk top hats) coincide with the entry into phase C, the repressive or what Turner calls "redressive" stage. The emphatic accentuation of normative dress (like a magistrate's cap and gown) in effect signifies the act of compulsory return to the rules governing ordinary time. Other concatenations may change the order of these three phases without transforming the process itself in the least. For instance a wedding, a *rite de passage* if ever there was one, begins with *formalities* (a procession with morning coats or tails, etc.) and may end with orgiastic rituals, possibly a masked ball.

In conclusion Leach emphasizes the alternating swing between life and death (from the beginning to the end of the year), then from death to life (during the brief moment of resurrection provided by Carnival).

The British anthropologist's analysis applies to the Carnival in Romans, not to mention European Carnivals in general. The St. Blaise festivities that marked the beginning of the Romans episode were unbridled *masquerades,* a dionysiac demonstration including crude face-painting, dances, brooms, rakes, flails, symbols of death. Then it moved on to the magical world of the rich men's kingdoms, the Land of Cockaigne of Provençal tradition, a wonderland of reversal where fine wines and dainty foods sold for a penny, while rotten herring was sky-high.[4] At the close of the festivities came the final parades of the Partridge Kingdom's military tribunal—king, judges, and soldiers—corresponding to the last stage, Apollonian *formalities* paving the way to a final, violent imposition of order, the return to everyday life. This three-part process characterized Carnival in both northern and southern France, on both sides of the Alps. First there would be masked collection of money. Then *Bonhomme de Carnaval* (a person disguised as the "Mr. Carnival" effigy) would distribute a wealth of hams and sausages during the middle phase. At the end the picturesque Carnival effigy became a scapegoat; a solemn tribunal was set up to try, hang, drown the *Bonhomme*. This prepared the participants to rid themselves of sin, to enter into the cheerlessness of Lent.[5]

As concerns the place of Carnival-Lent in the Christian time cycle, in the first chapter of this book I gave the definition I find best suited to the primordial concept of Carnival and the essence of Lent: burying one's pagan ways, having one last pagan fling before embarking on the penetential rigors of the catachumen's lententide, which would result in spiritual and baptismal rebirth at Easter. In short, the rites of Carnival were a logical prelude to their opposite: Lenten fasting and preaching. In Romans, as elsewhere, these festivities had been sandwiched into the Christian, more specifically the Catholic cycle. (The Protestants abolished Lenten fasting and were thus obliged to get rid of the preliminary feasting as well. As early as the sixteenth century they were making a spirited attempt at destroying all traces of Carnival.) The Catholic calendar ran from All Saints' Day to Advent and Christmas, then Carnival, Lent, Easter, and St. John's Day (Midsummer Day). Romans's 1580 episode was very much in line with this view of time. St. Blaise and the Holy Spirit were honored. The rich men's Mass was celebrated on *lundi gras*, with a few folk embellishments.[6] In Paris the League also organized religious yet lewd Mardi Gras processions; the people forced parish priests to take part in them.[7]

That is the crux of the question. Carnival's pre-Lenten yet anti-Lent functions made it antithetic to the ascetic values of Christianity. Lent exalts abstention from food and sex,[8] celebrates virtuous behavior. Historically it was a time of peace, the Truce of God.[9] Carnival, to the contrary, emphasized sins of the flesh, gluttony, and lubricity. It glorified feasting (the price list of foodstuffs, the "kingdom" banquets) and the release of sexual inhibitions (the maximum number of annual weddings and conceptions; dances; election of kings and queens; latent threats of rape and kidnapping against patrician ladies). Finally the trappings of war, real or imitation, were displayed (the poor people's sword dance, the elite's military parade). In this sense Carnival approached a system of pre-Christian or non-Christian givens (in other words folk or rustic, even pagan values). Insofar as its aim was to "bury pagan ways,"[10] it directly reproduced parts of the ancient winter festivities which had been adopted into the church along with the common folk as the countryside was converted during the first millennium, a period of prodigious cultural grafting. Among such pagan rites were the Saturnalian role reversals, the Lupercalian animal masquerades and floggings, the donkey ride, and so forth. But Christianity is after all a religion based on the concept of *sin*. It is not unusual, then, that it was able to digest these pagan rites so thoroughly, and that it had fully assimilated the peccant joys of Carnival, if only to banish them when Lent arrived.

These religious notions are pertinent, but they do not describe Carnival's existential content (seasonal, agricultural) or the class (or clan) struggle it incorporated.

For Carnival festivities were not only cyclical and annual, as Leach points out, or pagan plus Christian; they also had to do with the changing of seasons. They were specifically connected to the approach of the end of winter, a crucial moment for a society which was still semi-agricultural and thus nature-oriented. In this seasonal domain the reigning character was the Candlemas bear; it was in this disguise that Paumier briefly occupied a consul's seat in Romans's town hall. In Dauphiné as in Savoy, the bear predicted how much longer the cold season would last. On February 2 it came out of the den where it had been hibernating and looked at the sky. If it were cloudy, superstition maintained, the bear would decree winter was over. But if the sky were blue the cold would continue for forty more days, and the bear would lumber back into its den to sleep for a few more weeks.[11]

The Candlemas bear is an invention of the region of the great European mountain ranges (Alps, Pyrenees). In other western countries where the bear is not native, another hibernating animal serves as forecaster of the winter thaw. Ireland has a St. Bridget's Day (February 1) hedgehog. A groundhog emerges each February 2 or 3 in Pennsylvania (European settlers brought this folk tradition with them to North America). In both cases the rodent uses the sky to predict whether or not winter will last six more weeks, just like the Alpine Candlemas bear.

In the Pyrenees, the Candlemas-Carnival bear became a sheep-napper, and a "shooting" was staged as a symbolic measure of protection for the flocks. This bear is also a wild and hairy satyr, a sexual "wolf," sticking its paws into beehives and down women's dresses. In Romans, Paumier the Candlemas bear shifted from seasonal weather forecasting to political provocation. Some of his young supporters may well have had designs on the bourgeois ladies, but Paumier, more seriously, was concerned with the partial seizure of local power. Guérin hated him, but did not mistake him for a teddy bear.[12] Beneath his furry coat, Paumier was a political animal.

The object of Carnival was not only to give time a nudge, move the seasonal rhythm forward. It also dispensed fertility, for women and couples, crops, the community. It was at once symbolizer and purger of the various ills and sins which might affect the human body and soul, the social group, and the crops. This supported the Catholic scenario: Carnival embodied unbridled pleasure, the joys of life and the dance, the pagan sins of the flesh, and so on, which would be excrementally eliminated by Lent. In early February 1580 Romans's St. Blaise's Day dancers mimed the winter farm work of flailing, raking, and sweeping the threshing-floor. Even more specific was the role of the children carrying *brandons* (flaming wooden torches) during the mid-February massacre in Romans; their symbolic function was to exterminate parasites preying on fruit trees and cereal crops. These young torchbearers simultaneously warded off Paumier's men—the enemies of social order—and the moles or fieldmice attacking apples or grain. Well into the seventeenth century the old-style Carnival in France, from February 2 until the beginning of Lent, was packed with such propitiatory practices. Many of them were found in Dauphiné, for instance crêpes and blessed candles for Candlemas; the ringing of bells (more bells!) on February 5; a halt to spinning; aspersion with *andouille* (chitterling) broth; the burial of *carême-prenant* (the Provençal Carnival effigy); *brandons* and *fassenotes*. People did these things for all sorts of reasons: in hope of having a good supply of money during the year; to keep safe from lightning and evil spells of every sort; to prevent foxes from eating the chickens, mice from chewing up yarn; to make their Lenten fasting easier; guard the crops from fieldmice, tares, blight;

assure good yields from gardens and make onions grow big; help find brides and grooms for the young men and women of the village.[13] The idea of Carnival and more generally winter festivities as fertility rites has been developed in detail by several anthropologists and historians, such as Dumézil and Toschi, who contend that the macabre animal masks (bears, etc.) worn by a community's young people during the festivities in fact represented demons and dead souls. It was commonly believed that the dead moved among the living and could influence the next growing season. It was thus essential that everyone make offerings to these masked youths, so that the spirits they represented would guarantee a good year and good health to all, after which they would conveniently disappear. Dead souls, as we have seen, were also included among the masked revelers and agrarian *pantragnes* during Romans's Candlemas celebration. In 1580 they demanded their fair share of the urban wealth, amidst a macabre din of bells. It is obvious, however, that this notion does not necessarily imply that the people were resorting to long-defunct pagan practices. Medieval Catholicism admitted the people's firm belief in ghosts, devils, and their intervention in everyday affairs. Dumézil and Toschi have used this as the key to the original meaning of certain Carnival masquerades. We cannot say for certain, however, that the people of Romans in 1580 understood them *as masquerades*.[14] Carnival rites were rooted in custom, but their meaning was not always so clear.

Carnival, then, was agricultural, biological. But it was socially useful as well. The two are inseparable, just as the Maypole expressed an indissoluble bond between political power, phallic fertility, abundance of plant life. Baroja's definition of Carnival[15]—ambivalent and short but to the point—manages to include this bipolarity: the aim of Carnival, the Spanish folklorist writes, "is to maintain local society in working order"

(1) By eliminating harmful elements (biological, social, or sinful/anti-Christian) from the town as a preliminary to Lenten purification;

(2) Through enactment of the normal course of human life: birth, copulation, death, and rebirth (the cannibalistic dance in Romans, for instance, was not only a threat to the rich but also a transubstantiation fantasy);

(3) Through the imitation of agricultural or other work essential to group survival (plowing in some places, threshing in others, as in Romans) and through military parades;

(4) By representing animals of special importance to the economy (game, sheep, poultry, whose symbolic function, moreover, went far beyond the utilitarian, in Romans and elsewhere);

(5) Through activities producing the kind of noise which might aid in eliminating harmful elements, pursuing everyday affairs, etc.

Eliminating socially harmful elements, an extrapolation of sin, was accomplished through *satire.* It recurs in all our Carnivals, in Dauphiné, Italy, Switzerland, Occitania, around Bordeaux, Paris, etc. Scattered throughout Swiss history, for instance, are political or politico-religious Carnivals. During the fourteenth century the Carnivals attacked the rich, at the beginning of the Reformation the Pope, and in the nineteenth century Napoleon. In both northern and southern France, the last will and testament and sentencing of the Carnival effigy (which went by various names) provided an opportunity for a year's worth of complaints about adultery, usury, and so on, to be aired. Bordeaux's Carnivals in the mid-seventeenth century aided and abetted the powerful Ormée revolt there; Mazarin was satirized in Mardi Gras parades. And what about the long winter Saturnalia of rebellious Provence Carnivals during the French Revolution? From the sixteenth to the twentieth centuries, Carnival in Languedoc (Montpellier, Limoux)—like the holy city of Rome's own Carnival, perfectly in keeping with the Catholicism of the time—successively made fun of unfortunate local Jews, then of all the more or less secret vices of members of the community. Naturally satire, even that with a certain corrective slant, does not imply violence and bloodshed. Guérin was the one to introduce those elements in Romans, as he set his trap. None of the various festival entertainment committees had planned anything of the sort in February 1580. But satire is one of the most constant and common elements of Carnival from the fifteenth through nineteenth centuries. It is also present to a lesser extent in other winter or summer festivals.[16]

Banishing sin or evil from society (and preventing agricultural or biological ills in the bargain) is easier said than done. Controlling nature is one thing. Controlling control itself is another.[17] No one can argue with the fact that insect pests and fieldmice destroy crops, or that poisonous snakes and storms are threats to human welfare. A good sprinkling with chitterling broth on Mardi Gras or lighting a Candlemas taper are the appropriate steps everyone agreed should be taken to counteract these dangers.

On the other hand, as far as *social* welfare is concerned, here opinions swiftly diverged. For the craftsman a social ill might mean an indirect tax on meat or bread, while the municipal elite would consider the same tax beneficial. Inversely, the plebeians would find their own spirit of rebellion to be positive, but it would appear negative to the ruling class. As soon as Carnival ceased to be a purely agrarian phenomenon, as soon as it tried to define groups, express the urban or at least collective spirit of festivity, it inevitably implied social conflict. Carnival developed its own far from innocent terms for dealing with conflict.[18] In extreme cases a community might organize two separate Carnivals, even two separate Maypoles, one for the poor and one for the rich (a left- and right-wing pole, if you will). This is found in Périgord under Louis-Philippe, in a twentieth-century Normandy village, and in Romans in 1580. These "binary" conflicts, on the political and practical levels, were incorporated into Carnival's already established mythical-annual-seasonal function,[19] which aimed to symbolize and sometimes dramatize, the cyclical flow of time—of the years, growing seasons, religious holidays. The contests or jousts characteristic of Carnival glided effortlessly between the practical and the symbolic. Carnival tournaments or tennis games (in Florence), Shrove Tuesday soccer games (in the British Isles), matched two groups from within a town or within the ranks of the nobility. Other possible oppositions were two types of be-

havior (jolly versus sad); two age groups (married versus unmarried); two real or theatrically represented ethnic groups
(Englishmen versus Scots); the residents from a town's river-
banks or two rival neighborhoods, and so on. But binary conflicts could also represent a combat between two folk/religious
and chronological entities (not so different from the previous
case): Carnival versus Lent, pork versus cod; or two seasons,
such as summer versus winter. Again, we should keep in mind
that political life in Dauphiné, Languedoc, and Provence was
set in an annual, seasonal context. New consuls were elected
at the beginning of each year, as spring grasses began to replace
the dead straw—the stuff of which Carnival effigies were
made—of fall/winter. Symbolic and biological struggles between the seasons, then, reemphasized the practical and normative struggles between political factions, between outgoing
governments and malcontents shouting "get them out fast." All
this took place within a pre-Copernican thought system in which
social and cosmic time were inextricably mingled. Each regen-
erated the other through an anthropocentric view that subor-
dinated the central human microcosm to the engulfing macrocosm of the natural environment. "Symbolic systems," Lévi-
Strauss writes, "attempt to express certain aspects of *physical*
and *social* reality, and even more so the relationships the two
sorts of reality establish with each other."[20] And Carnival is
eminently endowed with symbolic systems.

And yet even in this world view combining the Universe and
the City of Man, the Cosmos and the Polis, a binary system
does not always apply. Sixteenth-century Italian peasants or
residents of the city of Berne acted out the annual sequence of
seasons, but instead of representing *two* major parts of the
annual cycle, such as Carnival/Lent or winter/summer, they
showed all *twelve* months of the year through the work done by
peasants during each (the same scenes appeared above cathe-
dral doors); or they represented the "twelve planets," and so
on.

From yet another perspective, Romans traditionally had a

pluralist Carnival, even when it was reduced to a confrontation between two opposing parties. The year 1580 was a clear example, with no fewer than five conflicting or colluding kingdoms. They embodied various quarters of town, confraternities, mock abbeys, age groups, factions, or social classes. The final struggle corresponded to an alliance between the Eagle-Rooster and Partridge kingdoms pitted against the Hare, Capon, and Sheep. This plurality would last through the centuries: when Calixte Lafosse described Carnival in Romans in about 1840, it still *enjoyed great fame* in the whole surrounding district. Now there were not five *reynages,* as in 1580, but *at least twenty singing societies having among their members poets and actors who went from square to square in Thespian chariots, each trying to outdo the other in song and verse. Fine entertainment for the public! They sang in every possible style, in patois* (Franco-Provençal), *in French, in gibberish, they sang comedy, tragedy, drama, political rhymes, racy refrains, masterpieces, nonsense. A free show! The best tunes would be sung for several months afterwards, then everything would die down until the next year's songs were readied. Today* (about 1869, when Calixte Lafosse was writing his memoirs) *all this has disappeared because of exorbitant printing costs* (to print up songs and skits) *and because of censorship. The plot of one of these Carnival vignettes might be, for instance, that a pretty young woman refuses to marry Mardi gras, who then dies of consumption, all this under the watchful eye of Father Jacquemart, a godlike character holding his see atop the tower of the same name. Now when Mardi gras dies Jacquemart deigns to come down to earth, entoning "The Eagle's companion am I in the airy reaches; my wish was to be a duck."* An Occitan chorus sang: *"If I were a prophet, I'd turn the Isère into cheap wine, and Romans's dirty gutter water into brandy and burgundy."*[21] We can see, then, that in 1840 a number of the Carnival customs were the same as those used in or inherent in late sixteenth-century Carnivals in Romans and/or Provence: reversal of the value of foodstuffs (good water turned into cheap wine, gutter water into good wine, etc.); the Carnival effigy's marriage, Jacquemart's descent from eagle into duck instead of Eagle-Rooster (there is in fact a statue of a domestic fowl at the foot of the present-day Jacquemart landmark in Romans). Even more conspicuous is the continuity of pluralism. There were twenty singing societies in 1840, five kingdoms in 1580. Carnival in Romans was never simply an opposition of old and young or rich and poor. Instead, as in Lyons or Italy, it represented a sort of comprehensive and poetic description of society, neighborhoods, professions, age groups, the young, males, and so forth. Embracing so many elements made Carnival particularly apt as an instrument of *social change*, which was slow but undeniable in sixteenth-century towns successively shaken by the Renaissance, the Reformation, the Counter-Reformation. In other words Carnival was not merely a satirical and *purely temporary* reversal of the dual social order, finally intended to justify the status quo in an "objectively" conservative manner. It would be more accurate to say it was a satirical, lyrical, epic-learning experience for highly diversified groups. It was a way to action, perhaps modifying the society as a whole in the direction of social change and *possible progress*.[22] In 1783, *Masques* in the revolting Vivarais protested against corrupt justice officials in the service of noble landlords. They fought for a true peasant and judicial system.[23] Masked doers of justice against greedy justice officials . . . It goes without saying, however, that *anti-Semitic* Carnivals (Montpellier, Rome) can hardly be deemed progressive. Popular festivities and social change do not always go hand in hand.

If Carnival is, then, a comprehensive, dynamic, oppositional description of a society, the organizers of Romans's 1580 Carnival used a variety of symbolic procedures in their description. Their followers understood and went along with them, in spite of or rather because of the animosity soldering them into conflicting groups. Among the symbolic systems was metaphor, a fundamental procedure of folk discourse.[24] *Food* symbolism appeared in the satirical price list Guérin's men or the judge himself drew up. Game, poultry, the best and freshest river fish, fine wine, spices, delicate fruits, and sugar symbolized the rich and their conspicuous consumption of food during Carnival. Food and drink that was sour, salty, rotten, stinking; common meats like mutton, beef, and pork; and animal feed like hay, straw, and oats were intended to represent the poor, momentarily and ironically "celebrated" by the high prices on the inverted list.

The use of live animals was less exclusive and more original. On one side were the bear, donkey, hare, and sheep (the poor); on the other were the eagle, rooster, partridge (the rich). In other words it was a contrast between castrated and noncastrated animals, or earthbound and airborne fauna.

Many other Carnivals made use of these methods of classification, but usually to chronological rather than sociological ends. The hog, for instance, would be contrasted to the cod (Mardi Gras/Lent). An impromptu fourteenth-century Italian poem contrasted the partridge, pheasant, capon, thrush, blood pudding, and pigeon (Carnival) to carrots, leeks, peas, tuna, and eel (Lent).[25] Classifications of this type were also used to sociological and satirical ends in the Carnivals of northern and southern Italy, so close to Dauphiné. Here not a group of animals, but the anatomy of an emblematic animal was used. A donkey, hog, turkey, wolf, etc., was supposed to will various parts of its body to a certain social category—the belly to priests, the genitals to women, the head to lawyers, and so on. In Montmorillon's 1795 Carnival, the town's residents appeared as sheep, and tax collectors were wolves.

The "symbolic grammar" of Carnival in Romans worked on three levels at once: for each animal in a given context there was a specific and special meaning, sometimes trivial. The rooster is virile, the bear is a "weatherman," the hare is bad luck, and so on. In the second place, the whole group of animals or creatures making an appearance during Carnival had a heraldic meaning, became a kind of grid or code "allowing for the use of the diversity of animal species as a conceptual support for social differentiation."[26] Here sociology gives way to zoology or botany, Marx yields to Tournefort. In the third place, the animal was a "scapegoat" for collective sins, or represented the challengers of the status quo. It was involved with the tasks of animal husbandry, the hunt, athletic/sporting activities (beheading of a rooster, killing of a sheep with sickles, partridge run). It had a role in the internal bonding of each of

the various social sub-groups as they partook of the animal's
flesh at their banquet. *Say it with meat,* the slogan might run. It
would be clear to everyone, even if meanings might vary. Rooster, eagle, or partridge made a simultaneously dramatic and
functional symbol, setting up a multilevel strategy, allowing
specific splinter groups to try and gain the upper hand in a
given situation. In 1580 this was the natural way of doing things
in Romans. The late Renaissance mentality was spontaneously
nominalist, better adapted to handling objects (maypole, sheep)
as it saw fit than dealing with abstract concepts such as class
struggle, reforms, etc. Guérin, the master of folk ceremonies,
knew all about this mentality, including how to exploit it.

Symbols, then, were as important as events in the political and
folk festival we call the Carnival in Romans. Might we go so
far as to say there were rich men's symbols and poor men's?
Yes and no. There was no great social distance between the two
groups in a small city, especially since hard times had affected
everyone, even the wealthiest citizens. At times it was even
possible for the two groups to exchange or share symbols. Their
view of the world was basically the same. In Romans in 1580
the poorer men used a donkey in their procession; the rich had
the prerogative of masquerading as Swiss Guards. But in Lyons
during the same period *both* donkeys and Swiss Guards appeared
in the printers' Carnival. Turks and holiday couriers were
united in Romans in 1580, but in conflict in Berne in 1523.
Consequently, it is impossible to assign fixed social categories
to Carnival objects, animals, or symbols.
   Social distinctions did, however, exist. The ultimately dichot-
omous division of the Provençal or southern Dauphiné folk
festival into a disordered segment, then an ordered one, was
clear in Romans as it was for Corpus Christi day in Aix-en-
Provence, or the *Tarasque* ceremonies at Tarascon. (Act I: the
tarasque—the effigy of a monstrous imaginary animal—lurches
wildly about, breathing fire; Act II: St. Martha breaks the
monster until it is tame as a lap dog.) The dichotomy was
chronological, but geographic as well. In Romans the orderly

Partridge Kingdom followed the disorderly Sheep displays. Furthermore, there was a split between north/south (St. Barnard, Jacquemart, the rich men's quarters), and east/west (craftsmen and plowmen in St. Nicholas, Le Chapelier). Even fire was divided in two: Candlemas tapers belonged to the plebeians, while the flaming brands of *lundi gras* were carried by children under the control of the rich.[27]

The common folk's use of symbol and satire is obvious. In a Carnival intended as a protest against a ruling caste, ordinarily the prime satirical instrument was the Carnival dummy or effigy made up to look like the enemy of the day: the Roman Pope, Luther, Napoleon III, a piglet as Louis XVI, a goat as Marie-Antoinette, and so on. The effigy was supposed to appear on Mardi Gras day. In 1580 it was not seen in Romans, for the Partridge slaughter the night before cut short the festivities. The poor had nonetheless displayed their symbolic system in various ways.[28] This involved the agrarian rites of St. Blaise's Day: flailers mimed the preparations for spring sowing and the symbolic annihilation of the rich. A procession led by a donkey had told the elite: "Your wives will beat you and make cuckolds of you." The blood-red mourning robes of the Holy Spirit confraternity had served to bury the departing year and announce cannibalistic intentions toward the rich. Symbolic nicknames were chosen for the popular leaders (Paumier, Pain Blanc). The paraders' faces were tellingly disguised with mud, ashes, and flour, transforming them into devils and ghosts. Protected by the anonymity of masquerade, the poor led the young people's ominous house-to-house search for alms, seeking vengeance against municipal exploiters, usurers, bloodsuckers of the people. Each of these rituals worked on both a mythical level (sowing, calendar of feasts, ghosts) and a political level (class struggles) by means of figurative representation. Actors replaced abstract concepts. The people immediately grasped Carnival drama. It was their specialty.[29]

The same goes for the sword dance, which ritualized a warlike confrontation. In Romans it took place on St. Blaise's day, and there was a connection between the date and the dance. Both sides of the Alps—the Piedmont and Dauphiné—attested to the connection.[30] Toschi and a few other scholars have made a thorough study of this "armed folk dance" of a type that was very common in Italy, Germany, England, Spain, and southern France.

(a) It was a *spatio-temporal rite.* The rose-window design made by the swords depicted the points of the compass and the heavens changing with the seasons. The death and resurrection of a character (a buffoon, harlequin) took place during the dance.

(b) It was an *agricultural fertility rite, and possibly a ritual dance to protect human health against various calamities.* This dance was linked to Carnival and the olive harvest in Provence;[31] in the Piedmont the sword traced a grain-growing furrow. At Cervières, in Dauphiné, it also coincided with the specifically anti-plague feast day of St. Roch, celebrated annually since the end of the Middle Ages.

(c) It was *a dangerous initiation into manhood for young males.* New members of trade confraternities were also initiated in this way. It characterized Carnival as a time of war or at least symbolic violence. Lent was by contrast a pacifist Truce of God[32] during which it was forbidden to slice up human "meat."

(d) It was a *statement of class struggles.* In the Piedmont the dancing sword put an end to the activities of an evil landlord who would terrorize peasants or rape their daughters. A nuptial theme also appeared: a girl would be carried off by one of the dancers, or freed from an evil seigneur (as above). (The sword dance was often mixed with the Turkish strain in folk theater, called *morisque* or *moresque.* But in Romans the characters disguised as Turks were on the other side, in the rich men's Carnival. Once again symbols appear moveable, if not interchangeable.)

During the Carnival of 1580 the last two meanings of the sword dance (symbolic violence and social conflict) were evidently emphasized at the expense of the first two (seasonal cycle and the fertility or prophylactic element), which nonetheless played a certain role.

As concerns Romans's sword dance on St. Blaise's day, it

was closely associated with the use of noisemaking and politically disruptive instruments: bells and drums. Both of these
were favorite weapons of folk protest rituals critical of the
dominant groups in Provençal or Franco-Provençal-speaking
areas. From this point of view, the people's Carnival had its
own rationale. To achieve its social goals, articulate its demands, it used the most effective or most audible means of
agitation possible considering the culture and psychology of
the times.[33]

In the face of such a challenge the rich men's Carnival pulled
out all stops to stage the elaborate Partridge processions (sim-
ulating the presence of a king, the high clergy, the army, justice
preparing to sentence Mardi Gras). In short, a whole battery of
hyperbole was at work beneath the caricature and masquerades.
The workingmen's kingdoms preached a return to older values,
those of Earth, Death, a primordial din, the symbolism of the
sword and cannibalistic violence. The elite's processional cor-
tèges were also aggressive in purpose. In addition they were "an
emphatic and celebratory collective," the parading metaphor
of a hierarchic society; instead of returning to the past, it exalted a systematic upward projection toward lofty concepts and
birds in flight. Thus, superstructure asserted itself in contrast
to infrastructure, the surreal in contrast to the subreal, the
brazen pot versus the earthen pot. It was a struggle between
two ideas of justice. The subsequent Lenten spectacle of the
executions of Paumier's comrades was no more than a logical
continuation of this; culture triumphed over nature. Guérin's
festival during the 1580 holidays drew on all the theatrical
traditions in Romans's Renaissance repertoire, and there was
certainly no lack of them: the quasi-medieval mystery play of
the early sixteenth century, royal entrances, devotional processions, the construction of a miraculous open-air Way of the
Cross. In 1580 there were burlesque improvisations within the
Catholic walls of St. Barnard and the Friary, even folk displays
of Moorish and Turkish inspiration. Judge Guérin was decidedly a first-class impresario, one of a kind. For him the end

(tragic as it might be) justified the means and subtended the comic or dramatic workings of Carnival. In any case the feast days were full of merriment until it came down to the business of cutting throats.[34] Death arrived cheerfully.

Now let us consider the problem of role reversal under these circumstances, wedged between the lower groups' reliance on caricature and the elite's use of hyperbole. According to anthropologists (Max Gluckmann, Marc Augé, Victor Turner, and others) role reversal represents Carnival's ultimate spasm. Turner paraphrases Van Gennep's discovery of "a moment when those being moved in accordance to a cultural script were liberated from normative demands, when they were, indeed, betwixt and between successive lodgements in jural political systems. In this gap between ordered worlds almost anything can happen."[35] This state he calls "liminality," the orgasmic interim when women and social roles could be exchanged. The poor took the place of the rich, and vice-versa, everything was inverted, the flow of the community discharged through the interstices of normative structures and ordinary hierarchy, which would be all the more solid for it once Lent arrived. In Romans, role reversal did in fact occupy a central position chronologically speaking (when the satirical price list was published); but it remained relatively superficial. The common folk made little or no use of it. The law and order party did use it, but only as tactical satire intended to mock the lower groups, whom they rightly or wrongly accused of wanting to equal the rich, turn the social and sexual order of things upside down. Romans's role reversal phase was one in which delicacies were supposed to sell for nothing. It was a brief foray into the Occitan Land of Cockaigne, where the digestive function was king,[36] where castles were made of sugar-candy, where dogs were tied up with sausages, where consumption was conspicuous. Cockaigne was to be one of the favorite themes of the Provençal *carême entrant* in the early seventeenth century. The relatively abundant food supply under good king Henri IV encouraged the popularity of Cockaigne as a theme far more than the more meager supplies of a war-torn year like 1580 could have.[37]

On our way through this "forest of symbols," as Baudelaire and Victor Turner would have it, we encounter the different important initiatives of the last few days of the Romans episode—Jacquemart and the Jacquemart–town hall connection. They revolved around the Carnival values of alliance, courtliness, romance.[38] Jacquemart itself was a very interesting neighborhood, a central sector, a hub: on account of individual vendettas about which we have little information, the quarter changed its allegiance, realigned its loyalties. It moved from the popular league (Paumier) camp to the law and order party (Guérin). In the beginning the Jacquemart kingdom was ruled by a rooster. Whether killed in a cockfight, beheaded by young men in a contest of skill, or stoned to death by schoolchildren, the rooster was one of the most common emblematic animals used in European Carnivals (Italy, Spain, northern and southern France, Germany, England, Scotland, as well as Dauphiné). The rooster was to Carnival what the bull is to Spanish culture. Swollen with meaning from head to spur, it was a symbol of bravery, of male sexuality. Romans's rooster was eager to service his hens; the eagle joined the partridge in a mating flight. The jousts, tilts to the ring, balls, and Carnival queens punctuating the final days of the festivities simultaneously expressed the young bloods' courtly devotion to the fair ladies of Romans, and the dangerous axis Guérin and Laroche would form in opposition to Paumier. The poor men, whose Carnival was exclusively masculine—they did not even dress up as women, although that was an elementary role reversal—fell into the trap. They had dealt with Catherine de'Medici in August, but in February they stupidly fell for the queen of the Partridge ball, the bait that lured them into ambush.[39] The union of festivity and political maneuvering was their downfall.

Today this union has almost entirely disappeared. Carnival folklore in Romans is virtually dead, although a very lively tradition subsisted through the nineteenth century. Before the Second World War there were still *pantragnes* in Romans, Mardi Gras parades of revelers, unsavory personages dressed in rags and tatters, their faces systematically dirtied, blackened, daubed with mud or ashes, gesticulating and marching through the streets, representing macabre characters, a wild march of young and old alike. The last *pantragnes* in 1930 were a marked contrast to the gilt-edged, perfectly ordered Carnival the urban elite was holding at the same time in the town theater.[40] Mud versus glitter, the street versus the ballroom. Some things never change.

XIII

A Word on the Peasants

The Carnival in Romans was more than the symbolic revelation, in miniature, of a certain urban consciousness. It was also a part of the larger movement flowing around it. A rural flow, because the Dauphiné peasant war was underway. A province-like urban flow, because Dauphiné's other large towns were also engaged in a struggle for fiscal equality (among other causes); they had the nerve to maintain that nobles should pay taxes like everyone else. This two-pronged Dauphiné movement has its place in a typology, in other words a classification of popular and peasant revolts during the sixteenth century.

These revolts are at the junction of two successive types of uprisings:[1] for simplicity's sake we shall call them Type I (mainly medieval) and Type II ("classic").

Type I includes Swiss insurrections of the late thirteenth century; the French Jacquerie of 1358; the great English peasant movement in 1381, and lesser revolts in Britain during the 1530s and 1540s; Catalan movements in the fourteenth and fifteenth centuries; and most notably the German peasant war of 1525. The various episodes have certain characteristics in common:[2] they permitted farming peasants in particular, and the village community in general—or one specific village faction—to assert control over the resources and elements of power present in the natural and social environment. Varying with circumstances, this could mean forests, hunting and fishing rights, communal pastures, or land abandoned during a recent economic crisis. It could also mean power over tithes, easing or controlling rather than doing away with them (the peasants did want parish priests and the poor to profit from tithes, but within reason); having a voice in naming a mayor, of course, but also the appointment of the parish priest, the bailiff, the seignorial judge; having a partial hold over justice, thus keeping the fines paid by rural inhabitants within limits. It could mean attacking whatever remnants of serfdom there were; lowering demands for the *corvée* (forced labor), the landlords' rents, inheritance taxes; having state taxes lowered as well; regulating inheritance procedures to guarantee that the peasant family could remain on one piece of land; possibly promoting a representative Estate or *Stand* on the regional level which would be specifically for peasants.

These various rural protest movements were generally centered on the peasant community. Although their goals and enemies were many, their greatest adversary was necessarily the seignorial system. The state, if one existed, was only a secondary target. Other scapegoats such as towns, Jews, and so on, ranked third. Peasant movements sometimes—but by no means always—justified themselves in religious terms, or as today's linguistic parlances puts it, had a religious code. In England in 1381, for instance, there were Franciscan slogans ("When Adam delved and Eve span,/Who was then the gentleman?"). There were evangelical and Lutheran slogans in Germany in 1525. Some of these movements even had a millennarian or apocalyptic tinge: the partly peasant but mainly urban revolution in Germany (1525) is an example. Its leader, Thomas Münzer, believed he could bring about a Last Judgment by totally and violently cleansing the world. Some of the movements in question knew victory, but they were the exception (the Swiss cantons, who won their independence by the thirteenth century). Other peasant movements were connected to lengthy periods of economic crisis (Catalonia in the fourteenth and fifteenth centuries). They were the carriers of certain communistic, libertarian, or simply democratic *invariables,* usually to a minimal but at times to a substantial extent. Writers such as Chomsky or Chafarevitch have pointed out that these invariables recur in all movements of social subversion since the beginning of history.[3]

In contrast to Type I revolts, which were especially prevalent between roughly 1300 and 1530, Type II includes the classic popular revolts recurring between 1520 to 1550 (the Acquitanian *Pitauts*, the *Communidades* in Castille) to the first decade of the eighteenth century (the last of the *Croquant* uprisings in southwestern France). As in the previous paradigm, the participants in these revolts wanted to maintain the power and financial autonomy of their corporate community. Like their predecessors, they launched an all-out attack, especially during and after the Wars of Religion, which were very rich in revolts. There were riots protesting the high price of grain; pro-Catholic religious revolts in western France, as well as uprisings against tithes in other areas; and struggles against the seignorial system, outlaws, towns, or financiers. Yet one characteristic was shared by nearly all the Type II revolts: to a much greater degree than the fourteenth and fifteenth century uprisings, they challenged the rising tide of modernity, meaning the centralized state, the government that was growing, enveloping, proliferating. Despite the rebels' often sentimental "royalism," they felt the government had grown too big to be honest, and they crudely attacked it. Protest was simultaneously aimed at the army (the crown army), taxes (direct or indirect), and the new bureaucratic elite of tax gatherers, land agents, clerks. The peasant and his urban allies, if any, had a comprehensive view of their enemies: the royal high judge who was their immediate target might also be a *châtelain* (constable of a castle-ward), financier, noble landlord, munitions dealer, and was attacked on all counts that applied. But the antigovernment coloring was almost always in evidence. It is like a litmus test showing whether or not a revolt is of the second type.[4] It indicated a rejection of the burgeoning government of the sixteenth and seventeenth centuries, a government that itself became a factor in a state of chronic social inequality.

The Carnival in Romans and the peasant war in Dauphiné are perfect examples of these phenomena. In keeping with the characteristics of the Type I revolt, they bluntly challenged the urban notables, as well as the nobility and even the seignorial system. In this way they were far more radical than the various *Croquant* outbreaks in southwest France during the seventeenth century, which specifically opposed taxes, but did not attack the nobility.

And yet in spite of sharing this Type I characteristic, the Dauphiné events were indisputably in the mainstream of Type II. They went beyond specifically urban and Carnival protests to unequivocally attack the government and taxes. The fight against taxes led the people of Dauphiné to clash with the nobility, whom they considered flagrantly exempted from tax.

The revolt in Romans and Dauphiné was double-edged: antinoble, antitax.

The Carnival in Romans was directed by a man (Paumier) who was not only an urban organizer, but also the charismatic leader of the surrounding rural communities. The revolt corresponded to a formidable peasant and antinoble awakening— in reaction to tax exemption and other privileges—which would continue in the countryside for several generations. In 1596, some fifteen years after the initial incidents, the extent of that reawakening was demonstrated in the *Cahiers* (petition of grievance) the rural third estate drew up in each larger village, mandate, or castlewick. These documents contain the declarations peasants and village residents made to strengthen the commoners' case as it would be presented to the king. The *Cahiers'* intention was to correct the fiscal imbalance between the third estate and the other two.[5]

Let us have a look at some of the angry statements contained in the 1596 petition (as seen in the microfilm of it preserved in the Isère *Archives départementales*, thanks to Vital Chomel). In Chabeuil (near Romans), 4,130 *sétérées* (nearly a thousand hectares, or about 2,400 acres) were owned by the nobility and clergy, and thus were tax-free. At La Côte–St. André, one-third of all the land had been bought up by privileged persons, especially nobles, and was henceforth tax-exempt. At Davajeu in 1599, a hundred hectares were in the same situation. Fiancey in 1596 had had about 500 hectares purchased by real or imitation noblemen since 1556, roughly the beginning of the Wars of Religion, which had put the knife to the peasants' throat and hunger pangs in their bellies. On top of that, the clergy had bought another 20 hectares or so. Taking into account what was already in noble hands before 1556, almost all of Fiancey was owned by noblemen. At Montléger, privileged persons held three-quarters of the land in 1596, the third estate one-quarter. Because of their weighty private and public debts, the town's common people had had to sell a good deal of land to the nobles. In Montmeyran that same year, the result of thirty years of heavy buying by clerics and nobles was that half of the land there belonged to them. The other half, still owned by taxpaying commoners, did not represent enough income or capital to pay the community's staggering debts. At Pariset close to 700 hectares were owned by the privileged groups. At Pipet, the nobility and the clergy held a quarter of the land. In the mandate of Quaix in 1596, a third of the land, and the best of it, had been bought by exempt individuals during the preceding fifty years. The truncated community nonetheless had 18,000 *écus* in debts. In Revel, the town debt was 12,000 *écus*; the nobles and the third estate shared the land fifty-fifty. In St. Paul-Trois-Châteaux, a town devastated by the wars, tax-exempt owners held 150 hectares of choice land.

In St. Marcellin and St. Etienne-de-St. Geoirs between 1570 and 1633, the nobles bought a third of the property belonging to commoners (St. Etienne) or a third of all land (St. Marcellin). Deeds included in the dossier under study (at the late date of 1633) allow us to see how these purchases were spread out over the years in St. Marcellin. Furthermore, these were both choice localities, one famed for its fields, the other for its pastures. Today St. Etienne-de-St. Geoirs, its fine, flat plainland perfectly suited to runways, is the site of an airport. St. Marcellin produces a famous cheese.

In Beaufort, a very active region in the 1580 protests, the

privileged class continued to buy up land and render it tax-free once the revolt was over. Commoners lost more than 300 hectares of fields, 40 hectares of meadows, 50 of woodland, plus vineyards. More than two-thirds of the purchases were made between 1580 and 1602. In Pisançon (just outside Romans) in 1596 the third estate owned 3,195 *sétérées* of land, the nobles and other privileged individuals 3,438 *sétérées*. The portion owned by the third estate was burdened with 4,978 *écus* in debts, or more than 1 *écu* per *sétérée*. A part of the tax-exempt land was made up of recent purchases from the commoners by persons of dubious nobility but real enough wealth. Among them was judge Guérin, now designated as "ennobled," buying 40 hectares. Then a Velheu, also ennobled, buying 3 *fauchérées* of meadowland; Gaspard Jomaron, another new noble . . . The same good old bourgeois dynasties in Romans, active in repressing the rebellion, now had blood that was slowly, surreptitiously turning blue.

Abbé Cavard has made a close study of the 1596 *Cahiers* for the Vienne regions, producing some precise details. For instance, the above-mentioned village of La Côte–St. André, a truly "central" one, was colonized by the urban elite from Grenoble, Vienne, Romans, and Crémieu; all of its meadowland belonged to the privileged class, including some fifteen noble residents and twenty-five noble outsiders. Six of these forty nobles were very new ones or bogus; nineteen were of not particularly old stock; three were illegitimate; the rest were perhaps authentic nobles. In St. Hilaire, some ten noble landowners made it even harder for the community to pay its 6,000 *écus* in debt. At Bellegarde (10,000 *écus* of town debt) fourteen nobles held two-thirds of the community's land. It comes as no surprise, then, that in 1579–1580 Bellegarde united behind the local notary in energetic protest against tax privileges! Elsewhere, in Septème the community literally did not know which way to turn: from 1576 to 1586, seventeen nobles bought more than 1400 *écus* worth of land in the district. It had become a nesting-place for noblemen. Like cuckoos, they laid their eggs in borrowed nests. The clergy, too, had extensive holdings in Septème. Furthermore, the community had 20,000 *écus* in debts, without counting private debt. Then the town of Vienne refused to allow its own residents owning land in Septème to pay tax there (the old city/country conflict over tax residency, which had flared up again after 1581).[7] Urban pressure thus compounded the nobles' efforts. Out of the seventeen nobles buying land in Septème, seven were ennobled crown officials, nobles "of the robe" who only slightly earlier had been members of the bourgeoisie.

In Cognée, the people gave up in despair: because of crushing debts and taxes, many of them abandoned their fields and homes. Witness the case of St. Symphorien–d'Ozon and Solaize; the residents were caught between heavy town debts (40,000 *écus*) and the extra taxes they paid because of the privileged group's tax exemption. The poor commoners of St. Symphorien and Solaize were squeezed *like a waffle in an iron*,[8] they claimed, and we have no reason to doubt them. The fortunate souls who enjoyed a permanent and total tax shelter in these two villages included two nobles of old stock, a parish priest, and the local representative of an abbey. But in addition there were the descendant of a prosperous innkeeper; the illegitimate son of a self-styled noble, and son-in-law of a rich man; an army captain, the son-in-law of an innkeeper; a doctor's son; two Italians, including one ex-gendarme; a notary's daughter, the granddaughter of butchers and cobblers; a judge's son; a farrier's son; a lawyer ... The tax-free "nobility" of St. Symphorien–d'Ozon, then, was truly a "mixed bag."

The important thing for our purposes, however, is not the exact details of these *Cahiers*, but the common people's state of mind, from which the petition flowed like so much lava. Two centuries before the start of the French Revolution, an "antinoble consciousness," at least as far as the new nobles were concerned, reached an apex with Dauphiné peasants. They rose up against the expansion of an agrarian capitalism centered on urban rents and urban outlets for agricultural products. Its proponents were new nobles whose money had originated with profits from an inn, a forge, a butcher shop. Covered by a noble coat of arms, this new capitalism ruined and undermined the peasant system, which was based on small family-run farms. The peasants reacted vigorously, the more so since Dauphiné had relatively representative institutions and a third estate tradition of grass roots organization, neither of which existed in the rest of France. Not to mention the fact that inspiring examples were close at hand (southern Dauphiné, Provence, Languedoc), providing a model of equitable taxation based on land rolls, and a lack of tax exemptions, meaning privileged citizens were scarce.

Dauphiné's particular brand of unrest was in marked contrast to the revolts and activist consciousness in the rest of France during the sixteenth and seventeenth centuries; they were much more timid, and more exclusively antitax. Comparing regions in this way naturally prompts a few qualifying remarks. The same antinoble feelings may have secretly existed in Picardy or Burgundy, but without representative institutions or ad hoc petitions of grievance, they found no expression. Dauphiné made its resentments perfectly clear, but the northern regions (say, Burgundy) would not be able to do so until the eighteenth century. What is more, we should not aggrandize Dauphiné's performance, for it was limited. At least in theory it remained respectful toward the true nobility, only opposing the counterfeit new nobles. Invidious tax exemptions were its main target. It was much less emphatic about seignorial rights. It did not (with good reason!) attain the level of Rousseau's thought that all men are born equal. With these reservations stated, I have no qualms about saying that even as it was, I find the performance of the Grenoble, Romans, and Vienne countryside inspiring. From about 1570 to 1640, Dauphiné—like Savoy, the Piedmont, Switzerland—was far ahead of the rest of "all Gaul," if not Germanic lands, in terms of a protest movement that by its very antitax nature was fairly antinoble, antiseignorial, antifeudal. The rural Dauphinois began with the same fiscal resentment that would set off the Normandy farmworkers' or *nupieds* revolt in 1639, the *Croquants* in southwestern France in 1637. But Dauphiné drew social or sociological conclusions that went much, much farther.

The two paradigms, I and II, that we find joined in the Carnival in Romans, are part of the long-term view of the three- or four-century span of the problem of revolts. As the 1596 *Cahiers* show, however, we might also consider the problem from a broad point of view, which would deal with fifty years, not three or four hundred. It would go beyond the narrow confines of the revolt itself to deal with the peaceful and legal environment in which they took place. Can we fully elucidate a collective antitax and antinoble movement like the one that took shape in Dauphiné between 1540 and 1640, and which culminated in Romans in 1580, by focusing on the only *violent* rebellion it entailed? If we do, we risk drawing attention only to the "primitive rebels," the down and out, brawlers, troublemakers, those quick to join in the infernal and often stupid cycle of atrocities.[9] We risk noting only the simplistic slogans of the struggle at hand, slogans that were all too often demagogic, if not dim-witted. In the reddish glow of burning castles, they recommended a return to a supposed golden age of old; they made their appeal to the good king, as opposed to the evil minister; they demanded the revival of pseudocustoms from the old days. For this reason they have been called, a bit too freely, "profoundly conservative," opponents of the "modern" state.[10] Historians who have studied the revolts—Bercé, Pillorget, Günther Franz—have lucidly pointed out the limitation of these demands.

There was, however, another, often more expressive, eloquent side to the protest activities. It was there in 1550, as in 1579, 1595, and 1634. It had to do with nonviolent petition of the *Conseil du roi* (royal council), with trials, litigation, legal battles. Skilled lawyers had unlimited opportunities to put forward a more sophisticated version of the arguments originally propounded by the protesters, by village governments, by Dauphiné's repressed social element, the bourgeoisie.[11] The *procès des tailles* (the "trial of the *taille*," a general term for the legal battle against unequal direct taxation) was exemplary in Dauphiné. As we have seen, it began in the mid-sixteenth century, was carried on in 1576, and culminated in 1579 just before our Carnival. It flared up again from 1591 to 1639, during the reigns of Henri IV and Louis XII, carrying on Jean de Bourg's efforts during the reign of Henri III. The royal decrees of 1634 and

1639 proclaimed the third estate's victory, which was at once partial and remarkable. The decisive royal texts stated that any commoners' property that nobles had acquired during a good many preceding years would henceforth be included in a land roll and be eligible for taxation from 1639 on. The *taille* would now be based on real property throughout the province, as it already was in southwestern Dauphiné, following the example of Provence and Languedoc. The privileged groups' tax exemption was not abolished (and would not completely disappear until 1789), but it was now much less comprehensive than during the sixteenth century, that difficult period when the nobility romped like a fox in the third estate's unprotected henhouse.

This study does not propose to describe the *procès des tailles*.[12] We will consider only a few of its outstanding features, the better to understand the Carnival in Romans[13] and its historical perspective. The *procès* did in effect yield a group of third estate intellectuals around 1576 (de Bourg), and another group around 1595 (followers of de Bourg). One of them was Claude Brosse, a rural *châtelain*, whose castle was at Anjou, on the Beaurepaire plain, close to stormy, revolutionary Valloire. His next job was as the syndic or trustee of Dauphiné villages from 1588 until the 1630s.[14] Another was Antoine Rambaud, a native of Die and lawyer attached to the Parlement of Grenoble, who later became a judge and an important personage in Die. Claude Delagrange, "hardworking small-town magistrate," was the *lieutenant particulier* (deputy magistrate) for the bailiwick of St. Marcellin. Jean Vincent, the nephew of the vice-seneschal of the Crest, was a lawyer with a degree from the University of Valence, and highly gifted as a teacher of law, although he never worked as one. Ennemond Marchier was also a Grenoble lawyer.[15] François Guérin or de Guérin practiced law in Vienne. He continued de Bourg's work in their home town.

At the forefront during one of the crucial moments of the *procès des tailles*, around 1595–1600, Delagrange, Rambaud, and Vincent were replaced thirty years later by a second generation of third estate lawyers, most notably François Guérin (no relation to judge Antoine Guérin) around 1634. Claude Brosse, the piece-worker of rural activism, formed an effective link between the 1600 lawyers and the 1630 generation. All of them were part of the strategic middle level of law practitioners, town judges, country castle constables; some of them (like judge Guérin) opted for the upward climb to nobility. Others (like François Guérin) instead turned toward their immediate inferiors on the social ladder and became leaders of the third estate. They put together an entire ideology which tended toward semi-egalitarianism, drawing all they could from the culture of the times. They placed this ideology at the disposal of the urban bourgeoisie and the village leaders. The majority of these crusading lawyers had been students of the great Jacques Cujas, the restorer of Roman law, when they were young men at the University of Valence around 1570. Judge Guérin had also studied law in Valence, but *before* Cujas began teaching there. This may explain the difference between Antoine Guérin's hierarchic and aristocratic mentality and the democratic and egalitarian turn of mind we encounter in the lawyers and judges defending the third estate around 1600.

An invaluable contribution to the peasant cause was made by Claude Brosse, a true rural leader, at the turn of the seventeenth century. So persistent was Brosse's campaign that he was briefly jailed by the officials of the Parlement of Grenoble, who defended and of course enjoyed tax privileges.[16] Brosse sent the king various petitions of grievance in the name of Dauphiné villagers in 1606 and 1608. He wrote them in his own hand; they were later printed and reprinted in Grenoble during the reign of Louis XIII. The author of this set of *Cahiers* took a great interest in tax exemption: he asked, as usual, that property bought by nobles no longer be automatically exempted from taxes; that the nobility's farmers and sharecroppers no longer be exempt; that back taxes owed since 1600 be excused.

Brosse was more than simply a tax-fighting Poujade. To a certain extent his writings were antinoble, antiseignorial. In this sense they are comparable to the *Cahiers* of the province of

Beauce, or Dauphiné's own, in 1576. They were much more daring than Champagne's 1614 *Cahiers*.[17] Claude Brosse was in fact only echoing peasant resentment as he had heard it from the general assembly of the corporate villages' consuls. The first problem was land. He asked the king to allow the third estate to buy back the property acquired by nobles, while guarding against swindles and speculation. Brosse asked that the villagers' creditors not be allowed to seize the peasants' wheat in payment; that the partial moratorium on interest on debts or hereditary rents, decreed by Henri IV, be observed. Claude Delagrange went one better than him, moving on to direct anti-seignorial protest. He stressed that many quit-rents or seignorial dues owed on land were really nothing but old debts which had carried interest. After the original debtor's death, his heirs became responsible for the debts and now-perpetual interest. The creditor's heir collected them as if they were a seignorial due.[18] The lawyers' guerrilla war against the seigneurs is readily apparent in Brosse's *Cahiers*. He was bent on having the peasants' right to hunt observed; he considered it a traditional Dauphiné right (the democratization of the right to destroy fauna and ruin the environment was always one of the objectives of the struggle against feudalism, unfortunately). Brosse asked that the *lods et ventes* (an inheritance tax paid to landlords) no longer be collected on land seized or sold for debts; that fifteen years' arrears in seignorial dues, originally assessed in grain, should not be collected (and what was worse, collected in money when grain prices were high). This partial challenge to the seignorial system extended to the seignorial and Parlement judges trying peasant cases (country folk particularly disliked provincial officials); it extended to virtual extortion by lesser officials as well.

As for the church, Brosse was of two minds. On the prochurch side, he wanted to see the numerous priestless parishes furnished with a pastor to tend to the rural folk's spiritual needs. On the antichurch side, he wanted to ease the payment of *décimes* (taxes paid by the clergy) on land that had once belonged to clerics; he wanted to do away with the tax exemption granted to land that paid annuities destined to fund the saying of

Masses. All in all, Brosse was in favor of parish priests, but against the clergy's tax abuses. His reasoning was classic and logical.

Finally, Brosse dealt with the problem of representation of the peasant order or suborder (to his mind the rural cause was completely distinct from the problems of town dwelling peasants) in the provincial governmental institutions. A demand of this type had already been articulated during the German peasant war of 1525, for a rural representative body or *Stand*. Brosse wanted to have *each* village represented in the provincial Estates by an ad hoc syndic or trustee, or by the *châtelain* who managed the *mandement* (mandate or territory) made up of several localities and containing the village in question. This was an unheard of demand. If it were applied, it would allow the immense peasant majority to counterbalance for the first time the noble, ecclesiastical, and urban minorities which had always dominated the Estates, particularly the first two groups. Once again we note that although *châtelains,* often commoners, may have been seignorial officials, Brosse considered them closer to the people they administered, and not the automatic supporters of the noble landlords who appointed them. After all, he had started out as a *châtelain* himself. In 1600, Brosse spelled out what the 1579 peasant rebels had only expressed orally. Their true discourse has been lost to history. The only recorded examples of the village protesters' speech that we have were noted in passing by Antoine Guérin, their enemy.[19]

XIV

Forerunners of Equality

The pleas of Brosse's fellow third estate lawyers between 1596 and 1630 offer a less detailed catalogue of grievances but a more complete vision of the world. Marmier, Delagrange, Vincent, Rambaud, and Guérin were not as close to the peasantry; they were more learned, more attuned to the urban bourgeoisie. Their main objective, of course, was the fight against the nobility's tax exemption on land acquired from commoners. However, they were also concerned about the workings of power and society. Their dislike of bureaucratic officials is what inspired them.[1] "They come from the very dregs; they are ennobled because of their position, their children with them; then they pay no taxes." Criticism was especially biting when it applied to very high officers of the *Chambre des comptes*—the sovereign fiscal court—and even more so when it was aimed at the Parlement of Grenoble,[2] whose members were accused of being judge and plaintiff at the same time. They had become privileged, free from taxes; yet as magistrates they handed down decisions on tax exemption—their own and that of other nobles. Vincent went so far as to challenge the practice of purchased hereditary office, or venality. The penal system (jailors torturing members of the third estate, putting hot irons to feet, needles under fingernails, scissors to eyelids, to make the prisoners hand over the taxes they owed) also drew its share of cirticism.[3] Even the *avocats consistoriaux* were accused in the process. They were the

highest-ranking barristers in Grenoble—the king's counsels—
with close ties to Parlement. They were condemned as lazy
penpushers who grew fat on the people's money while the good
merchants of the third estate sweated blood from Grenoble to
Indonesia to earn their meager profits!

If specific charges were rather picturesque, the general point
they made was more important: it concerned the government's
recent surge of growth.[4] It had been spreading like gangrene
since the days of good king Louis XII, that somewhat mythi-
cally idyllic era when there were seven times fewer officials
than in 1600; at the turn of the seventeenth century it seemed
tax men were everywhere, like bloodsuckers. Advancing this
argument, the men of Dauphiné's third estate were declaring
war against bureaucratic government, which had grown a great
deal over the past century. Yet they did not attack the *gabeleurs*
(tax officers), *fermiers généraux* (tax-farmers), financiers and
others of their kind, who were a favorite target of popular
revolts in other provinces after 1624. The only instance I find
of this in Dauphiné is Marmier's attack on commissioners and
financiers. Delagrange also laid blame on the professors at the
University of Valence: they were supposed to be dispensing
wisdom, but in fact they neglected their teaching duties.[5] They
had arranged to be exempted from taxes, while their colleagues
in Montpellier and Valence paid them.

Let us return to the question of power, of government. Popular revolts have often been described as essentially reactionary, opposed to the growth of centralized government and the
modernizing force, the progress it represented for society as a
whole. "These popular uprisings," Yves-Marie Bercé writes,
"tended to reject the modern state, seeking a return to an older
order, whose symbols and values were slowly but relentlessly
being replaced, much to the rebels' regret." They wanted to
turn back the clock, then stop it altogether, Bercé says.[6] René
Pillorget sees the revolts as a veritable bulwark of traditional
values.[7] Pierre Chaunu considers the Spanish *Communidades'* insurrection, similar to those we are studying, as a reactionary
retort to the modernizing state.[8] Mousnier holds that the revolts
of the sixteenth and seventeenth centuries were tied to the con-

cept of original sin and opposed to the development of the
state.[9] Günther Franz calls the German peasant war of 1525 the
combat of the custom-bound old right wing in the villages and
towns against the modern or territorial state, even against Roman law.[10]

There is no denying the direct link between the *procès des tailles*
and the peasant war of 1579–1580. The legal battle against
taxes peacefully pursued the Carnival struggle's aims over the
next two generations. Did the lawyers' case really have the
reactionary or custom-bound orientation Günther Franz and
Bercé have detected in popular revolts? In fact it did not. The
jurists in question were not so retrogressive. They were, of
course, opposed to unchecked growth of the government, resulting in unjust tax privileges, but their opposition was not
based on a love of the mythical good old days. They appealed
to the most modern forms of natural reason in their fight against
injustice: *It is not the custom of all antiquity which dictates form,*
Rambaud writes (p. 91), but instead *Reason, drawn from the*
wellsprings of natural wisdom (the mother of all true jurisprudence), which
does not change. And Delagrange writes: *To use custom, all too readily*
excessive and perverse, as a shield against Reason, would result in the
cruellest of tyranny. The more irrational the old practice the more
it *deserves vituperation!* The lawyers also attacked the nobles'
violent attachment to freedom from taxes. They even challenged
the privilege itself, saying that in time of need it ought to step
aside (J. Vincent). Supporting this argument are quotations
from Cicero's letters—the classics were fundamental—and an
example from ancient Greece: *The Spartans say that it is better to*
suppress customs than observe them to the detriment of the people (Delagrange, p. 15).

Today's historiography may assert that a reverent devotion to
custom was the reason for the tax protests, but the third estate's
counsels for the nobility around 1600—Expilly and du Fos—
substantiate this. They were out to tear the third estate's evidence to shreds, proclaiming it a *monstrous colossus full of refuse*
and cobwebs. To this end they proudly declared "Custom is the
legitimate King, the Law is a tyrant!" The custom in question,
which the nobles upheld with all their might, was of course

their own freedom from taxes. Vincent, a lawyer for the third estate, even mentioned *gothic* (in other words medieval) barbarism in discussing the nobles and their privilege. The disputed custom was no more than a worn relic which ought to be preserved, according to the nobles, or discarded, in the peasants' view.

The third estate counsels naturally modified their stance when it involved practice. They distinguished between certain privileges and customs which were still valid, while others were *excesses* or *corruptions of customs*. Delagrange, a subject of Henri IV, sounded like the Catalan rebels of the late Middle Ages. He even talked about *bad practices and evil customs*. Tax exemption was one of them, as was the *ipso facto* ennoblement of noble bastards, which was tantamount to legitimizing lechery. In the argument against evil customs, the king was presented not as the indiscriminate guardian of tradition, but as the extirpator of evil usages; his royal justice was always a legitimate recourse.

The lawyers' rational thought included an historic view which was familiar with the past but which preferred the present. In his modernist tract of 1599, Delagrange, with the support of his colleagues, answered the *avocats consistoriaux* (the pronoble king's counsel), who cited the *old days,* the *good friendship* of former times, when the third estate was not challenging the nobility: *Formerly, the question of tax exemption was not important. The tax burden was not heavy. But today the face of things has changed. Each and all must contribute* (taxes), *by right and by reason* (p. 279). This became a leitmotiv in Delagrange's pleadings (ibid., p. XIX, etc.). *Things have changed, taxes have greatly increased* since the fifteenth century; *nobles have bought the common people's land,* thus they ought to pay taxes, even if they did not before. And again: *No matter what antiquity might mean to the Nobles, law should conform to the present times.*[11] He thereupon notes the swiftness of historical change: *already the current times* (about 1600) *are different from those before the troubles* (before 1560). Tacitus, Seneca, and Ovid are called as witnesses, but quoting them only reinforces the present's primacy over the old days: *we praise our elders, but we live in our own time.*

These pleas against custom posed a delicate problem in relation to authority, which was central, monarchic, northern. The Dauphiné jurists despised the common law governing tax matters in northern France. It favored nobles and tax exemptions. Roman law, on the other hand, subjected all land, whether owned by nobles or not, to taxes, and Roman law prevailed or was supposed to in Languedoc, Provence, and Dauphiné. The lawyers would be in difficult straits if the king and his agents caught them making a public display of their dislike of common law, so they merely pointed out that in theory northern law did not extend beyond the Rhône, that it applied to the *Kingdom* (west of the Rhône) but not the *Empire* (east of the Rhône). Moreover, Jean Vincent and his friends gleefully noted that peoples considered more "barbarian" than the French, like the Poles and the Bretons, had their nobles pay taxes. Blaise de Vignère's work, *Description of Poland* (Paris, 1573) was a very useful source of information for Vincent, who was as well read in geography as Delagrange was in history.

Let there be no mistake about these lawyers: they were essentially champions of fiscal justice; there was no question of a "bourgeois revolution"[12] or the destruction of a *société des ordres*, the three-estate hierarchic society. This society, as described by Max Weber and Roland Mousnier,[13] was still very much a part of the mental horizon of the times, which with a few scandalous exceptions no one tried to cross. The third estate lawyers admitted—if sometimes hesitantly—that the priest and the noble were distinguished from the commoners by a first and second "degree of honor."[14] But these lawyer-authors wanted to put an end to the illicit manipulation giving the two privileged orders complete control of the provincial representative body (the Dauphiné Estates), where the third estate was reduced to playing bit parts. These lawyers were not, then, revolutionaries, but in the context of a hierarchical social structure they hoped to improve but not destroy, they appear to us as decided reformers. That was no mean feat.

It is true that Richelieu would later effectively dismiss both suits—the privileged group's and the commoners'—since he abolished the Dauphiné Estates *de facto* in 1628.[15] The third estate had more luck with its taxation demands in 1634 to 1639. Its 1600 argument against exemption did not step beyond the framework of a society structured according to rank. Since the province's three estates *voted* their tax contributions to the king, the lawyers said, law and reason dictated that all three orders should pay taxes, not just one of the three.[16] That was Rambaud's opinion, and he was not the only one entitled to it.

To the third estate counsels, the nobility brought to mind certain problems. The first was that of land, which is at the core of so many revolutions and peasant wars, overtly or secretly. Let us yield the floor to the commoner lawyers, Antoine Rambaud first of all:[17] *The Nobility has taken property from the king's domains, from the common people's fields, those of the Church* (that is, church lands were plundered by Huguenot nobles). *We are willing to serve as mules for you, Sire* (the king) *but not for the Nobles. . . . The law of Nature decrees that the propagations of one body be the decay of another. Thus the purchase of our property by the Nobility* (which furthered the propagation of the nobles as a body) *has lessened our property* (meaning the decay of the commoners) and in consequence it should *lessen* our taxes. Now for Marchier: he had an accurate view of the question, but he blew it out of proportion.[18] He claimed *the nobility has acquired peasant land,* which had become more valuable over the last hundred years because of inflation. *What was worth five sous is now worth one hundred écus* (or 6,000 *sous*; this seems an exaggeration, since the price of land had not multiplied sixty times). The result of the nobles' purchases was that now *one taxpayer must pay the tailles for a whole village* (because all the other landowners had sold to tax-exempt individuals). Claude Delagrange[19] held that the nobles had formerly *lived off their ancient domains.* But now, *despite obfuscation,* they could not hide that *they have taken our livestock and our livelihood, from widows and orphans* among others, they had snatched up *our land the excess of taxes had caused to depreciate;* the land could no longer turn a profit because of heavy taxes. That was why now, the counsels said, *we are acting;* the third estate had to act.

A generation later, around 1630, François Guérin[20] quoted specific figures: *during the last forty years, 187 Third Estate families have been ennobled.* . . . *The direct tax, or taille, has increased by 5,000,000 livres over the past few years, but taxable property has decreased by more than half* (?) *because of ennoblement and purchases of land belonging to commoners by nobles.* On this account, *in Chalon, Malleville, St. Baudille, the people have not an acre left;* the villages in the county of Albon were also in deep trouble because of these purchases. The same went for Valence: the tax-exempt nobles held twenty-six fiscal hearths in that town, meaning that many fewer persons paid the *taille.* One result of all this was that destitute villagers died or left their homes to wander as beggars. In four communities[21] the population had fallen from 1782 to 972 families during the first third of the seventeenth century, or a loss of 45.5 percent. On other of the aforementioned Albon lands, François Guérin continues, the nobles had bought work animals and arable land corresponding to 125 pairs of oxen (or a surface of between 1,000 and 2,000 hectares), resulting in a population loss of 192 families. Obviously the bold Guérin did not give a moment's thought to jumping from sociological causality to demographic effect. But although high death rates played a substantial role in the population decline, there is no doubt that tax pressure and social crisis, directly or indirectly brought about by land-grabbing nobles, also had much to do with the spread of poverty, death, and migration.

Occasional mention of specifics and figures aside, the third estate counsels' writings contain a great deal of heat, at times expressed in the plainest of terms. The same hatred and rancor were found in Provence, in southwestern France, in Normandy, in Beauce, even if they were not expressed in those regions.[22] In the same breath that they denounced land-grabbing, Vincent, Marchier, and Delagrange also spoke out against the public and private debts weighing down the peasantry. An example: in Pisançon, just outside Romans, each hectare of commoners' land owed debts to the capital equivalent to forty-four agricultural laborer workdays per hectare, and interest worth four workdays.[23] The third estate lawyers rather emphatically held the nobles responsible for these debts: *the Nobles own the greater part of our property, and the rest is pledged for debts to them.*[24] The counsels exaggerate the nobility's financial role; we know that the bourgeoisie more often than not also became moneylenders to the impoverished rural world. It is nonetheless perfectly true that nobles were still the best represented social group among the villagers' creditors in the late sixteenth century.[25]

Charges against the nobility easily made room for accusations against wealth. In a simplifying amalgam, the latter was deemed the synonym and begetter of the former. Antoine Rambaud (p. 12) equated them: *in fact the rich are the ones who become nobles. Freedom from taxes is an exemption of wealth, not nobility.* Jean Vincent (1598, p. 18) found *the Nobles are always round and plump, they have grown rich on our property.* Ennemond Marchier (P 362–365) carries the analogy even farther, almost to the point of paranoia: *the Nobility is plotting to ruin the Third Estate, sharing the debris of that fallen colossus.*[26] And Marchier concludes: *our ruin is their increase,* unwittingly quoting the slogan of his contemporaries, the Périgord *Croquants, our ruin is their wealth.*[27] Marx, too (outside the context of the seignorial system), characterized capitalism as the correlative accumulation of wealth at one extreme and poverty at the other. Delagrange's writings also include some pretty pieces of anti-aristocratic thought, mostly based on stereotypes, occasionally on reality. The nobles, Delagrange states, had taken advantage of their position; today we might say they had played the black market during the Wars of Religion. *They sold their foodstuffs and livestock higher in wartime than in peacetime.*[28] Thanks to their powerful connections, they had escaped being pillaged by soldiers: *While our land lay fallow, the Nobles cultivated theirs without danger.* Eustache Piémond's *Journal* substantiates that accusation (P 267). War damages sustained by the nobles were reimbursed by the third estate: *if the soldiers took some chickens from a gentleman, he would have the poor Third Estate folk of the village pay for it. There is not paper enough to tell all the inhumanities that we* (the third estate) *have suffered thus.* The nobles' perverseness went so far as helping the soldiery with the pillaging: *Some Nobles, to get their neighbor's property, beat him, had him pillaged by the men of war in the neighborhood, had his livestock taken away in payment of the whole village's taxes.* In addition the nobles were reputedly lazy, devoid of common sense and piety, licentious: *common sense is rare in the Nobility . . . The gentleman, a profligate and lecher, can have his bastard ennobled.*[29] An important reproach was that of noble pride and violence: *the Nobles use violence against the Third Estate . . . they hate peace, they wish to humble the rest of the people; they would like to have everyone under their thumb.*[30]

For all their violence, were the aristocrats really fighters? A good question, and one that gave the third estate counsels food for thought. The nobles brought up their estate's supposed role in war (the so-called blood tax) as the justification for their exemption from taxes in money. But Rambaud and Delagrange were not about to be fooled.[31] The third estate, said Rambaud, had seen even more action than the nobility during the Wars of Religion. *The Nobility of France has served in the army during the civil wars. The Nobility of Dauphiné has not.* (Here Rambaud exaggerated the Dauphiné/France contrast for purposes of his argument.) *If the Nobility is exempted from taxes because of its services in time of war, then the Third Estate which has fought as much and more should be even more exempt. . . . The Nobles say they are soldiers, but so are the people of the Third Estate. . . . Today's Nobility cannot be compared to the Roman legionnaires. They were always involved in a campaign,* professional soldiers that they were. *Our Nobles are not soldiers; therefore they have no right to the tax privileges the legionnaires enjoyed.* Delagrange is inexhaustible on this subject. He stresses the superiority of the third estate's military performance during the civil wars, due primarily to the preponderance of commoners. Delagrange was well aware of demographic reality. *In the civil war army for one Noble there were a hundred men from the Third Estate* (which did in fact account for more than 95 percent of the population). He went on: *the people of Dauphiné are good fighters. . . . Our role in victories has not been negligible. . . . Public dignity or majesty is too unsafe without the plebeian fighting forces and without the consent of the people.* (Delagrange borrowed this thought from Livy; the references he and his colleagues make to Latin texts are generally incorrect, but none the less apt for it.) The litany continues: *valiance has remained on the side of the people during the civil wars. . . . Even though one may be of low position, it is not unusual to find* (in the lowborn) *rare traits of goodness and virtue. . . .*

History bolsters the common people's claim to fame as warriors: Marcus Agrippa was low born, according to Tacitus, but valiant in war . . . most of Rome's senators were of the common people. Delagrange was familiar with Caesar's famous passage (*Gallic Wars,* 6–15) on Gaul's division into three estates (druids, knights, plebeians). And Caesar said *all the knights of Gaul served in time of war . . . which was not the case with our nobles,* the Dauphiné lawyer points out. Therefore the nobles did not have the right to the tax exemption granted to career soldiers.. The Middle Ages were mined for other pertinent examples. Dauphiné's Middle Ages: *The Daupineé statute* (fourteenth century) was the matrix for all the province's freedoms; it clearly indicated, Delagrange maintains, *that the Third Estate like the nobles also served in arms and in valiance.* The French Middle Ages: *at the battles of Crécy and Montlhéry, the foot Companies were composed of men of the Third Estate.*

What could the nobles honestly say to all this? One of their counsels, Claude Expilly, cited a proverb: *Noble lineage means a hundred years of the standard, a hundred of the bier.* This tends to indicate that the nobles did not have many illusions about the aptitudes of their eternally warbound brethen.[32]

In the final analysis, the third estate's counsels, its intellectuals, did not conceal their hatred of the nobility. They employed bitter invective. They were willing to concede a few virtues to authentic noblemen, but only those from the past, when knights were fearless and blameless like Bayard (Pierre du Terrail, seigneur de Bayard, 1470–1524; born in Grenoble, his valor won him the epithetic title *"chevalier sans peur et sans reproche"*). At the turn of the seventeenth century things had changed: *The Nobles plead Bayard, but Bayard loved the people.*[33] Vincent is more accommodating than Delagrange in this instance. He allows that the nobles *cling fast to the first rank in the province. It is their right by blood.*[34] However, he is intractable on the real point: *No exemption. Nobility is only a genealogical virtue.* Delagrange, on the other hand, does not even appreciate that virtue: *the Nobles bother everyone with their family trees and alliances which are more than half false.*[35] Delagrange is willing to make an exception for *the most civilized Nobles;* he acknowledges the existence of three ranks, *Clerics, Nobles, and Commoners;* but in the next breath he deplores *the quantity of Nobles* (sham, recent, newly ennobled) *is prejudicial to the real Nobles and their quality.*[36]

The third estate lawyers had an aggressive attitude toward the nobles. In relation to society as a whole, however, they adopted an "organicist" point of view. They treated it as a well-structured whole; the individual was a small part of the whole. Conflicts within society were to be avoided, theoretically. An illustration of their views, if an anachronistic one, would be to say they were very far indeed from the individualism of the Enlightenment and the concepts of class struggle advanced by Thierry, Guizot, Marx. But is that grounds for charging Delagrange, Vincent, Rambaud, et. al. with being "deeply conservative"?

I believe it would be out of order to do so. The lawyers used the concept of a unified social body to combat the nobles' pretentions to freedom from tax obligations. They also endeavored to restore the third estate's dignity as a full member of the three-part society. In this sense their objectives were progressive, even though the corrective measures they proposed, including a return to the ideal norms of the past, might now seem conservative to us.

In the lawyers' organicist view, the fundamental comparison was between society and the human body. It was a hasty translation of the medieval idea of the mystical body of the church, from sacred into political terms. Rambaud writes (p. 14) that *The Nobility is important as a decoration, a support and fortification of the mystical body of the State,* except for the fact their tax exemption *is contrary to the practice of all Antiquity.* Vincent echoes this church plus state vocabulary:[37] *we wish only to be recognized as members of the mystical body . . . this mystical body which has always had various portions and different ranks: the Senate and the plebeians in Rome; the druids, knights, and plebeians in Gaul.* Note that the third estate is asking for *recognition*, and recognition of its difference from the other categories as well.

Following the mystical body is the human body itself. The biological microcosm is likened to the social macrocosm which is itself in the image of the pre-Copernican world or universe. The *body*, Rambaud writes (p. 94–100), *is the police* (that is, organized society). *The head is the King. The arms are the Nobility. The feet are the Third Estate. The arms must carry food to the mouth;* which duty the nobles were not performing because of their infamous tax exemption. The mouth, so close to the royal head, was none other than the *common purse,* the royal Treasury. *The clergy is the heart. It is swollen with tithes; it will have to give some of them up* (the lawyers, incidentally, knew nothing of Harvey's theory of circulation; they did not see the heart as a pump but as an organ which was filled with humors and which rejected any excesses of them in order to remain healthy). As for the third estate, relegated to ground level, it supports the entire body: *the plowman, that is to say the man of the third estate who works the earth, is the most trodden upon.* For the social body to remain in good health this must be stopped, must be changed.

The province itself was a body. As Vincent writes (1598, p. 29), the health of the provincial "body" must be maintained *through the ordinary functions and the common aid of all its members together.* Marchier (p. 357) puts it in less corporeal terms: *the Nobility must participate in* (the upkeep) *of the province, the greater part of which it owns* (in land). Delagrange (1599–2, p. 14) returns to the body: *we do not deny the difference between the Nobility and the Third Estate but we deny that the third estate should be considered as nothing. It is the third member of the Body.* Then he embroiders the theme: *if one member* (for example the nobility) *receives all the body's humors* (all the wealth), *it decays. If the humors go to all the members, the body is healthy.* The corporeal point of view admitted hierarchy, on the condition that it was equitable (72–80). *The basis is reason. Each must be kept in his Estate* (or rank). *The Nobles must be content with handling the government* (that is, power) *and with the highest ecclesiastical posts.*

In second place after body imagery are the maternal and parental comparisons inevitably found in patriotic discourse:

nobles, the third estate counsel cries, do not bite the hand that has fed you, do not refuse to pay taxes to the province, our common homeland. *Our country is like our parents,* Vincent writes (1598, p. 16–22). *It must have a feeling heart. The three Estates are members of one body, of one province which is mother to all of them.* Borrowing a phrase from Tacitus, Vincent categorically rejects the notion of class struggle, of *disunion.* For the greater *unity* of the common body, the privileged members must pay their share of taxes. Patriotic quotations of St. Ambrose back up Tacitus (ibid., p. 31). *Natural instinct, the common desire of generous persons, nurtured in them since conception,* should incite the three orders *to go to the aid of their country, our mother.* Here both reason and nature informed a certain way of thinking prevalent in the West since the Aristotelian and Thomist Middle Ages.

Next come comparisons to plant life, an obvious enough choice for a largely agrarian population. Vincent (1598, p. 22) is adamant: *the province is an indivisible thing like a tree.* From Dauphiné's treelike indivisibility, he deduces that land rolls and fiscal equality should apply to its entire area, not just the canots of Gap, Embrun, Briançon. Then the tree is replaced by the vine (Vincent, 1598, p. 26). *The King is like a grapevine, in need of vineprops* (that is, the people!). Elsewhere the vine is metamorphosed into a cypress, surrounded by all kinds of flora: *The Nobles, these great poppies, defy the single cypress* (the king) *while the people hug the soil like purslane.*

Sun metaphors, already used in Jean de Bourg's 1576 *Cahiers,* compared the social setup with the structure of the universe. They indirectly permitted a bit of straight talk to the nobles: *The people are the sea. The Nobles are the wind* (stormy disturbers of the order of things). *The King is the sun, he is justice* (Rambaud). *The King is the Sun and the father of us all* (Vincent, 1598, p. 27). *The King is the sun, the Nobility is appointed to illustriousness, the Third Estate to feeding, the Church to Divinity. The three orders must thus contribute their persons, but also their property* (Rambaud, 1600, p. 16–17). This is not Copernicus's sun (the mechanical *center* of the system), but Ptolemy's, nothing more than a superior luminary. The worldview of the times was still thoroughly Aristotelian.

An entire series of "unifying" images also flowed from the counsels' pens. A selection follows:

Building imagery: Marchier declares (P 360) that *The people are as useful to the State as the Nobility. They are the cement holding the monarchy together.* Without the people, there would be *collapse* and *tyranny.*

The seignorial system: A landlord has three tenant farmers, Rambaud writes (1600), symbolizing the clergy, nobility, third estate. All three should go in together to *pay the shepherd's wages,* contribute toward *repairing the castle's rotten roof,* and so on. The meaning of this was clear to everyone: the nobility ought to pay taxes.

Stable imagery: it is not so important to change the mules (the third estate) *as to rein in the barbary horses and chargers* (the nobility), Rambaud states (1600, p. 108).

Shipping imagery: law in the Rhône region incorporated the Roman principle that in a sinking ship *everyone saves his neighbor.* The nobles ought to follow this example of obligatory assistance to those in danger, and help the other estates (Delagrange, pp. II, VIII, and 188). All of the silent partners in a shipwrecked vessel, under this law, had to pay a reasonable compensation for lost merchandise, with no exceptions (ibid.).

Finally, there were images of music, order, harmony: *the Nobles,* Delagrange writes (p. 225), *want to hold their fellow citizens in serfdom. They spoil everything concerning the harmonious proportions and the preservation of a State. . . .*

The usual smattering of Latin or Greek quotations notwithstanding,[38] *the counsels' references logically descend from Aristotle and his unifying notion of the city-state or polis.* The ideal is the common good, all parties or subgroups adapting to a social and natural whole. Delagrange (182) cites Aristotle by name (*Politics* 5-1). In every polity there must be a sharing of responsibility between the parts of this Republic. If we check the reference, we find mention of *justice, that is to say proportional equality.* This is rather close to the *official equality* between the orders de Bourg mentioned in his 1576 petition of grievance.[39]

Delagrange says that in practical terms that means *all privileges disappear in case of necessity,* or, again after Aristotle, *that the Nobles ought to succor their associates who are oppressed.* The third also recalls certain writings of Cicero and St. Ambrose: *he who does not defend his companion and takes no action against the harm that has been done him wrongs himself as much as if he abandoned his parents, country, friends.* Another Aristotelian feature was the desire for harmony within the city-state, immediately transposed into the ideal vision of Dauphiné life. As Aristotle and Delagrange (154, 159) saw it, *harmony* would consist in *maintaining a just temperament among the parts and members of the State, for fear that one part oppress the other and become too powerful.* From the need for this almost musical *harmonious proportion in the State* (p. 92), Delagrange drew the conclusion that *there is no State that can subsist without the people.* The same Aristotelian strain shows up in Rambaud (1600, p. 15): *harmony, justice, and proportion in the State* are necessary. Each part must *contribute to the preservation of the General* (the whole).

This vision of social matters, which were also tied to a *body,* engendered more specific applications, also derived from Aristotle at times. Vincent declared (1598, p. 28, and 1600, p. 53) *that Aristotle did not want tax exemptions in Sparta,* for they were contrary to piety and the public welfare. As for references to other authors, Delagrange (p. 182) quoted Plato (*Laws,* book 5): *The good citizen does not reject but gladly bears the responsibilities of the Republic.* Demosthenes is held to have been opposed to tax exemptions in Athens. It appears that Solon, the debtor's friend, expressed a similar opinion. Vincent is the one who quotes these two authors (1598, pp. 23, 38). Let us note in passing the idea of *public welfare:* Vincent, once again, proposes a general and monarchicodemocratic conception of *common welfare* or the common good, which the Jacobins later carried much farther: *The Nobles use the privileges of the province as if they were theirs alone* (1598, p. 36). *The Nobles think they are born only for themselves. But according to Pericles as quoted by Thucydides, one should love the public good above all,* and as Vincent neatly puts it, *consider oneself born not for the self but for the world.* Under these conditions, the *Multiple,* in other words society, must ultimately refer to the One, in the person of the king. *The Prince is the Father of the common Welfare* (ibid., 1600, p. 12). The people and the king are the subjects of God: *King and people are closely tied. To be in favor of the Nobles' tax exemption means being against the people, against their Right, against natural piety, against the very majesty of God, who is the patron of the Laws of human Society* (ibid., pp. 26–27).

Rambaud closes with remarks on the appeal of freedom, or the absence of slavery. The nobles' tax exemption, he says (1600, p. 15) represented *barbarian servitude* for the third estate. Greek thought, translated into Latin or French, was the source of this exaltation of liberty, which was also molded on theology developed since serfdom's final days, after St. Thomas of Aquinas and the Scholastics.

From Aristotle it was an effortless leap to the great Christian tradition and to St. Thomas, who was considered the Greek philosopher's Catholic disciple and shieldbearer. Our lawyers associated Antiquity (recently refurbished by the Renaissance) with medieval Christianity of the Thomist thirteenth century, which the Council of Trent had prolonged. Natural reason laid the foundation of harmonious balance of social categories, nobility, and third estate. It was also the common denominator between the two cultural currents, one originating before Christ, the other after. Delagrange cites St. Thomas by name (1599–2, p. 55); he writes: *law without reason is not law but perverseness. The prince's unjust high-handedness is not law but iniquity.* The doctors of the church inspired the lawyers to make Jesus the keystone of the three-estate society, since He had rendered unto Caesar. *Christ was a Cleric, and Noble* (son of God); *finally a lawgiver; and Christ paid taxes* (ibid., pp. 25, 26). Delagrange asserts that by refusing to pay taxes the nobles are traitors to religion and even more so to *charity toward our Country*, a simultaneously pagan and Christian notion (ibid., p. 1599–2, pp. 31, 105, and passim).

Like classical authors, the Bible and the Church Fathers were an invaluable source of quotations when it came to distinguishing between *custom* (possibly iniquitous) and *true law* (always just). King Solomon, in the *Wisdom of Solomon* 14, took a stance similar to those of Plautus, Cicero, and Seneca, writes Delagrange (1599–2, p. 55): *"Then the ungodly custom, grown strong with time, was kept as law,"* no matter how wrong it might be. St. Cyprian and St. Augustine agreed (ibid., p. 107): *God did not say: I am the custom, he said I am the way, the truth, the life.* Delagrange (1599–2, p. 27) took on a biblical tone to threaten tax-evading nobles and officials with divine punishment because they had made a custom of corruption. *The fathers of the Nobles began to corrupt our Law. They are now answering to God for it. Corrruption may become standard practice; that does not make it any better.*

Both Genesis and the Gospels make a fundamental appeal for unity among men. The point had not been lost on four-teenth-century rebels: *when Adam delved . . . who then was the gentleman?* With less of a flourish, but more details, Delagrange (pp. 31, 84, 121) elaborates on the theme. He brings Aristotle and Tacitus into it, but they are less help than the Old and New Testaments with their egalitarian creation and redemption stories. *Estates differ, but men are the same, Tacitus and Aristotle tell us. Commoners and Nobles are made of the same flesh, same blood, same bones. If the Nobles had inborn ingenuousness* (in other words innate nobility) *they would not need the blood of Jesus to redeem them. They would have to prove that Adam had a* (noble) *son before the fall* (before committing the original sin that put all men on an equal footing). N̲o̲b̲ility is not fundamental, *it had a beginning; the difference between Nobles and other men is not natural, nor substantial, but a human invention. According to Nature, all men are one . . . A beggar is just as much a man as a Noble. We are all descended from an original father. Nobility came afterwards.*

The third estate counsels' approach to Holy Scripture was far milder than the millennarism preached by Münzer and the Anabaptists, who based their social upheaval on the Apocalypse and the Book of Daniel. And yet . . . Dauphiné as well as Germany had rediscovered the Old Testament in the wake of Protestantism. Even though they were Catholics, the commoner militants had read the Psalms, the Wisdom of Solomon, Proverbs. In the Hebrew prophets they found vindication of the poor against the mighty, against nobles. Delagrange was inexhaustible on this count: in Proverbs 29 he found the theory of the good king, friend of the lowly: "*If a king judges the poor with equity his throne will be established for ever . . ."* The Pharoah was less harsh towards his people, selling them back their property, than the Nobles are toward the Third Estate (Delagrange, p. 164 and passim). He brings in the theory of the great dignity of the poor and the mystery of the wicked growing rich: *the Nobles hold the greater part of our land, they have never been anything but prosperous* (Delagrange, p. 217–218). He quotes Psalm 73: *"Their bodies are sound and sleek ...pride is their necklace.... Their eyes swell out with fatness, their hearts overflow with follies."* Then he turns to God; the king is but His earthly representative. Delagrange's *Just Complaint to God* (1597) entones Psalm 34: "The poor man cried, and the Lord heard him, and saved him out of all his troubles." The Church Fathers and other saints of the early days also chimed in with this chorus of protest: St. Ambrose, says Vincent (1598, p. 15, and 1600, p. 58–59), paid taxes, sold chalices if necessary to help the state. He preferred human welfare to precious metals. Shouldn't France's priests do as much? Then there was St. Salvien, a fifth-century bishop of Marseille, moralist, precursor of Jean-Jacques Rousseau, who said barbarianism was better than administrative injustice.[40] Delagrange (1599–2) tells us Salvien railed against the rich and the nobles who paid no taxes.

In the classical and theological context of 1600, where did demands for equality stand? De Bourg had already advanced them, clearly but cautiously, in 1576 (as we have seen, he asked for "official equality" of the three social categories).

Delagrange (p. 173–174) thought that *Nature has made us all equal.* The only *difference* between nobles and commoners was that the nobles were to hold the highest offices (that is why Parlement magistrates were automatically ennobled). Delagrange admitted (p. 174) *that the common people have less authority in the administration of public matters.* But that is as far as he would go. He did not think nobility an innate quality, as the aristocrats claimed, disregarding Christian doctrine. Nobility was simply a royal reward for service: *when the King honors the Nobles with honorary titles, it is for the service they effectively render him,* and for no other reason (ibid., p. 208). The nobles were foolish *to boast of the services performed by their dead ancestors, and rest on others' laurels* (ibid., 1599-2, p. 27).

All in all, Delagrange's egalitarian statements were tempered by the fact that he acknowledged the existence of a hierarchic society. *We* (the third estate counsels) *are not for government by the people, nor for equality, as the Nobles falsely claim. But our privileges* (referring to the original tax exemption for all Dauphiné citizens) *are equal to* theirs (Delagrange, 1599², p. 232). He considered equality an adjective rather than a substantive right, it would appear. He made a case for liberty, (nonservitude) rather than for power: *we do not aspire to Dominate, nor to band together against the Monarch....Nature's law is that we are all born free* (ibid., pp. 233–35).

Equality would simply mean that the tax burden would be proportional to each person's wealth and station in life. The apportioning would be accomplished by royal lawgiving, the great leveler which should ideally subject all citizens to taxes according to the formula "from each according to his ability." *The Edict of Hesdin* (under François I) *says that the King does justice without favoring or excepting anyone; he wants to maintain equality among his people, and wants each to bear the burden commensurate to his rank* (Delagrange, p. 253). In this instance the word *people* does not apply only to the lower classes, the common people. It takes in all three estates, nobility included.

As for Vincent, he is at once bold and reserved on this subject. He starts with a primitive communistic view of property: *in the beginning Nature made the land free and common to all men* (Vincent, 1598, p. 38). Less radical than Delagrange, he immediately acknowledges the notion of "difference" as longstanding: *Nature did not create all men to be the same. From time immemorial there have been different ranks: senators and plebeians in Rome; druids, knights, and plebeians in Gaul.* Vincent does not forget that distinctions also existed *within* the third estate. He even protests the notion of a basic equality between the social categories: *nothing is less equal than their equality!*

Nonetheless, Vincent comes back to the notion of a proportional equality—which all the third estate counsels held dear—

by citing Solon of Athens, the fifth-century B.C. liberator of debtors. *Harmony, the rule of proportion, is the cement of organized societies. Solon divided all the people into four categories, had property assessed, and for the sake of equality he ordered that each person bear the burden of the Republic in proportion to his property* (Vincent, 1600, p. 319–320). Once again, equality is on a par with liberty or nonservitude, and with justice: *we are not serfs, slaves under a Turkish and tyrannical domination. Justice is our passion* (ibid., p. 13, 17).

Marchier's 1595 challenge to Henri IV had already said all this more concisely: (Taxes) *are according to ownership* (of land) *resulting in equality between subjects* (nobles or not) *of a single State.* In other words, everyone should pay taxes based on his property. Marcheri's passion for equality did not prevent him, however, from having himself ennobled ten years later, in 1605.[41]

The idea of a *natural right* which guaranteed freedom for all, if not total equality, was already pronounced in Delagrange's writings, even before the concept was fully developed by the Dutch jurist Hugo Grotius. According to *Natural law,* Delagrange writes (235-39 and 1599, p. 255), *liberty is natural. No matter what the Nobility's defenders may think, servitude is unnatural, we are not serfs.*[42] Rambaud also agrees with the "natural" argument (in his *Second plaidoyer,* pp. 6–7). He stipulates the implementation of fiscal justice as provided for in Provence and Languedoc, but above all *native to the human race.*

Rambaud was a music-loving Aristotelian for whom equality was inseparable from the notion of musical harmony among social categories. *The Third Estate,* he writes (pp. 8[9]) *needs the rules of harmonics, not arithmetic. It does not want to make law of equality* (that would be "government by the people"). *It wants equal justice. But it does not want equal justice that follows arithmetic, with all things equal in weight and form. It wants the harmonic balance made up of different parts. Order and justice founded on proportional and harmonic equality, blending into one, are necessary to the survival of the State.*

Familiar with Bodin's work, Rambaud rejects the complexity of quantitative, mathematical harmony; he leaves that to the justice officials, more highly placed than himself and his commoner clients. *We do not seek to elevate our discourse to the level of considering the intellectual and mathematical harmony Bodin uses to construct the highest floor of the rich and sumptuous edifice of the Republic. It is too high and subtle a lesson for the crude Third Estate, and it is the province of the official magistrates* (Rambaud, *Second plaidoyer*, p. 9). Our author confines himself, then, to the musical metaphors he favors, and which the music-loving people understand: *we only wish to compare the just government of a State to the harmonious composition of Music for different voices, so that the people may hear and understand with ease* (ibid.). Fiscal equality, in good proportion, is like the never-dissonant complexity of an orchestra: *unless there is to be democracy, lawlessness, each must contribute in proportion to his property. Those who have little pay little; those who have much pay much. It is a lovely harmony of various tones. Aspiring to unity does not mean making everything equal. Unity in music is nothing other than Monarchy in a State.* This orchestra is conducted not by the people, but by the king, and ultimately by God. *As all the parts of a musical chord must lend support to one tone, the highest, thus the members of a State must look toward the Monarch to strengthen him. This royal unity* will lead, in conclusion, *to the sovereign Monarch of the Universe* (Rambaud, Ibid., pp. 10–11).

The third estate lawyers were undeniably egalitarian, but 1600 was not 1789, with its declaration of the Rights of Man: *All men are born free and equal in the eyes of the law.* The early seventeenth century was still anchored in a hierarchic society, even if the third estate pursued equality among the three categories[43] without destroying those categories. The individualism characterizing modern egalitarian thought, which grew with the influence of Hobbes, Locke, Rousseau, and Adam Smith from approximately 1650 to 1780 had not yet appeared. The Locke or Rousseau theory was that all individuals are of equal worth and deserve to be treated as equals. It would thus be anachronistic or premature to view the Daphiné militants as attempting a "bourgeois revolution" in 1575 to 1635, just as it is anachronistic to label the great German or Spanish sixteenth-century revolts "the first bourgeois revolutions." Dauphiné's third estate counsels refused, moreover, even to consider the Swiss revolt as a model. It had been too democratic, therefore was too compromising to their cause: *we do not want to treat the Nobles like the Swiss did* (plunder, perhaps kill them). On the contrary, Delagrange writes (1599, p. 269) *the nobles themselves want to break the King thus* (like the Swiss) *by taking all the property* (the third estate's) *without paying taxes on it.* The lawyers prefer to cite the Savoy example, one not of revolution but of reform. *Savoy's Nobility pays the tailles on the property it acquires from the Third Estate* (Delagrange, 1599-2, p. 30). The counsels' pro-Savoy ideal fit in with their defense of monarchy. It might be absolutist but at least it would guarantee the various *bodies* of society a minimum of just apportionment of taxes and of relative equality. Savoy's record was rather enviable: from 1584 to the eighteenth century, reforms in the duchy imposed taxes on the nobles' fields, instated land rolls, encroached on seignorial rights. However, the Dukes of Savoy were simultaneously putting strict limits on the representative assemblies' powers. They foreshadowed Richelieu's behavior toward Dauphiné's third estate: "if you allow me to abolish the provincial Assembly of the Estates which interferes with my absolute rule," the Cardinal suggested to the commoners, "I promise to do something about the nobles' tax exemption." *Hand over the Estates and I'll give you just taxation.*[44]

The third estate lawyers were monarchists, not democrats. They drew their inspiration from Bodin's theories of sovereignty, with which they were familiar. They acknowledged that in France sovereignty belonged to the prince, not the people. But they also pleaded sovereignty when they asserted that royal domination must not become tyranny. The prince was subject to law, he must not steal his subjects' property, he must respect the legitimate rights of Dauphiné's third estate.[45]

With their ideological base secured (it was classical[46] and Christian, rational, moderately but firmly prochurch and promonarchy), the Dauphiné lawyers could turn their attention to legitimate custom, from bastardized to lofty tradition.[47] Finally, they spoke of law with universal applications, a double reference to Dauphiné's tax privilege during the Middle Ages and to Roman law.

Following de Bourg's example, the consuls stressed the fact that the Dauphin (title of Dauphiné's counts before the province was annexed to France) had decreed a tax exemption in 1341 covering *all* residents, including the third estate. From then on, therefore, all taxes were supposedly voluntary contributions, that is, freely voted by the Assembly of the three estates. All these contributions were unanimous; in other words they should apply to everyone in the province, including the holders of the royal privilege. To a man the Dauphinois were theoretically free from the *taille*, and all of them, including nobles, were or should be voluntary taxpayers.[48]

Then the counsels left the decree of 1341 and climbed back into their time machine. They sped back through the thirteenth century and through the entire first millennium. They made a few points in passing; after all, they were educated men. They had read Pasquier, Fauchet, Grégoire de Tours, and other historians, so they did not neglect to mention that St. Louis, Chilprec, Childebert, in short the Capetians and Merovingians, had taxed the nobility and/or clergy.[49] Having established these precedents, they wasted no time getting down to their essential argument, which was rooted in Latin antiquity: a discussion of *Roman law*.

A scornful Marx said in his *18 Brumaire* that the French revolutionaries of 1789–1799 draped themselves in the tatters of the Roman republic, the remainders of a very distant past. But can we truthfully say the Roman law the third estate counsels preached was only a hand-me-down? It would be more accurate to call it a successful grafting of one great cultural tradition onto another. Modest jurists aside, Rome's example magisterially informed all modern legal thought.

The lawyers' argument on this subject was developed on two levels. First of all, it was historical: Vincent and Delagrange cited Roman statesmen in every era of the Republic and the Empire who subjected the aristocrats to taxes. They taxed wealth and land in general, without considering the rank of the rich person or landowner. The counsels' speeches were studded with Latin quotations: Servius Tullius polling property; Cato taxing jewels; Sylla selling the temple riches; Roman senators delivering their taxes in the form of copper coins heaped in a chariot; the second Punic war; Vitellius, Aurelian, and more, all pertinent. Rambaud and Delagrange may not have always been accurate in their references, but the facts they alluded to were there in the works of classical authors.[50] And while on the subject, the lawyers did not pass up the opportunity to brandish the rhetorical threat of a Roman-style intervention of people's tribunals, emphasizing the people's rights over those of the aristocrats.[51]

But Roman law and Dauphiné were not bound simply by juridical rationality. They lived together; they married for love. The people of Dauphiné, the jurists said, and they knew their Latin sources, had given themselves freely to the Roman Empire, in the days of Cottius, the good little Alpine king in the year 13 B.C. The best law minds in Die or Grenoble in 1570–1600 had been trained by Jacques Cujas, who had breathed new life into the program of studies at the University of Valence. They were comforted by the historian Pasquier. They had a decided penchant for the Romans, the *Italics* as they called them. They wore the toga, like the future members of the National Convention. They did not think of Caesar as having conquered their homeland. The residents of the province had become citizens of Rome of their own free will . . . consequently the Dauphinois were initiates of Roman law. Bolstered by this initial assertion or "certitude," the lawyers once again hopped on the toboggan of history. They made another dizzying trip through the ages, this time toward the present. They insisted that the perennial nature of Roman law in Dauphiné linked the province to Languedoc and Provence, which were descended from the old provinces of Norbonnaise and Viennoise. Moreover, the Provençal language, an offshoot of Latin, was spoken in Romans as well as in Aix-en-Provence or Montpellier. The

people of 1600 were well aware of this linguistic bond. Dauphiné had in fact remained part of the Empire, first the Roman
Empire which had included Viennoise and Narbonnaise, then
the Germanic Holy Roman Empire of the Middle Ages, whose
Kaisers were the legitimate successors of the Caesars. Dauphiné
may have been annexed to France during the fourteenth century
as the result of various vicissitudes; nevertheless, the third estate
lawyers maintained, it was still part of the Empire. The counsels were on very solid ground in this case: the most insignificant boatman heading down the Rhône, as late as the nineteenth century, knew that on his left was the Empire and his
his right was the kingdom.[52]

Being subject to Roman law was of the utmost importance.
It meant not paying the forced, personal, humiliating tribute
due from vanquished peoples, that shameful tribute called the
taille. Let the French pay it; they were Gauls. But we Dauphinois, in our Roman togas, *voluntarily* pay *real* contributions on
the land we own in *allodium,* in other words full and entire
property in the Roman style ("quiritary" property). Even if the
land were held in *emphyteusis* (a perpetual share in someone
else's property), it amounted to real ownership for the peasant
or bourgeois tenant. The lawyers stood fast on this point.

And of course Roman law, written law, real taxes, also
implied the existence of *land rolls.* They were much more equitable than analogous registers in Normandy or Île-de-France.
Called *cadastres* or *compoix,* they were found in Languedoc, Provence, and in southern and southeastern Dauphiné. With a little
effort, the lawyers told their Dauphiné compatriots, soon *all* of
you can have land rolls, throughout the province, as would
have long since been the case had Grenoble followed the provisions of Roman law; to the south, in Die, Embrun, Briançon,
the third estate had been courageous enough to safeguard those
provisions. Is it any wonder that the town of Romans was
christened *citadel of the land roll?* Situated on the Isère, on Dauphiné's Mason-Dixon line, if you will, sixteenth-century Romans clung tight to the principle of a rigister of property listing
the fields, houses, vineyards, chestnut trees, shops, of one and
all . . .[53]

The writings of the lawyers evidence the third estate's heightened, enriched consciousness, as compared to the more condensed, primitive, perhaps more moving material in de Bourg's egalitarian *Cahier* of 1576. A quarter of a century later, in the days of Henri IV, antinoble feelings were running higher than ever, were more circumstantial and detailed. The third estate had more self-esteem after its role in the Wars; the line between the two opposing groups—nobility and commoners—was more clearly drawn. Around 1600 there was a synthesis of a Christian or biblical outlook, which our lawyers summoned to their aid, and the Greco-Roman thought which had been de Bourg's sole source of cultural themes. What is more, Roman law and the history of France made a decisive entrance into the commoner's battle against the privileged groups. In Rambaud and Delagrange, then, de Bourg had successors worthy of him. They kept his heritage of political and cultural combat thriving. As for Claude Brosse, he was very active between 1600 and 1630; he articulated specifically rural complaints and demands. He also helps to acquaint us with peasant thought, bits of which judge Antoine Guérin had recorded along with his own malicious comments.

The development of a well-reasoned protest ideology during the last two decades of the sixteenth century was not completely steady, nonviolent; quite to the contrary. The "organicist" third estate lawyers and intellectuals and a yawning gap in their argument.[54] For a while it had threatened to engulf them, and even now it troubled them each time they looked over their shoulder. The peasant war (1579–1580), the Carnival in Romans, the massacre in Moirans . . . They were unpleasant memories, "original sins" the nobles were always ready to fling in the commoners' face like bitter reproaches.

The lawyers remembered the incidents well. If the privileged groups raised the Carnival in Romans as an objection, an example of threatening behavior, the third estate counsels would have to explain it. So they tried to reinterpret it, since they could not wish it away. They did their best to dissociate themselves from it. Delagrange was outstanding at this intellectual exercise. An eminent bourgeois who opposed the nobles but was also adverse to the disorders the lower strata of commoners easily got involved in, a man of learning though not steeped in folklore, he made a few disdainful but slightly awkward allusions to the Romans affair. His main argument was that it was in fact the third estate notables, the rich commoners, with judge Guérin (in his pre-ennoblement days) in the lead, who were the ones credited with killing Paumier. This was their way of restoring order in the streets of Romans. They had won their strikes as respectable bourgeois; all the notables—nonnobles as well as aristocrats—had profited from the newly found social peace. The nobles ought to have been grateful to the elite commoners (whom they wrongly snubbed) for risking their lives to assure the nobles' safety. In short, Delagrange told the nobles "you owe us your lives. Without our help the peasants and craftsmen would have gotten rid of you long ago. What a nerve you have to make sure you are exempt from taxes and have us pay them for you." But we should let Delagrange's text speak for itself (1599, p. 53). *Romans residents of the third estate alone cut the throat of the captain* (Paumier) *who was the chief of certain madmen and peasants in control of the town and who had perpetrated several pieces of impudence in and around Romans. Not only were they aggressive toward the Nobles, but also toward those of the Third Estate richer and more honorable than themselves. Everything these men saw ripe for the taking, they took. If the Third Estate had not undertaken to punish them, it is certain that the Nobles never would have been able to hold them off. Therefore, my lords, cease to put forward the doings of these sadly mistaken madmen; speak no more to us of the League.*

Elsewhere (1599, p. 264), Delagrange again mentions the *outbreak of certain rustics and workmen of little consequence and small numbers who rose up in Dauphiné in 1579,* in opposition to *the Nobles and some of the most Notable citizens of the Third Estate.* Satisfied with his precise if unflattering description of the revolting craftsmen and peasants, Delagrange reiterates it (pp. 87, 103–104, etc., and 1599-2, p. 26) several times: *the rising and fury of this bunch of senseless and erring workers and rustics was put down by the notable persons of the Third Estate in each town, and that is what protected Noble persons from the league . . . . The principal and most sensible citizens of the Third Estate put a stop to the rising of their inferiors in Romans in*

1580. In Valence, it was not the town and its notables, *it was Bonniol the miller of the Abbon mill a half-league from Valence,* who was responsible for the local unrest, *but the King's justice won out* (ibid., p. 25). We should add that the third estate lawyers were sometimes less hostile towards the rebels than Delagrange was. Some of them accused the nobility and its oppression of causing the popular uprisings: *the Nobles wrong the people, that is the source of the sedition, which makes the people the nobles' equals.* Even more radically, Marchier, flouting Henry IV, suggested that the third estate and the villagers, exasperated with the nobles' behavior, might rise up once more against the most recent outrages.[55]

When the lawyers reflected on the 1570–1580 revolt, or other social phenomena, they were highly aware there was a difference, even a gap, between the well-off bourgeois and the lower groups of commoners; the latter were quick to violent action. Delagrange, for instance (p. 99), makes an intelligent analysis of the *octrois* (tolls) and other consumer taxes (on meat, flour, etc.). They affect the poor, he says, in contrast to the real taxes based on land rolls which equitably take some of the unfair excess enjoyed by the rich and the notables. Rambaud does not upset third estate solidarity in any way. But he puts himself on a bourgeois pedestal to speak out against *the dull and lowly condition* (of the third estate) *which prevents it from seeking justice* (other than through the obligatory channel of a counsel such as Rambaud) *directly from His Majesty* (p. 92).

So much for the craftsman/bourgeois distinction. As for peasant/towndweller contrasts within the third estate, they surface once again in the lawyers' discourse on tax problems. Since the Romans agreement of 1583, signed in the name of the third estate by all of Dauphiné's towns and villages, the tax dispute between town and country had been decided in the latter's favor. The agreement stated that city dwellers owning land in rural villages would pay the appropriate taxes in the village in question. That would keep the local peasants from being unduly overburdened. It was an irrevocable concession by the urban third estate to the rural third estate. In all loyalty, it sealed the alliance of the third estate as a whole against the nobles. But it did not completely do away with internal conflict—open country against city—which had been long and bitter.[56]

These various social contradictions were silhouetted in the background of the Paumier-Guérin Carnival in Romans; to various degrees they survived beyond 1580–1600. They should not be viewed only in one dimension. They were carried along in a time flow which included the Carnival as one decisive but fleeting instant. If we wish to go beyond the *événementiel* (narrative of historical events) we should immediately appeal our case to the remarkable chronological paradigm of protest and revolt which Eli Barnavi of the University of Tel Aviv[57] has proposed for the hierarchic societies of the past. He has applied it to a wide variety of rebellions: the Taborites of Bohemia, Anabaptists in Munster, the Spanish *Communidades,* the Neapolitan revolt of Masaniello, and the Parisian League, among others.

In this paradigm the starting point, Barnavi holds, is the emergence of a *united front,* with peaceful rather than violent aims at first. In Dauphiné it was the union of the third estate, town and country, craftsmen and bourgeois, against the nobles and other tax-exempt groups (the clergy, Parlement officials, etc.). The situation existed in the 1550s and was forcefully revived in 1576 by de Bourg, whose charismatic personality unified the village and town communities in support of the petition of grievance. Next, as the movement entered a more violent phase, the first *signs of internal dissent* appeared: they were evident in Montélimar by the summer and autumn of 1578, between the upper and lower groups of commoners, between Colas and Barletier. Properly speaking, *internal dissent* was apparent during all of 1579. While the peasants carried on their own fight against the nobles and landlords, Romans's commoners split into two camps, the notables on one side, craftsmen and farmworkers on the other. At the bottom of this social division were local politics and finance. There was a confrontation between two leaders of two different social echelons, Guérin and Paumier. The judge was a bourgeois, educated, Machiavellian; he was well on his way to ennoblement; at the same time he was the uncontested chief, the boss of the local political machine.[58] Paumier, with his peasant background, was a successful master-craftsman; he wanted a legitimate portion of local power for himself and his group. Guérin had set his sights on nobility; Paumier's marriages show he hoped to become part of the bourgeoisie.

During this internal dissent phase of the paradigm, man's "changeless instincts"[59] come to light. Almost anything can fire them: the sixteenth-century German peasants found their revolutionary theory in the Anabaptists' apocalyptic and biblical teachings. The Dauphiné common folk armed themselves with Carnival ammunition and traditions. The village *reynages,* the folk and religious expression of the peasant community and the youth groups, mobilized against the excesses of the great noble and patrician landowners. In Romans, the urban festivities from Candlemas to Mardi Gras were an aesthetic accompaniment and symbolic turning to account for the two conflicting camps.

After internal dissent comes *armed conflict,* plebeian and peasant groups against the elite. It raged in Dauphiné during the winter and spring of 1580. It was accompanied by a *shift in alliances,* which Delagrange and his fellow lawyers precisely analyzed twenty years after the fact. The general rule in towns, particularly in Romans, was that the upper stratum of the third estate went over to its former enemies (abandoning the good fight for the abolition of tax privileges). Among their new allies were the nobles, Maugiron, the Parlement, the ultra-Catholics, and so on. Inversely, the plebeians and peasants tried to cover themselves with a back-handed alliance. As Catholics, they played it both ways, joining forces with Lesdiguières's Huguenots to fight for the ruling class.[60]

But they were beaten in the end; a return to the initial phase of the paradigm then takes place gradually. Patched together again, the third estate resumed its struggle as a united front, leaving behind its violent internal quarrels. The fight against the nobility and the Parlement, ensconced in their tax privileges, was resumed. Naturally this was not purely and simply the start of a new cycle; each concrete situation has its irreducible originality. Centralized government in the persons of Henri II (during the 1550s) and Catherine de'Medici (1580) had stoutly upheld tax exemption for the nobles, who were considered the natural mainstays of the throne. With Richelieu, during the 1630s, the ship of state changed course: to a certain extent the Cardinal yielded to the third estate's fiscal requests. The financial side of government had an interest in fleecing taxpayers no matter what their rank; it won out over the justice—or rather, injustice—side of government in Dauphiné, which had consolidated the iniquitous forces of social order, in the days of Catherine or of Henri II.

These diachronic paradigms and contrasts nevertheless leave the deep unity of the protest process intact in synchronic terms (its own particular structure at a particular time). Though full of cracks, chips, and disjointed pieces, Dauphiné's third estate remained a solid block. Even as internal dissent began to plague it in August 1580, a character like Gamot, the Grenoble attorney, could appear as a living and unifying synthesis. The hotheaded attorney, flanked by the barber-surgeon Bastien who echoed his sentiments, functioned as the leader of the popular and "antifinancier" leaguers in Grenoble's bustling world of the *basoche*, lesser lawyers, court clerks, sergeants, and so on.[61] A good number of them supported the cause of Romans's rebel craftsmen, against the Parlement of Grenoble "bigwigs" who were on the aristocrats' side. Smack in the center of their violent diatribe, Gamot and Bastien inserted the slogan which from 1560 to 1640 represented the common denominator of the people's grievances: the fight against the two upper estates' tax privilege. "Messrs. of the Nobility, if you do not want to pay taxes, there will be a slaughter of 100,000 nobles," Gamot and Bastien said in substance, after having cited the bloody precedent of the Swiss revolts (later it was even claimed that Gamot had spent a training period in the Swiss cantons so that he would be able to serve as an antinoble agitator in Dauphiné!). Yet this Gamot, a troublemaker to be sure, was the kind of Carnival character Romans would have welcomed as one of its own. In 1579 he walked the streets of Grenoble in full regalia, with a rake (agricultural implement and social leveller), a green bough (Maypole, fertility, peace) . . . and even wreaths of onions (an ordinary food, antidysentery, of the people). A tireless militant, Gamot stood for every symbol; he *was* the symbol personified.

Far from being completely disowned by the local bourgeoisie, who were nonetheless afraid of what the craftsmen and law bureaucrats might do, Gamot, after being sentenced to death by Parlement, was pardoned, freed, given amnesty, thanks to intercession on the part of the towns and their notable consuls. They considered Gamot a "worthy man and devoted to the people."[62] Even in Romans, division did not exclude synthesis. Paumier and Guérin were mortal enemies; still they communed intellectually through a Carnival folklore which constituted their "code," linguistically speaking. They played contradictory roles in the Carnival, but it was the natural element for them both. Despite their rivalry to the death, they were cultural brothers.

That, to me, is the current electrifying the Romans episode: the same craftsmen sporting masks of mud and flour in February 1580 had been the most determined supporters of the third estate's petition of grievance the year before (A 44). An isolated incident, the Carnival in Romans illuminates, reflects on the cultures and conflicts of an era. These include strictly urban struggles, municipal problems which set the craftsmen and the butcher trade in opposition to the patrician ruling group; traditional peasant agitation molded into an assault on a system of landholding that was becoming aggressive, capitalistic;[63] the violent rejection of the government and taxes, both revealing of social conflict. There was also a place for the Catholic, medieval, Renaissance, and soon to be baroque folk traditions of festivity; the bourgeois, semilearned and semiegalitarian ideologies drawing inspiration from classical authors . . . The Carnival in Romans makes me think of the Grand Canyon. It shows, preserved in cross section, the social and intellectual strata and structures which made up a *"très ancient régime."* In the twilight of the Renaissance it articulates a complete geology, with all its colors and contortions.

Appendix

Dauphiné roman?

GUERIN d'azur au pommier arraché de sinople au chef d'arg. chargé au point d'hon... d'une oublie... de cettye de 2. plattes ou besans de g...

omnia & uno)

Chonet.

1

1/ Guerin's coat of arms; the first line contains a reference to an uprooted apple tree, *pommier* (Paumier) *arraché*. Bibliothèque Nationale.

2/ A dispute between Paumier and the consular authorities in February 1577. The first word in the fourth line is Paulmier (Paumier). ACR, GG 44/23.

2

3/ Jean de Bourg's one-hundred-article Petition of Grievance, 1577. The second line begins ". . . l'égalité laquelle est requise en toute société . . . ," (The equality which is required in any society). ADD, C1023.

4/ Signature of the bandit Laroche, "bon amy et voisin," (your good friend and neighbor), February 1579. ADD, E 3387.

5/ Signature of Guillaume Robert-Brunat, the Romans craftsman leader, "pour le peuple," (for the people), 1579. ACR, FF 19.

6/ Signature of Geoffroy Fleur
the butcher, another leader
of the revolt, 1579. ACR,
FF 19.

7/ The imperious signature of
Judge Antoine Guérin, 1579.
ACR, FF 19 (63).

8/ Text and signature of
Jacques Colas, the
Montélimar league leader
(about the outlaw Laroche),
1579. ADD, E 3387.

Chapter Notes

Chapter I

1. ADD, E 1169 = ACR II₄.

2. Martine Perrochet, in her unpublished thesis on Romans in the fifteenth century, calculated five persons per hearth, and in addition, a figure of 0.67 of a person to allow for the nobles and poor not counted in the hearth roll. Multiplying by 5.7 would give 6,594 inhabitants. I find a basis of five too high. I have reduced it to 4.5, retaining the extra 0.67, for a total of 5.17. This is simply a question of gradation. See M. Perrochet, l'Ecole des Chartes thesis on Romans in the fifteenth century (Romans Public Library).

3. ADD, E 3592, for 1366.

4. Figure from Perrochet, thesis.

5. ACR, CC, tax rolls for the years cited above; and Thomé de Maisonneuve, *Histoire de Romans*, II, p. 571.

6. ACR, CC 81.

7. ACR, BB for this date (courtesy of M. Rossiaud).

8. The plague killed approximately 4,000 people in Romans from June 1564 to January 1565. This accounts for the demographic deficit of 1566 to 1557, despite a swift recovery due to an immediate influx of people from the country, and the no less immediate remarriage of widows who quickly bore new babies (see G. Delille's thesis on this subject).

9. ACR, CC, tax roll for 1566.

10. ACR, CC 90, tax roll for 1570.

11. ACR, CC 93. The 1578 tax roll is classified ACR, CC 92.

12. ACR, CC 94. Within its sixteenth-century ramparts, Romans covers 37.68 hectares (courtesy Mme. Francine Mallet).

13. ACR, CC 361. Presuming a decrease in number of persons per household occurred.

14. R. Gascon, *Grand commerce*, I, p. 350.

15. ADD, E 3804.

16. P. Laslett, *Household and Family in Past Time.*

17. ACR, CC 92, for 1578. Same division in the other tax rolls (e.g., ACR, CC 93, for 1582).

18. In terms of the value of their property, recorded as upkeep, I calculate their actual payment at 314 *écus* out of a total of 1932.4 *écus* tax paid by Romans in 1578. Land roll values assess four-fifths or more real estate and less than one-fifth moveable personal property (ADD, E 11689 = ACR, FF 53).

19. Marc Venard, *L'Eglise d'Avignon*, p. 1758.

20. Information on sixteenth-century commerce in Romans courtesy M. Rossiaud.

21. On Romans's four or five notaries, see also ACR, GG 19 for 1591.

22. Or 358.2 *écus* tax out of 1932.4 according to my tally based on 1578 records. The count made at the time showed 379.3 *écus* or 19.4 percent.

23. ACR, BB 13, f^0 317 v^0(=311v^0). Meeting of March 25, 1577. Request (refused) of Jean Thomé, Gaspard Jourdan, and Michel Servonnet, drapers, to move from the third into the second rank.

24. For the entire paragraph, see Venard, *L'Eglise d'Avignon*, pp. 1766 ff.

25. ADD, E 11600 (ACR EE 10, June 1577), and P. E. Girard, *Procédure*, BSASD, 1866, pp. 400 ff.; ADD, E 3794 for 1547. For similar excommunications, compare to J. Adhémar, *Montlaur*, BSASD, September 1972, p. 353.

26. All of these details from Venard, *L'Eglise d'Avignon*, pp. 1771 ff.

27. On farm protests, see ACR BB 14, December 1579–February 1580.

28. One *écu* equals 5 *florins* or 3 *livres* (pounds).

29. But perhaps less so than the France of today, even though it was not famed for its just distribution of wealth, with the top decile controlling 30.5 percent of revenue (today's measure). In Sweden, the most egalitarian of Western democracies, the share is only 18.6 percent (Malcolm Sawyer, report for the Organization of Economic Cooperation and Development, as quoted in *Nouvel Observateur*, September 9, 1976.) Jean Fourastié has recently disputed inegalitarian distribution of wealth in France.

30. R. Gascon, *Grand commerce*, I, p. 63.

31. Ibid., and M. Lacave in *Annales*, Nov.–Dec. 1977.

32. ACR, CC 4, CC 5, CC 6.

33. ACR, CC 11, 12, 13, 14.

34. ADD, E 3608.

35. ACR, CC 2 and CC 3.

36. J. Soubeyroux, *Thesis.*

37. Venard, *L'Eglise d'Avignon,* p. 1786.

38. The 1578 tax roll shows 17 of the 137 heads of household in the second rank paying less than 0.8 *écu* tax.

39. ACR, CC 94, tax roll for 1583, and ACR, CC 5 (tenants).

40. ACR, CC 5 and CC 94.

41. My calculation, averaged from numerous indications in ACR, CC 5, for the St. Nicholas quarter. A building assessed at 50 *écus* yields a rent of 3.

42. Antoine Nicodel as he appears in Chapter VII owns no property. His widow does—a sign of prosperity, however slight.

43. See also below, Chapter VII, the study directly relating to craftsmen sentenced in 1580. They appear as minor property owners, but not poor.

44. AC Vienne, no. 45, in Cavard, *Vienne,* p. 216 (March 17, 1579).

45. From 1569 to 1580, the governor of Romans was Philippe Philibert, lord of Cervières St. André, who had zero influence. In 1584 Antoine de Solignac, lord of Veaune, was governor; he was one of Guérin's men.

46. Theoretically, the judiciary in Romans was divided between the royal judge and a judge appointed every second year by the Chapter of St. Barnard, co-lords of the town. See for example, Bouchu, 1968, in BSASD 1873, p. 6 and n. 1. In fact, Guérin was "king" of the judiciary.

47. Père Archange de Clermont, *Mémoires pour l'histoire des huguenots de Romans* (Romans: 1887), p. 26 no. 2.

48. ACR, FF 19, March 5, 1577.

49. ADD, E 3598: decree of the Parlement of Grenoble (February 25, 1559) on consular elections in Romans.

50. A member of one of the two upper ranks was more or less born to a stint as consul, for example, the Guigou, Coste families. For a member of the third rank, there seem to have been two prerequisites during the period from 1565 to 1585: (1) be on good terms with Guérin; (2) be a trade confraternity member and have some experience collecting indirect municipal taxes. Consider the case of Jean Magnat, baker. In 1576 and 1577, he was in charge of collecting the town tributes levied on food producers and others. In the political year ending in spring 1579 he became third counsul of Romans (ACR, FF 19; ACR, CC 53, Magnat's accounts).

51. ADD, E 3597 (March 25, 1536)(in 1366, 430 attended according to ADD, E 3592).

52. ADD, E 3596 (May 19, 1542). Much further evidence confirms this text, most notably in 1622 (ADD, E 3598).

53. ADD, E 3737 (text of July 26, 1558).

54. ACR, BB 14, f⁰ 69 v⁰, 70, 71 v⁰, municipal decision of May or spring 1579, mistakenly bound in volume BB 14, which is supposed to begin at November 1579. (A 34). This partly destroyed text upholds the testimony of Antoine Guérin (A34), which a recent historian of Romans has quite wrongly contested (Thomé de Maisonneuve, BSASD, vol. 18, 1943–1945: 219).

55. Ibid. f⁰ 69 v⁰. See the capital text in ADD, B 1709 on the appointment of these captains, a prerogative of the consuls and the town council, except in revolutionary times such as 1579 when the "poor people" had captains "agreeable to the people" appointed.

56. L. Gruppi, in *Dialectiques* 17, winter 1977, p. 40; cf. also Michel Foucault, *Histore de la sexualité*, I, (Paris: 1976), p. 123: "Power . . . is not a certain quality certain people have. It is one name for a complex strategical situation in a given society."

57. Drought of 1504, plague of 1505; *Les Trois Doms* staged in Romans, Pentecost 1509; (Canon U. Chevalier, *Mystère des Trois Doms à Romans en 1509* (Romans: 1887).

58. See the much later ACR, BB 23 (January 6, 1610) and BB 24 (December 29, 1617); and especially BSASD, vol. 16, 1882, p. 386 (fine account of a 1517 miracle); vol. 4 p. 476; see U. Chevalier, *Notice historique sur le Mont-Calvaire de Romans* (1883).

59. Père Archange, *L'histoire des Huguenots*.

60. Ibid.

61. ADD, E 3668, doc. 14.

62. ADD, E 11599 (=ACR, EE 9); see also below, Chapter VII.

63. *Dictionnaire de Spiritualité*, published by Beauchene, see Carême (Lent).

64. On this chronology, see Venard, *L'Eglise d'Avignon*.

65. A. Lacroix, *Romans et le Bourg-de-Peage* (Valence: 1897), Chapter 17. See also ADD, E 11649 (=ACR, FF 13 and FF 15); ADD, E 11748 and 11749 (=GG 45 and 46). On the municipal nature of urban schools in sixteenth-century France, later replaced by Jesuit and Oratorian schools, George Huppert is currently writing a refutation of F. de Dainville (S.F.), *Naissance de l'humanisme moderne* (Paris: 1940).

66. ACR, CC 491.

67. ACR, GG 21: One of the first parish registers in Romans, with signatures recorded for weddings.

68. Fustel de Coulanges, *L'Alleu*, pp. I–IV.

69. R. Brenner in *Past and Present*, 1975, p. 63 n. 80.

70. Estimates of the demographic percentage of noble and clerical landlords and the statistics I have come up with on property belonging to nobles before 1602 and the clergy before 1605 are based on figures in an unpublished study by Perier and Rossi on elections in the districts of Romans (106 communities) and Vienne (165 communities).

In hectares:	Romans	Vienne	Total
A) Noble holdings before	10,059.34	22,297.24	32,356.58
1602, clergy before 1635	%A/C 34.12%	%A/C 40.85%	%A/C 38.49%
B) Total taxable property (incl. holdings exempted in 1658 and 1693–95)	19,420.92	32,290.33	51,711.25
C) Total	29,480.26	54,587.57	84,067.83

For more detailed information, Bernard Bonnin's forthcoming thesis on the agrarian history of Dauphiné should be consulted. Bonnin's work takes an entirely new slant on the subject and renders further comment by me unnecessary.

71. Comparison courtesy Bernard Bonnin, thesis dossier 22.

72. Bernard Bonnin, dossier 21.

73. The following counts are based on data collected by Perier and Rossi. Certain points refer to Rossi's work.

74. These remarks owe much to conversations with my friend Bernard Bonnin.

75. The archives are full of mentions of such exemptions occurring when a taxpayer becomes a noble of the robe. For example, in 1580 Henri Gigou acceded to an office in the local administration of the royal treasury and was exempted. Only one of many such cases between 1570 and 1580 (ACR, CC 354 for 1580; cf. ADI B 185 to 95).

76. René Valentin de Cheylard (1960), pp. 273–284; cf. J. B. Wood (1977).

77. J. Nicolas, thesis, p. 866.

78. Vienne, Archives Civiles, CC 95, ff.

79. Remarks to me by V. Chomel (1977).

80. Retrospective confirmation for the period under study: in 1579 the Parlement of Grenoble lowered a similar tithe from 6.6 percent to 3.2 percent (AD de L'Isère, B 190: case of the abbé de Valcroissant). Also, a keeper of the books of their estate in Vienne (ADI, 4E, 245/62) in 1576, asked that the tithe be brought into line at 4.8 percent (or one-twenty-first). As far as the protests of 1579–1580 are concerned, the tithe was of little importance compared to the antinoble theme.

81. ADI, B 190, for 1579. In 1562, even the Huguenots wanted to confiscate the tithe, not abolish it.

82. All the preceding statistics are my own, arrived at with figures provided in the invaluable work of Perier and Rossi.

83. I have not gone into the question of the overall amount the peasant had to hand over. There were royal taxes and tithes and seignorial rents and dues, plus taxes farmed out and interest on debts, if applicable. A quarter to a third of the gross agricultural product, perhaps, but not half? See Bernard Bonnin's thesis for an exhaustive and convincing answer.

84. Lawrence Stone, *The Causes of the English Revolution* (London: 1972).

Chapter II

1. A 29. The term *élévation populaire* (rising of the people) is indicative of the stratified nature of Romans society, as well as the lower classes' attempts at climbing. Guérin uses the term, and so does the baker Jean Magnat, third consul of Romans in 1579. Thus, a case of a notion common to both the bourgeois and lower-class elements of Romans.

2. Lesdiguières, *Letters*, I, p. 31. Lesdiguières's base of operations at the time was Gap. It must be emphasized that the peasant leagues sometimes played the role of pawn, a hostile or friendly pawn depending on the region, in the complex game Lesdiguières was conducting. "He was the behind-the-scenes ally of the Duke of Savoy (who was, however, a Catholic). Savoy was eager for influence in Dauphiné. Lesdiguières was also in league with the Maréchal de Bellegarde, who was scheming to get control of the Marquis de Saluce's land in nearby Piedmont" (A. Dussert [1931], p. 13031).

3. Chevalier (1876), pp. 40–41.

4. Ibid.

5. Ibid., p. 36

6. Dussert (1915, 1922, 1931).

7. G. Franz, *Baurenkrieg*; Y. Bercé, *Histoire des Croquants*, II, pp. 679, 680, 687.

8. Dussert (1922), pp. 43–46 and 282–85

9. Dussert (1915), p. 73.

10. Dussert (1922), p. XIV.

11. Same situation at the Estates of Vivarais (Dauphiné's neighbor); see A. Molinier, *Thesis*, p. 41.

12. Compare with Molinier's calculations, *Thesis*, p. 40: the Vivarais Estates were mainly taken up with war and tax questions from 1562 to 1580; in 1743 to 1779 they dealt with local commerce, industry, transportation.

13. Van Doren, papers, I, pp. 26–27, 76 (see Bibliography).

14. Van Doren, papers, I, pp. 15 and 27, and my Graph I; Dussert (1922), pp. 43–46, 183–84, 214–15, 282–84, 331.

15. Dussert (1922), pp 241, n. 2; Van Doren, papers, I, pp. 21, 25, 27.

16. Dussert (1922), pp. 241–43, 296–97; Van Doren, papers, I, pp. 21–29, 32, 39 n. 103.

17. Van Doren, papers, I, p. 32, 53, ns. 100, 122; Dussert (1922), p. 297.

18. Compare to J. E. Brink (1975).

19. Dussert (1915), pp. 335–339; Van Doren, papers, I, pp. 32 ff.

20. Van Doren, papers, II.

21. Cavard (1950), pp. 125, 183.

Chapter III

1. Cavard, (1950), p. 175.

2. AD Drôme, C 1023: 100—Article text (November 24, 1576, and March 16, 1577). Scott Van Doren kindly lent me a copy which I also compared to the original.

3. Example of an acquisition of this type, but limited to six or nine years, in a letter of Catherine de'Medici dated August 4, 1579, to Henri III about Gaspard de Laval (*Lettres de Catherine de Médicis,* vol. VII, p. 70).

4. Dussert (1922 and 1931).

5. Exception: the *Ormée* in Bordeaux in the seventeenth century is replete with classical references (C. Jouhaud [1977]).

6. C. Lefort, *Les formes de l'histoire* (Paris: 1978).

7. On requests for *equalization* between 1530 and 1560, see the texts quoted in Dussert (1922), p. 214 n. 1, 288 n. 2, 289, 291 n. 2, 296 ns. 3 and 4, 197; cf. also Scott Van Doren, p. 88 and n. 98. It was certainly in the state's interest to promote "equalization" in order to bring in more tax revenues; it would mean income in proportion to the wealth of regions, estates, and social groups. Richelieu realized this (see below, Chapter IX; and, for Provence, Pillorget pp. 355, 358–359). See also ACR, BB 15, August 4, 1580, request for general equalization throughout the area of debts due to the military occupation of Romans.

8. ADD, C 1024, and A. Lacroix, *Procès des Tailles.*

9. De Bourg had his reasons, less than lofty, for *not* referring to the generalization of real taxes proposed by Pasquier. An urban bourgeois, de Bourg did not not oppose a real *taille* in itself, but would not have wanted to see it too generally applied as that would conflict with the interests of the urban bourgeoisie, touching their rural property. We have seen that de Bourg favored the place of residence as a tax base, and with reason.

10. This text concerns the clergy who "by old privilege should not enjoy the privilege of exemption." It thus seems to contrast the "good" older privileges and the "bad" newer ones.

11. Bercé, *Histoire des Croquants*, II, *in fine*.

12. Ibid., I, pp. 274 ff.

13. The following after Dussert (1931), p.134.

14. All in Dussert, 1931, *in fine*. See also Bibliothèque Nationale, manuscrits français 15561, p. 22: a neutral summary, by Avançon, Archbishop of Embrun, of the third estate's position.

15. Art. 1 to 14, 28, 30 to 34, 36 in Dussert (1931), p. 166 ff.

16. A. Dussert (1931).

17. Below, Chapter III.

18. Art. 20, 23, 24, 31, 32, 40 of the 44 articles.

19. P. Chaunu, *Histoire économique et sociale de la France,* ed., F. Braudel and E. Labrousse (Paris: 1977), vol. I, pp. 35–39.

20. Cavard, *Vienne*, p. 217 ff.

21. Piémond, pp. 74–76; Dussert (1931), p. 144.

22. Bibliothèque Municipale de Grenoble, ms. R 80, vol. XVI, fol. 64. A less complete version of this text is in Cavard, pp. 221–222.

23. The preceding after *Lettres de Catherine de Médicis,* vol. VII, July–August 1577; Cavard, pp. 210–230; Dussert (1931); Piémond, pp. 72–85. On Switzerland, see above; compare to Alfred Berchtold *et al., Quel Tell?* (Payot, Lausanne: 1973, introductory chapters.)

Chapter IV

1. Bercé, *Histoire des Croquants.*

2. Pont-en-Royans was subsequently terrorized by Laprade, another outlaw, but Maugiron trusted the town to resist, even though it was Protestant (ADD E 3671, 2, Maugiron's letter of January 1, 1579, kindly pointed out to me by Scott Van Doren).

3. According to A. Lacroix, *l'Arrondissement de Montélimar,* vol. VI, p. 173. On the same subject see Jean de Bourg's 1576 *Cahier.*

4. See J. Goy and E. Le Roy Ladurie, *Les fluctuations du produit de la dime.*

5. AC Montélimar, BB, August 22, 1578, according to A. Lacroix, *Arr. de Montélimar.*

6. AD Drome E 3387 (letter by the consuls of Bollène, March 8, 1578). AC Donzère, BB 2 in ADD, E 6849, for June 1577 to October 1578. On the segmented organization of the original union, see the letter by the consuls of Sauzet (October 19, 1578) in Baron de Coston's *Histoire de Montélimar,* p. 392. Compare to Bercé, *Histoire des Croquants,* I, p. 275 (same segmentary character in Acquitaine).

7. Thomé de Maisonneuve, BSASD (1943–1945), p. 113 and n. 25.

8. According to A. Lacroix, *Arr. de Montélimar*, vol. VI, p. 174 (on Montélimar's *commune*) and Baron de Coston, *Histoire de Montélimar*, p. 392.

9. According to A. Lacroix, *Arr. de Montélimar*, vol. II, p. 128, decision at Donzère, February 2, 1579; see also A. Lacroix, *Arr. de Montélimar*, vol. V, p. 113, and ADD E 6849, BB 2, June 14, 1577 and April 4, 1580.

10. This paragraph on Jacques Colas is almost entirely taken from Coston, *Histoire de Montélimar*, pp. 272, 366 ff.; and from Colas de la Noue, *Jacques Colas*.

11. Colas, *Colas*, pp. 38–39 quoting Lestoile, vol. I, pp. 197–199.

12. Colas, *Colas* (letters), pp. 157–161.

13. Thomé de Maisonneuve (1943–45), p. 111. Maisonneuve mistakenly read and recorded La Cloche for Laroche (ADD, E 3387, documents of February–March 1578).

14. ADD, E 3387, Catherine de'Medici, letters of August 1578 and February to March 1579.

15. Catherine de'Medici, *Lettres*, vol. VII, p. 49.

16. This text is found in Colas, *Colas*, pp. 181–185.

Chapter V

1. Van Gennep, *Manuel* (Carnival-Lent).

2. Charles de Coynard, *Les Guérin de Tencin*, p. 26. See also below, Chapter VIII.

3. The Swiss or Savoy shepherd's trumpet (there is one in the museum at Chamonix) is a wooden horn about 40 cm. long in the shape of an elongated cone with holes in both ends, sometimes reinforced with metal rings.

4. On the Grand Prior see also B.N., ms. fs. 15561.

5. See below, Chapter VII.

6. A. Van Gennep, *Revue d'ethnographie* (1924), p. 136 ff.

7. On agrarian feasts in January–February in Dauphiné, see also Pilot de Thorey, pp. 12–13.

8. Van Gennep, *Revue d'ethnographie*.

9. The date given by the Anonymous Author (Guérin); an (incorrect) note at the bottom of Piémond's published texts says February 10. Thomé de Maisonneuve, also mistakenly, puts the election on February 11 according to Guérin (!) in BSASD (1943–1945), p. 164.

10. Piémond, p. 65. Another Serve, related to Paumier, was significantly known as Montmirail: Guillaume Serve, called Montmirail (ACR, CC 92, tax roll of 1578, third rank, f⁰ 16 v⁰).

11. Brun-Durand, *Biographie du Dauphiné*, p. 349.

12. Pilot de Thorey, p. 12. Compare to M. Agulhon, "Jeu d'Arquebus à Aix. . ." On the popinjay kings in Romans, see also ACR, BB 23, June 12, 1611, March 25, 1612; BB 24, April 28, 1614; BB 27, April 1, 1628, etc; ACV, BB 9, July 13, 1579, Romans arquebusers from the popinjay games come to compete in Valence.

13. Thomé de Maisonneuve (1943–45), pp. 223–224.

14. Brun-Durand, *Biographie du Dauphiné*, p. 350.

15. See below, Chapter VI.

16. Valloire: plain and valley farm region north of Romans.

17. *Marchand* (merchant) and not *méchant* (wicked) (Piémond's editor's mistake. I checked the text against BN ms. fs. 3319, f⁰ 79 v⁰-81 1⁰ by comparing the appearance of the same letters as written in other words).

18. All based on Piemond, p. 65 and especially J. Roman, *Catherine de Médici en Dauphiné*, p. 7.

19. See above, Introduction.

20. Piémond, p. 65: footnote taken from the record (now lost) of proceedings of Romans's council, February 2, 1579.

21. Thomé de Maisonneuve sums up this text (1943–1945), p. 218. The 1582 taille roll or tax roll shows 484 farmers out of 1,335 taxpayers (ACR, CC 93). This very high figure helps us understand why the Romans protests were finally best expressed through an agrarian, Catholic folklore, rather than the initial stirrings of the Protestant craftsmen.

22. Piémond, p. 65 n., citing the town register "BB," today lost, for February 2, 1579.

23. On this subject see Thomé de Maisonneuve (1943–1945), p. 218.

24. ACR FF 19; ADD, E 3743 (57), November 12, 1579 (decision at Romans, text furnished by S. Van Doren); see also above, Chapters III and IV.

25. Piémond, pp. 65–66, 65 n.

26. A 32, n. 1.

27. Ibid. See above, Chapter I, in the same sense de Bourg's *Cahiers*.

28. Roman, *Catherine de Médici*, p. 9; and BSSI (1890), p. 316.

29. ACR, CC 491 (58).

30. ACR, FF 24; see also ACR, FF 10, FF 11, FF 15, FF 49.

31. ACV, BB, February 4, 1579, in Piémond, p. 65 n. 2.

32. Roman, *Catherine de Médici*; Piémond, p. 57.

33. ADD, E 3744/2 (February 13, 1579); Thomé de Maisonneuve (1943–1945), p. 221. Compare to J. Roman, *Documents*, BSSI (1890), doc. 177–178.

34. ADD, E 3744 (3).

35. Thomé de Maisonneuve (1943–1945), p. 223 n. 49, and (1941–1942), pp. 78–80.

36. Ibid., p. 221, 224.

37. Thomé de Maisonneuve, *Histoire de Romans*.

38. Thomé de Maisonneuve, 1943–1945; quoting from the lost register (BB) of proceedings of the Romans council.

39. My account may sometimes use the terms "rebels" and "mutineers" which I borrow from the original sources (*rebelles* and *mutins*); while they are not necessarily exact, they are convenient.

40. The following is based on Brun-Durand, *Biographie du Dauphiné*, entry for *La Prade*.

41. Lesdiguières, *Correspondance*, vol. I, pp. 13–15, 33 (Lesdiguières's protestations against the capture of Roussas by Colas).

42. Decision of March 3, 1579 in Romans, in Piémond, p. 66 n. 1.

43. Piémond, p. 66 n. 1 (Romans session of 3.3.1579, lost register). Cf. also AC Chabeuil, CC 2–2 (42) (reference courtesy of Scott Van Doren).

44. It is noteworthy that it was the third (craftsman) rank's consul, the baker Jean Magnat, who was charged with the expenses incurred by Romans's expedition to Châteaudouble, jointly supported by the town government and the league. Romans's very archaic system of accounting made each of the four consuls responsible for a part of the receipts and payments, therefore making such an assignment of expenses possible. Another explanation is that Magnat's sympathies lay at least partly with the craftsman faction, though Magnat was certainly less radical than Paumier. (ACR, CC 353, spring 1579. Jean Magnat and his three colleagues' terms expired around March–April 1579).

45. A 40 n. 1. On Gordes, see Piémond, p. 563.

46. Châteaudouble was the administrative seat of a *châtellenie* made up of several parishes (Brun-Durand, *topog.*, Drôme). On the problems between Lesdiguières and Laprade, see Piémond, p. 67 n. 2.

47. On all the preceding see A 39; and J. Roman, *Doc.*, BSSI, 1890, p. 305.

48. Piémond, p. 67 and A 39 are unanimous. Same phenomena in Vendée (R. Aron, *Clausewitz*, II, p. 107).

49. Piémond, p. 67 n. 2, Romans session of March 10, 1579; Piémond, p. 68 and BSSI (1890), pp. 309–310.

50. ADD, C 1023 for this date. See also BSSI (1890), p. 307.

51. Piémond, p. 67 n. 2; 68 n. 1.

52. Brun-Durand, *Biographie du Dauphiné*, entry for La Prade; Piémond, p. 69; A 38–39 n. 1.

53. See also Chorier's false version of Laprade's death, II 657, in Piémond, p. 69 n. 1.

54. A 40 and Piémond, p. 69. The fall of Châteaudouble had great repercussions since a song was written about it, in French, no doubt (?) shortly after the event. It celebrates the common people's unity with the third estate (for the complete text see Colas, *Colas,* quoting Le Roux de Lincy). See Le Roux de Lincy, *Recueil de chants historiques français* (Paris: 1842), vol. II, pp. 383–388.

55. A 38 n.; and above.

56. Lesdiguières, *Correspondance*, I., p. XXVI.

57. In fact, with this conciliatory spirit reigning, a royal *pardon* was eventually granted the leaguers. Though they had risen up during the winter of 1578–79, their victory over Laprade was for the cause of law and order (Chevalier, in BSASD X [1876], pp. 42–43).

58. Piémond, p. 70 n. 1.

59. Ibid. (Romans decison of March 16, 1579, lost register).

60. Ibid.

61. Ibid.

62. ADD, E 6414.

63. Texts of 1579, quoted by Lacroix, *Arr. de Montélimar*, vol. V, pp. 111–114.

64. Le Roy Ladurie, *Paysans de Languedoc*, pp. 393–394.

65. See ACR, CC 491 (64). Basset's letter of May 12, 1579. He congratulates the Romans consuls on the order that reigns in their town, compared to the rural atrocities. Basset says law and order will help Romans advance the cause of the *Cahiers*.

66. Piémond, p. 74, n. 1, and A 42.

67. Piémond, p. 75 n. 1, and ADI, B 2339, f⁰ 6800, May 11 and 20, 1579; Dussert, p. 152; Van Doren, thesis, p. 60.

68. Cavard, *Vienne*, p. 221.

69. ACR, CC 491 (=ADD, E 11534).

70. J. Nicolas, *Thesis.*

71. See above, Chapter I; and BN, MF, 15.561, f⁰ 22; as well as the text published by Colas.

72. Above, Chapter I.

73. On these events see Piémond, pp. 73–74 n. 1.

74. ADD, E 3620.

75. ACR, CC 92, for the year 1578: François Rochas (the ropemaker Laroche) pays 7 *florins* tax. Paumier and Brunat, the two leaders of the revolt, who became Laroche's enemy, were more or less in the same tax bracket, Brunat paying 6 *florins* and Serve-Paumier 11 *florins* 3 *sous*.

76. Also see Piémond, p. 88: "The rich, *guignant qu'il fallait restituer* . . . ."

77. Same idea in the *Cahiers* of de Bourg (above, Chapter I).

78. Compare to the revolt of the armed *masks* of Vivarais against the law and order party in 1783 (Sonenscher, 1971, pp. 254–255; Molinier, *Thesis*, p. 914).

79. On justice in Romans and the relationship between the king and the Chapter, see Thomé de Maisonneuve, BSASD (1941–1942), pp. 78–80.

80. Arnaud, *Histoire des protestants,* for the year 1572.

81. Piémond, p. 65; A 29.

82. Thomé de Maisonneuve, BSASD (1941–1942), pp. 80–82.

83. ADD, B 1709 (beginning of seventeenth century in Romans).

84. See above, Chapter I.

85. V. Chevalier in BSASD (1875), pp. 42–43.

86. Ibid., p. 44.

87. ACR, FF 19, November 5, 1579.

88. All according to a comparative study of the lists of consuls and council members: ACR, BB 15 (general meeting of the new Council formed in spring 1580); and BB12 (end of the register, proceedings of the general meeting of March 23, 1579, mistakenly bound in BB 12).

89. Paul Van Dyke, *Catherine de Médicis,* II, 250 ff; Edith Sichel, *Cath. Méd.* (London: 1908), p. 316; J.H. Mariéjol, *Cath. Méd.,* (Paris: 1922), p. 290; Irene Mahoney, *Madame Catherine* (New York: 1975), p. 248 (very detailed); Ivo Luzzatti, *Cath. Med.* (Milan: 1939), p. 376; Jean Heritier, *Cath. Med.* (Paris: 1959); J. Castlenau, *Cath. Med.* (Paris: 1954), p. 204; Mezeray, *Hist. de France,* editions d'Ales (1844), I, p. 468.

90. BN, ms. fs. 3319, p. 123.

91. J. Roman, "Catherine de Médicis en Dauphiné," *Bull. de l'acad. delphinale,* Dec. 1, 1882 (published in 1883).

92. Ibid., p. 7; this bastion implied a partial or total preponderance around Gap, in Champsaur, Trièves, Barronies, around Die, and "a good part" around Valence.

93. J.C. Brieu, 1868–1869.

94. *Lettres of Catherine de'Medici,* vol. VII, texts of July 1579.

95. All the preceding after the letter dated July 18, 1579 in Baguenault de Puchesses, *Lettres de Cath. de Méd,* vol. VII, pp. 48–51. References to Catherine's letters are to this edition.

96. Ibid., vol. VII, p. 50.

97. The word is in fact *marchand* (checked against the original ms., BN, ms fs. français 3319) and not *méchant drapier*, J. Brun-Durand's erroneous reading in a footnote in his edition of Piémond (p. 80). Indeed, Catherine was much less hard on Paumier than on Colas (*fol*) or de Bourg (*factieux*). Paumier was not instantly repulsive to the ruling class, with the exception of Guérin. Quite the contrary.

98. Guuérin (A 44 ff.); Piémond, pp. 78 ff.; Catherine de Médicis, *Lettres*, dated July 18 and 20, 1579 from Romans. The admirable agreement of these three sources gives a very high value to Guérin and Piémond's testimony, Guérin's prejudices notwithstanding.

Chapter VI

1. Catherine de'Medici, *Letters*, September 6, 1579.

2. ACR, CC 534 (=ADD, E 11 577).

3. ACR, FF 19 (and BB 13, f⁰ 273 ff.).

4. ACR, BB 13, f⁰ 230 v⁰.

5. It was "formidable" according to the sixteenth century's moderate criteria; in the twentieth century it would seem "normal"!

6. ACR, GG 44.

7. Dussert (1931), p. 123.

8. With reason: witness the feasting and the dance held in the town hall in February 1580.

9. ACR, FF 19 (77).

10. Ibid., and A 41.

11. ACR, CC 353, accounts of one of the four consuls, Bernardin Guigou, 1579; he collects fines, etc. (211 *écus* in receipts); he pays the gatekeepers, the schoolmaster (315 *écus* expenditures).

12. One *écu* equals 3 *livres*.

13. Guérin (A 40–41): once again the judge has the facts straight, tendentious as his interpretations might be, and ACR FF 19 confirms them. See also, below, the list of animals associated with the various *reynages* (sheep, partridge, capon) which Guérin and which a text in the archives of the Parlement of Grenoble (ADI, B 2039, in Piémond, p. 98, note) verifies.

14. Decree signed Fustier, by the court, in Parlement May 18, 1579 (ACR, FF 19).

15. *Taille* roll for 1583, ACR, CC 94.

16. ACR, BB 12, fol. 250, March 23, 1579 (1579 proceeding bound in with registers from another year).

17. The following draws on ACR, BB 14 for the dates indicated.

18. On this subject see register ACR, BB 14 for the period November 1579 to February 1580.

19. See above, Chapter I.

20. ACR, FF 19 (July 2, 1579).

21. ARR, FF 19 for that date.

22. Catherine de'Medici, *Lettres,* Vol. VII, pp. 120–121 (September 6, 1579).

23. The butchers' and bakers' tax strike in Romans was attested to by November 12, 1579 (ADD, E 3743, doc. 57, f^0 2 r^0; copy kindly provided by S. Van Doren).

24. There was also a strike on dues from the weighing of flour (ACR, CC 491, 52) in December 1579.

25. All the above draws on ACR, FF 19 (especially for September 10, 1579 and February 22, 1580).

26. Piémond, p. 87; Devic, XI-1 o, 679; Pontbriand (1886), ch. IV.

27. BSSI (1890), p. 384.

28. V. Chareton, *La Réforme en Vivarais,* p. 85 ff.

29. BSSI (1890), p. 383.

30. See Le Roy Ladurie, *Peasants of Languedoc* (1966), (original French edition), pp. 607 ff. (revolt led by Roure, a noble, in Vivarais, 1670).

31. Devic, XI-1, p. 564, and Guérin in BSSI (1890), p. 384.

32. Ibid., and Devic, XI-1, pp. 668–669 and notes.

33. BSSL (1890), p. 385.

34. ACV, BB, f^0 251.

35. Ibid., f^0 257 and 259.

36. Ibid., f^0 276.

37. BSSI (1890), p. 382.

38. Ibid., p. 391.

39. Fourmenteau, *Finances,* Book III, p. 405 (according to Littré). There were about 100 or 120 men to a "banner."

40. Piémond, p. 86, and Guérin in BSSI (1890), p. 385.

Chapter VII

1. AC Romans, BB 14, for the months in question.

2. Pierrette Crouzet (unpublished doctoral thesis on *lettres de rémission,* Sorbonne).

3. BSSI (1890), p. 385.

4. Paolo Toschi, *Le origini del Teatro Italiano.*

5. A 152 n. I was told by one person I interviewed (but only one, unfortunately) that there was a flail dance in Romans as late as 1938 in Romans, on Mardi Gras, along with the burning of a mannequin.

6. P. Duparc, *St. Esprit*; Lorcin, pp. 161–163.

7. Van Gennep (1924).

8. Scenes of fantasized or occasionally real cannibalism turned up fairly regularly in various popular risings; see Le Roy Ladurie, *Paysans de Languedoc,* pp. 398–399.

9. The French reads *qu'ils voulaient tout tuer* and not *tout tenir,* a misreading by J. Romans in his edition of Guérin's "anonymous" manuscript. The original manuscript (BN, ms. français 3319) verifies this.

10. Toschi, *Le origini.*

11. For all the preceding, see BSSI (1890), p. 391.

12. Ibid., pp. 386–392 (Bellièvre and Maugiron's letters of February 10 to 12, 1580).

13. Piémond, pp. 88–89.

14. This was true in Languedoc as well as Dauphiné, where Carnival (buffoons, sawhorses, cloth animals, and so on) was also essentially between men (D. Fabre, *Fête en Languedoc*).

15. There is no trace of Laroche in the archives, but Jean (or François?) Rochas (most probably the "Laroche" Guérin mentions) turns up as an extraordinary member of the craftsman audience at the fabled town assembly of September 9, 1576 (ACR, FF 19 for this date, and BB 13 f° 273).

16. Bouges, *Histoire de Carcassone,* for 1579.

17. AC Romans, BB 14, f° 19, proceedings of February 17, 1580.

18. Philippe Gardy, *Thesis* (on the works of the Occitanian Carnival playwright Brueys, who wrote at the beginning of the seventeenth century).

19. ADD, E 3745 (for 1588); and above, Chapter II.

20. R. Chartier and M. Julia in *l'Arc* (1976), no. 65.

21. Ibid.

22. Marc Augé (1977).

23. M. Marion, *Dictionnaire des Institutions*, p. 453; S. Clémencet (1958), p. 11.

24. Marion, *Dictionnaire*, p. 265. And also: the *Grand Conseil*, "the highest court of appeals" (above the Parlements, etc.), was separated from the king's *Conseil étroit* in charge of political and administrative tasks; "It was a college of councillors; it became an administrative tribunal for *exceptional* contests and

it went everywhere the Court did (i.e., the royal court). It was very active in the sixteenth century. The Parlements hated it as the servile tool of state power.'' It included counsels, lawyers, clerks, attorneys, process-servers; it was often on the road during the sixteenth century. Following the king in 1629, it even met in Montélimar (Jean-Paul Laurent, in *Guide des recherches judiciaires*, pp. 29 ff.).

25. Catherine de'Medici, *Lettres*, vol. VII, p. 48.

26. Gardy and Albernhe, *Thesis*, I, p. 178 (on Brueys).

27. See also the authentically and simultaneously sacred and burlesque ceremonies, starring nudes piously daubed in black for a religious feast in Vienne during the renaissance (Cavard, *Vienne*, in the chapter on the Protestant Reformation).

28. Jean Bodin, *De la république*, Latin edition (Paris: 1586), end of book III, p. 362 (this text is not included in the French edition).

29. Ibid., continuation of text.

30. An error by Piémond's editor, Brun-Durand, who mentions a rooster (Piémond, p. 88 n. 2).

31. Romans's municipal proceedings during the sixteenth century contain allusions to slingshot games played by the town youth (ACR, FF 67).

32. There were similar characters, based on current events—in Berne's 1523 Carnival (*Fêtes de la Renaissance*, CNRS, I, p. 363).

33. A. Van Gennep, *Folklore du Dauphiné* (Paris: 1932), p. 176; Natalie Davis, *Society and Culture*, ch. IV and V.

34. The same duality appeared in Berne earlier in the sixteenth century (*Fêtes de la Renaissance*, CNRS, I, p. 364).

35. See Le Roy Ladurie, *Paysans de Languedoc*, I, pp. 398–399 (in John Day's translation, pp. 196–197).

36. Piémond, p. 98, end of n. 2.

37. I read Guérin's manuscript here as *héraut* and not *homme* (J. Roman's misreading): B.N. ms. fs 3319 f⁰ 145 v⁰.

38. Guérin's ms., BN, ms. français 3319, f⁰ 145 v⁰; J. Roman omitted this passage.

39. The original reads *à son aise* (at will) and not *à son aire* (in its eyrie or on the ground); J. Roman's misreading of Guérin's ms. 3319 f⁰ 145 v⁰.

40. See Littré on the sexual meaning of the word *couvrir* (cover; cf. modern English for horses).

41. Toschi, *Le origini*. See also, for all of the following, the Bibliothèque Nationale's *Heraldry* catalogue.

42. ACR, HH 3, 1579–1580.

43. ACR, proceedings, BB 14, for the months of December 1589 and January–February 1580.

44. BSSI (1890), pp. 392–394 (two missives).

45. Ibid., p. 391: Maugiron's letter to the king, February 12, 1580.

46. J. Rossiaud (1976 a and b).

47. J. Rossiaud, "Prostitution. . . ," *Annales* (March 1976).

Chapter VIII

1. Two-hundred and seventy-eight taxpayers contributed a total of 555 *écus* (the 1583 *taille* roll by quarter is AC Romans, CC 94). Let us bear in mind that the tax shares assigned to each head of household in the 1583 document are not the same in absolute value as in the *taille* roll of 1578, for instance, used elsewhere in this work. The relative ranking of taxpayers and shares, however, remains analogous.

2. "Quartier commençant à l'hôpital Sainte-Foy descendant à la grande rue de Jacquemart finit à la petite place tout ce qui est à main droite en descendant" (f° 46 of the 1583 taille roll, ACR, CC 94).

3. "Troisième quartier commençant à la maison de Paradis fin(it) à Bonandaud et descendant par la grande rue de Portefere à la boucherie; finit à la maison du sieur André Flandrin tout ce qui est à main droite" (1583 *taille* roll, f° 29, ACR, CC 94).

4. See above, Chapter VII, on the Carnival price list.

5. The Dijon uprising took place in effect during Carnival, from February 19 to 28, 1632. See B. Porchnev, *Soulèvements populaires en France* (Paris: 1963), pp. 135–140.

6. See "Le gros *chapon de pallier*" (play on Chapelier?) in Guérin's inverted price list (A 157).

7. A. Griemas, *Sémantique structurale*, p. 128. On the fertility of crops and livestock, insured by the brands, see the decisive texts collected by R. Vaultier, *Folklore pendant la guerre de Cent Ans*, pp. 47–50; and also the texts and data gathered for all of France by Mannhardt (1875), and Van Gennep, *Manuel*, volume on *Carnaval-Carême*.

8. Michel de Certeau, *L'écriture*, pp. 275 ff.

9. Charles de Coynart, *Les Guérin de Tencin*, first chapter devoted to Antoine Guérin.

10. In the 1583 *taille* roll (ACR, CC 94) the list for this quarter includes Guillaume Espinier living *on* the Isère bridge and a town gatekeeper.

11. R. Pillorget, *Mouvements*, p. 334, gives the example of seventeenth-century

Aix-en-Provence, pillaged by peasants who forced their way into town after a revolt in 1630.

12. ACR, BB 12, proceedings of March 2 or 12 (?), 1580, mistakenly bound into this volume.

Chapter IX

1. All of the preceding based on BB 14, proceedings of February 22–29, 1580.

2. ACR, BB 14, f⁰ 22 r⁰, February 18, 1580.

3. ACR, BB 14, February 22, 1580, extraordinary council meeting.

4. In English in the text (*translator*).

5. Chorier, II, 697.

6. Piémond, pp. 105 and 110; Chorier, II, 701.

7. BSSI (1890), p. 399.

8. Ibid., p. 423.

9. Ibid., p. 420 (7/18/1580).

10. See above, Chapter II, and Chorier, II, 701.

11. BSSI (1890), p.444.

Chapter X

1. On April 28, 1580, Henri III sent Maugiron "letters of clemency and abolition" (i.e., abolition of proceedings) for the ex-rebels. His reasons were simply humane, but he also feared the new alliance between the remaining leaguers and the Protestants; while formerly, he notes, the Huguenots were frightened of the leaguers (Bibliothèque municipale de Grenoble, R 80, vol. 16, f⁰ 76).

2. Romans, no doubt thanks to Guérin, had a rather violent St. Bartholomew's Day; but Vienne did not (Cavard, p. 165, and Arnaud, *Histoire des Protestants* for the year 1572).

3. ACR, EE 9.

4. Only 12 of the 128 taxed paid 20 or more *livres*; the remaining 91 percent of all Huguenots paid less.

5. J. Estèbe, *Thesis*: From 1568 to 1585, out of 128 Huguenots of known profession in Vienne 77 (60.2 percent) were craftsmen; 20.3 percent bourgeois of various kinds; 14.1 percent merchants; 2.3 percent plowmen and winegrowers. Compared to their real numbers in the town, the craftsmen and bourgeoisie are over-represented, while the urban peasantry, in fact such a large group (36 percent of Romans's population, for instance) steered almost

entirely clear of the Reformation (these percentages and figures are my own, based on Cavard's list in his *Vienne*, p. 419 ff.).

6. See Mandrou's map in *La Revue suisse de l'histoire* (1966).

7. ACR, CC 92; see above, Chapter I.

8. The 1578–79 tax shares are not the same as in the 1583 *taille* roll, a year of heavier taxes. I used the 1583 roll for my study of Romans's quarters (Chapter VIII).

9. To tell the truth, one member of the second rank was sentenced to hang (and defaulted) in 1580, once again Michel Barbier (alias Champlong); in a flagrant exception to the rule, he was taxed a second time in the merchant rank (he had already been included in the first rank) because of a house or piece of land he had bought from a member of the second group. But let me reiterate that Michel Barbier was not in any way involved in the *urban* revolt in Romans.

10. ADI, B 2039 furnishes the bulk of the following data.

11. Ibid., three *sétérées* in vineyards makes 72 *écus*.

12. ACR, CC 354 (1580).

13. On this apple tree *(pommier)*, later a less flagrant laurel or olive tree, see Coynart, *Les Guérin de Tencin*, p. 47; G. de Rivoire, *Armorial du Dauphiné*, p. 295; and the various *Armoriaux de Dauphiné* (early eighteenth century) in the Bibliothèque nationale's manuscript department. Guérin's *lettres d'anoblissement* date from October 1581 (*Annales de la ville de Romans*, p. 172). Piémond makes ready use of *Pomier* as the spelling of the rebel leader's name.

14. G. Brunat was commissioned by the consuls (Letter of J. de Gillier, ACR, CC 491[79], May 25, 1579).

15. ACR, CC 93, for the year 1578: Guillaume Brunat rented a house owned by Ennemond Chosson du Perrier.

16. ACR, FF 19, text of November 1580 (settlement of the estate of G. Fleur, executed).

17. ACR, CC 491 (48), July 11, 1579.

18. ACR, FF 19 (contract for the butcher trade).

19. In Chapter I, I used a slightly higher threshold of prosperity than in this paragraph, taking into account the first decile of Romans society, while here I am simply identifying the upper group of farmers, above 0.6 *écu*, above which level we find no prosecuted farmers.

20. The result of the repression was that the special court caused eleven persons to be hanged by the neck until dead, not counting Paumier who was hanged in effigy. There were also thirty-three persons sentenced to death but not executed (defaulters). See A 170; A. Lacroix in BSASD (1897), p. 394; U. Chevalier, BSASD (1876), p. 68.

21. Mousnier (1958); Mousnier (1954), p. 460.

22. Six-hundred and thirty-seven craftsmen plus 478 farmers equals 1115 out of 1304 total taxpayers (see above, Chapter I). Again, there is a very large percentage of farm workers (36.7 percent), explaining Romans's agrarian folk character, among other things. I am using the terms "folk" and "folklore" in their general or etymological sense, without the slightly pejorative nuance J. Favret-Saada gives them (for perfectly legitimate reasons) in his admirable study *Sorcellerie* (J. Favret-Saada, *Sorcellerie* (1977), pp. 15–16 ns. 2 and 3.

23. On Romans's poor, see above, Chapter I. Municipal proceedings of December 1579 and January–February 1580 (ACR, BB 14) devote much space to the problem of almsgiving, lacking at the time; thus they are concerned with the poor.

24. Jean-Claude Brieu (1868–1869).

25. The same was true for Provence, where the leaders of popular revolts were sometimes officials but never priests or nobles of the sword (as opposed to nobles of the robe); see Pillorget, *Thesis*, p. 393.

26. Rural leaders: Cussinel, a noble from Moras; Buisson, miller of Hauterive; the court clerks of St. Vallier; Beaurepaire, the castle steward of Moras; the royal notary of Bellegarde, sentenced to hanging and 1000 *écus* fine; Michel Barbier, lawyer, of St. Paul; a bourgeois (of Curson); an innkeeper and miller also from that town, etc.; and two plowmen. On these leaders see L. S. Van Doren's remarkable work: *Thesis* (pp. 321, 353), and his article in *Sixteenth Century Journal* (1974). See also Piémond, pp. 96, 98, 179.

27. Brun-Durand, *Dictionaire biographique de la Drôme*, under *Bouvier* (A. de).

28. Catherine d'Medici, *Lettres*, vol. VII, September 6, 1579.

Chapter XI

1. Ibn Khaldun; I refer to the 1967 French translation, vol. II, pp. 777–779.

2. René Pillorget, *Mouvements*, pp. 528 ff.

3. Ibid., pp. 587–631.

4. Ibid., pp. 388–389. The most frequent urban movements in the Provençal sphere of influence were those directed against consular authority, local justice officials (Guérin, in Romans), indirect crown taxes, and military authority, in that order. Romans was admirably typical from this point of view.

5. Ibid., pp. 170–171.

6. Romans was at the northern limit of the Occitan-speaking area, at the southern limit of Franco-Provençal.

7. Pillorget, *Mouvements*, pp. 333–334.

8. Ibid., p. 7; see also, Le Roy Ladurie, *Peasants of Languedoc*, vol. I, pp. 502, 608 (in John Day's translation, pp. 266, 274).

9. See the American historian R. Benedict's recent dissertation on "Rouen in the 16th century" (Princeton University).

10. P. Ansart (1977), p. 105.

11. For all the above section: on comparative studies see R. Chartier, "L'ormée de Bordeaux," in *RHMC* (April 1974), p. 279 ff. (a review of S.A. Westrich's book *The Ormée . . .* and J. Cavignac's translation, *Cahiers de L'I.A.E.S.*, no. 3, 1973, Bordeaux); S. Bertelli, "Oligarchies et gouvernement dans la ville de la Renaissance," *Social Science Information* (1976) XV, 4–5: 601–624; on misfits and drifters in Dauphiné towns: AC Tain, BB 1, August 3–9 1578; see also M. Mollat and Philippe Wolff, *Ongles bleus . . . et Ciompi* (Paris: 1970); Charles de la Roncière, *Florence* (unpublished thesis), Book III; E.P. Thompson, "Mode de domination . . . en angleterre," *Actes de la recherche en sciences sociales* (June 1976), and *The Making of the English Working Class* (London: 1963), pp. 162–172; A. Soboul, *Sans-culottes*, p. 442. On the Geneva craftsmen and Rousseau, see *Histoire de Genève*, Paul Guichonnet, ed. (Toulouse: 1974), pp. 237 ff; on craftsmen in east central France and their political role, see R. Gascon, *Grand commerce . . . au XVIe siècle, Lyon* (Paris: 1971), p. 421; on the typology of southern French revolts, R. Pillorget, *Mouvements*, pp. 151, 420, 427 (Bacon text), pp. 48–51 (cooptation in the councils) p. 58 ("les plus apparents," the most outstanding), pp. 182, 198, 223, 233; pp. 52 and 169 (Auriol in 1599); pp. 512 (cabaretiers' strikes); p. 630 (butchers); p. 630 (Aix revolt of 1630); p. 846 (Draguignan in 1659, clash between peasants and craftsmen, each backed by a faction of the elite); p. 656, 666 (tanners in Aix in 1651); p. 717 (struggles of dominant factions and peasant movement in Aubagne, 1656); p. 508 (the people against the power elite over the breaking of the Arles bridge in 1637); pp. 162, 164, 169, 930 (on the infrequency of wage-related protests, prevalence of antimunicipal protest; cf. Y. Castan, *Honnêteté*, p. 333); p. 320, 333, 344 (peasants' storming of Aix in 1630); pp. 386–388 (statistics on popular movements); pp. 7 and 429–31 ("revolutionary" attacks against the rich); and p. 982. On the starvation riots *after* the period under discussion, see also Bercé, *Histoire des Croquants*, I, p. 231 (common folk revolting in Villefranche-de-Rouergue); Ibid., pp. 294–45, 326, 334 (revolts in Bordeaux, Agen). On Anabaptism, see A. Friesen, "The Marxist Interpretation of Anabaptism," in *Sixteenth Century Essays*, Carl S. Meyer, ed. (St. Louis: 1970), vol. I; and Hans J. Hillerbrand, *Thomas Münzer, a Bibliography*, in *Sixteenth Century Bibliography*, vol. 4 (St. Louis, Center for Reform, Research: 1976). On the general subject see Plato, *Republic* IV (rich versus poor in a town); Roland Barthes, *Fragments d'un discours amoureux* (Paris: 1977), p. 244 (deviation from the goals of war); Robert Dahl, *Who Governs* (New Haven: 1975) (the transfer of urban power from patricians to plebeians).

12. The list of Catholic confraternities drawn up by the Huguenots during their attempt to suppress them, in 1562, shows in addition to the four confraternities I discuss here a St. Crispin society (perhaps for shoemakers?), St. Nicholas, St. Foy (two of the town's parishes), St. Sebastian (antiplague and

popinjay?), St. Catherine, Notre-Dame-de-Mars, St. Claude, St. Stephen, and unspecified "others" (text in BSASD, Vol. 9 (1875), p. 138). Compare to R. Pillorget, *Thesis*, p. 94–95; Natalie Davis has shown in her *Thesis* that after 1560 Lyons's Catholics favored trade confraternities, which helped the faith.

13. ACR, HH 8, HH 9, and HH 10 (dossiers of the St. Matthew confraternity from 1578 to 1583); ADD, E 3796 (the same for 1614 to 1616).

14. Cavard, *Vienne*, p. 10; compare to R. Pillorget, p. 24.

15. Piémond, p. 98.

16. Dossiers of Romans's Maugouvert-Bongouvert abbey, ADD, E 3797; ACR, GG 41 and GG 42.

17. ACR, BB 22, a text characteristic of the whole holiday period from December 11, 1606 to February 16, 1607. On Bongouvert's financing of Lenten preachers, see BSASD, I (1866), p. 335.

18. ACR, BB 13, April 1577.

19. ACR, BB, according to notes kindly furnished by M. Rossiaud.

20. On *charivaris* in the mid-Rhône basin during the *ancien régime* as young males' opportunity to win women, see A. Molinier, *Thesis*, pp. 696–697. See also the ATP colloquium on the *charivari* in 1977.

21. The description of Maugouvert-Bongouvert draws on the ADD, E 3797 dossiers; and ACR, GG 41 and GG 42. See also Georges Duby, *Cathédrales,* pp. 315–317; M. Ozouf, *Fête.;* M. Eliade, *Traité,* Ch. VIII; J. Rossiaud (1976).

22. ADD, E 3796, February 1613.

23. J. Rossiaud (1975) illustrated this point using other examples.

24. Duparc (1958); see also M. Vovelle, *Fêtes,* p. 49.

25. On the link between the Holy Spirit confraternity and incorporated citizens in southeastern and central France, during both the Middle Ages and the Renaissance, see Duparc (1958).

26. P. Amargier, "Mouvements populaires . . . à Marseille," *Cahiers de Fan-jeaux,* vol. 11, pp. 305–319.

27. See the work of Von Wiese, Schmalenbach, etc., as in A. Cuvillier, *Manuel de Sociologie,* vol. I, pp. 142, 147, 149–150.

28. Von Tönnies, in A. Cuvillier, I, p. 147.

29. The term *reynage* might be thought of as analogous to the *krewes* in New Orleans's Mardi Gras *(translator)*.

30. A. Dauzat, *Le Village et le paysan de France* (Paris: 1941), p. 153 (map).

31. P. Veyne.

32. The king in our *reynages* is not entirely assimilable to the feast-day king described in Frazer's *Golden Bough.* Frazer's king assured the fertility of crops through his existence and primarily through his violent death. But current

research holds this view is too limiting as to such kings' functions (R. De-tienne, *Jardins d'Adonis*, pp. 9 ff).

33. On *reynages* and related problems see R. Bautier (1945); L. Lamarche (1958); A. Lacroix (1881); A. Van Gennep, *Folklore Auvuergne* (1942), pp. 179–194; J.P. Gutton (1975); A. Dauzat (1941), p. 153; A. Lacroix (1880); L. de Nussac (1891); J. Rossiaud (1976) *in fine*; and of course the writings of Guérin and Piémond (on the Romans incidents); M. Vovelle, *Fêtes*, p. 52; ADD, E 11822, GG 1; and E 11949, GG 4; E 11952, BB 2; E 12033, GG 2; M. Ozouf, *Fête*; S. Freud, 1962 edition, pp. 96–97; R. Barthes, *Mode*, p. 263; B. Bettel-heim, *Interview* (1977); Shakespeare, *The Tempest*, II, 1 (143–163); G. Duby, *Cathédrales*, pp. 21–23.

Chapter XII

1. On the Provençal influence and similarities between Provence and Dau-phiné in terms of culture and dialect, see André Devaux (1892), (1968 edition), pp. 440–441. Romans was at the northernmost limit of Occitan-speaking territory, as we have seen.

2. A. Prudhomme, "Du commencement de l'année . . . en Dauphiné," *Bul-letin historique et philosophique du Comité des travaux historiques et scientifiques* (1898), pp. 279 ff.: in the Vienne region the year began on March 25 until the sixteenth century.

3. A. Van Gennep, *Les Rites de passage* (Paris: 1909), published in English as *The Rites of Passage* (London: 1960), notably Ch. I and IX; E. Leach, "Sym-bolic Representation of Time," in *Rethinking Anthropology* (London: 1961); Victor Turner, *Dramas, Fields, and Metaphors* (Cornell University Press: 1975), pp. 38–39, 78–79, ff.

4. On the land of Cockaigne see the work of the Occitan poet Claude Brueys, published in Aix in 1628, as presented in H. Albernhe and P. Gardy's *troisième cycle* doctoral dissertation (unpublished), *Caramentrant*, vol. I (Universi-té de Montpellier: 1970); and J. Delumeau, *Mort des pays de Cocagne* (Paris: 1976), p. 13. On role reversal in Carnival as a means of reinforcing posts of social authority by deindividualizing them, temporarily giving them to persons normally much lower on the social scale, see C. Carozzi's article on the medieval poet Adalbéron, forthcoming in *Annales*.

5. This three-part schema also fits many other village Carnivals in the Drôme, as late as the nineteenth and twentieth centuries (cf. Van Gennep's papers, file on Drôme, archives of the ATP museum).

6. On Lenten preaching by mendicant friars in Romans, see ACR, GG 39; and BSASD, I (1866), p. 335; in general, refer to Peter Weidkuhn, *Carnaval de Bâle* (on Protestant suppresssion of Carnival); and T. de Bèze, *Histoire ecclésiastique*, vol. 2 (*idem* for Rouen).

7. L'Estoile's *Journal* for February 14, 1589.

8. Cabourdin, *Thesis,* I, pp. 358–361; A. Molinier, *Thesis,* p. 620; C. Cros, 1976–I, p. 41.

9. G. Duby, *Cathédrales,* pp. 69–70.

10. Ibid., Ch. I.

11. Ibid., and A. Van Gennep, *Folklore du Dauphiné,* vol. I, p. 228.

12. On the Candlemas bear, a weather forecaster in Dauphiné and Savoie, see for this feast A. Van Gennep, *Folk. Savoie; Folk. Dauphiné; Manuel;* and the Van Gennep papers in the ATP museum (file on Drôme). On Candlemas as "the beginning of the end" of winter, in the fourteenth through eighteenth centuries, cf. Vovelle, *Fêtes,* p. 100; and Cavard, *Vienne,* p. 5. On the Candlemas-Carnival bear in the Pyrenees, see Van Gennep, *Manuel;* V. Alford, *Pyr. Fest.,* and Daniel Fabre's recent ethnographic films; see especially D. Fabre's admirable study *Jean de L'Ours* (1969), part 2. On the *groundhog* in American folklore see *Encyclopedia Americana;* on the hedgehog in the Irish St. Bridget's Day, see C.O. Danachair, *The Year in Ireland* (Dublin: 1972); and S.O. Suilleabhain, *A Handbook of Irish Folklore* (1942).

13. All this data is taken from the *Traité des superstitions* by Rev. Jean-Baptiste Thiers, published in 1679. Francois Lebrun, in a brilliant article (*Annales de Bretagne,* [1976], pp. 456–457), brought together the above references to specific customs appearing in the 1777 edition of Thiers's book. Cf. P. Toschi, *Origini,* and also *Folklore italiano* (Rome: 1963), pp. 275 ff. (on Candlemas); J-C Bringuier, *Provinciales* (Vendée), TF I, November 30, 1976, Candlemas crêpes intended to keep hens laying all year (interview with an old Vendée woman); *Histoire rurale de France,* IV, p. 332; H. Vincenot (1976), pp. 61–64 (Candlemas and Carnival as fertility rites); see entry for *Fastnachtshär* in Funk and Wagnalls *Dictionary of Folklore;* Moulis (1975), pp. 36, 65, 67, 71, 76, 79, 85, 93; Van Gennep papers, ATP, Drôme file (Candlemas); Mannhardt, *Wald und Feld Kulte,* pp. 535–538 (*brandons*); O. Erich and R. Beitl, *Wort. Deutsch. Volksk.* (1955), p. 193.

14. On the preceding see Toschi, *Origini;* Mannhard, *Wald und Feld Kulte;* Jeanmaire, *Dionysos,* p. 38; G. Dumézil, *Le Problème des Centaures,* pp. 11–13; despite his obsession with plant demons, J. G. Frazer, *The Golden Bough,* is still important, see 1916 edition, vol. I, p. 137, IV, p. 252, etc. (unfortunately he has greatly extrapolated from Mannhardt's solid *in situ* observations). On Frazer see M. Détienne's criticism (1972), pp. 9 ff. English "Halloween" is a better remnant than any in France of the link between masked young people and demons or evil characters.

15. Baroja, *El Carnaval,* p. 277.

16. A satirical Carnival was not necessarily violent: Pillorget, *Mouvements,* pp. 407–408; satirical Mardi gras play (1627) ridiculing the bordello owned by the Bishop of Riez: Pillarget, *Mouvements,* p. 256; Carnival *lazzi* in Italy: Toschi, *Origini,* p. 725; political Carnivals in Switzerland: *Fêtes de la Renaissance,* CNRS (1973), I, pp. 361–364; A.N. BB 30–423 (1860); P. Weidkuhn,

pp. 43–50; anti-Semitic Carnivals: *Félix et Thomas Platter à Montpellier* (1892), pp. 196, 399, and in Rome: Mme. Boiteux's article and Toschi, *Origini*, pp. 333–340; anti-Mazarin Carnivals in Bordeaux in 1651, see the unpublished work of M. Jouhaud; and F. Loirette (1972) (effigy of Mazarin formally beheaded); *cheval-jupon* satire in Mantois's Candlemas celebration: Bougeatre, p. 231. Satirical last wills of Harlequin, animals, and other Carnival personages in Toschi, *Origini*, pp. 228–243. Other satirical winter festivals in Provence: Pillorget, *Mouvements*, pp. 588, 791 (St. Sebastian and St. Valentine's days, 1649 and in Aix-en-Provence, 1659).

17. This expression *(maîtriser la maîtrise)* is Michel Serres's.

18. P. Ansart (1977), p. 30.

19. Distinction between mythical/practical: A. Greimas, *Sémantique structurale*, pp. 128, 149, 150. On two Carnivals, two Maydays, see Fayolle, *Limousin*.

20. C. Lévi-Strauss, *Introduction à M. Mauss*, p. XIX.

21. This entire passage is taken from the Calixte Lafosse papers in Romans's Bibliothèque municipale (public library).

22. On the role of youth groups (their role did not exclude other age groups from being active in Carnival) see Toschi, *Origini*, pp. 98–99; G. Duby, preface to *Fêtes en France*, p. 15; on a conception of Carnival (which I find incomplete) as essentially conservative, cf. P. Weidkuhn, pp. 45 ff; A. Poitrineau in *Autrement*, July, 1976, p. 189; A. de Gaudemar, *Autrement*, July 1976, p. 81; F. Raphael, in *Contrepoint* 24 (1977), p. 124; on the *plurality* of urban Carnivals see Toschi, *Origini*, p. 95 (Florence); on the representation of the twelve months, the twelve planets, and not only the two seasons involved, see also *Fêtes de la Renaissance*, I (Berne; 1906), p. 362.

23. A. Molinier, *Vivarais* (thesis), p. 354 and *passim*, emphasizes the "objectively" antiseignorial aspect of the 1783 *Masques;* Sonenscher (1972).

24. P. Fontanier, *Figures du Discours* (1977), p. 157.

25. Toschi, *Origini*, pp. 150–195, 251–266; Bercé, II, p. 585.

26. C. Lévi-Strauss, *Le Totémisme*, p. 101; and A. Radcliffe-Brown (1965), Ch. VI. See also on the problems of symbolism, in my bibliography below, Victor Turner's important work; and M. Ozouf, *Fête;* M. Douglas, *Implicit Meanings*, p. 261; Greimas, *Sémantique structurale* and *Sém. Sc. Soc.*, p. 49; A. de Vries (1974), p. 238; S. Ossovsky, *Struct. de class.*, p. 64 and *passim;* on the respective signification of the various animals in Carnival, cf. for example (on the bear) Pliny the Elder, *Natural History*, Book 8, Ch. 54; on the "polysemy" of symbols see U. Eco (1977); see also the fine work of J.B. Fages, J. Le Goff, "Gestes symboliques," p. 737; T. Todorov (1977), p. 181 and *passim;* R. Barthes, *S/Z,* pp. 12, 18, 49, 126, 166; and in *Communications*, 4–1964; G. Duby, *Cathédrales*, p. 131; R. Robins (1976), p. 224; C. Geertz (1973), p. 141.

27. On these questions see M. Vovelle, *Fête en Provence*, p. 53 *et passim;* on donkeys and Swiss Guards in Lyons, cf. Natalie Davis, *Thesis;* on Turks and

couriers, *Fêtes de las Renaissance,* I, p. 363 (cf., for Romans, A 156 and A 160).

28. On the satirical/political Carnival effigy in northern and southern France see the data gathered by R.J. Bezucha, *Masks of Revolution;* cf. also A.N. BB 30, 362 (reference courtesy of C. Tamiason); AD Haute-Garonne, B, SP 741, Goudargues year 1743, according to Yves Castan, *Honnêteté* and M. Agulhon (1848 Carnival), in *Autrement,* July 1976, p. 203 ff; M. Ozouf, in J. Le Goff and P. Nora, *Faire de l'histoire,* III, p. 265.

29. On the use of flails for symbolic destruction, see G. Duby, *Hist. France rurale,* III, p. 39; flails and straw (straw effigy) as symbols of winter or Lenten *brandons:* Frazer, *Golden Bough,* abridged edition, p. 368; Bercé, *Hist. Croquants,* II, p. 645; agrarian rites of the Carnival period in the Alpine regions, Vovelle, *Fête,* p. 57, and Van Gennep, *Manuel,* Carnival-Lent; flail dance in Romans's Carnival until about 1930, *interview;* on the donkey: Vovelle, *Fête,* p. 114; Flandrin, *Familles,* p. 123; Van Gennep, *Folkl. dauphinois,* vol. II, p. 176; donkey ride in Lyon, sixteenth century, N. Davis, *Thesis;* Cleber, G. Guige, etc. (cf. bibliography below); Rossiaud, *Abbayes,* p. 86, on St. Blaise, Vovelle, *Fête,* pp. 45, 58; A. Van Gennep (1924), pp. 136 ff.; Pilot de Thorey, *Usages;* A. Wright and T.E. Lones, *Brit. Cal. Customs,* vol. II (Candlemas-St. Blaise); G. Long (1930), p. 18, *The Gentleman's Magazine,* 1885 (see bibliography below); Toschi, *Origini,* p. 142. On death rituals (Carnival and other) see E. Leach, *Lévi-Strauss, pp. 287–288; M.* Douglas, *Implicit Meanings,* p. 146; cannibalistic symbolism: Pillorget, *Mouvements,* p. 337; Piémond, pp. 424–425; L. Kurtz (1934); on funeral rites of the Holy Spirit confraternity: Duparc (1958); on Dauphiné funeral banquets, on graves, see Pilot, *Usages;* see also G. Duby, *Cathédrales,* pp. 287–288. On rituals: V. Turner, *The Drums of Affliction; Dramas,* pp. 50–60; *Forest of Symbols,* p. 96; Duby, *Hist. France rur.,* II, 542; P. Weidkuhn (1976), p. 34; on vengeful masquerades and face-painting, see Bercé, *Histoire des Croquants,* I, p. 214; *pantragnes:* Calixte Lafosse papers, B. M. Romans; Vovelle, *Fête,* p. 98; and especially M. Sonenscher's admirable *Masques armés du Vivarais en 1783* (1972).

30. Toschi, *Origini,* p. 78.

31. Comte de Villeneuve, *Statistique des Bouches-du-Rhône,* vol. III, pp. 26–27.

32. G. Duby, *Cathédrales,* pp. 69–70.

33. On the sword dance in general, see *Standard Dict. of Folklore* under *Sword Dance;* in Dauphiné, Lajoux's ethnographic film (St. Roch's Day in Cervières, Dauphiné); and A 152; Vovelle on Provence, p. 61; Villeneuve, *Stat. B.-du-R.,* III, pp. 209–210; in the Piedmont and Italy in general, Toschi, *Origini,* pp. 78, 98, 329, 473; in England, E. P. Thompson, *Charivari,* p. 11; in Alsace (connected to crafts and trades): Poitrineau, *Autrement* 7 (1976); in Germany, K. Meschke, *Schwerttanz* (Berlin: 1931); in Sweden (Carnival), *Kult. hist. Lexik.,* IV (1959); in Scotland: V. Turner (interview); cf. also Tacitus, *Germany* 24; and Xenophon, 6-1-5 (connection with danger). In general see Clastres,

Libre, 1977–1. On bells and other Carnival *charivari* instruments, see Baroja, *Carnaval,* p. 257, and ethnographic films; Pillorget, *Mouvements,* pp. 339, 343, 401. On the passage from nuptial to political *charivari,* cf. N. Belmont, speech at the *Charivari* colloquium; AN Côte d'Or, 8 M 29 (reference courtesy of Charles Tilly).

34. On Carnival hyperbole and judiciary satire, see Castan, *Honnêteté,* pp. 52, 424–425, 583; Barthes, *Mode,* p. 25; on Turk or Saracen figures see Vovelle, *Fête,* p. 79; J. Estèbe, *Tocsin,* p. 105; on the role of the sacred (Catholic) in urban space, N. Davis, *Exposé;* on the municipal role of the judiciary elite, see R. Dahl, *Who Governs;* on "royal" or solemn processions analogous to those in Romans, P. Van Dyke, *Catherine,* I, pp. 214, 250; Bercé, *Histoire des Croquants,* I, p. 208; on Romans theater in the sixteenth century see J. Chocheyras, *Théâtre;* royal entries into Romans in the sixteenth century: BSASD, 1873, pp. 79–80; Romans's way of the cross: U. Chevalier (1882); and in general M. Ozouf, *Fête,* p. 265, and *Autrement* 7 (1976), p. 201.

35. Translator's quotation: Turner, *Dramas,* p. 13.

36. M. Bakhtine, 1970 tranlation, Ch. IV, V, VI.

37. On role reversal in Carnival, see Bercé, *Histoire des Croquants,* II, pp. 585–592; V. Turner, *Ritual Process,* pp. 188 ff., and *Forest of Symbols,* p. 125; M. Gluckmann, *Order* (1963); MacKim Marriott, in M. Singer (1966); E. Ehmke, *Perceptions* (1975); A.T. D'Embry, *Hermaphrodites;* M. Doublas, *Meanings* (1976), p. 162; H. Cox, *Feast* (1969). On the *pays de cocagne* in Occitan and Carnival folklore, see P. Gardy's thesis.

38. Toschi, *Origini,* Ch. XI *et passim.*

39. On tilts to the ring and other Carnival games see bibliography on *Ring* and *Heraldry;* on the rooster M. Agulhon, *Imagerie (1975);* Toschi, *Origini,* p. 96; Rudwin, *Origin* (1920); E. Cros (1975); R. Wright, vol. I, (1936) (Mardi gras); C. Geertz, *Cockfight* (1975); Pilot de Thorey, p. 17; and P. Rivière, *Moi,* p. 42; Baroja, *El Carnaval; British Calendar Customs,* vol. I, p. 13; and vol. II (Scotland), tome 2, p. 156; Poitrineau, in *Autrement,* July 1976, (cockfights in northern France and Champagne).

40. Calixte Lafosse's Romans glossary, manuscript in Romans's library, under *pantragne.* My own interviews in Romans, notably of M. Bourne, substantiated this.

Chapter XIII

1. My main interest in this paragraph is "molecules" (peasant wars and other uprisings) rather than "atoms" (in other words the various forms these uprisings took, such as the drawing up of *cahiers,* festive gatherings, market riots, burning of castles or land registers, etc.). Each "molecule" is by definition a grouping of "atoms" (Charles Tilly is writing a thesis on this subject).

2. D. Sabean (1976).

3. P. Vilar, *Catalogne* I: 464, 497, 499; Brenner (1976), p. 62 (English revolts of the sixteenth century); S. Sabean (1972); S. Luce, *Jacquerie*, pp. 56–57; *Les 12 articles des paysans allemands* (1525) in K.C. Sessions (1968), p. 17; Chomsky (1977), pp. 160–165; Chafarevitch (1977); R.B. Dobson (1970), p. 270; M. Mollat and P. Wolff, p. 87.

4. On this question there is an extensive bibliography. Refer to Porchnev, Mousnier, Bercé, Pillorget (see bibliography below); my contribution to Braudel and Labrousse, *Histoire Economique et Sociale de France*, I-2, Ch. V; and M. Lagrée (1976).

5. ACV, CC 42 (in ADI, microfilms, MI 105). See also exemptions of land in Romans for local patrician families such as the Loyrons, Velheus, Costes: ACR, FF 26, 27, and CC 499. On the extent of exempted noble landholdings, see ADD, E 11819, 11828, 11955, 12104, 12019, 12025: the percentage of this land in comparison to all cultivated land in the villages mentioned in the dossiers varied between 14.4 percent and 56 percent (with an average of 32.1 percent.) See also, for the period of this study, ADI, B 190, on exemption from the *taille* and protest against tithes.

6. Cavard, *Vienne*, pp. 395 ff.

7. Chomel (1963), p. 309.

8. Cavard, *Vienne*, p. 396.

9. R. Cobb (1970).

10. Bercé, *Histoire des Croquants*, I, p. 462.

11. The following passage on the extremely rich theses of the third estate lawyers is based on the works and speeches of C. Delagrange, A. Rambaud, C. Brosse, E. Marchier, and, in contrast, C. Expilly and J. Dufos, lawyers for the nobility. On these texts see the bibliography below.

12. Vital Chomel, archivist of the Archives departementales de l'Isère, is writing an important study on this subject.

13. "The incidents in Romans, Montélimar, the Valloire, can only be understood in the perspective of the development of the tax conflict," V. Chomel in B. Bligny, *Hist. du Dauphiné*, p. 233.

14. A. Lacroix, *Procès des tailles*, which complements C. Laurens, *Procès des tailles*, and A. Rochas, *Biog. du Dauphiné* (on Brosse, Rambaud etc.).

15. Piémond, p. 354; and Chomel, in Bligny, *Histoire du Dauphiné*, p. 245.

16. Brosse, 1606, 1611, 1621.

17. On the 1576 Dauphiné *Cahiers*: see above, Chapter I. The peasant *Cahiers* in the Beauce, the same year, were decidedly antinoble; they were aimed at country gentlemen, considered looters, violent; they were charged with commandeering provisions, competing with commoners for the right to farm great domains (J.M. Constant has informed me); the Champagne *Cahiers* in 1614

did not come out against the nobles to any extent, or oppose the landlords, perhaps because the *seigneurs* controlled the drawing up of the said petition (R. Chartier and J. Nagle, in *Annales,* 1973, pp. 1490–91).

18. C. Delagrange, pp. 88–89.

19. A 149–50 *et passim.*

Chapter XIV

1. Marchier, in Piémond, pp. 361–363; Vincent (1600), p. 49; Delagrange, 1599, p. 261.

2. Marchier, Piémond. pp. 355–359; Rambaud, p. 73–75; Delagrange, p. 14 *et passim.*

3. Vincent (1600), p. 48 (venality); Marchier, p. 363 (torture).

4. P. Chaunu in F. Braudel and E. Labrousse in *Histoire Economique et Sociale de France,* I, 1, Ch. III and IV; F. de Guérin, p. 105; Vincent (1600), p. 185; Delagrange, 1599-2, pp. 92, 103.

5. Delagrange, 1599-2, pp. 133–134.

6. Yves-Marie Bercé, *Histoire des Croquants,* vol. II, pp. 634, 636.

7. R. Pillorget, *Mouvements,* p. 445.

8. P. Chaunu, *L'Espagne de Charles Quint* (Paris: 1973), p. 236, 240, 244.

9. R. Mousnier, *Fureurs,* pp. 308, 350.

10. G. Franz, *Bauernkreig* (1956 edition), pp. 1–3.

11. The same was true of the next generation, see F. Guérin, p. 30; the tax burden increased from 1600 to 1630, meaning there was *social change;* thus a need for *real* taxes.

12. On this point I differ with excellent historians such as Joseph Perez and M. Steinmetz (see bibliography below).

13. M. Weber (1971 edition), p. 244; and R. Mousnier, *Hiérarchies sociales.*

14. On this subject see also A. Jouanna (1977), p. 65. Jouanna's book, focusing on racial myths in sixteenth-century France, points out how original Dauphiné's egalitarianism really was—even though it was moderate—in comparison to the "hierarchic" mentality prevalent in the rest of France, excepting Paris.

15. F. Guérin stresses that the province lost both its Estates and the control of its *gabelles* in 1628; the management of salt tax was granted to financiers who were not necessarily Dauphinois.

16. On the preceding see Delagrange, 1599, pp. 42–43, 123, 155, 283, 286–287 *et passim;* Rambaud, pp. 50–51.

17. Piémond, pp. 30, 102, 106.

18. In Piémond, pp. 359–360.

19. Ibid., pp. 126, 147, 189, 192, 196, 268, etc.

20. Ibid, pp. 34–37.

21. Morestel, Valouse, Demptezieu, La Batie.

22. M. Foisil, pp. 30–31; Y. Bercé (1974), I, p. 277; R. Pillorget (1975), pp. 103, 107; Piémond, p. 136; M. Constant (orally informed me on the Beauce region, where there was more antinoble than antiseignorial feeling).

23. Pisançon, 1596 (AC Vienne CC 96); 3,438 *sétérées* of land belonged to nobles; 3,915 to the third estate, carrying 4,987 *écus* in debt. For the above figures I calculated the hectare at 4 *sétérées*, the wages of an agricultural worker at 7 sous per diem (as in *Paysans de Languedoc*, I, p. 273), the *écu* at 3 *livres* and the interest rate at 9 percent (*Paysans de Languedoc*, vol. II, p. 1024).

24. Delagrange, pp. 217–218.

25. Hickey (1976), graph.

26. Piémond, pp. 362–365.

27. Third estate letter in Y. Bercé, *Histoire des Croquants*, vol. II, p. 701.

28. These quotations and those which follow are from Delagrange, 1599, (in order) pp. 270, 161, 96.

29. J. Vincent (1598), p. 32; Delagrange, 1599, pp. 199, 204.

30. Marchier, p. 355; Delagrange, pp. 61, 123, 128.

31. Piémond, pp. 13, 14, 32, 38, and *passim*, for the texts hereafter.

32. C. Expilly, p. 400; the preceding texts are from Delagrange, pp. 128, 129, 130, and Delagrange (1599–2), pp. 103, 112, 241, 267.

33. C. Delagrange (1599), p. 254.

34. J. Vincent (1598), pp. 26, 40.

35. C. Delagrange, p. 79.

36. C. Delagrange, pp. 95–95 and Delagrange (1599–2), p. 105.

37. J. Vincent (1598), p. 39. On the *mystical body*, notably from the thirteenth century onward, see the entry for this term in *Dictionnaire de spiritualité*, Beauchène (Paris: 1953), Vol. II, *(corps mystique)*.

38. Marchier is especially pedantic from this point of view.

39. See above, Chapter II.

40. *Vie des Saints*, Letouzey (1949), vol. 7.

41. Piémond, p. 358, and index.

42. On the true (medieval) origins of *franchises* and nonservitudes in Dauphiné, see V. Chomel, "Francs" (1965).

43. "Equalitarian intimacy based on the group [and not] on the individual," F. Furet and P. Nora, in *Daedalus*, winter 1978, p. 329.

44. On Savoy, see J. Nicolas, *Thesis;* P. Defournet, Bassy, vol. I., p. 47; P. Guichonnet, *Histoire de la Savoie* (Toulouse: 1973).

45. Delagrange (1599 and 1599–2) p. XXV, 105, 227–231; Vincent, p. 232; Rambaud, pp. 37–49; Bodin, *République,* book I, Ch. 8, quoted by the lawyers.

46. See also the capital role of antiquity (60 percent of historical references) in the arguments of the *Ormée* ideologues in Bordeaux in 1651 (C. Jouhaud, 1977).

47. Péguy, quoted by Jacques Julliard, *Contre la politique professionnelle* (Paris: 1977).

48. F. Guérin, p. 6; Delagrange, pp. 39–45, 63, 106–108, 187, 223, 228; and Delagrange (1599), p. 73; (1599–2), p. 62; Vincent (1598), p. II; (1600), pp. 40–49.

49. Rambaud, pp. 23–25 using E. Fauchet, *Antiquités gauloises;* Delagrange (1599–2), p. 148.

50. F. Guérin, p. 9; Delagrange (1599–2), pp. 6, 7, 24, 54, 92, 122–23; Vincent (1598), pp. 14, 16, 25, 28–29; and (1600), pp. 99, 218–220; Rambaud, pp. 87–89; and (1600), p. 26–27; on the question of *real* equity of taxes in Rome, which does not concern us here, see G. Ardant, *Histoire de l'impôt* (Paris: 1971), vol. I.

51. Vincent (1598), pp. 6–7, 28, 71.

52. On the continuity of the notion of an empire in southeastern Gaul, from the Romans to the Germanic emperors, with the Merovingians, see M. Werner's exposé in the *Empires* colloquium organized by M. Duverger (University of Paris I: 1977).

53. On the Roman origins of Dauphiné's *cadastres,* the lawyers' texts were literally innumerable and reinforced by Etienne Pasquier's writings (see A. Lacroix, *Procès des tailles,* and Charles Laurens, *idem*). See Rambaud, pp. 29, 51–52; Vincent (1598), pp. 8–9, and (1600), p. 51; F. Guérin, p. 4; Delagrange, pp. 67, 70, 76–78, 119, 138–141, 146, 170, 191–192; and (1599), pp. 255; (1599–2), pp. 2–3, 106–197, 112–114. On the more specific problems of Dauphiné's Occitan regions see Delagrange, p. 139; on "quiritary property," Delagrange, pp. 79, 150; Vincent (1600), pp. 107–109; on the problems of Narbonnaise, Languedoc, Provence, and *cadastres,* see Rambaud (1599), pp. 31, 70–73; Vincent (1598), p. 25; and (1600), pp. 86, 135–136, 203, 210; F. Guérin, pp. 8–11; Delagrange, p. XLI, and (1599–2), p. 19.

54. On the continuity of third estate action in Dauphiné from 1579 until the end of the sixteenth century, see Ramabud, p. 64.

55. Marchier, p. 366; see Delagrange, p. 146; (1599), p. 228; (1599–2), pp. 23, 90. One of the nobility's counsels' principal objections to the third estate concerned the revolts (C. Expilly, pp. 361–381; J. Dufos, p. 24).

56. The text of the 1583 agreement is in ADD, E 11 535 (ACR, CC 492). See

also on this conflict, called the "Montbonod" affair, Delagrange, pp. 73, 152; (1599), p. 288 and (1599-2), pp. 75, 94, 242; C. Expilly and J. Vincent (1600), p. 222; Rambaud, pp. 33.

57. I wish to thank Eli Barnavi for all he told me (in private conversations) about his as yet unpublished paradigm.

58. "le *boss*, la *machine* politique locale . . ." in the French *(translator)*.

59. J. Michelet, *Histoire de France* (Rouff), II, pp. 153, 154.

60. See for example the contradictory attitude of Lambert, deputy from St. Antoine: he pretended to quit the popular league, but in fact rejoined it and allied himself with Lesdiguières in August 1580 (J. Roman, in BSSK (1890), pp. 399, 423; Piémond, p. 95).

61. Letter from Lyonne to Hautefort in BSSI (1890), p. 305 (March 3, 1579).

62. On Gamot, cf. A. Lacroix, *Procès des tailles*, p. 23; E. Piémond, p. 366, no. 1; Delagrange (1599-2), p. 25; J. Dufos (1601), p. 24; (and above, Chapter I); Van Doren, *Thesis*, p. 317; Prudhomme (1888), p. 399; Catherine de'Medicis, *Lettres*, VII, pp. 71-73; Piémond, pp. 82-83; Cavard, p. 221, etc.

63. They "rose again" in the seventeenth century: Hémardinquer (1977), p. 88; and of course during the eighteenth century and in 1789.

Manuscript Sources

The manuscript sources cited in this work are primarily found in the Archives Communales de Romans, preserved in the town's Bibliothèque Municipale, and other manuscripts in that library (Calixte Lafosse collection); in the Archives Départementales de la Drôme; in the Archives Départementales de l'Isère; in the Archives Communales de Valence; in the manuscripts of the Bibliothèque Municipale de Grenoble; in the Bibliothèque Nationale's "manuscrits français" collection.

Precise references to these sources appear in the footnotes to each chapter. In connection with the final chapter, I examined but did not utilize the original of the historian Étienne Pasquier's valuable unpublished text (ADD C1024) on the rights of Dauphiné's third estate. I would like to stress the importance of the regional survey found in the Archives Communales de Vienne, CC 39 to CC 44 (on microfilm in the Archives Départementales de l'Isère, Mi 104 to Mi 107).

Abbreviations

A 41	(Example): "Anonymous," p. 41; refers to the anonymous account of the events in Romans (which was in fact the work of Judge Antoine Guérin), edited by J. Roman, BSASD, 1877 (see bibliography).
P 22	(Example): "Piémond," p. 22; refers to the journal of the royal notary Eustache Piémond (see bibliography).
ACG	Archives Communales de Grenoble.
ACM	Archives Communales de Montélimar.
ACR	Archives Communales de Romans.
ACV	Archives Communales de Valence.
ADD	Archives Départementales de la Drôme.
ADI	Archives Départementales de l'Isère.
BSASD	Bulletin de la société départementale d'archéologie et de statistique de la Drôme.
BSSI	Bulletin de la société statistique de l'Isère.
VD	Refers to work by the American historian L. Scott Van Doren (see bibliography).

Bibliography

*Alphabetical Index of Works
Consulted and Cited*

1) Books and Other References

The following list is by no means an exhaustive bibliography on the topic of Carnival in general. For a more complete bibliography on this subject see Baroja, Toschi, etc.

Agulhon, M. *Pénitents . . . de Provence*. Paris: 1968. (See also his contributions in Duby, Georges. *Histoire de la France rurale*. vol. 2, pp. 145–147; and in *Autrement*, below.)

Albernhe, H., and Gardy, P. *Les Chansons de Carrateyron*. Paris: 1972.

Alibert, Louis. *Dictionnaire Occitan-Français*. Paris: 1966.

Allard, Guy. *Bibiothèque de Dauphiné*. Grenoble: 1797, and *Dictionnaire du Dauphiné*. Grenoble: 1864.

Annales de la ville de Romans: see Chevalier, Dr. U.

Archives historiques du département de la Saintonge. vol. 46, p. 35. (About a noble revolt during Carnival.)

Ardant, G., *Histoire de l'impôt*. Paris: 1971.

Arnaud, Camille. *Abbaye de la jeunesse . . . .* Marseille: 1858.

Arnaud, Eugene. *Histoire des protestants du Dauphiné.* 3 vols. Paris: 1875–1876.

Aron, J. P.; Dumont, P.; and Le Roy Ladurie, E. *Anthropologie du conscrit français.* Paris: 1972

Artus, T., sieur d'Embry. *Description de l'île des hermaphrodites.* Cologne: 1724.

Baby, F. *La Guerre des demoiselles en Ariège.* Carcassonne: 1972.

Baguenault de Puchesse, see Catherine de'Medici (lettres).

Bakhtine, M. *L'Oeuvre de François Rabelais. . . .* French translation. Paris: 1970.

Barthes, Roland. *S/Z.* Paris: 1970.

Bautier, Philippe. *Les Reynages.* Guéret: 1945 (Important.)

Belmont, Nicole. *Mythes et croyances dans l'ancienne France.* Paris: 1973.

Bercé, Yves-Marie. *Histoire des Croquants.* Geneva: 1974.

―――. *Croquants et Nu-pieds.* Paris: 1974.

―――. *Fête et revolte.* Paris: 1976.

Berchtold, A., et al. *Quel Tell?* Lausanne: 1973.

Bezucha, R. "Masks . . ." in Price, Roger. *Revolution and Reaction.* 1948 (London: Croom Helm; New York: Barnes and Noble).

Biraben, J. N. *Les Hommes et la peste.* 2 vols., vol. 1. Paris: 1976. p. 119. (On the plagues of 1564 and 1586 in France.)

Blanc, André, *La Vie en Valentinois (1500–1590).* Paris: 1977.

Bligny, Bernard, ed. *Histoire du Dauphiné.* Toulouse: 1973. (See especially the contributions of Chomel, V., and Bonnin, B.)

Bodin, Jean. *La République.* Latin edition. 1586.

Boni, M. *Carnaval de Nice.* Nice: 1876 (animal figures).

Boudignon, Michele, et al. *Fêtes en France.* Paris: 1977 (with a preface by Georges Duby).

Bougeatre, E. *Vie rurale dans le Mantois . . . .* Meulan: 1971 (revised by M. Lachiver; very valuable for information on folklore).

Bouges, Father. *Histoire de Carcassonne.* Paris: 1741 (especially p. 363).

Boussel, P. *Guide de la Bourgogne. . . .* Paris: 1976, p. 333 (on the *Mère folle* in Dijon, related to Romans rituals).

Braudel, Fernand. *La Méditerrannée et le monde méditerranéen à l'époque de Philippe II.* 2 vols. Paris: 1966.

Braudel, F., and Labrousse, E. *Histoire économique et sociale de la France* (= HESF). Tome 1. Paris: 1977 (the first two volumes, by Chaunui, P.; Gascon, R.; Le Roy Ladurie, E.; and Morineau, M).

Brosse, Claude, *Cahiers des villages.* Grenoble: 1606, 1608, and the 1611, 1616, 1621 editions (Bibliothèque Nationale).

Brun-Durand, J. *Dictionnaire topographique de la Drôme.* Paris: 1891.

Brun-Durand, J. *Dictionnaire biographique de la Drôme.* 2 vols. Grenoble: 1900 (cf. articles on *Guérin, Serve,* etc.).

BSSI, 1890, cf. Roman, J., 1890.

Burel, Jean. *Mémoires.* Le Puy: 1875.

Cabourdin, Guy. *Terres et hommes en Lorraine.* Université de Lille III: 1975.

Calderón de la Barca, P. *L'alcade de Zalaméa.* 1645 (play about a peasant revolt against marauding soldiers).

Carnival in Sweden: cf. *Nordisk cultur,* no. 22, 1938; and Nilsson, P., *Arets folkliga fester* (1936) (my thanks to Börje Hanssen for this reference); and *Kulturhist. lexik. för nord. medeltid.* vol. 6. Malmoe: 1959.

Carnevale, article in *l'Encicl. del. Spettacolo.* vol. 3. Rome: 1956.

Caro Baroja, Julio. *El Carnaval.* Madrid: 1965.

Castan, Yves. *Honnêteté . . . en Languedoc.* Paris: 1974.

Catherine de'Medici, *Lettres.* Tome 7. Paris: Baguenault de Puchesse, 1899.

Cavard, P. *La Réforme et les guerres de Religion à Vienne.* Vienne: 1950.

Cesaire D'Arles, *Opera Omnia.* vol. 1. 1973 edition, p. 743 (winter festivities, with masquerades, during the first millennium A.D.).

Chafarevitch, I. *Le Phénomène socialiste.* Paris: 1977.

Chareton, V. *Réforme et guerres civiles en Vivarais.* Paris: 1913.

Charivari (symposium on). Musée des Arts et Traditions Populaires. (This museum is also referred to in footnotes as ATP.)

Chaunu, P. *L'Espagne de Charles Quint.* Paris: 1973.

Chaunu, P. *La Mort à Paris.* Paris: 1978, p. 203.

Chevalier, Dr. Ulysse. *Hôpitaux de Romans.* Valence: 1865 (and BSASD, 1866, p. 114).

————. *Un Tournoi à Romans en 1484.* Romans: 1888 (account of a Turkish "sultan" in Dauphiné).

————. *Mystère des Trois Doms, du Chanoine Pra, en 1509 à Romans.* Lyons: 1887.

Chocheyras, Jacques. *Théâtre religieux en Savoie, et en Dauphiné.* Geneva: 1971.

Chomel, Vital. See his essential text in Bligny, 1973.

Chomsky, Noam. *Per ragione di stato.* Turin: 1977. Also *Dialogues avec M. Ronet.* Paris: 1977; and *Réflexions sur le langage.* Paris: 1977. (Interesting speculations on the genetic nature of sentiments of liberty and equality.)

Chorier, N. *Histoire générale de Dauphiné.* Lyons: 1672, p. 697 (interesting on the subject of Jean Guigou, who was a protester in 1579 but against Paumier in 1580).

Clement, S. *Guide des recherches dans les fonds judiciaires de l'Ancien Régime.* Paris: 1958.

Clermont, Père Archange de. *Mémoires.* Edited by J. Chevalier. Romans: 1887.

Cobb, R. *Police and the People.* Oxford University Press: 1972.

Cocchiara, Giuseppe. *Paese di Cocagna.* Turin: 1955 and 1969.

Colas de la Noue, E. *Jacques Colas.* Paris: 1892 (important appendices).

Coloni, J. M., of Romans. *Prévoyances...jusqu'a 1582.* Avignon: 1575.

Constant, J. M. unpublished exposé on the Beauce *Cahiers de doléance* for 1576 (the peasants' hatred of the *nobles*, rather than the seigneurs as such).

Coston, Baron de. *Histoire de Montélimar.* Montélimar: 1883.

Cox, Harvey. *The Feast of Fools.* Cambridge, Massachusetts: 1969.

Coynart, Charles de. *Les Guérin de Tencin.* Paris: 1910.

Cros, Edmond. *L'aristocrate et le Carnaval des gueux.* Centre d'études socio-critiques, Université Paul Valéry, Montpellier: 1975.

Cultures (Unesco, Paris), vol. 3, 1976, no. 1: *Les grandes traditions de la fête.* (Especially the articles by J. Duvignaud and P. Weidkuhn [Carnival in Basle]); no. 2: *Fêtes et cultures.*

Cuvillier, A. *Manuel de sociologie.* Paris: 1967.

Dahl, Robert. *Who Governs?* New Haven: 1969.

Da Matta, Roberto. "Carnaval," in his *Ensaios de Antropologia estrutural*. Petropolis: 1973.

Dauzat, A. *Village et paysan de France*. Paris: 1941.

Davis, Natalie Z. *Society and Culture in Early Modern France*. Stanford: 1975; fundamental bibliography: pp. 296–309.

Delacenal, R. *Histoire de Crémieu*. Grenoble: 1889 (p. 481, Appendix 12: text of the Crémieu petition of grievance for 1579; interesting).

Delagrange, Claude (counsel for Dauphiné's third estate during the *procès des tailles*). *Juste plainte*. . . . Lyon: 1597; *Responses* . . . Paris: 1599; *Deffense* . . . *et response à la réplique*. Paris: 1601. (See Lagrange [Cl. de] in the Bibliothèque Nationale catalogue.)

Delumeau, J. *Mort des Pays de Cocagne*. Publications de la Sorbonne, tome 12, notably Ch. 1. Paris: 1976.

Desroche, H. *La société festive*. Paris: 1975.

Detienne, M. *Les Jardins d'Adonis*. Paris: 1972.

Devaux, Andre. *Essai sur la langue vulgaire de Dauphiné*. Lyons: 1892, p. 440–441 (and Slatkine Reprints, Geneva: 1968).

Devic, Claude, and Vaissette, Jacques. *Histoire générale de Languedoc*. Vol. 11-1. Toulouse: 1872–1892 (events of 1579–1580 in Dauphiné, Vivarais, and Gévaudan).

Dictionnaire de Spiritualité, by M. Villier et al. (Beauchesne, Paris: 1953; tome II, entry for *Carême*).

Dobson, R. A. *The Peasants' Revolt of 1381*. London: 1970.

Dochier, J. B. *La taille en Dauphiné*. Grenoble: 1783, pp. 5, 51, *et passim*.

———. *Origine de Romans*. Valence: 1813.

———. *Recherches sur l'impôt . . . en Dauphiné*. Valence: 1817.

Douglas, Mary, *Implicit Meanings*. Boston: 1976.

Dreyfus, Paul. *Histoire du Dauphiné*. Paris: 1976.

Drouout, Henri. *Mayenne et la Bourgogne*. Paris: 1937.

Duby, Georges. *Le temps des cathédrales*. Paris: 1976 (cf. also his *Histoire de la France rurale*. Vol. 2, p. 542, and vol. 4, p. 332. Paris: 1977; and his preface to M. Boudignon, above).

Dufos, Julien. *Défense de la noblesse*. Paris: 1601;

———. *Secondes Ecritures*. Grenoble: 1602.

Dumézil, G. *Le problème des Centaures*. Paris: 1929.

Duparc, P. *Annecy jusqu'au XVI* siècle. Annecy: 1973 (provides interesting comparisons).

Dussert, A. *Les Etats de Dauphiné aux XIV* et XV* siècles*. Grenoble: 1915, p. 24 and *passim*.

———. *La Mure*, Paris and Grenoble: 1902.

Duvignaud, J. *Fêtes et civilisations*. Geneva: 1973 (cf. also *Le Don de Rien*. Paris: 1977, pp. 134–137).

———. see *Cultures*.

Ehmke, E.G. "Order and Disorder in 17th Century France." Symposium on

France at the Newbury Library, Chicago, October 10, 1976.

Eliade, M. *Traité d'histoire des religions.* Ch. 8. Paris: 1975.

Erich, Oswald A., and Beitl, R. *Wörterbuch der deutschen Volkskunde.* Stuttgart: 1955, entry for *Fastnacht.*

Expilly, Claude. *Plaidoyer (pour la noblesse)* and the collected edition of his *Plaidoyers.* Paris: editions of 1612, 1619, etc.

Fabre, Daniel. *Jean de l'ours.* Travaux du laboratoire d'ethnographie et de civilisation occitanes, Institut d'Etudes Méridionales de la Faculté des Lettres de Toulouse, editions Revue *Folklore.* 2, Carcassonne, summer 1969. (Important.)

Fabre, D., and Lacroix, J. "Vie quotidienne des paysans de Languedoc au XIXe siècle." Paris: 1973.

Fabre, Daniel. *La Fête en Languedoc.* Toulouse: 1977 (see also his films and those of Lajoux on Carnival in both northern and southern France).

Faure, Alain. *Paris carême-prenant.* Paris: 1978 (excellent).

Faure, Claude. *Recherches sur l'histoire du collège de Vienne.* Paris: 1933.

Favret-Saada, J. *Les mots, la mort, les sorts: sorcellerie en Bocage.* Paris: 1977.

Fayolle, G. *Vie quotidienne en Périgord.* Paris: 1977, p. 274 (on a double Maypole celebration, politically both left and right wing). *Fêtes de la Renaissance,* Editions du CNRS. 3 vols. Paris: 1956, 1975.

Filippini, Maria N. *Cuisine corse.* Vico: 1965 (especially the important paragraph on *elections*).

Firth, R. *Symbols.* Ithaca: 1973.

Fontana, A. "La Scena," in *Storia d'Italia.* I. Turin: 1972, p. 866.

Foucault, Michel. *Histoire de la sexualité, I, La volonté de savoir.* Paris: 1976 (cf. also his *Moi, Pierre Rivière . . .* p. 42, on cockfights).

Franz, Günther. *Der deutsche Bauernkrieg.* Darmstadt: 1952.

Frazer, J. G. *The Golden Bough.* London: 1916 (especially in the index of the final volume, the word *Carnival,* with references interspersed through all eleven volumes of the work). See also abridged edition.

Furet, F., and Ozouf, J. *Lire et écrire.* Paris: 1977.

Gaignebet, C. *Le Carnaval.* Paris: 1974 (stimulating). See also his article in *Annales* (March 1972) on "Carnaval et Carême."

Gamon, Achille. *Memoires.* In Michaud and Poujoulat. *Nouvelle collection des Mémoires pour servir l'Histoire de France.* Vol. 8. Paris: 1838. See also the Valence edition, 1888.

Gascon, R. *Grand commerce et vie urbaine à Lyon au XVIe siècle.* Paris: 1971.

Gay, Gaspard. *Mémoires des frères Gay. . . .* Montbéliard: Jules Chevalier, 1888.

Geertz, C. *Myth, Symbol, and Culture.* New York: 1975 (especially his chapter on cockfights).

Geiger, Paul. *Deutsches Volkstum in Sitte und Brauch.* Berlin: 1936 (on masquerades).

Giesey, Ralph E. *Royal Funeral Ceremony in Renaissance France.* Geneva: 1960.

Glotz, Samuel, ed. *Le Masque dans la tradition européenne.* Belgian Cultural Ministry: Binche, 1975.

Gluckman, Max. See his works on Africa, interesting on the topic of ritual role reversal; in particular, *Order and Rebellion in Africa*. Glencoe, Illinois: 1963.

Gomme, G.L. *The Gentleman's Magazine Library, English Traditions and Foreign Customs.* London: 1885 (especially p. 65: St. Blaise; and p. 244 on Carnival in Florence, with many points of comparison to Romans rites).

Greimas, A. *Sémantique structurale.* Paris: 1966.

————. *Sémiotique et sciences sociales.* Paris: 1976.

Guenée, B., et al. *Entrées royales . . . 1328–1515.* CNRS. Paris: 1968.

Guenée, B. *L'Occident aux XIVe et XVe siècles, les Etats.* Paris: 1971 (important for comparing Dauphiné's Estates to others in France at the time).

Guérin, François (de). *Trés humbles remonstrances.* Paris: 1634 (also contains the council's decrees on the *taille*).

Guichonnet, P., ed. *Histoire de Genève.* Toulouse: 1974 (see p. 168 for a study in comparative demography).

Heers, J. *Fêtes . . . à la fin du Moyen Age.* Montreal and Paris: 1975.

Humbert, Gen. Jacques. *Embrun.* Gap: 1972.

Ibn Khaldun. *Discours sur l'histoire universelle.* Translated by Monteil. Vol. 2. Beirut: 1867.

Jacquot, J. See *Fêtes de la Renaissance*.

Joisten, C. *Contes populaires du Dauphiné.* Paris: 1971.

Jouana, Arlette. *L'Ordre social dans la France du XVIe siècle.* Paris: 1977.

Joutard, Philippe, Estèbe, J., et al. *La Saint-Barthélemy.* Neuchâtel: 1976.

Konigson, E. *L'espace théâtra médiéval.* Paris: CNRS, 1975 (see p. 131: monograph on the "Mystère des Trois Doms" in Romans: 1509).

Kristeva, Julia. *Le texte du roman.* Paris and The Hague: 1970 (on a medieval Carnival text).

Kurtz, Leonard. *The Dance of Death.* 1934 (Geneva, Slatkine Reprints, 1975).

Lachiver, M.: See Bougeatre.

Lacroix, André. *Romans avant 1890.* Valence: 1897.

————. *L'arrondissement de Montélimar.* Valence: 1868–1893.

Laslett, P. et al. *Household and Family in Past Time.* Cambridge: 1972.

Latreille, A., ed. *Histoire de Lyon.* Toulouse: 1975.

Laurens, Charles. *Le Procès des tailles.* Grenoble: 1867.

Leach, Edmund. *Rethinking Anthropology.* London: 1961.

Leach, Maria, et al. *Standard Dictionary of Folklore.* New York: 1972, entries on *Carnival, Fastnacht, Sword Dance,* etc.

Lebigre, Arlette. *Les grands jours d'Auvergne.* Paris: 1976 (especially p. 102, on seigneurial oppression).

Lefort, Claude. *Les formes de l'histoire.* Paris: 1978, p. 235 (on the forerunners of equality in Florence around 1400: Bruni and Salutati).

Le Goff, Jacques, and Nora, Pierre, et al. *Faire de l'histoire.* Paris: 1974. (See also J. Le Goff in *Pour un autre Moyen Age.* Paris: 1977, "Le rituel symbolique," pp. 335 ff.)

Leon, Pierre. *Naissance de la grande industrie en Dauphiné.* Paris: 1954, p. 51, 67, *et passim.*

Le Roy Ladurie, Emmanuel. *Les Paysans de Languedoc*. Paris: 1966.

Lesdiguières, François de la Bonne de. *Actes et correspondances*. 3 vol. published by Count Douglas and J. Roman, Grenoble: 1878.

L'Estoile, Pierre de. *Mémoires*. Paris: 1975-1976.

Levi-Strauss, Claude. *Le Totémisme aujourd'hui*. Paris: 1962.

_____. Introduction to Marcel Mauss, *Sociologie et Anthropologie*. Paris: 1966.

Long, George. *The Folklore Calendar*. London: 1930.

Long, J.D. *La Reforme et les guerres de Religion en Dauphiné (1560– 1598)*. Paris: 1856, and Slatkine Reprints, Geneva, 1970.

Lorcin, M.T. *Les campagnes lyonnaises (XIVe–XVe siècles)*. Lyon: 1974.

Luce, Siméon. *La Jacquerie*. Paris: 1859.

MacKim, Marriot. "Feast of Love." In Milton Singer, *Krishna Myths*. Honolulu: 1966.

Macleod Banks, Mrs. M. *British Calendar Customs, Scotland*. 2 vols. London: 1939.

Mannhard, W. *Wald und Feld Kulte*. Berlin: 1875 (fundamental, and too often obscured by Frazer's work).

Manteyer, G. de. *La terre de Jarjayes* . . . . Gap: 1946.

Marmier, third estate counsel; see the text of his *plaidoyer* appended to Piémond, below.

Mauss, Marcel. *Essai sur le don*. Paris: 1968.

Mermet, Thomas the Elder. *Histoire de Vienne*. 1853.

Michelet, Jules. *Histoire de France*. Vol. 3 (book 4, Ch. 5 through 18), especially pp. 153-154 in the 19th-century Jules Rouff edition.

Mollat, R., and Wolff, Philippe. *Ongles bleus, Jacques, et Ciompi*. Paris: 1970.

Monier, Abbé Eugène. *Etudes monographiques sur le Charlieu*. Valence: 1907.

Mousnier, R. *Fureurs paysannes*. Paris: 1967 (see also his contribution to *Histoire de France*. Paris: Larouse, 1954).

Mousnier, R. *Précurseurs du contrat social*. EDHIS, 23 rue de Valois, Paris: 1978 (on anti-absolutist writings in the 16th century.)

Muchembled, R. *Culture populaire et culture des élites dans la France moderne* XVe–XVIIe siècles). Paris: 1978 (similarities between Carnival in Dauphiné and northern France).

Nicolas, Jean. *La Savoie au XVIIIe siècle*. Paris: 1978 (see also by the same author "Ephémerides du refus," an article in *Annales historiques de la Révolution française*. 1973, p. 593, and 1974, p. 111).

Nora, Pierre: see Le Goff, Jacques.

Ossovski, S. *La Structure de classe* (translation). Paris: 1971.

Ozouf, Mona. *La Fête revolutionnaire*. Paris: 1976 (see also her contribution in *Autrement* and in Le Goff and Nora, 3, pp. 266 ff.)

Pansier, P. *Theatre populaire d'Avignon*. Marseilles: 1973, p. 5 (excellent data on the possible origin of *reynages*, at the feast of Epiphany, as early as 1373).

Peacock, J. L. *Rites of Modernization*. Chicago: 1968.

Perez, Joseph. *La révolte des Communidades*. Bordeaux: 1970.

Perier, Augustin. *Recueil de documents relatifs à l'histoire du Dauphiné.* Vol 1. Grenoble: 1881, pp. 1–5.

Piémond, Eustache. *Mémoires.* Edited by J. Brun-Durand. 1885. New edition from Slatkine Reprints, Geneva: 1973.

Pillorget, Rene. *Mouvements insurrectionnels en Provence.* Paris: 1975 (a fundamental work).

Pilot de Thorey, J. *Usages, fêtes . . . en Dauphiné.* Grenoble: 1882.

Les Plaisirs de l'Ile enchantée. 1664 (see G. Saffroy).

Félix et Thomas Platter à Montpellier, Montpellier: 1892.

Ponsoye, Charles. *Quelques pages de notre passé.* Valence: 1941, pp. 133–150.

Pontbriand, A. de. *Le Capitaine Merle.* Paris: 1886.

Porchnev, B. *Soulevements populaires en France.* Paris: 1963.

Poueigh, J. *Le Folklore des pays d'oc.* Paris: 1952.

Prudhomme, Auguste. *Histoire de Grenoble.* 1888; new edition, Marseille: 1975.

Rambaud, Antoine, third estate counsel. *Plaidoyer . . . .* Lyons: 1598; *Lettre . . . .* Paris: 1598; *Second plaidoyer.* Paris: 1600 (all three of these texts appear in the 1600 edition).

Ring, Tilts to the, cartels, tournaments, etc.: cf. Bibliothèque Nationale Lb 36 149; Lb *37* 3475 (Perrault, carousel of 1662); LB *36* 3460; Ye 13861; Lb 36 1377 (Louis XII, 1620); BN, Fantanieu, 120 (Savoy in 1608). See also *infra,* Piémond, p. 135; Colas, p. 67; Vovelle, p. 79; *La Princesse de Cléves* (on Mme. de Valentinois); Bercé, *Histoire des Croquants,* I, p. 214; Duby, *Cathédrales, p. 246; see also below,* G. Saffroy.

Rivoire de la Batie, G. *Armorial du Dauphiné.* Lyon: 1867.

Rochas, Adolphe. *Abbaye joyeuse. . . .* Grenoble: undated (*ca.* 1870).

Roman, J. *Catherine de Médicis en Dauphiné.* Grenoble: 1883.

Rudwin, Max. J. *German Carnival Comedy.* New York (Stechert): 1920.

Sabean, D. *Landbesitz am Vorabend . . . . des Bauernkriegs.* Stuttgart: 1972.

Saffroy, Gaston. *Bibliographie généalogique, heraldique, et nobiliaire. . . .* Paris: 1968; cols. 3301–3374 (tilts to the ring); and cols. 3456–3515 (heralds).

Salmon, J. H. M. *Society in Crisis, 16th Century France.* New York: 1975.

Servier, J. *Portes de l'année.* Paris: 1962.

Sessions, Kyle C. *Reformation and Authority (the Peasants' Revolt in Germany).* Lexington, Mass.: D.C. Heath, 1968 (especially p. 17).

Simler or Simmler, Josias. *La République des Suisses.* Translated by I. Gentillet. 1577 (interesting for its antinoble content, made explicit by the translator who was a sympathizer in the Dauphiné revolts).

Soboul, Albert. *Les Sans-culottes parisiens . . . .* Paris: 1968 (role of craftsmen in urban popular movements).

Sonenscher. "Masques armés de 1783 en Vivarais." Montpellier: Université Paul Valery, 1972.

Sperber, D. *Le symbolisme aujourd'hui.* Paris: 1974.

Thiers, J.B. *Traité des superstitions.* Paris: 1679, 1700, and 1777.

Thomé de Maisonneuve, P. *Histoire de Romans.* 2 vols. Romans: 1937–1942.

Thompson, E. P. *The Making of the English Working Class.* London: 1963.

Tilly, Charles. "Rural Action in Modern Europe." In J. Spielberg and S. Whiteford, *Forging Nations*. Michigan State University Press: 1976.

Todorov, Tzvetan. *Théories du symbole*. Paris: 1977.

Toschi, Paolo. *Le origini de Teatro italiano*. Einaudi: 1955 (by the same author: *Invito al folklore italiano*. Rome: 1963, pp. 275 ff.).

Turner, Victor. *The Ritual Process*. Chicago: 1969.

———. *Dramas, Fields, and Metaphors*. Ithaca: 1974 (see also his *Drums of Affliction*).

———. *The Forest of Symbols*. Ithaca: 1974, p. 28 *et passim*.

Van Dyke, Paul. *Catherine de' Medici*. New York: 1922.

Van Gennep, Arnold. *Le Folklore des Hautes-Alpes*. Paris: 1946.

———. *Le Folklore de Dauphiné*, 2 vols. Paris: 1932 (see also his *Folklore de l'Auvergne et du Velay*. Paris: 1942, p. 179 [*reynages*]).

———. *Manuel du folklore français* (volume Carnival—Lent); see also his *Rites de passage*, and the Van Gennep collection in the ATP (his work on the Drôme).

Varagnac, A. *Civilisation traditionnelle*. Paris: 1948.

Vassal. *Les Paladins du diable*. 12th Aigues-Mortes Festival: August 1976.

Vaultier. *Le Folklore d'après les lettres de rémission*. Paris: 1965.

Veyne, Paul. *Le Pain et le cirque*. Paris: 1976.

Videl, L. *Histoire de Lesdiguières*. Paris: 1638.

Vilar, P. *La Catalogne dans l'Espagne moderne*. Paris: 1962 (Vol. 1 has a chapter on revolts).

Villadary, A. *Fête et vie quotidienne*. Paris: 1968 (good bibliography).

Villeneuve, Count of. *Moeurs des Provençaux*. Nyons: 1972 (re-edition).

Vincenot, H. *Vie quotidienne des paysans bourguignons* . . . . Paris: 1976.

Vincent, Jean, third estate counsel from Grenoble. *Discours*. Paris: 1598; and *Réplique*. Paris: 1600.

Vovelle, M. *Métamorphose de la fête en Provence*. Paris: 1976.

de Vries, A. *Dictionary of Symbols*. London: 1974, under *Hare*.

Walter, G. *Histoire des paysans de France*. Paris: 1963.

Weber, Max. *Economy and Society* (French edition). Paris: 1963.

Wright, A. R. (with T. E. Lones), *British Calendar Customs, England*. 2 vols. London: 1936–1938 (see also above Mrs. MacLeod Banks).

Wunenburger, Jean-Jacques. *La fête, le jeu, et le sacré*. Paris: 1977.

Yardeni, Myriam. *La Conscience nationale pendant les guerres de Religion*. Louvain: 1971.

Ziegler, Jean. *Une Suisse au-dessus de tout soupçon*. Paris: 1976.

2) *Articles*

Agulhon, M. "Le jeu de l'arquebuse à Aix . . ." offprint. (1977); and "Imagerie civique . . ." in *Ethnologie française* 5 (1975): 39; the rooster.

Albernhe, H., and Gardy, P. "Carnaval en litterature occitane." *Revue des langues romanes* (1971).

Amargier, A. "Sur la confrérie du Saint-Esprit au Moyen Age." *Cahiers de Fanjeaux* 2 (1976):305.

Auge, Marc. "Quand les signes s'inversent." *Communications* 28 (1978):66 (and by the same author, *Pouvoirs*. Paris: 1977).

Autrement. Special issue. *La Fête, cette hantise*, August 1976.

Boiteux, Martine. Article on the Roman Carnival in *Annales*, March 1977, and *Mélanges Ecole française de Rome* 2 no. 88 (1976).

Bonnin, Bernard. Article on "L'endettement des communautés dauphinoises au XVIIe siécle." *Bulletin du centre des recherches historiques et sociales de la région de Lyon* (1972).

Brenner, R. "Agrarian Class Structure ..." *Past and Present*, February 1976.

Brieu, J. C. "Assassinat du sieur de Callas, 1579." *Bulletin de la société des études scientifiques et archéologiques de Draguignan* 8 (1868–1869):101–134.

Brink, J. E. "A Tax Loophole, Montpellier, 16th century." *Meeting of the Western Society for French History*. Denver 1975 (see also an article by the same author in *Annales du Midi*, July 1976: 287, on the Estates in the Midi).

Burke, Peter. "Festivals and Protest, Italy, 1647." *Social History Society Newsletter*, Spring 1977: 2.

Ça cinéma. 11, no. 10 (1976). Article on the Carnival in Romans by Blon, Philippe; Farges, J.; and Le Roy Ladurie, E.

Caisson, Max. "L'hospitalité corse." *Etudes corses* 2 (1974).

Carozzi, C. ". . . Adalberon de Léon." *Annales*, July 1978.

Casanova, Antoine. "Sur le Carnaval corse." in Hommages à Geores Fournier, *Annales de Littérature de l'Université de Besançon*. Paris: 1973.

Chartier, R. "Noblesse française et états de 1614: réaction aristocratique?" *Acta Poloniae historica* 36 (1977).

Chartier, R. and Julia, D. "Le Monde à l'envers." *L'Arc* 65 (1976).

Chartier, R. and Nagle, J. "Les de doléance de 1614." *Annales*, November 1973.

Chevalier, Dr. Ulysse. "Cordeliers de Romans." *BSASD* (1867–1868).

―――. "Le pont de Romans." *BSASD* (1867).

―――. "Les statuts de Saint Barnard de Romans." *BSASD* (1880).

―――. "Généalogies romanaises: Velheu." *BSASD* (1882).

―――. "Annales de Romans pendant les guerres de Religion." *BSASD* (1875–1876).

―――. "Les Abbayes laïques de Romans." *BSASD* (1882): 27.

Cholvy, G. "Sentiment religieux populaire." *99e congrès de la société savante*. Besançon (1974): 293.

Chomel, V. "Le Dauphiné sous l'Ancien Régime; publications historiques, 1935–1962." *Cahiers d'histoire*: 303 (important).

Chovet, P. and M. "Le ligue des Vilains de Romans." *Le Peuple français* 26, April–June 1977 (see also no. 6 of *Le Peuple français*).

Clastres, Pierre. "La Guerre et les sociétés primitives." *Libre* 1 (1971).

Cros, Claude. "Démographie historique de Saint-Priest." *Bulletin de la société d'ethnographie du Limousin*, January–June 1976: 41.

Dalet, G. "Guerre des paysans de Valloire." *Bulletin mensuel de l'académie delphinale*, November 1972.

"Le Dauphine en 1698." (Bouchu survey), in *BSASD* (1873).

Dufour, A. "Nobles dauphinois pendant la Ligue." *Cahiers d'histoire* (1959), p. 227.

Dujet, A. "Antoine Rambaud," *BSASD* (1922–23): 197.

Duparc, P. "Confréries du Saint-Esprit." *Revue historique de droit français et étranger* (1958) (two important articles).

Dussert. A. "Catherine de Médicis et les Etats de Dauphiné."*Bulletin de l'académie delphinale* 5th series, tome 13, 2, (1922, published in 1923).

Erhard, J., and Viallaneix, eds. *Fêtes de la Revolution. Société des études Robespierre*. Paris: 1977.

Entrée royale, Francois I. Account of 1533 royal entry published in *BSASD* (1973): 79.

Esmonin, M. "Sur la taille réelle." *Bulletin mensuel de la société de l'histoire moderne*, January 1913: 176 ff.

Fejoz, J. "Fêtes locales . . . en Savoie." *Monde alpin et rhodanien* 1 (1976).

Foisil, Madeleine. "Harangue . . . d'Antoine Segnier." *Annales de Normandie* March 1976.

Gallier, Anatole de. "La Baronnie de Clérieu." *BSASD* (1969–1970). Cf. also his "Imprimerie à Tournon." *BSASD* (1877), on the beginnings of the local "press" in the 1580s.

Gardy, Philippe. "Carnaval d'Oc." *Europe*, Paroles occitanes (1976–1977); see also Albernhe.

Gauvard, Claude, and Gokal, A. "Charivari au Moyen Age." *Annales*, May 1974.

Giraud, P.E. "Procédure contre les chenilles à Romans, 1547." *BSASD* (1866).

Grinberg, Martine. "Carnaval et société urbaine, XIVᵉ–XVIᵉ siècles." *Ethnologie française* IV, 3.

Gurevitch, A. Y. "On the Nature of the Comic." *Medieval Scandinavia*. 9–76.

Gutton, J.P. "Reynages . . ." *Cahiers d'histoire* XX (1975).

Hemardinquer, J.J. "Guerre aux châteaux (Bretagne, 1675)," *Communications des travaux historiques et scientifiques*. Nantes 1972 in the Bibliothèque Nationale, Paris 1977 (on an antiseignorial revolt).

Hickey, D. "The Routes of Renaissance Dauphiné." *Canadian Journal of History*. 6-2, September 1971. See also the paper given by D. Hickey at the 1976 congress of the Historical Society of Canada, "Procés des tailles . . . en Dauphiné au XVIᵉ siècle."

Lacroix, Andre. "Canton du Grand-Serre: La Valloire." *BSASD* (1868).

_____. "Claude Brosse et les tailles," *BSASD* 31 to 33 (1897–1899) (fundamental).

_____. "Les de Fructu . . ." *BSASD* (1880).

_____. "Reynages et vogues," *BSASD* (1880):421.

Lagree, M. "Structure pérenne en Bretagne." *Revue d'histoire mediévale et contemporaine*, July 1976: 394.

Lamarche, L. "Reynages." *BSASD* 74 (1958): 104.

Lebrun, Francois. "Le Traité . . . de J.B. Thiers." *Annales de Bretagne*, 3, no. 83 (1976).

Le Camus (Monsignor), seventeenth-century text on the use of *brandons*, etc., in *Monde alpin et rhodanien* 1–4 (1977): 64.

Lecoq, A. M. "Citta festeggiante." *Revue de l'Art* (1976).

Loirette, F. "Mazarinade . . . et Carnaval de Bordeaux (1651)," *Bulletin et Mémoire de la Société archéologique de Bordeaux.* 66 (1972): 83.

Mandrou, R. "Cartographie des protestants réfugiés à Genève après 1592." *Revue Suisse d'histoire* (1966), (on the extent of the Protestant exodus from Romans).

Mentzer, R. Article (in English) on the socioprofessional makeup of the Protestant population in southern France during the sixteenth century. *Bibl. d'humanisme et Renaissance* 29, Geneva 1977.

Merriman, John. Article on the "guerre des demoiselles" in *American History Review* (1975).

Notices et livre de raison du couvent des Cordeliers de Montélimar. (Excerpts). *BSASD* (1870): 375–455.

Nugues, Charles. "Le festival." (Good bibliography). See *Autrement.*

Nussac, L. de. "Quelques reynages en Limousin." *Bulletin de la société de l'histoire et archéologie de Corrèze.* 13 (1891): 463.

Poitrineau, A. See his article in *Autrement*, above.

Prudhomme, Auguste. "Commencement de l'année en Dauphiné." *Bulletin historique et philosophique du Comité des travaux historiques et scientifiques.* (1898): 260.

Radcliffe-Brown, A. R. "Sociological Theory of Totemism." *Structure and Function in Primitive Society.* New York: 1965.

Richet, D. "Conflits religieux, Paris, seconde moitié du XVIᵉ siècle." *Annales*, July 1977 (especially p. 779).

———. "Elite et Noblesse." *Acta Poloniae historica.* 36 (1977).

Roman, J. *Documents sur la Réforme et les guerres de religion en Dauphiné.* published by *BSSI*, third ser., tome 15 (= 26), Grenoble (1890) (fundamental).

———. "La guerre des paysans en Dauphiné, 1579–1580." *BSASD* (1877) (fundamental: contains Guérin's text, with a few errors and omissions I detected in comparing it with the original, BN, ms. fs. 3319).

Rossiaud, J. "Prostitution . . . au XVᵉ siècle." *Annales.* (1976): 289.

———. "Fraternités de jeunesse." *Cahiers d'histoire.* 1–2 (1976): 67 (important).

Sabean, D. "Communal Basis of Peasant Uprisings." *Comparative Politics*, April 1976.

Sage, C. and M. "Saint-Jean d'Avelanne." *Monde alpin et rhodanien.* 1–2 (1976) (Dauphiné folklore).

Sidro, Annie. "Carnaval de Nice (1294–1889)." *Lou Sourgentin.* Nice, February 1976 (important).

Terrebasse, H. de. "Mont-Calvaire à Romans . . . miracle de 1517." *BSASD* (1882): 383.

Thomé de Maisonneuve, P. "Les libertés municipales de Romans." *BSASD* (1939–1945). (A series of articles over those years; those written in 1943–1945 are essential, although they contain some errors.)

Turner, Victor. "Symbolic Studies." *Annual Review of Anthropology.* 4 (1975): 145 (important). See also his article in *Daedalus* 1 summer 1977: 61.

Vallentin du Cheylard, R. "Ban et arrière-ban, 1594, Valentinois-Disois." *BSASD* (1950): 273.

Van Der Wee, H. "Economy and Revolt in Southern Netherlands." *Acta neerland* (1968).

Van Doren, Liewain Scott. "Revolt and Reaction in Romans, 1579–1580," *Sixteenth Century Journal*, April 1974 (fundamental).

––––––. "The Royal Taille in Dauphiné, 1494–1559," and "The Royal Taille in Dauphiné, 1560–1610," articles which the author kindly allowed me to study in manuscript form. The former was published in *The Proceedings of the American Philosophical Society.* 121, no. 1, February 1977, pp. 70–96; the latter appeared in the *Proceedings of the Third Annual Meeting of the Western Society for French History*, December 1975 and 1976, pp. 35–53. In the footnotes to this book I have sometimes referred to these articles as Van Doren, *Papers.*

Van Gennep, Arnold. "Le culte de Saint Blaise en Dauphiné et Savoie." *Revue de l'ethnologie et des traditions populaires* 5 (1924): 136–148.

Venault, Philippe. "Plaisir de l'historien." *Ça cinema* 12–13.

Vilar, P. "Motin de Esquilache." *Historia iberica* (undated offprint, on a festival revolt in the eighteenth century).

Vossier, J. "Claveyson." *BSASD* (1882) (on the plague of 1586).

Weidkuhn, P. "Carnaval de Bâle." *Cultures* III, I (1976) (on role reversal).

Westrich, S. A. "L'Ormée de Bordeaux, Bordeaux." Translated by J. Cavinhac. *Cahiers de l'I. A. E. S.* 3 (1973).

Wood, James B. "Mobility among the Nobility of Modern France." *Sixteenth Century Journal*, April 1977: 3.

3) Theses

Albernhe, H., and Gardy, P. "Carementrant dans la littérature occitane." Doctorat de Troisième Cycle thesis, Université de Montpellier, 1970.

Benedict, Phillip. "Protestants in Sixteenth-Century Rouen." Ph.D. dissertation, Princeton University, 1975.

Bonnin, Bernard. His forthcoming thesis on the history of modern Dauphiné sheds new light on the entire topic.

Boutier, Jean. "Révoltes bas-limousines à la fin du XVIIIe siècle." Doctorat d'Enseignement Secondaire thesis, Université Paris VII.

Davis, Natalie Z. "Protestants in Lyons, Sixteenth Century." Ph.D. dissertation, University of Michigan, in the university's microfilm collection. Contains an extensive bibliography on the folklore of central eastern France.

Defournet, P. Doctorat de Troisième Cycle thesis on Bassy (in Savoy). L'École des Hautes Etudes en Sciences Sociales, 1970 (see especially vol. I., p. 47).

Delille, Gerard. "Vourey (XVIᵉ–XVIIᵉ siècles)." Doctorat d'Enseignement Secondaire thesis, Université de Grenoble, 1968, (on the progression of noble land acquisition in rural areas).

Estèbe, Janine. "Protestants du Midi (1559–1598)." Doctorat d'Etat thesis, Université de Toulouse–Le Mirail, 1977.

Grinberg, Martine. "La fête en France à la fin du Moyen Age." Doctorat de Troisième Cycle thesis, L'École des Hautes Etudes en Sciences Sociales, (includes an essential bibliography on the subject).

Hickey, Daniel. "Warfare, Stagnation, and Mobility in Valentinois-Diois." Ph.D. dissertation.

Le Baron, Christian. "Formes . . . de Carnaval en Provence." Doctorat d'Enseignement Secondaire thesis, Université de Paris-VIII (Vincennes).

Marrot, Jacques. "Fête à Carcassonne." Essay for the Diplôme de L'École des Hautes Etudes en Sciences Sociales, 1976.

Molinier, Alain. "Le Vivarais sous l'Ancien Régime." Doctorat de Troisième Cycle thesis, L'École des Hautes Etudes en Science Sociales, 1977.

Perier, Mme. "L'élection de Romans vers 1701." Doctorat d'Enseignement Secondaire thesis, Université de Grenoble (ADI, 2 J 73).

Perrochet, Martine. "Romans au XVᵉ siècle." Thesis for the Diplôme de l'École des Chartes, 1974 (copy in Romans's Bibliothèque Municipale).

Rossi, M. "L'élection de Vienne en 1607–1706." Doctorat d'Enseignement Secondaire thesis, Université de Grenoble (ADI, microfilms, 2 J 55).

Soubeyroux, Jacques. "Les Pauvres à Madrid au XVIIᵉ siècle." Doctorat d'Etat thesis, Université de Montpellier, 1976.

Van Doren, Leiwain Scott. "War, Taxes, and Social Protest . . . in Sixteenth-Century Dauphiné." Ph.D. dissertation, Harvard University, 1970.

Venard, Marc. "L'Église d'Avignon au XVIᵉ siècle." Doctorat d'Etat thesis, Université de Paris-I, 1977.

Venault, Philippe, "Scenario based on Carnival in Romans," essay for the Diplôme de L'École des Hautes Etudes en Sciences Sociales, 1977.